M-Blk.St.

A
Nation
within a
Nation

A Nation within a Nation

Amiri Baraka

(LeRoi Jones)

and Black Power

Politics

Komozi Woodard

The University of North Carolina Press *Chapel Hill and London*

Manufactured in the United States of America
This book was set in Janson and Franklin Gothic
by G & S Typesetters, Inc.
The paper in this book meets the guidelines for
permanence and durability of the Committee on
Production Guidelines for Book Longevity of the
Council on Library Resources.

Library of Congress
Cataloging-in-Publication Data
Woodard, Komozi.
A nation within a nation: Amiri Baraka
(LeRoi Jones) and Black power politics /
by Komozi Woodard.
p.   cm.
Includes bibliographical references (p.   ) and index.
ISBN 0-8078-2457-7 (cloth: alk. paper)
ISBN 0-8078-4761-5 (pbk.: alk. paper)
1. Baraka, Imamu Amiri, 1934–   2. Afro-American
political activists—Biography.   3. Revolutionaries—
United States—Biography.   4. Afro-Americans—
Politics and government.   5. Black nationalism—
United States—History—20th century.   6. Black
power—United States—History—20th century.
I. Title.
E185.97.B23 W66   1999
818'.5409—dc21   98-22833
[B]   CIP

03 02 01 00 99   5 4 3 2 1

To the memory of
Almasi Mkalimu Woodard (1972–1995),
who came forward like a flower out of the
midst, full of mystery and wonder. He made
everything beautiful in his days and filled our
lives with so much love and laughter.

The sun rises and sets. The tide climbs
and falls. The moon waxes and wanes. And
man is born and dies, but our life force endures
forever with no beginning and no end.

For my parents,
Theodore and Helen Woodard

For my children,
Kuza Akili, Malik Babu, Adimu Komozi,
and Zawadi Jua

Contents

Illustrations

Preface

Amiri Baraka (LeRoi Jones)—author of over twenty plays, three jazz operas, seven books of nonfiction, a novel, and thirteen volumes of poetry—is best known as a major cultural leader, one of the African American writers who galvanized a second Black Renaissance, the Black Arts Movement of the 1960s, making an indelible contribution to modern African American culture and consciousness. Literature professor William J. Harris writes that "as a contemporary American artist Baraka must be ranked with the likes of John Coltrane, Ralph Ellison, Norman Mailer, Toni Morrison, and Thomas Pynchon"; as the Father of the Black Arts Movement, Baraka "almost single-handedly changed both the nature and the form of post–World War II Afro-American literature."[1] Biographer Arnold Rampersad places Baraka alongside Phyllis Wheatley, Frederick Douglass, Paul Laurence Dunbar, Langston Hughes, Zora Neale Hurston, Richard Wright, and Ralph Ellison "as one of the eight figures . . . who have significantly affected the course of African American literary culture."[2]

In Maya Angelou's judgment, Amiri Baraka is the world's greatest living poet.[3] He is a singular lyrical poet whose work, as Henry C. Lacey suggests, reveals a special gift of "emotive music" with a passionate and incantatory beauty.[4] Lacey explains that Baraka's work is concerned with the "sounds of black life" and that probably "more than any other writer, Baraka captures the idiom and style of modern urban black life."[5]

Clearly, Amiri Baraka is a remarkably prolific writer; his work is important in several genres, including modernist fiction, essays, music criticism, and drama. His pathbreaking social history of African Americans, *Blues People*, is only one indication of his role as one of America's most profound music critics. Moreover, from the beginning of his career, he made crucial contributions to the American stage, winning the 1964 Obie Award for *Dutchman*, the drama that Norman Mailer thought "the best play in America."[6]

In his writing and drama Amiri Baraka's personal yearning for individuality and meaning captured the imagination of a generation of African Americans because to varying degrees that group was experiencing similar tensions—between moods ranging from spiritual ennui, personal malaise, and identity crisis on the one hand to racial kinship, black consciousness, and cultural regeneration on the other. Thus, one of Baraka's most important creative achievements is his "artistic reordering" of the African American odyssey in search of identity, purpose, and direction.[7]

For the purposes of this study, the most important dimension of Baraka's avocation is his role in developing the politics of black cultural nationalism. The ideological and political transformation of Amiri Baraka into a militant political activist in the 1960s was as influential as that of Paul Robeson in the 1930s. "More than any other American writer, white or black," writes Werner Sollors, "Baraka is the committed artist *par excellence.*"[8] Baraka's formative political influences are an interesting blend, ranging from Fidel Castro and Mao Zedong to Julius Nyerere and Sekou Toure. While his ideological and literary ancestors are Richard Wright, Langston Hughes, Paul Robeson, Harry Haywood, and Aimé Cesaire, Baraka's own generation of militant literary and intellectual influences include Askia Muhammad Toure, Jayne Cortez, Walter Rodney, Amilcar Cabral, Ngugi Wa Thiong'o, and Sonia Sanchez.

During the Black Power era, Amiri Baraka assumed "the stature of the people's hero and rebellious outlaw," becoming, in Sellors assessment, "the symbolic heir to Malcolm, the 'Malcolm X of literature.'"[9] The increasing radicalization of the Black Revolt and the rise of the Black Arts Movement pulled LeRoi Jones from relative political obscurity in the Beat circles of Greenwich Village, swept him into the center of the Black Power movement, christened him Imamu Amiri Baraka, and ultimately propelled the foremost black literary figure into the ranks of black national political leadership. Because of the power and popularity of his cultural and political activities, Imamu Baraka's trajectory to cultural nationalism became one of the most striking and influential models for self-transformation in the Black Power movement. Harold Cruse explains that the young intellectuals, artists, writers, poets, and musicians of the 1960s were "actually coming of age into a great intellectual, political, creative and theoretical vacuum. They would enter the arena of activity in search of leadership . . . One of the most outstanding of them, LeRoi Jones, learned in such a personal way as to epitomize within himself all the other things his generation learned either empirically or vicariously."[10]

Baraka's influence on the political dynamics of cultural nationalism was both immediate and fundamental. While the Harlem Renaissance of the 1920s treasured the accomplishments of the black establishment and counseled racial moderation, the Black Arts Movement celebrated the folk culture of blues people and preached black revolution. In contrast to the Harlem Renaissance, the Black Arts Movement was aimed at black America rather than white critics and audiences.[11] "In essence, Baraka and the Black Arts Movement have had a profound and lasting philosophical and aesthetic impact on all postintegrationist black art," explains William Harris, "they have turned black art from other-directed to ethnically centered. Thus the contemporary [African American] artist writes out of his or her own culture and, moreover, is self-consciously an [African American]."[12]

This study of the dynamics of black cultural nationalism examines how Amiri Baraka's cultural politics contributed to the Black Power experiments in the 1960s and influenced the course of black nationality formation in the 1970s. In *The Dynamics of Cultural Nationalism*, John Hutchinson defines the cultural nationalist as one who sees the essence of a nation as its distinct civilization, generated by its unique history and culture. In a metaphoric sense, the cultural nationalist understands the nation as an *organic* entity, a natural solidarity expressing the spirit of a people. Such cultural nationalists as Malcolm X and Amiri Baraka emphasized the importance of winning some measure of self-determination in order to create the conditions for the flowering of the African personality.[13] Furthermore, Hutchinson observes that "cultural nationalism is a movement of moral regeneration which seeks to re-unite the different aspects of the nation—traditional and modern, agriculture and industry, science and religion—by returning to the creative life-principle of the nation."[14] For Baraka's cultural nationalism, the black conventions represented the core of the *nation-becoming;* those assemblies were the gatherings at which the nation took definitive shape. Thus, the black political assemblies were the centerpiece of Baraka's politics of cultural nationalism, that is, the heart of the strategy of nationality formation.

Before the black assemblies, the politics of cultural nationalism was confined to small circles of students, artists, and intellectuals; in terms of black nationality formation, it remained a *head* full of radical ideas but separated from the *body* of the black community. However, between 1965 and 1970, more than 500 urban uprisings galvanized a new generation in the struggle for black liberation. The massive tumult of the ghetto revolts set the stage for the fusion between the nationalism of small circles of radical artists and intellectuals and the grassroots nationalism of the broad urban masses; out of that explosive mix came a new generation of militant Black Power organizations, demanding self-determination, self-respect, and self-defense. In the midst of the uprisings the politics of black cultural nationalism and the Modern Black Convention Movement took form, unleashing the dynamics of nationality formation. During those turbulent years, Amiri Baraka's poetry raised the slogan, "It's Nation Time!"

The black conventions were an essential component of the Black Power movement, which included the bold cultural, political, and economic programs proposed and developed by the Black Arts Renaissance, the Black Panther Party, the US Organization, the Republic of New Africa, the Revolutionary Action Movement, the Nation of Islam, the Organization of Afro-American Unity, and the League of Revolutionary Black Workers. Together these cultural and political formations galvanized millions of black people in the broadest movement in African American history. High school and college youth organized black student unions; writers and artists established the black arts; professors and educators created black studies programs; athletes mobilized protests against poverty and racism; workers fashioned militant unions; welfare mothers demanded power and dignity; soldiers resisted army discipline; and during prison uprisings such as Attica, politically conscious inmates saluted Malcolm X and George Jackson.[15] Clearly, the agitational effect of Black Power as a slogan was unprecedented.

During the Black Power era, the politics of cultural nationalism took advantage of that momentum by proposing a strategy of black liberation that involved the struggle for regional autonomy in urban centers, in alliance with oppressed people of color in the United States, particularly Puerto Ricans and Mexican Americans. From these semiautonomous urban enclaves, the conventions sought to accelerate the process of black nationality formation through the rapid spread of independent black economic, institutional, cultural, social, and political development. One basic driving force in that process of nationality formation was the increasing degree of conflict between the black communities on the one hand and both the welfare and police bureaucracies on the other.[16] Another major driving force in that process was the collapse of basic government and commercial services in the postindustrial ghettos. In response, the cultural nationalist strategy of African American radicals was to develop parallel black institutions in the void left by the urban crisis, emphasizing the failure of the American government and mainstream economy in providing basic services and offering black nationalism and cooperative economics as alternatives.

The story of the phenomenal rise of black cultural nationalism as a mass movement is told here with an eye toward the broader context in which that development unfolded: the strength, persistence, and cancer of institutional racism; the violent antagonism of racial and ethnic conflict in the political arena; the effect of the 1965 Voting Rights Act on the nature of black political mobilization; the impact of black migrations on urban ethos; the import of increasing population concentrations of African Americans in the cities; and the crucial influence of international developments on African American identity and black consciousness.

Acknowledgments

I am indebted to a number of institutions and individuals who made this book possible. In terms of institutions, study and research grants from the New Jersey Historical Commission, the University of Pennsylvania, Northwestern University, and Sarah Lawrence College were essential. I am particularly indebted to the New Jersey Historical Commission Research Grant; the Flik International Travel Grant, Hewlett-Mellon Research Grant, and Simpson Research Grant from Sarah Lawrence; a postdoctoral fellowship from Northwestern; and the Fontaine, W. W. Smith, Burnham, and Mellon Fellowships from the University of Pennsylvania.

The following libraries and archives were more than generous and supportive. The Moorland-Spingarn Research Center at Howard University has seventy-two boxes in its Amiri Baraka Collection; the Beinecke Library at Yale University has two boxes of Langston Hughes's LeRoi Jones/Amiri Baraka files in the James Weldon Johnson Collection; the Deering Collection at Northwestern University has important LeRoi Jones/Amiri Baraka files; the Schomburg Center for Research in Black Culture in New York holds the Larry P. Neal Papers, the Hubert H. Harrison Papers, and the files of the National Negro Congress; the Dr. Martin Luther King Jr. Memorial Center held the King Papers before they were sent to Stanford University; Blacksides, Inc. has important Gary Convention files from its production of the documentary film *Eyes on the Prize;* and any study of Amiri Baraka's politics must consult the newspaper clippings of the Newark Public Library. I am also indebted to the library staffs at Columbia University, the Dayton Public Library, Iona College, Mount Vernon Public Library, Newark Public Library, New York University, New School for Social Research, Northwestern University, Princeton University, Rutgers University, Sarah Lawrence College, the University of Chicago, the University of Cincinnati, the University of Pennsylvania, and Yale University.

Extraordinary intellectual support was provided by these colleagues: Shakoor Aljuwani, Tamu Aljuwani, Scot Ngozi Brown, Mindy Chateauvert, Kathleen Cleaver, Amy Cohen, Alan Dawley, John Dittmer, Barbara Ehrenreich, Bill Fletcher, Leon Forrest, Herb Fox, Van Gosse, Rob Gregg, Allen Green, Henry Hampton, Jaribu Hill, Ngoma Hill, Lori Hunter, James Weusi Johnson, Ira Katznelson, Jeff Kerr-Richie, Robin D. G. Kelley, Miriam King, Karimu Lewis, Rasuli Lewis, Louis Masiah, Louise

Newman, Charles Payne, Marsha Pickett, Paulette Pierce, Frances Fox Piven, Aaron Porter, Gail Radford, Mfuasi Reed, Safi Reed, Terry Kay Rockefeller, William Sales, Bobby Seale, Libby Smith, Max Stanford, Monica Tetzlaff, Helene Tissieres, Kwame Ture, Jacqueline Wade, Cornel West, Michael West, Howard Winant, Almasi Woodard, Kuza Woodard, and Suzanne Woodard. Moreover, the professors at both Rutgers University and the University of Pennsylvania are a remarkable treasure, especially Elijah Anderson, Mary F. Berry, Linda Brodkey, Lee V. Cassanelli, Richard S. Dunn, Robert F. Engs, Evelyn Brooks Higginbotham, Walter Licht, Clement Price, and Said Samatar.

A year at the African American Studies Program and the Center for Urban Affairs and Policy Research at Northwestern University helped me deepen my understanding of both persistent urban poverty and new developments in Africana Studies. Moreover, teaching at both the New School for Social Research and Sarah Lawrence College put me in contact with both exceptional students and two superb faculty writing circles, led by Louise Tilly and Lyde Sizer, respectively. I learned important lessons from Charles Tilly and Ira Katznelson in the circle at the New School. And, with Lyde Sizer and Robert Desjarlais at the helm, the faculty writing group at Sarah Lawrence is producing a number of important works by Chikwenye Okonjo Ogunyemi, Musifiky Mwanasali, Sandra Robinson, Mary Porter, and Paul Josephson.

Sarah Lawrence College is a noble intellectual community. I am deeply indebted to my colleagues, particularly Cameron Afzal, Janet Alexander, Regina Arnold, Paola Bacchetta, James Bowen, Bella Brodzki, Gary Burnley, Robert Cameron, Dominick Carbone, David Castriota, Persis Charles, Emmy Devine, Annie-Claude Dobbs, Roland Dollinger, Daphne Dumas, Omar Encarnacion, Charling C. Fagan, Joseph Forte, Luis Francia, Margery Franklin, Raymond Franklin, Suzanne Gardinier, Mason Gentzler, Fawaz Gerges, Alice Ilchman, Susan James, Barbara Kaplan, Shirley Kaplan, Marilyn Katz, William Melvin Kelley, Randall Kenan, Judith Kicinski, Robert Kinnally, Arnold Krupat, Mary LaChapelle, Eduardo Lago, Cassandra Medley, Nick Mills, Priscilla Murolo, Alice Olson, Leah Olson, Judith Papachristou, William Park, Gilberto Perez, Marilyn Power, Charlotte Price, Debra Priestly, Elfie Raymond, Sandra Robinson, Shahnaz Rouse, Prema Samuel, Joelle Sander, Raymond Seidelman, Judy Serafini-Sauli, William Shullenberger, Amy Swerdlow, Peter Thom, Rose Anne Thom, Pauline Watts, Sara Wilford, and Horatio Williams.

My editorial and research assistants were Crystal Byndloss, Tara Crichlow, Wednesday Guyot, Barbara Hickey, Ingrid McFarlane, Nicole

Morris, Anita Rich, Heather Scott, Tanya Sutton, Toni Tysen, Carol Whitehead, Vanessa Whitehead, Almasi Woodard, and Kuza Woodard. Moreover, the professional and technical support that I received from Dennis Penn and Linda Cardoso at the Duplicating Service Center of Sarah Lawrence was essential to the production of this manuscript.

Just as important as libraries and archives were the oral sources of this history; the following activists, teachers, and scholars spent hours in interviews and discussions helping get the story of the black liberation movement straight: Shakoor Aljuwani, Tamu Aljuwani, Muminina Akiba, Sababa Akili, Sam Anderson, Ahmad M. Babu, Amina Baraka, Amiri Baraka, David Mtetezi Barrett, Sanjulo W. Ber, Tamu Bess, Unita Blackwell, Fahamisha Brooks, Naisha Brooks, Scot Ngozi Brown, C. C. Bryant, Eugene Campbell, Stokely Carmichael/Kwame Ture, Dorothy Cotton, John Henrik Clarke, Harold Cruse, Robert Curvin, Dennis Dahmer, Imarisha Davis, Kamau Davis, David Dennis, James Farmer, Vicki Garvin, Larry Hamm, Vincent Harding, Curtis Hayes, Harry Haywood, Greg Hite, Taalamu Holiday, Wynona Holman, Maisha Jackson, June Johnson, Maulana Karenga, Karimu Lewis, Rasuli Lewis, Charles McDew, Haki Madhubuti, Jeledi Majadi, Cheo Mfalme, Bob Moses, Baba Mshauri/Russell Bingham, Saladin Muhammad, Simba Mwenea, Diane Nash, Kasisi Nakawa, Saidi Nguvu, Obiodun Oyewole, Sgt. William Reynolds, Jamala Rogers, William Sales, Muminina Salimu, Michael Pili Simanga, Sonia Sanchez, Bobby Seale, Archie Shepp, Sekou Sundiata, Cheo Taalamu, Malaika Thazabu, Donald Tucker, James Turner, Sala Udin, Eulius Ward, Richard Wesley, Preston Wilcox, Terry Williams, and Jalia Woods.

Another set of colleagues assisted in the illustrations for this book. The Congress of African People's photography department, Sura Wa Taifa (which is Swahili for "Images of the Nation") took many of the best pictures of Baraka's Pan-African movement. One of the key photographers in that department was Zachariah Risasi Dais, who took the photographs in the Baraka family collection. Amiri Baraka graciously permitted the use of that photography collection in this book.

Finally, mentors are a special gift, and through the years I have been especially endowed by these devoted teachers: Helen Woodard, Theodore Woodard, John W. P. Collier, Baba Mshauri, Harry Haywood, Vicki Garvin, Amiri Baraka, Robert F. Engs, Vytautas Kavolis, Taalamu Holiday, Weusi Johnson, Jalia Woods, and Michael B. Katz.

A Nation within a Nation

Introduction

It is a peculiar sensation, this double consciousness, this sense of always looking at one's self through the eyes of others, of measuring one's soul by the tape of a world that looks on in amused contempt and pity. One ever feels his two-ness,—an American, a Negro; two souls, two thoughts, two unreconciled strivings; two warring ideals in one dark body, whose dogged strength alone keeps it from being torn asunder.
—W. E. B. Du Bois, *The Souls of Black Folk*

Each generation must, out of relative obscurity, discover its mission, fulfill it, or betray it.
—Frantz Fanon, *The Wretched of the Earth*

These young people were actually coming of age into a great intellectual, political, creative and theoretical vacuum. They would enter the arena of activity in search of leadership. . . . One of the most outstanding of them, LeRoi Jones, learned in such a personal way as to epitomize within himself all the other things his generation learned either empirically or vicariously.
—Harold Cruse, *The Crisis of the Negro Intellectual*

The Dynamics of Black Nationality Formation

During the 1960s and the 1970s, Amiri Baraka (LeRoi Jones) rose to national leadership in the Black Revolt at the head of the Modern Black Convention Movement. The Modern Black Convention Movement began in 1966 with the Black Arts Convention in Detroit and the National Black Power Conference planning summit in Washington, D.C. Under Baraka's leadership, elements of the Black Arts Movement and sections of the Black Power Movement merged to fashion the politics of black cultural nationalism in the Modern Black Convention Movement.

In the aftermath of hundreds of African American urban uprisings, black nationality formation developed quickly on the municipal level. In June 1968, 1,000 African Americans drafted a black political agenda at the Newark Black Political Convention. In November 1969, African American and Latino leaders joined at the Black and Puerto Rican Political Convention, selecting a "Community Choice" slate of candidates for municipal offices in Newark. By June 1970, the black and Puerto Rican convention candidates won the municipal election in Newark and broke an historic, executive political color bar by installing the first black mayor in a major northeastern city. By 1972, the Modern Black Convention Movement in Essex County, New Jersey, had created a new congressional district, expanding the space for black political representation in America. Eventually, U.S. Representative Donald Payne, an African American, replaced white incumbent Peter Rodino as the Democrat in that congressional seat.

In Newark, Baraka's movement developed numerous organizations and institutions to accelerate the process of black nationality formation: several political groups, including the United Brothers and the Committee For A Unified NewArk (CFUN); a number of youth organizations, including the Simba Wachunga (Young Lions) and the NewArk Student Federation; cultural centers, including the Spirit House and Hekalu Mwalimu (Temple of the Teacher); a repertory group, the Spirit House Movers and Players; two newspapers, *Black NewArk* (local) and *Unity and Struggle* (national); a journal of jazz criticism, *Cricket*; independent black publishers, including Jihad Publications; the *Black NewArk* radio and television programs; several independent and autonomous African Free Schools; and a host of cooperative stores, shops, and other business developments, including a housing complex. Two apartment developments planned by Baraka's organizations, Kawaida Towers and Kawaida Community Development, became explosive in the political arena.

During the 1970s the politics of black cultural nationalism emerged from its local urban enclaves to become a national phenomenon. The Modern Black Convention Movement hastened black nationality formation by helping to create a black national political community. While black elected officials on the local, state, and national levels developed structures like the Congressional Black Caucus to enhance their political positions, black grassroots organizations rallied their forces to define their own agenda.

Consequently, on the national level, the Modern Black Convention Movement produced four critical organizations: the Congress of African People, the African Liberation Support Committee, the National Black Assembly, and the Black Women's United Front. The Congress of African People (CAP) represented the culmination of years of annual National Black Power Conferences. Three thousand black nationalists and civil rights activists gathered in Atlanta, Georgia, in 1970 to launch that organization, supported by a broad united front of leaders who included Amiri Baraka, Louis Farrakhan, Jesse Jackson, Whitney Young, Coretta Scott King, and Betty Shabazz. One of the most formidable Black Power groups of the 1970s, CAP mobilized around black nationalism and Pan-Africanism and established branches in twenty-five cities in the United States. In May 1972, CAP joined with an even broader front of black nationalists and Pan-Africanists to organize the first African Liberation Day in support of national liberation parties in Zimbabwe, Angola, Mozambique, Guinea-Bissau, and South Africa. This mass demonstration of 60,000 black people produced the African Liberation Support Committee (ALSC), which established numerous chapters in Canada, the West Indies, and the United States.

While the ALSC took the initiative in foreign policy, for African Americans the most popular domestic thrust in the U.S. political arena was the National Black Assembly (NBA). The NBA was founded at the March 1972 National Black Political Convention in Gary, Indiana, which gathered between 8,000 and 12,000 black political leaders to develop the National Black Political Agenda. Representatives of the NBA presented the Black Agenda to both the Republican and Democratic national conventions in the 1972 presidential election. The independent momentum of black politics created by the NBA contributed to the remarkable rise in the number of black elected officials during the 1970s. In the aftermath of the 1974 "African Women Unite" Conference in Newark, New Jersey, Amina Baraka (Sylvia Jones) led more than 800 women and men in CAP, ALSC, and the NBA, representing twenty-eight states, in founding the Black Women's United Front (BWUF), with the aim of developing an autonomous political and ideological agenda for African American women. At a series of summit meetings, the BWUF analyzed the chief causes of the oppression and exploitation of black women and, from an African American perspective, defined the targets and objectives of women's liberation in the United States.

This book looks at several fundamental issues. First, if sociologists predicted that African American urbanization would lead to assimilation, then why was there such a phenomenal spread of black nationalism in the 1960s? Second, what role did black cultural nationalism play in the Black Revolt? This question has a number of dimensions. Theodore Draper insists that the African American idea of a black nationality in the United States is at best a political mirage and at worst an escapist "fantasy." Was it essentially escapist, or was it, as some major sociologists and historians have suggested, ambivalent, illogical, dysfunctional, or pessimistic?[1] Was black cultural nationalism progressive and democratic, or was it reactionary and fascist?[2] Did black nationalism and the urban uprisings cause the demise of the Black Revolt in 1968? In other words, what role did the politics of black cultural nationalism play in the black freedom movement of the 1960s: did it accelerate or retard the process of black nationality formation? And how so?

Third, what are the dynamics between black nationalists and black Marxists? There is a long history of rivalry between these two camps, dating back to the struggles between Marcus Garvey's Universal Negro Improvement Association and the American Communist Party. However, there is also a history of ideological borrowing between black nationalism and socialism, which is a major theme in the development of such leading black figures and organizations as Hubert H. Harrison and W. E. B. Du Bois in the American Socialist Party, Cyril Briggs in the African Blood Brotherhood, A. Philip Randolph in the National Negro Congress, and more recently Huey P. Newton in the Black Panther Party and Amiri Baraka in the Congress of African People. How do we make sense out of these peculiar dynamics of both rivalry and interpenetration?

And finally, what is the relationship between black people and America? Are African Americans an ethnic group along the same lines as Irish Americans, Jewish Americans, and German Americans, destined to be assimilated into American society? Or do they constitute an oppressed nationality locked out of White America, fundamentally in conflict with the established social, economic, and political order of the United States?[3]

With an eye toward these questions, this study examines Amiri Baraka's cultural approach to Black Power, the rise and fall of the Modern Black Convention Movement, and the phenomenal spread of black nationalism in the urban centers of late twentieth-century America. During the 1960s and 1970s, Amiri Baraka led in the development of some of the most important Black Power organizations in America. The dynamics of black nationality formation interwove the rich networks resulting from the Black Power conferences and the black political conventions of the 1960s and 1970s into the impressive fabric of the Modern Black Convention Movement.

While Clayborne Carson and some other historians have claimed that black nationalism was the cause of the early demise of the Black Revolt, this book argues that the politics of black cultural nationalism and the dynamics of the Modern Black Convention Movement were fundamental to the endurance of the Black Revolt from the 1960s into the 1970s.[4] Hundreds of black rebellions and scores of black assemblies established the matrix for the African American political culture that led to the brief hegemony of the politics of black cultural nationalism. At the head of the Modern Black Convention Movement, Amiri Baraka's politics of cultural nationalism became one of the cutting edges in the struggle for political democracy. Thus, an analysis of the politics of black cultural nationalism is essential to an understanding of the spectacular spread of the Modern Black Convention Movement. This study traces the dramatic transformation in Baraka's cultural nationalist politics that facilitated the burgeoning black conventions.

In the mass assemblies of the Modern Black Convention Movement, the different socioeconomic classes in the black community revealed something of their political physiognomy as it seemed as if each force was compelled to candidly articulate and fight for its own interests in the struggle for power. At first in his leadership capacity, Amiri Baraka attempted to restrain the tensions between the competing political interests in the Modern Black Convention Movement. Between 1972 and 1975, however, the political and ideological conflicts within the Modern Black Convention Movement sharpened, and in the context of increasing antagonism, the grassroots momentum for a black national political community unraveled. By 1974, Baraka's faction of the Congress of African People moved to the Left, repudiating black nationalism and embracing a revolutionary Third World Marxism. The momentum of the Modern Black Convention Movement collapsed tragically and traumatically as the construction of Baraka's Kawaida Towers and the Kawaida Community Development were halted by a lethal three-way combination of racial violence by white vigilantes, political treachery by black elected officials, and American apartheid practiced by the federal government. In the aftermath of those catastrophic events and with the loss of its grassroots political center, the black national political community became increasingly confused, fragmented, and anguished by the debacle of Black Power.

The Argument

In this narrative history I suggest several major propositions about the modern dynamics of black nationality formation. African Americans are an oppressed nationality subjugated by racial oppression in the United States.[5] Black nationality consciousness took form in the context of slavery, racial oppression, and group conflict in America.[6] Moreover, this study shows that the chief sources of contemporary black nationality formation are urban.[7] African American nationalism has spread quickly in the cities because of the nature of urban bureaucratic competition and conflict in a multiethnic capitalist society.[8] As blacks migrated to the North, they were not absorbed into White America; instead they developed a distinct national culture and consciousness. Unfortunately, uncritical discussions of assimilation serve only to obscure the fact that in the twentieth century African Americans were urbanized and modernized in a very separate manner, which laid the foundations for a distinct black national political community.

There are several reasons for this. In the twentieth century, black ghetto formation generated a new black ethos and contributed to an unprecedented degree of African American nationalism in the urban areas. Moreover, in contrast to a great deal of American sociological prognosis, certain aspects of cultural assimilation contribute directly to black nationality formation. Ernest Gellner suggests that in modern urban society, nationality formation is accelerated as dominant nationalities monopolize positions of wealth, power, privilege and construct bureaucratic ethnic boundaries that exclude other nationalities, particularly those oppressed groups that are considered as different language communities.[9] Scholars agree that Black America is not only one of the most oppressed groups in the United States but also one of its most distinct language communities.[10] As African Americans migrated to northern urban industrial centers in unprecedented numbers and raised their level of education, these bureaucratic ethnic boundaries combined with white racism to exclude a rising group of educated black Americans. Anxious for their place in the sun, an emerging black intelligentsia increasingly sought to establish *parallel* institutions where they might find appropriate positions. In key political and economic arenas these same dynamics were expressed in growing demands for *proportional representation* in the corporate and government bureaucracies. The threadbare discussion of assimilation, presumably as the logical opposite of nationalism, tends to obscure the complexity of these crucial dynamics. In contrast to a great deal of received wisdom, the pace of black nationality development actually accelerated as African Americans were urbanized and acculturated.[11] Rather than explain these developments, some of the earlier approaches toward urbanization and assimilation tended to evade them by simply designating black nationalism as either irrational or dysfunctional. Unfortunately, those theories remain forceful in American scholarship.[12]

But if black nationality formation takes place in those segments of the oppressed intelligentsia that are excluded, that does not explain why other segments of that intelligentsia, particularly those that were nominally "integrated" into the system, became important proponents of black nationalism. In other words, how do we explain the dynamics that led such figures as Amiri Baraka, once in the center of the integrated Greenwich Village literary circles, into the ranks of black nationalism? British sociologist Anthony D. Smith identifies the logic that helps account for these dynamics in terms of a conflict between *bureaucratic nationalism* and *romantic nationalism*.[13] During the civil rights revolution to destroy Jim Crow racism, an impersonal U.S. bureaucratic nationalism penetrated into new dimensions of the social and cultural life of Black America, attempting to impose conformity. During the 1960s, as more and more black students appeared at the national universities and colleges of white America, black nationalism spread at an unprecedented pace among African American college students, artists, and intellectuals. Many of those people were alienated as the bureaucracy demanded that African Americans replace their black identities with white ones in order to find a slot in the land of opportunity. In other words, they resented the implication that blacks had to become "white" in order to *make it* in America. Rather than conform to fit into those slots, many of those youths bolstered the forces of black cultural nationalism.

If black students and intellectuals saw one face of American bureaucratic nationalism, the grass roots saw quite another face as federal urban renewal schemes threatened to destroy many black communities. Thus, as many metropolitan centers sought to modernize the inner cities with urban renewal, they unwittingly accelerated the processes of black nationality formation. By setting in motion these grassroots communities and a radical black intelligentsia at the same time, the 1960s witnessed an unprecedented fusion between the nationalism of the grass roots and the nationalism of the emerging college-educated elite. Since a number of these college students grew up in the black ghettos, that fusion prepared the conditions for the development of a grassroots intelligentsia. As that new breed of black students sought its identity, it was particularly receptive to Malcolm X and his "Message to the Grass Roots."

Another critical reason for the acceleration of black nationality formation since the 1960s is group conflict in the American political arena. Group conflicts have helped shape ethnic political traditions for Irish Americans and Jewish Americans and forge nationality consciousness for African Americans.[14] Nationalities, argues Louis Wirth, are essentially conflict groups.[15] The emergence of black politics in America was accompanied by "group trauma," the kind of "collective suffering" that stimulated the development of a collective nationality consciousness. Peter

Eisinger observes that at the early stages of nationality formation the group's development proceeds much faster than the power structure's willingness to incorporate them into the polity; that situation renders the group politically *invisible*. Consequently, emergent groups advocate violent and/or radical solutions to their problems.[16] In line with this pattern, during the 1960s and 1970s Black Power groups proposed a number of radical solutions to racial oppression.

The basic strategy of the politics of black cultural nationalism reflected a radical sense of the urban crisis of the 1960s. The black nationalists of the 1960s viewed the members of liberation movements in the Third World not only as allies but as brothers and sisters in the struggle. Identifying with the battles for self-determination in Africa, Asia, and Latin America, the politics of cultural nationalism proposed a strategy of black liberation involving struggles for regional autonomy in urban centers, in alliance with oppressed people of color in the United States, particularly Puerto Ricans and Mexican Americans. Tactically, this stratagem involved mass social mobilization for black self-government at the municipal level and for proportional representation at higher levels of government. From these semiautonomous urban enclaves, the African American cultural nationalists sought to accelerate the process of black nationality formation through the rapid spread of independent black economic, institutional, cultural, social, and political development. One important driving force in that process was the collapse of basic government and commercial services in the second ghetto. The cultural nationalist strategy of African American radicals was to develop *parallel* black institutions in the void left by the urban crisis, emphasizing the failure of the American government and mainstream economy in providing basic services and offering black nationalism and cooperative economics as rational alternatives. Considerations of strategic allies revolved around other communities that experienced similar urban dynamics.

Therefore, looking at these issues from a broad view of American history, the Black American nationality took shape in the crucible of racial oppression, nationality conflict, and ethnic competition in the United States. White racism and group antagonism are not temporary distortions of American democracy; they are fundamental features of U.S. society. Thus, the black freedom struggle is a *protracted* collective effort to abolish racial oppression and to advance black equality. The black freedom movement is *heterogeneous* by nature. In 1948, Harry Haywood defined the black liberation movement as "the sum total of the efforts of all organizations, groups, and agencies among Negroes which strive in any manner and to any degree to realize the ideal of Negro equality. Included in this concept is the struggle against all tendencies which conflict with the basic conditions for the achievement of this aim."[17] By implication, such a movement for black liberation is a united front effort, embracing a broad range of the different religions, philosophies, ideologies, and politics within the black national community. Thus, the black freedom movement is the entirety of African American efforts to knock down the barriers to black equality in the U.S. and to overcome the obstacles to the social, cultural, and economic development of peoples of African descent. While in the nineteenth and early twentieth century the classical Black Convention Movement helped create a black national consciousness and contributed to the early development of the black freedom movement, in the 1960s and 1970s the Modern Black Convention Movement played a crucial role in the Black Power Revolt and in African American nationality formation.

Black Nationality Formation

For the purposes of this study, nationalism is an "ideological movement for the attainment and maintenance of autonomy and individuality for a social group, some of whose members conceive it to constitute an actual or potential nation."[18] Although many intellectuals yearn for a pure nationalist ideology, they are probably longing for the impossible, because nationalism is heterogeneous. Typically, nationalist movements embrace various elements of the influential philosophies of their age. As Rudolf Heberle observes, "The more important social movements tend to absorb a great deal of the social thought of their time and their ideologies therefore tend to become rather complex aggregates of ideas."[19] The findings in this study confirm Heberle's conclusion on this score. In fact, as Konstantin Symmons-Symnolewicz observes, in nationalism "the number of combinations . . . is potentially unlimited."[20] Thus, the key is to understand the configuration of the distinct blend or amalgam of any particular nationalist movement, including black cultural nationalism in America. In the 1960s, black cultural nationalism embraced elements of Third World Marxism.

But these definitions are not necessarily the same as criteria for analysis: how would one know if a black nationalist movement is weak or strong? In other words, how would one measure the degree of success of any particular movement that fell short of sovereignty? Nationality formation is the standard yardstick applied to such movements today. Looking at nationalist movements in various countries, Anthony Smith surmises that one important way to distinguish the strength of their role in nationality formation is by the variations in their "intensity, duration, extent, force, and clarity." Consequently, he suggests that the research agenda for an understanding of the dynamics of nationality formation must involve "the extent and intensity of their activities; the complexity of their organizations; the extent to which their ideology is diffused to the group and the number of their adherents; the unity and dedication of the hard core of the membership; the clarity and articulation of their goals; the importance of nationalist issues to both members and their group [vis-à-vis] non-nationalist issues; and, the consistency and duration of the movement as a whole."[21]

By those measures, a more developed nationalist movement hastens the process of turning a specific population into a nationality; however, a less developed movement plays a negligible role in that course of events or even retards the process. In the worst cases, such movements may actually contribute to the disintegration of a community. Hence, Smith concludes that strong nationalist movements develop four essential components: a dedicated hard core imbued with the new nationalist values and tastes; an array of institutions and organizations; a set of clearly articulated myths and rituals, distinguishing its nationalism from other ideologies, and a fairly broad diffusion in the cities.[22] By these criteria, the politics of black cultural nationalism played a substantial role in nationality formation between 1960 and 1976.

In his sociology of nationalism, Symmons-Symnolewicz suggests that the best approach to the subject of nationality formation is to examine "the dynamics of nationalism, that is, the factors which underlie the origins of nationalist movements, shape their development and determine their success or failure."[23] Moreover, Harry Haywood suggests that students of nationality formation approach the subject with "an eye towards examining the particular *history* of a nation or national group and understanding its particular *features*, *dynamic* and *future direction*."[24]

Historical Background

There have been at least five distinct phases in the historical process of black nationality formation in the United States. The first phase was the ethnogenesis of African Americans during American slavery; this established the social and cultural foundation of Black America. The second was the black nationalism that flowered before the Civil War among the small literary and abolitionist circles of free blacks in the urban North, inspired by the Republican principles of the successful American and Haitian revolutions.[25] A third phase resulted from the failure of the Civil War and Reconstruction to guarantee full citizenship for African Americans; under racial oppression and Jim Crow segregation, a subject nation developed in the Black Belt areas of the South.[26] That black nationalism was vividly expressed by the great Kansas Exodus after the collapse of Reconstruction. The fourth phase of black nationality formation resulted from the Great Migration of perhaps 1.5 million African Americans to competitive, urban, industrial centers and from the development of large, compact, black concentrations in the ghettos of America; the flowering of this urban nationalism coincided with the colonial uprisings of the First World War, a global sense of nationality graphically expressed in the Garvey Movement of the 1920s. The fifth phase of black nationality formation ensued from the migration of 4 million black Americans from the South between 1940 and 1970 and the development of dozens of *second ghettos*, which generated hundreds of urban uprisings during the 1960s; this modern sense of nationality was heralded by the Black Power Movement and the politics of black cultural nationalism. This phase of black nationalism entered into the political arena around the 1965 Voting Rights Act, expressing solidarity with the radical liberation movements in Africa, Asia, and Latin America. Consider each of the five phases of black nationality formation in turn.

Ethnogenesis

In contrast to white ethnic groups, African Americans were forced to migrate to America as slaves. While other groups left an oppressive situation behind, black Americans were thrust into the house of bondage. This is a crucial difference between the foundation of Black America and that of any white ethnic group. During slavery, African Americans began developing into a distinct nationality as the result of complex processes of *ethnogenesis*; various West African ethnic groups were forged into one people in American bondage.[27] In contrast to the other New World slave systems, which produced multitiered, racially stratified social orders in Latin America and the Caribbean, racial slavery in British North America produced a singular two-caste system, a dynamic of racial formation dividing groups into *whites* and *blacks*.[28]

Unfortunately, that crucial dimension of the ethnogenesis of Black America has received the least attention. Nevertheless, a clearer picture is emerging: the definitive two-caste division into the categories of black and white was not uncontested. According to W. E. B. Du Bois, E. Franklin Frazier, Joel Williamson, F. James Davis, and James Oliver Horton, the distinct two-caste system in the U.S. persevered over a challenging alternative racial arrangement, a three-caste system. The most striking cases of a Caribbean-style, three-caste structure in the Slave South were in New Orleans and Charleston.[29] During Reconstruction, while that triple-caste arrangement prevailed in Louisiana, Eric Foner observes the beginning of the integration of light and dark African Americans in the midst of the revolutionary cultural situation in South Carolina. Influential sectors of the biracial elite began repudiating caste arrangements and opting instead for class formation within the black community. Thus, Foner explains that a distinct pattern of ethnogenesis for Black America unfolded as the "sons and daughters of prominent free families, mostly young people in their twenties, fanned out into the South Carolina countryside as teachers and missionaries":

> Several thereby acquired positions of local political leadership, and later returned to Charleston as constitutional convention delegates and legislators. Thus the children of the Charleston elite cast their lot with the freedmen, bringing, as they saw it, modern culture to the former slaves. This encounter was not without its tensions. But in the long run it hastened the emergence of a black community stratified by class rather than color, in which the former free elite took its place as one element of a new black bourgeoisie, instead of existing as a separate caste as it had in the port cities of the antebellum Lower South.[30]

Of course, outside those exceptional situations in New Orleans and Charleston, the integration of light and dark African Americans flowered subtly within the processes of family formation and community building on thousands of farms and in hundreds of towns in the Upper South. That pattern of ethnogenesis is evident in the manuscripts of the 1880 agricultural census in North Carolina, where the census taker noted a wide spectrum of colors and hues within many farm households as light-skinned African Americans found kinship within the embrace of Black America. However, key vestiges of that three-caste arrangement survived even in the North, where an exclusive, fair-skinned caste persisted for decades against the forces of black nationality formation. Horton examined the various patterns within those three-caste arrangements in antebellum Cincinnati, Buffalo, and Boston. While W. E. B. Du Bois observed a privileged, blue-veined elite in late-nineteenth-century Philadelphia, David Katzman reports a similar exclusive pattern in Detroit before the Great Migration. Ultimately, the interplay between the forces of white racism and the dynamics of black nationality formation was stronger than the three-caste system in the United States. On the one hand, increasingly,

Jim Crow racism made little distinction between light and dark African Americans after the Civil War. On the other hand, the Great Migration created the conditions for the triumph of class formation within Black America; the rise of a ghetto business sector mortally wounded the foundation for color caste privilege, mixed light and dark elites, and laid the basis for the "Browning" of the black middle class. The cultural foundation for a new "Brown" aesthetic was strengthened by the creative works of W. E. B. Du Bois at the turn of the century and of the Harlem Renaissance during the 1920s. The most devastating blow to the prestige of the color caste system was delivered by the Black Arts Movement, which insisted upon, as the poet Haki Madhubuti (Don L. Lee) put it, "the integration of light and dark Black people." In that sense, the Black Arts Movement represented the zenith of African American nationality formation, returning many to the bosom of the black community.[31]

To sum up, in the U.S. matrix of ethnic conflict and racial domination, the different West African groups became one African American people, developing a rich group life of culture, family, community, religion, folkways, and consciousness. Indeed, Lawrence Levine argues that under racial slavery, "the preliterate, premodern Africans, with their sacred world view, were so imperfectly acculturated into the secular American society into which they were thrust, were so completely denied access to the ideology and dreams which formed the core of the consciousness of other Americans, that they were forced to fall back upon the only cultural frames of reference that made any sense to them and gave them any feeling of security."[32] The development of a collective culture under these circumstances of racial bondage was facilitated by the fact that despite the ethnic diversity of their West African ancestors, these early African Americans "shared a fundamental outlook toward the past, present, and future and common means of cultural expression which could well have constituted the basis of a sense of common identity and world view capable of withstanding the impact of slavery."[33] That strong African American foundation generated a distinct sense of nationality that extended into the free black communities where former slaves clustered in the North.

Antebellum Black Conventions

As black nationality formation entered its second phase, its contours were suggested by the *range* and *diversity* of expressions of identity and solidarity in the black conventions. These sentiments indicate that African Americans viewed themselves as an oppressed black nation, deflected from its historical path by the formidable obstacles of the Atlantic slave trade,

American slavery, and white racism. The Ethiopianism of this early phase of black nationalism ranged from the radicalism of David Walker to the conservatism of Alexander Crummell, as its proponents heralded a return to a golden age of African civilization.[34]

Generations of African American leadership articulated their sense of black nationality and group identity in the expressive politics of the nineteenth-century black convention movements and in the twentieth-century black freedom movements. The black conventions began locally at least as early as 1817 in Richmond and Philadelphia.[35] Called together by Bishop Richard Allen, Reverend Absolom Jones, and entrepreneur James Forten, 3,000 African Americans rallied in Philadelphia at Mother Bethel African Methodist Episcopal Church in January 1817 to discuss their national destiny in the face of the proposals of the American Colonization Society. Privately, James Forten favored black settlement in Africa; he felt that the African Americans would never become a people until they "come out from amongst the white people."[36] It was the same national sentiment echoed later by J. Mercer Langston: "We must have a nationality, before we can become anybody."[37] However, the vast majority at that black convention protested the plans of the American Colonization Society to settle free blacks in Liberia. The black assembly proudly declared its sense of identity, birthright, self-worth, and critical republicanism:

> Whereas our ancestors (not of choice) were the first successful cultivators of the wilds of America, we their descendants feel ourselves entitled to participate in the blessings of her luxuriant soil, which their blood and sweat manured; and that any measure or system of measures, having a tendency to banish us from her bosom, would not only be cruel, but in direct violation of those principles, which have been the boast of this republic. . . . we never will separate ourselves voluntarily from the slave population in this country; they are our brethren by the ties of consanguinity, of suffering, and of wrong; and we feel that there is more virtue in suffering privations with them, than fancied advantages for a season.[38]

Thus, black Americans were one distinct people and they would rise out of bondage together; those who were free would not go "voluntarily" to Africa leaving their own people in chains.

The black conventions did not become national in scope until the fledgling assemblies of the 1830s. African American leadership came together under crisis conditions; it met in the aftermath of the monstrous attacks of savage white mobs in Cincinnati, Ohio, who in 1829 forced half of the black community to escape to Canada.[39] That crisis reached catastrophic proportions as state after state passed legislation against incoming black migration. Leon Litwack reports that a leading Cincinnati lawyer "explained to Alexis de Tocqueville that the severe restrictions on Negroes constituted an attempt 'to discourage them in every possible way.' Not only had the laws provided for their expulsion, the lawyer declared, 'but we annoy them in a thousand ways.'"[40] Thus, midwestern states alternated between anti–black migration legislation and mob violence. According to Litwack, "Three states—Illinois, Indiana, and Oregon—incorporated anti-immigration provisions into their constitutions."[41] Ominously, during the Illinois state constitutional debates, one person warned that the people in the southern portion of the state "would take the matter into their own hands, and commence a war of extermination." Similarly, at the Indiana state constitutional convention, one person argued that "it would be better to kill them off at once, if there is no other way to get rid of them." Thus, force was employed in southern Ohio to frustrate the settlement of 518 emancipated slaves from Virginia.[42] Although increasing racial oppression in the North set the stage for the spread of the African American assemblies, the Black Convention Movement refused to be discouraged.

At the first national convention in Philadelphia in 1830, the summit declared "That we do most cordially rejoice that the bond of brotherhood, which rivets a nation together in one indissoluble chain, has collected so large a portion of our people together."[43] As a center for political debates about the destiny of African Americans, the semiautonomous Black Convention Movement was one of the principal training grounds for such leaders as Frederick Douglass, Mary Ann Shadd, Henry Bibb, Mary Bibb, John S. Rock, Henry Highland Garnet, and Martin R. Delany. The strategy, tactics, and orientation of the black struggle for equality were debated heatedly at the black conventions of the 1840s and 1850s as African American leadership attempted to forge an independent stance regarding black destiny. At one Independence Day rally, Frederick Douglass asked white Americans:

What have I, or those I represent, to do with your national independence? Are the great principles of political freedom and of natural justice, embodied in the Declaration of Independence, extended to us? . . . What, to the American slave, is your 4th of July? I answer; a day that reveals to him, more than all other days in the year, the gross injustice and cruelty to which he is the constant victim. To him, your celebration is a sham; your boasted liberty, an unholy license; your national greatness, swelling vanity; your sounds of rejoicing are empty and heartless; your denunciation of tyrants brass fronted mockery; your prayers and hymns, your sermons and thanksgivings, with all your religious parade and solemnity, are to him, mere bombast, fraud, deception, impiety, and hypocrisy—a thin veil to cover up crimes which would disgrace a nation of savages.[44]

Speaking at one of the antebellum black summits in the 1840s in "An Address to the Slaves of the United States," Henry Highland Garnet argued that "no oppressed people have ever secured their liberty without resistance." He thundered:

Brethren, arise, arise! Strike for your lives and liberties. Now is the day and the hour. Let every slave throughout the land do this, and the days of slavery are numbered. You cannot be more oppressed than you have been—you cannot suffer greater cruelties than you have already. Rather die freemen than live to be slaves. Remember you are FOUR MILLIONS! . . . Let your motto be resistance! resistance! RESISTANCE![45]

For most African Americans breaking the bonds of slavery, resistance was indicated by a profoundly symbolic act of self-determination and self-definition. According to Orlando Patterson, the ritual of the *social death* of slaves involved the loss of their names in bondage; however, the process of rebirth pivoted upon the descendants of Africa *naming* themselves.[46] In *Slaves Without Masters*, Ira Berlin reports that free blacks

commonly celebrated emancipation by taking a new name. A new name was both a symbol of personal liberation and an act of political defiance; it reversed the enslavement process and confirmed the free [black's] newly won liberty just as the loss of an African name had earlier symbolized enslavement. Emancipation also gave blacks the opportunity to strip themselves of the comic classical names that had dogged them in slavery and to adopt common Anglo-American names. Very few Caesars, Pompeys, and Catos remained among the new freemen. In bondage, most blacks had but a single name; freedom also allowed them the opportunity to take another.[47]

Creating a new identity was a component part of establishing a new life and building the free black community. As Gary Nash explains, "Names are filled with social meaning, reflecting in many cases . . . 'personal experiences, historical happenings, attitudes to life, and cultural ideas and values.'" It is easy to forget that in many ways black emancipation was remarkable. As Nash puts it, "inventing a family name for oneself is an extraordinary act that few people experience." This process of cultural redefinition involved two stages: "first, the symbolic obliteration of the slave past; and second, the creation of a unique Afro-American identity."[48]

At the black conventions, leaders defined the group situation of African Americans as that of an oppressed nationality, similar to that of other oppressed people around the world. Martin R. Delany argued, "We are a nation within a nation;—as the Poles in Russia, the Hungarians in Austria; the Welsh, Irish, and Scotch in the British dominions."[49] Frederick Douglass explained that African Americans were an oppressed nation, a divided national group held in captivity:

> This people, free and slave, are . . . becoming a nation, in the midst of a nation which disowns them, and for weal or for woe this nation is united. The distinction between the slave and the free is not great, and their destiny seems one and the same. The black man is linked to his brother by indissoluble ties. The one cannot be truly free while the other is a slave. The free colored man is reminded by the ten thousand petty annoyances with which he meets of his identity with an enslaved people, and that with them he is destined to fall or flourish. We are one nation, then. If not one in immediate condition, at least one in prospects.[50]

Similarly, the Michigan black state convention call insisted on national self-determination:

> For as we are an oppressed people wishing to be free, we must evidently follow the examples of the oppressed nations that have preceded us: for history informs us that the liberties of an oppressed people are obtained only in proportion to their own exertions in their own cause. Therefore, in accordance with this truth, let us come up, and, like the oppressed people of England, Ireland and Scotland, band ourselves together and wage unceasing war against the high handed wrongs of the hideous monster of Tyranny.[51]

The black abolitionists established this sense of national identity and global consciousness as part of the foundation of Black America. Generation after generation have expressed this awareness of African nationality as they attempted to fashion black united fronts against white domination.

Civil War and Reconstruction

African Americans have been involved in a protracted struggle against Herrenvolk democracy: democracy for the ruling race but tyranny for the subjugated groups. And one of the persistent psychological tendencies in American history has been the inclination to make the U.S. a homogeneous all-white nation.[52] However, Americans have been divided about the national destiny of African Americans, particularly the ruling circles in Washington. As late as April 1865 at the end of the Civil War, President Lincoln reconsidered the colonization of black people. Clearly, in his earlier political career, Lincoln had favored colonization; however, there is some controversy about his stance after African American soldiers in Union uniforms shed their blood on the nation's battlefields.[53] Nevertheless, General Butler reports a meeting he held with Lincoln in April 1865 at which the president wondered, "But what shall we do with the Negroes after they are free? . . . I can hardly believe that the South and North can live in peace unless we get rid of the Negroes." Lincoln concluded that, "I believe that it would be better to export them all to some fertile country with a good climate, which they could have to themselves. . . . What . . . are our difficulties in sending the blacks away?" Of course, when General Butler looked into the logistics of shipping more than 4 million black people overseas, he reported back to Lincoln that it was impossible.[54]

Likewise, the Republican proposal in the 1862 *House Report on Emancipation and Colonization,* which recommended internal colonization of blacks and a policy of racial containment in the South, was politically impractical. For example, one perspective in the Republican circles was manifest in General William T. Sherman's Special Field Order No. 15, outlining the colonization of black people on the Sea Islands of South Carolina and Georgia and on a strip of land thirty miles inland on the East coast from Charleston, South Carolina to Jacksonville, Florida.[55] The decree provided black settlers with "possessory titles" to forty-acre lots on lands abandoned by Confederate owners. Leon Litwack reports that, on January 12, 1865, General Sherman and War Secretary Stanton held a summit meeting with twenty black ministers in Savannah; Sherman requested that the African Americans clarify "in what manner you would rather live, whether scattered among whites, or in colonies by yourselves."[56] Speaking for the majority of the delegation, one spokesman responded, "I would prefer to live by ourselves, for there is a prejudice against us in the South that will take years to get over."[57] As George Fredrickson notes, "If Sherman's order had been carried out on a permanent basis and if the area had been enlarged or the concept applied to other regions, the resulting separation of the black and white populations in the South would have drastically altered . . . the future history of the region."[58]

However, ultimately, this rigid kind of *internal colonization* was rejected for several reasons, ranging from white paternalism to practical politics. According to George Fredrickson, the most rigid plans for Yankee apartheid languished in Washington, D.C., because they would have "required a coercive power greater than the government was thought to possess," and because those crude arrangements would have "smacked too much of the . . . discredited doctrines of the colonizationists." Moreover, many influential Republicans rejected a rigid plan for colonization at the end of the Civil War: the Radical Republicans were the most hostile to colonization ideas, because they precluded the possibilities of full black American citizenship; the moderate Republicans understood that the black presence in the political arena was necessary "to make the Southern states loyal and desirable members of the Union."[59] With the Fourteenth Amendment and black citizenship, which made the "three-fifths of a man" clause on representation null and void, the South received an unprecedented number of new congressional seats. Voting black Republicans in the South were necessary to secure national power for the party; without their votes the Republicans would have won the war only to lose the White House and the Congress. Thus, the Reconstruction aim of bringing the South back into the Union pivoted on black participation in the national political community. In this sense, for the first time the prospects for African Americans' incorporation into the American nation were promising. Finally, the most fundamental reason that the *absolute* colonization plans were rejected is that black labor was the foundation of the Southern economy. Slavery was not only a system of racial domination; it was an economic mode of production. In reconstructing the war-torn Southern economy, the situation of black labor was critical. Fantastic, racist schemes of building that regional economy without African Americans simply courted catastrophe.[60]

As the second phase of black nationality formation drew to a close, many black nationalists were overwhelmed by the new situation and lost their bearings on the unexplored terrain created by the Civil War and Reconstruction. Some militant nationalists joined the Republican Party; the warnings of others like Henry Highland Garnet were dismissed. In one important case, Martin Delany became a conservative in the South Carolina political arena.[61] Indeed, black nationalists encountered unprecedented competition for the loyalties of black people at the end of the Civil

War as African Americans were swept into the political arena by the Fifteenth Amendment. The Republican Party, the party of Lincoln, established hegemony over the black vote during Reconstruction.

In some counties in the South, blacks enjoyed considerable social and economic benefits from black political power. For instance, in Beaufort, South Carolina, black rice workers struck for higher wages and decent living conditions. In the light of black political power in that state, Governor Chamberlain refused the rice planters' demand that he send in troops to crush black labor resistance. Moreover, the black workers were emboldened by the support of such black elected officials as Congressman Robert Smalls. According to Eric Foner, Robert Smalls, the Civil War hero, "was a living symbol of black power, of the revolution that had put the bottom rail on top, at least in local politics."[62] When twentieth-century proponents of the civil rights movement called their efforts the Second Reconstruction, they hoped for new leadership of the political stature of U.S. Representative Smalls.

Retreat from Reconstruction

However, at the end of Reconstruction, the National Republican Party abandoned its political supporters in the South to the tender mercies of the planters and Klansmen in the 1870s. The collapse of national support for Reconstruction doomed the possibilities of African American civil rights for nearly a century. (In fact, the situation was so dismal that in 1962 when the Student Nonviolent Coordinating Committee reached Fannie Lou Hamer on a Mississippi plantation, she told them she did not know that she had the right to register to vote.[63]) Earlier historiography suggested that the collapse of Reconstruction was caused by the 1876 Hayes-Tilden Compromise, the "Gentlemen's Agreement" in the Washington circles that solved the presidential election crisis of 1876. According to this line of argument, the Republicans sold out African Americans principally by the withdrawal of federal troops from the South, opening the way for a racist bloodbath and the overthrow of Republican governments in that region. However, historical evidence demonstrates that there were many others factors involved in the collapse of Reconstruction. William Gillette explains that there were several major indications of the northern retreat from Reconstruction:

the waning of popular support and the waxing of conservative sentiment; the increasing desire for reconciliation on the part of northerners despite terrorism and repression in the South; the gradual reduction of federal troops in the South, accompanied by the collapse of federal election enforcement; the resurgence of racism in political campaigning, which speeded up the displacement of Republican governments in the South by Democratic ones and helped bring about conservative victories in the North; the restriction on federal action imposed by judicial decision; and finally, the initiation of a conservative southern policy by design and by default in 1875."[64]

Perhaps, the two principal reasons for the demise of Reconstruction are these: first, the Republican Party attempted to act as if an essentially military situation was one of *politics as usual;* second, the North lacked the will, commitment, and endurance necessary for a protracted fight for Black American rights over white Southern resistance.[65] Since any successful struggle for African American equality must be *protracted,* "Black Reconstruction" was doomed.

Thus, African Americans were left to fight for themselves against Klan terror as they were forged into a distinct national group during a third and crucial phase of black nationality development. During the 1870s, when Henry Adams, a grassroots political organizer for the Republicans, arrived at the Louisiana home of his friend, Joe Johnson, he found the house burned down. Mrs. Johnson told Henry Adams that some fifty or sixty white terrorists had burned and shot her husband to death because he stood up for his political rights as a black leader. When she asked Henry Adams if the terrorists would be brought before the law, Johnson was filled with grief to realize there was no longer any justice for black people. Mrs. Johnson beseeched God to "help us get out of this country and get somewhere where we can live."[66]

Frustrated with the betrayal of blacks by the Republican Party and the naked terrorism of the Democratic Party, Henry Adams became one of the grassroots leaders who led the mass mobilization for the Kansas Exodus out of the Deep South in the 1870s. At one point Adams estimated that some 98,000 people were preparing to join this movement to flee Southern terror. In Tennessee, the mobilization to form black colonies in the West was led by a faith healer, Benjamin "Pap" Singleton. Many black people felt abandoned by the black elite during this ordeal; as the black establishment counseled them to stay in the South, tens of thousands of poor African Americans joined the emigration movement. They believed that land ownership was the only guarantee to full citizenship rights. Although nearly 10,000 blacks from Kentucky and Tennessee emigrated to Kansas, the vast majority were so desperately poor that they could not raise the resources for the exodus.[67]

The tragedy of the North's retreat from the promise of Reconstruction was that it allowed the racists in the South to subjugate the African American people and to establish a relationship between blacks and whites that was essentially one of *internal colonialism*.[68] Harvard Sitkoff explains that "After acting to provide . . . [black people] with freedom, equality, and the vote, it permitted the white South to reduce [them] to a state of peonage, to disregard [their] rights, and to disenfranchise [them] by force, intimidation, and statute."[69] The Congress, the Supreme Court, and the two major political parties closed their eyes while white terror beat black people into semicolonial subjugation. The Congress refused to intervene as the South robbed African Americans of the franchise; in fact, in the early decades of the twentieth century there was *no* African American in the Congress. The Supreme Court weakened the force of the Fourteenth and Fifteenth Amendments by severely limiting their application; the Court also nullified the Civil Rights Act of 1875 and crippled state law barring Jim Crow segregation. Finally, since neither the Republican nor the Democratic party considered black votes important to national elections, the *civil rights* of African Americans were dropped from the national political agenda until the New Deal.[70] To make matters worse, the socialist labor movement joined in the surge of white supremacy, as 3,220 black people were lynched between 1880 and 1930.[71] Indeed, Sitkoff notes:

> Nor could blacks turn with hope to the Socialists. Jack London wrote often of Negro inferiority, claiming he was "first of all a white man and only then a Socialist." Victor Burger, insisting "that the Negroes and mulattoes constitute a lower race," employed themes of white supremacy to win the votes of white workers.[72]

Although most African Americans lost their voting rights with the collapse of Reconstruction in the South, those blacks who could vote cast their ballots for the Party of Lincoln until the Depression. However, the situation was not bottomless, and black people were in motion. During the first decades of the twentieth century, some 1.5 million African Americans migrated to the northern industrial centers in search of a better life. That migration stream created strategic black urban concentrations that influenced the course of national politics, and in the process awakened a new black consciousness. Before long, a number of former adversaries—in particular, the communists, the labor unions, and the Democratic Party—

sought the membership and support of the black masses in the industrial and political arenas. Thus, liberalism, communism, and trade unionism became the main ideological rivals of black nationalism in the twentieth century.

Twentieth-Century Black Nationality

At the turn of the century there was a resurgence of black nationalism as African American nationality formation entered a fourth phase marked by increasing class formation, rapid urbanization, unprecedented ghetto formation, and anticolonial unrest. Although the 1884 Berlin Conference signaled the European scramble for Africa, that imperialist contest helped rekindle the concept of *Africa for the Africans*. In his historical and cultural efforts to vindicate the image of Africa, the Liberian intellectual Edward Blyden pioneered the concept of the *African Personality*. In his writings he conveyed the conclusions drawn from his research in Africa: that black Africans had built the Great Pyramids; that Islam had been more beneficial for Africans than Christianity; that African culture and civilizations were wholesome; and that the African people contributed a distinct spirituality to world civilization that was manifest in their cultures, customs, and concepts.[73]

In America, Bishop Henry McNeal Turner taught black nationalism and Pan-Africanism to thousands. Turner was a religious nationalist who dreaded the idea of black people praying to a God who looked like the men who sought to lynch them; he insisted that God was black.[74] Bishop Turner spread his message of black pride in Africa through the African Methodist Episcopal Church's missionary work; in fact, white authorities feared him so much that they made the hysterical claim that Turner's influence was responsible for the Ethiopian movement turmoil at the turn of the century in South Africa.

In 1903, W. E. B. Du Bois made an indelible contribution to African American identity, black nationality formation, and Pan-Africanism with his publication of *The Souls of Black Folk*. Contributing to the concept of the African Personality, Du Bois explored the distinct psychology of black folk and argued that the precious legacy of black culture was manifest in the spirituals. Working alongside Henry Sylvester Williams, Dr. Du Bois pioneered the earliest Pan-African summits at the turn of the century, beginning with the one in London in July 1900, followed by five international Pan-African summits between 1919 and 1945: the first Pan-African Congress, held in Paris in February 1919; the second held in London, Brussels, and Paris in September 1921; the third held in London, Lisbon, and Paris in 1923; the fourth in New York City in 1927; and the fifth in 1945 in Manchester, England. The fifth summit, attended by such future leaders of Africa as Nnamdi Azikiwe, Kwame Nkrumah, and Jomo Kenyatta, contributed to the momentum of African independence. The groundwork for that momentum was established by the anticolonial unrest of the First World War.[75]

During the First World War many black radicals, both nationalists and socialists, expressed their sense of African nationality as they observed uprisings in Egypt, Iraq, Iran, Afghanistan, Turkey, Korea, Mongolia, China, Russia, and Ireland. This was the vision of revolt expressed by the Father of Black Radicalism, Hubert H. Harrison. Harrison was one of the 142,868 West Indian immigrants who entered the United States between 1899 and 1932; 46 percent of those black immigrants lived in New York State.[76] If there was an early possibility of a blending of black nationalism and socialism, that prospect was represented by Harrison. He spread his political activities between the black struggle and the socialist movement. Harrison was a self-educated, working-class, socialist intellectual who developed into a black nationalist; he left the socialist party because the white radicals refused to struggle against racism. While some socialists thought that African Americans represented a reactionary economic and political force in American life, others thought that at best the black struggle for equality was a subsidiary of the labor question.[77] Harrison left the socialist party convinced that it was imperative for African Americans to fashion their own politics. Faced with a racially divided labor market in the United States, Harrison concluded that black workers had interests different from those of white workers. Men like Harrison began the Harlem street corner oratorical tradition, which was institutionalized by the time Malcolm X arrived. As hundreds of thousands of black migrants assembled in urban centers, they began to develop a new sense of themselves; these political agitators appealed to their increasing sense of black nationality.

By 1920 a new black middle class had developed in the context of increasing concentrations of black people in the ghetto and rising nationality consciousness. In contrast to the old, colored middle stratum that was tied to the white community, the new Negro middle class was commercially linked to the black community. August Meier explains that, "There was a real burgeoning of Negro enterprise after 1890 and especially after 1900, though it was based more on the Negro market than were the earlier enterprises."[78] Booker T. Washington was one of the leading proponents of the racial consciousness necessary for the economic solidarity and business foundation of that new middle class. The structural link between the black middle class and the African American community further stimulated black nationality formation.

However, Mr. Washington also counselled political resignation for black folk; thus, in 1905 W. E. B. Du Bois and the Niagara Movement criticized the Wizard of Tuskegee and vowed to defend the civil rights of African Americans. Similarly, Hubert H. Harrison argued that, "Political rights are the only sure protection and guarantee of economic rights. . . . Every fool knows this. And yet, here in America today we have people who tell us that they ought not to agitate for the ballot so long as they still have a chance to get work in the south."[79] Known as the "Black Socrates" of the Harlem Renaissance, Harrison formulated the "New Negro Radicalism" of the period, fashioned the slogan "Race First," and introduced Marcus Garvey to the Harlem political community.[80] Harrison invited Garvey to speak at his Liberty Party rally in Harlem. The charismatic Jamaican orator stole the show, and that speech before Harrison's independent black party launched the Garvey phenomenon in the United States.

Marcus Garvey had already made contact with the colonial liberation movements in London, where he studied African history and anticolonial nationalism under Duse Mohammed Ali, the Egyptian intellectual and editor of the *Africa Times and Orient Review*. Garvey arrived in the United States at a time when Harlem was becoming the center of black culture and African American protest; that metropolis was developing an impressive concentration of vanguard writers, newspapers, and civil rights leadership. As Nathan Huggins explains, "The circumstances that made Harlem and New York appear a viable center of Negro cultural, intellectual, and political life were in part the result of the large migration of talented blacks to the city in the years before the war. But, more important, what distinguished Harlem from the several other burgeoning black metropolises were changes, seemingly centered in Harlem, in the character of Negro protest and thought."[81] Harlem drew W. E. B. Du Bois and James Weldon Johnson to the helm of the NAACP; Charles S. Johnson to the National Urban League and the Harlem Renaissance; A. Philip Randolph to the legendary Brotherhood of Sleeping Car Porters and the radical newspaper *The Messenger*; Cyril V. Briggs to the militant African Blood Brotherhood and its newspaper, the *Crusader*. Indeed, Cyril Briggs's newspaper served as the inspiration for the militant Robert F. Williams's *Crusader* in the 1960s.

The rising black population in Harlem was part of a major national urban phenomenon. The Great Migration of between 500,000 and 1.5 million black people from the South to northern and western urban centers had a profound national impact on black consciousness; those African Americans were the foundation for the black ghettos, which became a major feature of urban American life. As Kenneth Kusmer notes, one consequence of this new black urban situation in the ghetto "was the sense of common destiny prevalent to some extent in all socioeconomic classes in the black community."[82] As the processes of African American nationality formation unfolded in urban areas with compact concentrations of African American population, that new sense of black consciousness was the basis for the flowering of the Garvey Movement and for the spread of black nationalism. By 1920, there were 34,451 black people in Cleveland, 35,921 in Newark, 37,725 in Pittsburgh, 40,838 in Detroit, 109,458 in Chicago, 134,229 in Philadelphia, and 152,467 in New York City.[83]

In that context, Marcus Garvey raised the issue of black nationalism and self-determination so forcefully that it swept him center stage in the rising African American ghetto. Garvey articulated the vision of anticolonial resistance in his own inimitable way, linking the destiny of the urban black migrants with the fate of the colonial subjects, and that fired the imagination of millions of people in the black world. One of the greatest political agitators of the twentieth century, Garvey asked, "Where is the Black Man's government?" His Universal Negro Improvement Association (UNIA) spread its branches in thirty-eight states in North America as well as in forty-one countries outside the United States.

In his early years, Garvey inspired a broad-based black united front, embracing both the Moorish Science Temple Movement and the African Blood Brotherhood (ABB). The Moorish Science Temple Movement, founded by Noble Drew Ali in Newark, New Jersey, in 1913, spread to Philadelphia, Pittsburgh, Detroit, and Chicago, paving the way for the emergence of Elijah Muhammad and the Nation of Islam. Looking to Islam for inspiration, Noble Drew Ali argued that black people in the United States were a distinct nationality. Similarly, the ABB, founded by Cyril Briggs, insisted that black people in the United States were a nation within a nation and demanded self-determination. Briggs and the ABB, which was in communication with the Irish Republican Brotherhood (IRB), initiated black involvement in the American communist movement; a young member of the ABB, Harry Haywood, became a leading theorist of black nationality for the American Communist Party and the Communist International.[84]

After the phenomenal rise and fall of the Garvey movement, black nationalism encountered overwhelming competition for the loyalty of

African Americans. In the contest for the allegiance of black workers, the American Communist Party was forced to make concessions to nationality consciousness; without that flexibility the Marxists would have made no headway among African Americans. By 1930, radical groups like the League of Struggle for Negro Rights, led by Harry Haywood and Langston Hughes, articulated the demands of black workers, women, youth, soldiers, professionals, students, artists, writers, clerks, small business people, and nurses for equality. Its program insisted on equal rights, decent housing, jobs, education, and culture. The League declared that African Americans were a subject people:

> We proclaim before the whole world that the American Negroes are a nation—a nation striving to manhood but whose growth is violently retarded and which is viciously oppressed by American imperialism.
>
> For three hundred years the American Negroes have been enslaved. The same blow which struck the shackles of chattel slavery from them hammered on the chains of a new slavery. After three-quarters of a century of supposed freedom the Negro people must still fight for that liberty which should have rightly been theirs after the Civil War.[85]

The Left also fashioned a new strategy for mobilizing African Americans in industry. In the days of Hubert H. Harrison, black radicals realized that class solidarity was precluded by the American split labor market, which had divided workers into two rival and antagonistic racial camps. However, in the 1930s in laying the foundation for the Congress of Industrial Organizations (CIO), young, white radical organizers attempted to develop a strategy to unify the ranks of labor. While the American Federation of Labor had sanctioned segregated locals for black labor, the CIO organizers recruited black workers into the same union locals as white wage earners. The CIO strategy was informed by hard lessons learned from years of defeat in strike struggles, particularly in meatpacking plants, steel mills, and coal mines. In the mid-1930s, John L. Lewis's United Mine Workers made an important and unprecedented effort at union organizing by seeking the support of black leadership, by employing black organizers in their campaign, by electing black officers, and by demanding equal pay for equal work, regardless of race.[86] David Dubinsky used the same approach in organizing black workers into the International Ladies' Garment Workers Union (ILGWU) in the mid-1930s. Indeed, Dubinsky protested the discrimination against black delegates at a Chicago union convention by moving the assembly to a new meeting place.[87] A number of the other unions withdrew from the American Federation of Labor (AFL) and pursued this new strategy of organizing.

Labor leaders who practiced what they preached won new respect in the black community. John L. Lewis won respect by endorsing civil rights legislation and supporting the crucial organizing efforts of A. Philip Randolph and the Brotherhood of Sleeping Car Porters; these workers had been desperately fighting for union recognition from the railroad industry since the 1920s. Much of the success of the CIO's new reputation came from the quality of its organizers. Many were radical, young labor intellectuals, communists, socialists, and idealists. They viewed the CIO as a democratic social movement. For example, Victor and Walter Reuther organized their first protest against racial discrimination at Detroit's City College; later they joined the movement to unionize auto workers.[88] At the cutting edge of these changes were the American communists; this was their golden age in the struggle for racial equality in industry. According to Harvard Sitkoff, no group within the CIO crusaded for racial justice more than the communists. For instance, the radical Harry Bridges of the Marine Workers Industrial Union realized that because of the large number of black maritime workers, the only successful strategy was interracial unionism. Moreover, the communists did the most to elect African Americans to union leadership positions. Taking the lead in the fight for African American representation in union leadership were black communists like Ferdinand Smith in the National Maritime Union, Jesse Reese in the Steel Workers Organizing Committee, Revel Cayton in the longshoremen's union, and Henry Johnson in the packinghouse workers union. These radical innovators also convinced the white union leadership to contribute money to the civil rights movement. This new strategic effort forced a major breach in the racial caste system in American industry and forged an important link in the development of the black and labor coalition which eclipsed black nationalism after the decline of Marcus Garvey's UNIA.

In reality, these progressive initiatives were possible because of the life-and-death situation of American labor during the Depression; the CIO would have failed without a black and labor alliance. As Sitkoff explains, "The congress trod the path of necessity. The large numbers of black workers in the mass production industries made unionization imperative. Outside the unions they constituted a dangerous strikebreaking—perhaps fatal—union-busting force."[89] The clearest examples of this situation were in the auto, meatpacking, and steel industries. Twenty percent of the steel workers were African American. To succeed at its union organizing campaign, the Steel Workers Organizing Committee employed an elaborate strategy to win over the black community.[90] The National Negro Congress helped forge the basis for a black and labor coalition, providing black organizers to recruit African American labor into the steel workers' union drive in Chicago. The CIO Packinghouse Workers Organizing Committee (PWOC) followed suit, using the same strategy as the steel workers.

Furthermore, in these labor struggles African Americans learned important political lessons about the force of mass action, particularly about the powerful potential of boycotts and disruption. Thus, the 1930s was a decisive turning point in the relationship between the labor movement and the black community.[91] Nevertheless, African Americans remained an autonomous force, with their own agenda. During the 1930s many black people rallied against the Italian fascist invasion of Ethiopia, and in the 1940s they supported the Council on African Affairs as W. E. B. Du Bois and Paul Robeson championed the cause of independence for Africa. In his political and cultural work, Robeson evoked Edward Blyden's idea of the African Personality and began the important transformation of cultural nationalism from an elite literary current into a philosophy that celebrated African American folk culture. Robeson explained that he wanted to be an African and that black identity and spirituality was a life-long mission. He warned black Americans that "it is not as imitation Europeans, but as Africans, that we have a value."[92]

One of the most important black united fronts in the twentieth century was the National Negro Congress (NNC), founded in Chicago in 1936. Some 8,000 people, both blacks and whites, gathered to support the development of a program for black equality. The NNC's global consciousness is indicated by its identification with antifascist movements in Europe and anticolonial struggles in Latin America, Africa, and Asia. The founding meeting of the NNC received greetings from around the world. In a message condemning the fascist invasion of Ethiopia, Mao Zedong said, "I greet . . . the First National Congress of the fighting Negro people, 12,000,000 strong in America against every form of national and racial oppression."[93] The NNC established a broad movement that recognized that although African Americans had many organizations with different programs and tactics, what was necessary was a common front to struggle for a minimum program of unity. A. Philip Randolph was elected the first president of the National Negro Congress.

Unfortunately, the American communist movement made a momentous mistake in interfering with the autonomous political development of the NNC on foreign policy issues. While the NNC opposed fascism around the world, under the influence of Stalin, the American communists inside the NNC aligned that black organization with the Hitler-Stalin Pact. In protest, A. Philip Randolph resigned, charging that the American Communist Party had violated the organizational independence of the NNC. In his resignation speech, Randolph warned black people of the dangers of depending on whites for the financial support of their leading organizations.[94]

During the Second World War, A. Philip Randolph began the March on Washington Committee, threatening that unless President Franklin D. Roosevelt issued an executive order banning discrimination in hiring by unions and employers and ending segregation in the armed services, 10,000 African Americans would march on Washington. When the overwhelming response from black people encouraged Randolph to build the momentum for a march of 100,000, the White House attempted to co-opt the black labor leader. Roosevelt did not want to lose the moral edge in the ideological part of the war against fascism in Europe. However, Randolph firmly demanded an executive order. When negotiations failed to divert the march, President Roosevelt conceded and issued Executive Order 8802 and the Fair Employment Practices Committee (FEPC) in June 1941; however, this measure was so weak that in May 1943, Roosevelt issued Executive Order 9346, which established the President's Committee for Fair Employment Practices. These executive mandates emboldened black workers to resist racist attacks from white wage earners in the railway and shipping industries.[95]

The Raw Deal: The Second Ghetto

One of the major setbacks for black Americans during the New Deal was the severe racism and segregation institutionalized in federal urban policy.[96] The extreme segregationist policies of the federal government treated African Americans as *internal colonies* in urban areas, laying the groundwork for American apartheid.[97] At the same time, a second great black migration resulted in the urbanization of 4 million more African Americans between 1940 and 1970.

These structural developments set the stage for a *fifth* phase of black nationality formation. The political and cultural dynamics of this phase of black nationalism were profoundly affected by the Third World Revolution in Africa, Asia, and Latin America. As Black America's identification with the Third World unfolded, African American nationality formation spread a new radical brand of black cultural nationalism, one distinct from the elitist nineteenth-century nationalism that stood aloof from the grass roots; in contrast to the classical bourgeois black nationalism, which shunned the black masses, this new cultural nationalism embraced, celebrated and developed black folk culture as the foundation for a black nation.[98]

These developments took place in tandem with the rise of a second type of black ghetto in the United States. The *second ghetto* is an essential concept pioneered by Arnold Hirsch. In contrast to the *first ghetto*, which was a product of open racial antagonism between whites and blacks in the cities of the U.S., particularly after the First World War, the second ghetto is the result of systematic public policy aimed at racial segregation. Hirsch found that the mold for the government policies that resulted in the second ghetto was forged in the midst of the racial antagonism in Chicago, where a combination of business, civic, and political leaders as well as university officials developed urban policy and legislation designed to concentrate and contain the African American population in the ghetto. He explains that the second ghetto, which was the Chicago solution to the urban race problem, became the model for federal housing legislation.[99] On a national level, the second ghetto developed as a component part of federal urban policy: beginning with the New Deal in the 1930s, the federal government facilitated the persistence and extension of high levels of residential segregation. Between 1935 and 1950, the federal government displayed an intense racialist consciousness and insisted upon discriminatory practices as a precondition for support from federal housing agencies. This federal intervention in housing segregation made a dramatic difference. As Hirsch reports, "Combined with the slum clearance, urban renewal, public housing, and highway construction programs of the 1950s and 1960s, these government initiatives encouraged and subsidized white flight to the suburbs, helped strip older towns of their middle classes, and practically ensured that blacks would remain locked in economically weakened central cities." These ghettos were much larger than the first segregated communities. They covered vast areas in major cities, and by 1980 fourteen of these urban centers contained at least 200,000 African Americans.[100]

Black Consciousness

One logical effect of the growth of the ghetto and the increased awareness of race that accompanied the migration from rural to urban areas was a new kind of black nationalist consciousness.[101] One former Garveyite explained to this writer that before migrating from Omaha to Chicago, his nearest black neighbor in that South Omaha section was several miles away; in South Omaha where African Americans were sparse, the sense of black community was generated by the church. In contrast to the 10,315 black people of Omaha in 1920, Chicago, where he joined the Garvey movement, had 109,458 African Americans, one of the largest concentrations of people of African descent in the world.[102] Black nationalism's emphasis on racial unity, according to Kusmer, "appealed to many urban blacks who were, for the first time, living in a social environment that *resembled* (even if on a rather small scale) an all-black nation."[103]

While the first ghettos had a dramatic impact on black consciousness, the second ghetto was an even stronger social foundation for black nationalist sentiments. Kusmer observes:

> One feature of black life that would outlive the decade of the twenties . . . was the sense of common destiny prevalent to some extent in all socioeconomic classes in the black community as a result of the consolidation of the ghetto. In the twenties this new racial consciousness created the Harlem Renaissance and the Garvey movement. Four decades later, in a much more explosive setting, it would produce black revolutionaries and cultural nationalists with . . . a good deal more militancy than Garvey. In both cases, the underlying social foundation of these phenomena was the urban ghetto.[104]

By 1970 there were major concentrations of African Americans in many cities in the U.S.: roughly 138,000 in Newark; 214,000 in St. Louis; 250,000 in Cleveland; 335,000 in Los Angeles; 411,000 in Washington, D.C.; 482,000 in Detroit; 529,000 in Philadelphia; 812,647 in Chicago; and 1,088,000 in New York City.[105] As black people concentrated in these ghettos in large numbers, they generated African American communities with their own distinctive sets of attitudes, values, and cultures.[106]

Mapping out the folkways of Harlem in the 1960s, Amiri Baraka reported quite tastefully:

> There are hundreds of tiny restaurants, food shops, rib joints, shrimp shacks, chicken shacks, "rotisseries" throughout Harlem that serve "soul food"—say, a breakfast of grits, eggs and sausage, pancakes and Alaga syrup—and even tiny booths where it's at least possible to get a good piece of barbecue, hot enough to make you whistle, or a chicken wing on a piece of greasy bread. You can *always* find a fish sandwich: a fish sandwich is something you walk with, or *"Two of those small sweet potato pies to go."* The Muslim temple serves bean pies which are really separate.[107]

The new urban generation felt that black Americans were just as distinct in their music and dance as in their cuisine. In Black America a new *soulful* music was central to the development of an *imagined community* of African Americans.[108] In his study of this period, William Van Deburg explains that "as an indigenous expression of the collective African-American experience, it served as a repository of racial consciousness. Transcending the medium of entertainment, soul music provided a ritual in song with which blacks could identify and through which they could convey important in-group symbols."[109] Thus, for the new artists and writers *the music* and musicians became central to their very sense of being.[110]

Furthermore, in his book *Blues People*, Amiri Baraka explains the impact of urbanization, modernization, radio, and race records on black nationality formation; in this new framework the interplay between the different provincial blues traditions nourished the development of national African American musical styles:

> [One] important result of race records was that with the increased circulation of blues, certain styles of singing became models for a great many aspiring blues artists. Before race records, blues form was usually dependent on strictly local tradition. . . . the race recordings really began to put forth extra-local models and styles of blues-singing which must have influenced younger [blacks]. (Even in rural areas of the South, there was always at least one family that had a "victrola," which drew their neighbors from miles around. The coming of radio . . . also had a profound effect on blues in a similar fashion.) . . . The phonograph record increased one thousandfold the widespread popularity and imitation of certain blues singers; and because of this, phonograph records themselves actually *created* whole styles of blues-singing. And even though the local traditions remained, the phonograph record produced the first blues stars and nationally known blues personalities. . . . It is easy to see how this must have affected the existing folk tradition and created another kind of tradition that was unlike any other in the past.[111]

Thus, in many complex ways the rise and expansion of the black ghetto generated a new black ethos and contributed to an unprecedented degree of African American nationality formation in the urban areas. As blacks migrated to the North, they were definitely *not* assimilated into white America; instead, they developed a distinct national culture and consciousness by synthesizing various elements selected from their regional and provincial backgrounds. In other words, ambiguous discussions of assimilation only serve to obscure the fact that in the twentieth century African Americans were urbanized and modernized in a very separate manner that laid the foundations for a black national political community.

Institutional Racism

Tragically, these cultural developments were undermined by the institutional racism that structured the emergence of the second ghetto. The structural meaning of *blackness* reflected gross inequities in the racial allocation of power, authority, and wealth.[112] These inequities were felt most painfully in the ghetto. The new black ethos of the 1960s reflected the very distinct tension between the promise of freedom in the North and the harsh realities of the segregated, dark ghettos. In his autobiography, Claude Brown asks: after fleeing racial tyranny in the South, where could African Americans run to if they were already in the northern promised land?[113]

The physical surroundings in the black ghetto mocked the new sense of pride and camaraderie that was developing in these semiautonomous black communities. In his autobiography, Huey P. Newton, a founder of the Black Panther Party, painfully recalls the interior of ghetto housing: "I slept in the kitchen. That memory returns often. Whenever I think of people crowded in a small living space, I always see a child sleeping in the kitchen and feeling upset about it; everybody knows that the kitchen is not supposed to be a bedroom. That is all we had, however. I still burn with the sense of unfairness I felt every night as I crawled into the cot near the icebox."[114]

Similarly, in *Home*, Amiri Baraka maps out his confinement in Black America with a sense of profound anguish:

These streets stretch from one end of America to the other and connect like a maze from which very few can fully escape. Despair sits on this country in most places like a charm, but there is a special gray death that loiters in the streets of an urban [black] slum. And the men who walk those streets, tracing and retracing their steps to some hopeless job or a pitiful rooming house or apartment or furnished room, sometimes stagger under the weight of that gray, humiliated because it is not even "real."[115]

Baraka's writing contributed to his generation's sense that these ghettos were all connected:

Sometimes walking along among the ruined shacks and lives of the worst Harlem slum, there is a feeling that just around the next corner you'll find yourself in South Chicago or South Philadelphia, maybe even Newark's Third Ward. In these places life, and its possibility, has been distorted almost identically. And the distortion is as old as its sources: the fear, frustration, and hatred that [blacks] have always been heir to in America. It is just that in the cities, which were once the black man's twentieth century "Jordan," *promise* is a dying bitch with rotting eyes. And the stink of her dying is a deadly killing fume.[116]

Thus, ghetto oppression had become a national racial oppression for black Americans.

Moreover, for African Americans the grip of racial oppression reached beyond the second ghetto into the work place to structure a special brand of labor exploitation. During the New Deal the failure of the Roosevelt administration and Congress to establish a *national* labor market placed another major racial burden on people of African descent and thus contributed to the modernization of the colonial relationship between blacks and whites. At first the National Industrial Recovery Act (NIRA) sought to establish a national labor market and national minimum wage in the United States; however, in order to get the legislative approval of powerful Southern politicians, the Roosevelt administration compromised on the race question. With the 1933 NIRA, the United States established *regional* wage standards, retaining the legacy of slavery and caste in the Southern labor market by paying blacks lower wages than whites for the same work. The impact of the inequities in that New Deal legislation has been disastrous on the black working class, undermining the health and security of generations of African Americans. Protesting this institutional racism at congressional hearings, the NAACP demonstrated that the prime motive beneath the organization of regional wage standards was the institutionalization of lower wages for African Americans. The civil rights group declared that the boundaries of the "southern region" shifted to the north in each industry where black workers were concentrated. In effect, the New Deal established a *dual* labor market in legislation like the NIRA. During the NIRA hearings, southern businessmen warned the nation that if the government forced employers to grant equal pay for the races, black workers would be replaced by white wage earners.[117] William Harris has pointed out the far-reaching consequences of this New Deal legislation:

It must also be kept in mind that inequities established during the early New Deal would affect workers a generation later. Social Security, the federal agency established to provide old-age insurance for workers, also exempted from coverage those job classifications in which blacks were heavily employed. [The rules omitted agricultural and service employment.] [118]

Many African American laborers were forced out of work at the end of the war boom. In the early 1950s, radical black workers led the resistance of African Americans in the workplace. In 1951, more than one thousand militant black workers, representing tens of thousands more, met to form the National Negro Labor Council (NNLC). The Council's strategy was to remain in multiracial unions, while building independent black caucuses in order to fashion the special demands of black workers. During these difficult struggles, since the American communist party opposed their activities, the issue of black *autonomy* in the communist movement remained a burning issue for African American activists who were mobilizing these black labor united fronts.

Endorsed by Paul Robeson, some of the leading figures in the NNLC were Bill Hood, representing the United Auto Workers at the Ford River Rouge plant; "Big Red" Coleman Young, the militant Detroit UAW organizer who later became that city's first black mayor; Ernest "Big Train" Thompson, a militant United Electrical, Radio and Machine Workers (UE) organizer representing labor in Bayonne, New Jersey; Clarence Coggins, a political organizer in Newark, New Jersey, who later helped organize the election of that city's first black mayor; and Vicki Garvin, the brilliant executive secretary of the NNLC in New York City, who later worked for African liberation with Maya Angelou and W. E. B. Du Bois and subsequently with Malcolm X.[119] The NNLC organized itself into twenty-three local councils, challenged the Jim Crow policies of many of the big companies, and fought in hundreds of local struggles on political, economic, and social fronts. A nationwide campaign against Sears Roebuck, for example, was successful in defeating that company's discriminatory hiring policy. Moreover, the NNLC specifically worked to stop discrimination against black women in industry.[120] At the October 1951 summit of the NNLC, Bill Hood read a speech written by Vicki Garvin that insisted on the hard-won power of black labor leadership:

The day has ended when white trade union leaders or white leaders in any organization may presume to tell Blacks on what basis they shall come together to fight for their rights. . . . Three hundred years has been enough of that. We Black people in America ask for your *cooperation*—but we do not ask for your *permission* [emphasis added].[121]

The National Negro Labor Council's work was not limited to industrial organization; some of its best work was accomplished in black residential communities. For instance, in its political work in the community, during the early 1950s the New Jersey Negro Labor Council provided the unity and organizational framework for the election of Irvine Turner, the first black city council representative in Newark, New Jersey. Clarence Coggins led a complex struggle for democracy and representation. First, the NNLC successfully mobilized broad-based support to change the structure of Newark's government from an at-large commission into a mayor-council ward system that allows for some proportional representation. Mindy Thompson explains that "under the commission form it had proven impossible for Blacks, women and other minorities to gain representation and the government remained in the hands of a small ruling clique."[122] Under the new system, Newark's government included council representatives of five wards. Most black people lived in the ghetto in the Central Ward (then the Third Ward). Turner campaigned as a progressive anti-McCarthy candidate criticizing the H-bomb and was swept into office by a black and labor alliance. During the political mobilization, the New Jersey branch of the NNLC held a neighborhood political convention, perhaps Newark's first black political assembly, to select Turner as a candidate. According to Thompson, Turner's election was the "first time that a Black had broken through the solid white front of municipal government in New Jersey," triggering black political mobilization for representation throughout the state: "Black people became more conscious of the question of dignity and the power they would win in struggle."[123] At any rate, those early developments may help explain why the Modern Black Convention Movement took root so quickly in Newark during the Black Revolt of the 1960s.

However, with the collapse of the American communist movement, the NNLC disintegrated. Many of the political gains made by that movement in black communities were absorbed by ethnic political machines; in Newark, Irvine Turner became the Negro boss of the Central Ward.[124] Moreover, the NNLC was attacked by the House Un-American Activities Committee (HUAC), and abandoned by the American Communist Party. In Washington, HUAC threatened the careers of many black artists and intellectuals, including W. E. B. Du Bois, Paul Robeson, and Langston

Hughes. While Hughes recanted his early radicalism, Robeson was stripped of his passport. In the hysteria, HUAC maligned W. E. B. Du Bois, then a leading anti-nuclear war activist in his eighties, calling him a menace to America. In 1951, Dr. Du Bois, who had chaired the Council on African Affairs, was actually "tried in federal court on charges of being an unregistered agent of a foreign power."[125] Later, the American Communist Party diluted its demands for black self-determination, and the party's central leaders purged Harry Haywood, the leading black communist proponent of a radical African American claim to national equality and black liberation, while Haywood was living in exile in Mexico.

These developments set the stage for a severe estrangement between communists and black nationalists. Furthermore, the official communist and socialist contempt for black nationality aspirations doomed cooperation and established a Chinese wall between the two movements on the eve of the Black Revolt of the 1960s. Many of the leading veteran cultural nationalists of the 1960s had felt betrayed by the communists and socialists during the 1950s. Queen Mother Moore abandoned the communist movement to become a leading black nationalist and Pan-Africanist; Abner Berry, an important communist, helped Max Stanford and other young black militants build the African People's Party in Philadelphia. After his association with the Left, John Henrik Clarke became a leading black historian and an important advisor to Malcolm X in the Organization of Afro-American Unity. Similarly, Harold Cruse became a leading black nationalist intellectual, warning the Black Power generation about the heinous dangers of embracing Western Marxism.

Internationally, the strength of revolutionary nationalism grew phenomenally in the anticolonial movements. In China, the communists and the nationalists forged an alliance against the invasion of Japan. In Vietnam, the communists and nationalists established the Viet Minh, an alliance to drive out the French. However, in other areas key leaders who were overthrowing Western colonialism became increasingly suspicious of Soviet motives as well. Aimé Cesaire, one of the founders of the Negritude Movement and a leading communist in Martinique, resigned from the French Communist Party in a public letter to Maurice Thorez on October 24, 1956, criticizing both the Soviet and French parties. Making a cogent case for ideological, political, and organizational independence from the French Communist Party, Cesaire explained that he was *not* repudiating Marxism or Communism but rather insisting that oppressed nations could not "delegate anyone to think for [them]; to do [their] searching, to make [their] discoveries":

We cannot henceforth accept that anyone at all, be he our best friend, answer for us. If the aim of all progressive politics is someday to restore their freedom to colonial peoples, then the day by day activities of progressive parties must at least not contradict the supposed objective and not every day wreck the very bases, the organizational as well as the psychological bases, of this future freedom; and those bases boil down to one postulate: the right to take the initiative.[126]

While Cesaire took pains to distinguish between the philosophy of Marxism and the practice of opportunism, many other radical and progressive nationalists made no distinction between the ideology of Marxism-Leninism and the official policies of the French, Soviet, and American communist parties.

Civil Rights Resistance

Thus, in many quarters among the people of color, Western Marxism was discredited during the 1950s. Meanwhile, Black America took its fate in its own hands, spearheaded by Thurgood Marshall's NAACP legal strategy. The 1954 *Brown v. the Board of Education* ruling by the Earl Warren Supreme Court set the stage for a new level of struggle over the immediate issue of school desegregation and the long-term question of black citizenship. Privately, President Eisenhower, who had the executive responsibility for enforcing the *Brown* decision, was firmly opposed to the Court's ruling; in fact, he called his appointment of Earl Warren to the Court "the biggest damfool mistake I ever made."[127] Thus, Eisenhower provided no national leadership on the crucial civil rights issue of his day. In 1956, 101 of the 128 congressmen from the former confederacy issued the "Southern Manifesto," urging white resistance to the federal government on civil rights issues.[128] That political leadership paved the way for the massive development of the White Citizens' Council, which savaged the NAACP in the South. While the Klan focused on physical terrorism and assassinations, the middle-class White Citizens' Council engineered the financial annihilation of southern civil rights organizations and leaders.[129]

However, African American protest seized the initiative in 1955 when the resistance of Rosa Parks sparked the Montgomery Bus Boycott. Rosa Parks was supported by both Jo Ann Robinson, a leader of the Women's Political Council, and E. D. Nixon, a former Garveyite and a president of both the local Brotherhood of Sleeping Car Porters and the local NAACP. The Montgomery leadership drafted a young and inexperienced Martin

Luther King Jr. to spearhead the protest. The black working people of Montgomery, particularly women domestic workers, strode toward freedom rather than sit in the back of the bus; they boycotted the buses for 381 days.[130] By the 1960s, Dr. Martin Luther King Jr.'s Southern Christian Leadership Conference (SCLC) and James Farmer's Congress of Racial Equality (CORE) had rejuvenated the legal struggle for civil rights by taking the issues into the streets and forcing the federal government to intervene in crisis situations.

The racial crisis stirred wave after wave of protest, sparking the most widespread black awakening in African American history. The February 1, 1960, student sit-in at Woolworth's in Greensboro, North Carolina, rekindled black youth activism, and paved the way for the birth of the Student Nonviolent Coordinating Committee (SNCC). The SCLC organizer, Ella Baker, made certain that SNCC established itself as an independent organization so that it could find its own bearings in the struggle for equality. This phase of the civil rights movement represented a new bold defiance of the caste system among African Americans and their allies.

SNCC made a major breakthrough in the civil rights movement when Bob Moses applied the organizing philosophy of Ella Baker in Mississippi. Baker argued that the mission of civil rights organizing should be self-emancipation, that people had to be prepared to become their own liberators. When Moses arrived in Mississippi, he discovered that there was a long tradition of resistance and deep networks of black struggle.[131] In Mississippi, even the NAACP was, for the most part, an *underground* organization during the 1950s.[132]

These tactics appealed to an active minority who built the Mississippi Freedom Democratic Party (MFDP), particularly such staunch grassroots women leaders as Fannie Lou Hamer, Victoria Gray, Unita Blackwell, Ruby Hurley, and Winnie Hudson. In 1963, 80,000 black people voted for the MFDP candidates; the Mississippi Council of Federated Organizations (COFO) used a South African freedom tactic of organizing disfranchised voters in parallel elections.[133] The MFDP's challenge to the segregationist official Mississippi Democratic Party at the 1964 National Convention in Atlantic City, New Jersey, was a major turning point in the black freedom struggle; when President Johnson strong-armed the votes of liberal Democrats to reject the official seating of the full MFDP delegation, that ordeal began the radicalization of a new generation of student activists angered by the betrayal of the Liberal establishment. James Baldwin raised one of the most challenging issues of identity, purpose, and direction for the civil rights movement: "Do I really *want* to be integrated into a burning house?"[134]

By 1965, that radicalism was barely contained as Dr. King's SCLC took the initiative for a national march on Selma, Alabama, after state police savagely attacked nonviolent demonstrators on the Pettus Bridge on "Bloody Sunday," March 7, 1965. The Selma march rallied public opinion for the 1965 Voting Rights Act; ironically, that was a milestone in the history of African American nationality formation.[135] After the Voting Rights Act, black nationality formation increasingly unfolded within the political arena. The Watts uprising in August 1965 announced the awakening of a new force, as the country watched African Americans shouting *"Long Live Malcolm X!"*[136]

Moreover, SNCC used the Selma march as a springboard for its political mobilization in Lowndes County, Alabama; they assisted local people in the organization of the Lowndes County Freedom Organization, whose symbol of defiance was a black panther. According to Cleveland Sellers, the Lowndes County experiment consolidated "widespread agreement that it was time for SNCC to begin building independent, black political organizations."[137] Those are the roots of the Black Panther Party. After James Meredith was shot attempting a March Against Fear from Memphis to Jackson, a number of the civil rights organizations—including CORE, SNCC, and SCLC—rushed to Mississippi to continue the demonstration. During that march on June 17, 1966, the differences within the civil rights movement bubbled to the surface; SNCC's new chairman, Stokely Carmichael, electrified rallies of African Americans with a new agitational slogan, "Black Power."

The Black Power Experiments

The "Black Power" slogan was the most effective instrument of political agitation in Black America since Marcus Garvey's mass mobilization during the 1920s. In their book *Black Power: The Politics of Liberation in America*, Stokely Carmichael and Charles Hamilton explained that the text was never meant to be a blueprint or program for the Black Revolt: "We do not offer a blueprint; we cannot set any timetables for freedom. This is not a handbook for the working organizer; it will not tell him exactly how to proceed in day-to-day decision making." Nonetheless, critics of the programmatic implications of Black Power found the book an easy target. Instead of a program, the *profession de foi* called for "broad experimentation in accordance with the concept of Black Power," anticipating that those experiments would be the basis for new programs for black liberation.[138]

At the outset of the Black Power phenomenon, SNCC activists raised several key organizing issues for radicals. Too often scholars forget how unclear the issues looked in 1966, and they neglect the initial concerns that remained unanswered at the time. The vanguard activists wanted to know if the concept of Black Power, which had grown out of their political work in rural Mississippi and Alabama, was actually relevant to mobilizing and organizing in northern black ghettos. They asked what would be the value of the black vote in urban areas and around which issues African Americans could be organized. They also wondered if African Americans would attempt to develop alternative or parallel political structures in urban areas, as SNCC had done with the Mississippi Freedom Democratic Party and the Lowndes County Freedom Organization in the rural South. Moreover, SNCC wanted to identify the "levers of power for poor Blacks." And it asked what was the relationship between corporate wealth and urban poverty.[139]

Keeping these issues in mind, the serious study of Black Power must begin with an examination of its most important experiments along these lines. This book is one effort toward that goal. Specifically, this history of the leadership of Amiri Baraka and the dynamics of black cultural nationalism investigates how those activities contributed to the Black Power experiments in the 1960s and influenced the trajectory of black nationality formation in the 1970s. As an innovator in the politics of cultural nationalism, Baraka helped forge the political culture of the Modern Black Convention Movement.

This book explores the rise and fall of the politics of black cultural nationalism between 1960 and 1976. The following chapters trace the emergence of those politics, developing from the confines of small isolated circles of artists and radicals in Greenwich Village and Harlem in the early 1960s into broad-based mass movements spearheaded by formidable Black Power organizations in the 1970s. The rise and fall of the leadership of Amiri Baraka and his organization, the Congress of African People (CAP), were directly related to the trajectory of the Modern Black Convention Movement. Before the black conventions, most of the black cultural nationalists remained in obscure, isolated sects that had little or no influence in the political arena. However, in the aftermath of the 1967 urban uprisings, Amiri Baraka rose to the ranks of black national leadership as the black conventions mounted. As the process of nationality formation unfolded, Baraka led in the development of the United Brothers and the Committee For A Unified Newark in the *municipal* political arena, and in the emergence of the Congress of African People, the Black Women's United Front, the African Liberation Support Committee, and the National Black Political Assembly in the black *national* political arena.

Part I looks at the politics of black nationality formation at the local level. Chapter 1 examines several crucial dimensions of Amiri Baraka's political development, including his trip to Cuba. Baraka's early attempts to launch a mass black political movement in New York City were ill-fated. Although he was unsuccessful in building a mass political movement in Harlem, the years between 1960 and 1966 constitute a formative period that established the ideological foundation for the Modern Black Convention Movement that later took root in Newark. During those seminal years a new generation of leaders raised in black ghettos began to identify the destiny of the black freedom movement with the fate of revolutionary nationalist movements in Fidel Castro's Cuba, Mao Zedong's China, and Patrice Lumumba's Congo. Moreover, in charting its self-transformation, that generation looked to such paradigmatic figures as Frantz Fanon, Malcolm X, and Amiri Baraka. Attempting to spread that process of self-reconstruction, the black cultural nationalists stressed the urgency of "cultural revolution" as a component part of black liberation. In the aftermath of Malcolm X's assassination, young writers pioneered the Black Arts Movement, which portrayed the African American working people, the grass roots, as the leading force in the Black Revolution. Nevertheless, the Harlem Black Arts Movement failed to secure the minimum political support necessary to endure the ghetto dynamics of New York City. By 1966, Amiri Baraka had fled Harlem to return to his hometown, Newark, New Jersey.

Chapter 2 describes how Baraka began to find his bearings under the influence of Stokely Carmichael's initiation of the Black Power experiment, Huey P. Newton and Bobby Seale's development of the Black Panther Party in Oakland, and Maulana Karenga's inauguration of the US Organization in Los Angeles. Returning after a semester as a visiting professor in the pioneering black studies program at San Francisco State College, Baraka was propelled into the political arena by the 1967 Newark uprising. He was foremost among the leaders who linked the fate of the black freedom movement to the political momentum generated by the African American urban uprisings of the 1960s. That momentum was linked to the

Modern Black Convention Movement as the 1967 National Black Power Conference opened in Newark in the aftermath of one of the most severe rebellions in United States history.

Chapter 3 traces the entrance of black nationalism into the political arena. In 1968, the politics of black cultural nationalism embraced the Modern Black Convention Movement as an essential forum of black liberation. Those black assemblies became an important part of the process of legitimating African American leadership and an essential method for reaching a consensus on the black political agenda.

Chapter 4 recounts how Baraka's group established an alliance with the Young Lords Party and created an effective political coalition between the black and the Puerto Rican communities. By rejecting much of the old sectarianism in cultural nationalist politics, Baraka built a new type of organization, the Committee For A Unified NewArk (CFUN), in order to mobilize the African American community in the struggle for power. In 1970, the Black and Puerto Rican Convention candidate, Kenneth Gibson, became the first African American mayor of a major northeastern city.

Part II of this book examines the politics of black cultural nationalism at the national level and then explains the consequences of those developments for local politics. In this context, the ideology of some of the leading black cultural nationalists developed in the direction of national communism.[140] Chapter 5 traces the development of the Congress of African People, the African Liberation Support Committee, and the Black Women's United Front and pinpoints the 1972 National Black Political Convention in Gary, Indiana, as the zenith of the politics of black nationality formation.

Chapter 6 analyzes the dilemmas faced by Amiri Baraka and his organization. This is the tale of the rise and fall of both Kawaida Towers and Kawaida Community Development, Baraka's major attempts at urban renewal as well as housing and economic development. The chapter ends with the disintegration of the Modern Black Convention Movement. The book's conclusion, "Winter in America," assesses the Black Power experiments in Newark in terms of African American nationality formation. At the end of this history, I attempt to identify the most serious pitfalls in the political dynamics of black cultural nationalism, suggesting the dangers in the confusion and conflation of black self-determination with segregation, and of African American nationality formation with American apartheid. Institutional racism established a relationship of internal colonialism with black people in the ghetto. Therefore, without the broadest possible effective and protracted political, social, and ethical struggle for black equality and full democracy, institutional racism and political opportunism will easily diminish the struggle for self-determination by transforming it into the perpetuation of segregation and will tranquilize the fight for black nationality by changing it into the supervision of impoverished bantustans. Navigating through these submerged rocks is the formidable challenge for contemporary black leadership.

Part I
Rise

CHAPTER I

Groundwork

The Impact of Fidel Castro, Patrice Lumumba, Robert F. Williams, and Malcolm X on Amiri Baraka and the Black Arts Movement

Colonial subjects have their political decisions made for them by the colonial masters, and those decisions are handed down directly or through a process of "indirect rule." Politically, decisions which affect black lives have always been made by white people—the "white power structure."
—Stokely Carmichael and Charles V. Hamilton, *Black Power*

Afro-Americans were caught up in an assertive drive for a viable, collective identity adapted to the peculiar conditions of their development in the United States and their African background. Further, it was a drive to recover a cultural heritage shaped by over 300 years of chattel slavery and a century of thwarted freedom.
—Harry Haywood, *Black Bolshevik*

By 1970 the dynamics of the Black Revolt had propelled Imamu Amiri Baraka (LeRoi Jones),[1] the prolific poet and playwright, into the ranks of national black leadership and transformed his organization, the Newark Congress of African People (CAP),[2] into one of the most formidable Black Power groups in the country.[3] The meteoric rise and fall of the leadership of Amiri Baraka and CAP (1966–1976) is the history of the interplay between the dynamics of cultural nationalism and the development of the national Modern Black Convention Movement.[4] The history of the Congress of African People was an odyssey for thousands of politically active students, street youths, veterans, workers, artists and intellectuals, as they searched for new strategies, tactics, and forms of organization and leadership for black liberation. Their struggles in Newark's grassroots social movement prepared the way for their leadership of the Modern National Black Convention Movement, where they joined others at the center of the broadest and most explosive awakening of black consciousness in U.S. history.[5]

In *New Day in Babylon*, William Van Deburg argues that Malcolm's life represents *the* paradigm for the Black Power movement's process of self-realization.[6] As the fire prophet of the Black Revolution, Malcolm X set the pace not only for the younger generation of black activists, but for a generation of intellectuals and artists as well. Malcolm X represents the path of the grass roots to self-transformation and ethical reconstruction through the power of black consciousness. For a generation of black American artists and writers, Malcolm X's example inspired its faith in the potential of the black masses to make their own history—that they would become the self-conscious agents of their own liberation. It was a confidence in the power of black consciousness to transform black people into world historical actors, in tandem with the revolutionary upsurges in Africa, Asia, and Latin America.[7] In other words, Malcolm X had an indelible impact on the younger generation of leadership with his emphasis on the logic of self-determination, self-defense, and self-respect.

While Malcolm X represented the primary paradigm for the self-transformation of black consciousness, there was certainly another important model for change; and that was the path of the revolutionary intellectual to the national liberation movements. For the Black Revolution, Frantz Fanon, the psychiatrist who left his career to join the Algerian Revolution and who wrote *The Wretched of the Earth*, represented another way to revolutionary self-transformation. Similarly, many looked to the lives of Kwame Nkrumah, Julius Nyerere, and Amilcar Cabral as examples of radical intellectuals who returned to their people and led movements for liberation.

Imamu Amiri Baraka's path to black consciousness was different from that of Malcolm X; it represents the other important route to black nationalism, the road traveled by students and revolutionary intellectuals. Baraka's outlook on black nationalism began to take shape in the early 1960s with his visit to Cuba and his associations with Fidel Castro, Robert F. Williams, Mohammed Babu, and Malcolm X. Imamu Baraka's encounters with these revolutionary leaders challenged his identity both as a writer and as a man. As a result of a profound process of *identity transformation*, a metamorphosis second only to that of Malcolm X, Amiri Baraka became the foremost proponent of the politics of black cultural nationalism in the 1960s.

Unfortunately, black radical intellectuals emanate from small isolated, social, cultural, and political circles, without effective ties to mass organizations. Lacking mass support, a small circle is similar to a head without the strength of the body of the nation.[8] The first phase of Amiri Baraka's political development was a formative period during which he emerged as a revolutionary artist and a radical intellectual; however, Baraka did not develop as an effective political leader until the Newark uprising in 1967. In Newark, Baraka rose as the head of the Modern Black Convention Movement; before that mass movement, many black nationalist intellectuals experienced important personal transformations, but they had extreme difficulties translating their radical beliefs into sustained mass political action.

Nonetheless, the influential personal transformations of writers were essential; they set the stage for the larger battles to come. In the initial phases of black nationality formation, the next wave of black activists were influenced by the moving narratives of individual transformation articulated by Malcolm X in *The Autobiography of Malcolm X*, Eldridge Cleaver in *Soul on Ice*, and Amiri Baraka in *Home* to construct a radical black identity, purpose, and direction. Narrative, poetic, and dramatic accounts of self-transformation inspired millions in the black national community to *imagine* black *nationhood* in White America.[9] Furthermore, Baraka's work as both an artist and a cultural theorist, in association with Askia Muhammad Toure and Larry Neal, sparked the explosive Black Arts Movement, which galvanized thousands of African American artists and writers; this upsurge prepared the path for the politics of the Modern Black Convention Movement.

For many African American artists and intellectuals as well as black students, Imamu Amiri Baraka represented this second paradigm for self-transformation. John Hutchinson notes that in the process of nationality formation, the artist is usually "the paradigmatic figure of the national community."[10] As the Father of the Black Arts Movement, Imamu Baraka's personal yearning for identity, purpose, and direction captured the imagination of a generation of African American readers because to varying degrees it was experiencing similar tensions between feelings ranging from spiritual ennui, personal malaise, and identity crisis to racial kinship, black consciousness, and cultural regeneration.

Imamu Amiri Baraka was born Everett Leroy Jones on October 7, 1934, during the Great Depression in Newark, New Jersey. There he attended Barringer High School and Rutgers University before studying at Howard University in Washington, D.C.; it was at Howard University that Everett *Leroy* Jones changed his name to *LeRoi* Jones.[11]

After leaving Howard and serving in the United States Air Force, Jones found his way to Manhattan's Greenwich Village in the 1950s to become a major poet, editor, and music critic. In Greenwich Village, he married Hettie Cohen; this interracial marriage produced two children, Kellie and Lisa Jones. Soon Jones became identified with the leading writers and poets of the Beat Generation, including Jack Kerouac and Allen Ginsberg, and he wrote a number of his early works, including his award-winning play, *Dutchman*, and his pioneering history of African American music and cultural ethos, *Blues People*. As the publisher of *Yugen* and *Floating Bear*, Jones became one of the most influential editors of the new Beat poetry.

Although many commentators found it strange that LeRoi Jones's trajectory toward black nationalism passed through the Beat poetry circles and jazz sessions of Greenwich Village, Anthony D. Smith, a leading sociologist of nationalism, observes that part of the pattern of modern cultural nationalism involves its origins in the romantic rejection of the conformities of bureaucratic society.[12] In this sense, Jones's early development in Greenwich Village as well as his increasing yearnings for black identity and for what Amilcar Cabral once called "a return to the source" are component parts of a nationalist pattern.[13]

Ideological Transformation

Harold Cruse writes that "the great transformation in LeRoi Jones was brought on by the Cuban Revolution."[14] The generation that created the Black Arts cultural revolution was profoundly influenced by the image of a young, rebellious Fidel Castro and the early fire of the Cuban Revolution. Amiri Baraka confirms as much in his autobiography when he writes, "The Cuban trip was a turning point in my life."[15]

At the invitation of the black journalist Richard Gibson in July 1960, a 25-year-old LeRoi Jones joined Harold Cruse, John Henrik Clarke, Sarah Wright, Ed Clark, Julian Mayfield, Dr. Ana Codero, and Robert F. Williams to see the Cuban Revolution firsthand. Many of these black writers had contributed to a special July 4th issue of the newspaper supplement, *Lunes de Revolución*.[16] Jones was watching Robert F. Williams, the hero of the self-defense groups in the Black Revolt because of his courageous stand against Klan terror in Monroe, North Carolina.

Harold Cruse, however, was watching Jones to see what impact that historic journey to the Sierra Maestra would have on the younger generation. Cruse recalled, "In Havana it was noted that Jones made a very favorable impression on the revolutionary intelligentsia of the Castro regime." The senior writer thought it remarkable that the young Cuban rebels and LeRoi Jones had so much in common: "they actually talked the same 'language.'" And he concluded that "for Jones's impressionable generation, this revolutionary indoctrination, this ideological enchantment, was almost irresistible."[17] But, it seems that even such seasoned political veterans as John H. Clarke and Harold Cruse were fascinated by the July 26th journey to Sierra Maestra to meet Fidel Castro. Cruse was the most skeptical of any of the writers, yet even he wrote:

> We were caught up in a revolutionary outpouring of thousands upon thousands of people making their way up the mountain roads to the shrine of the Revolution, under the hottest sun-drenching any of us Americans had probably ever experienced. . . . Nothing in our American experience had ever been as arduous and exhausting as this journey.[18]

Intrigued by the new attention given to African American writers, Cruse remarked that "the ideology of a new revolutionary wave in the world at large had lifted us out of the anonymity of lonely struggle in the United States to the glorified rank of visiting dignitaries."[19]

Nonetheless, Harold Cruse would not identify with that generation of Third World rebels in quite the same manner as LeRoi Jones. Jones's encounters with such leaders as Fidel Castro in Cuba, Mohammed Babu in Tanzania, and Robert F. Williams and Malcolm X in the Black Revolt challenged his identity both as a writer and as a man. As far as Jones was concerned, he was on the path to finding himself, and it all revolved around the sense of kinship that he felt with that generation of radicals in Cuba, Africa, and Asia. Their problems would become the heartfelt concerns of LeRoi Jones and his wing of the black liberation movement. Later he would express the same spirit of identification with young African writers like the Kenyan Ngugi Wa Thiong'o. In this passage, Ngugi captures the impact of the upheaval in the Third World on his generation of African writers. For both African and African American writers, intellectuals, and students, the 1950s was "the decade of the high noon of the African people's anticolonial struggles for full independence."

> The decade was heralded, internationally, by the triumph of the Chinese Revolution in 1949 and by the independence of India about the same time. . . . In Africa the decade saw . . . armed struggles by the Kenya Land and Freedom Army, Mau Mau, against British colonialism

and by FLN against French colonialism in Algeria; intensified resistance against the South African Apartheid regime, a resistance it responded to with the Sharpeville massacre; and what marks the decade in the popular imagination, the independence of Ghana in 1957 and of Nigeria in 1960 with the promise of more to follow. . . . in [the] USA, the Fifties saw an upsurge of civil rights struggles spearheaded by Afro-American people.[20]

LeRoi Jones and Richard Gibson were becoming increasingly identified with the liberation movements of the Third World. So much so that when Jules Feiffer of the *Village Voice* criticized Richard Gibson's support for Robert F. Williams and Cuba, Jones began a critique of Left liberalism. In Jones's writings the Black Revolt and the Third World Revolution were increasingly linked. Full of resentment, he wrote, "I get the feeling that somehow liberals think that they are peculiarly qualified to tell American Negroes and other oppressed peoples of the world how to wage their struggles. No one wants to hear it. . . . As Nat Cole once said, 'Your story's mighty touching, but it sounds like a lie.'"[21]

Increasingly, Jones expressed his identification with the rise of Third World revolutions: "The new countries of Asia, Africa, and Latin America are not interested in your shallow conscience-saving slogans and protests of moderation or 'political guarantees.' As a character in Burrough's *Naked Lunch* says, 'You think I am inarrested in contracting your horrible ol' condition? I am not inarrested at all.'"[22]

And significantly, Jones was focusing on the *revitalization* theme in the Third World revolution: "Fidel Castro, Kwame [Nkrumah], Sukarno, Nasser, and some others have actually done something about these ills, in their own countries." And they were not concerned about what liberals "[had] to say about the way they are conducting the resurrection of their people."[23]

Further, Jones was intrigued by the white liberal preoccupation with black identity in the 1960s. He wondered why there was so much "fuss" about black people calling themselves "Afro-Americans."[24] However, the uproar about a new black identity was probably stimulated by the United Nations demonstration, protesting the murder of Patrice Lumumba; and Jones was right in the center of those arrested at that protest.

The Congo Crisis

In 1960, Patrice Lumumba, the charismatic premier of the newly independent Republic of the Congo, held a singular fascination.[25] Lumumba rose from simple origins in a remote Congolese village. Like Malcolm X, he had no university degrees, but with his courage and determination by 1960 he had become a man of the people and a burning symbol of African nationalism. Many of the students of color identified with Lumumba, a young man with high aspirations despite the humiliations of white colonialism.

He experienced the Congolese form of dual consciousness as he struggled to make something of himself in the civil service. In the Belgian Congo, they developed a name for an upwardly mobile class of urban Africans which was particularly telling; they were called "evolué," meaning civilized, with the implication that most Africans were not.[26] During one episode, when a young Patrice Lumumba wandered into a segregated white area in his own homeland, he was mortified when a white woman settler screamed that he was a "dirty monkey." Such experiences had a special resonance to young black people in South Africa and the United States. But despite such barriers to his development, Patrice Lumumba seemed unstoppable in his rise to political leadership in the Congo and to acceptance in the hearts of young people around the world.

Just as the rise of Lumumba inspired devotion in many people, it disturbed some Western interests. The United States made no secret of the fact that it backed secessionist forces aiming to dismember the Congo in order to keep its mineral wealth in the hands of Europeans. Soon after Lumumba's election as prime minister, violence erupted in the new nation. As he traveled around the world, seeking support for the young republic, Lumumba spoke in several cities in America. He was warmly received in July, as he talked to an audience of black students at Howard University about the crisis in the Congo.[27] And when he spoke on July 24, 1960, in New York City, stressing the strategic value of his nation's resources, black people were drawn to Lumumba and the fate of the mineral-rich Congo.[28] In effect, for a generation of students whose attention was riveted on the struggle to control Africa's mineral wealth, the Congo Crisis was a crash course in world political economy. They learned that some Western interests would stop at nothing, including the use of mercenaries, to control African mines.

But through all of that conflict, for African Americans Patrice Lumumba was the Nelson Mandela of that day. John Henrik Clarke sought to explain the overwhelming attraction for Lumumba in the black community:

> Patrice Lumumba became a hero and a martyr to Afro-American nationalists because he was the symbol of the black man's humanity struggling for recognition. . . . When the Congo emerged clearly in the light

of modern history he was its bright star. Lumumba was a true son of Africa and was accepted as belonging to all of Africa, not just the Congo. No other personality has leaped so suddenly from death to martyrdom.[29]

In fact, the life and death of Patrice Lumumba had such an impact on black people that John Henrik Clarke argues that his murder rekindled the flame of Afro-American nationalism. Clarke observes that the new Afro-American nationalism was introduced to the political arena by the "riot in the gallery of the United Nations in protest against the foul and cowardly murder of Patrice Lumumba."[30]

The political ferment among African Americans had some time to develop during the Congo Crisis, lasting from 1960 up to the murder of Patrice Lumumba in 1961. The protests mounted around the world as the situation worsened in the Congo. As the Belgian interests usurped power in the Congo, outrageous reports poured out of Africa about the death of Lumumba's daughter and soon about the brutal treatment of Premier Lumumba himself in captivity. The whole world watched helplessly as they destroyed Lumumba's vision of a unified Congo.

And finally, with the news of Lumumba's murder, young people around the world were deeply moved. A storm of international protests and demonstrations erupted in many of the major world capitals. They expressed their outrage all over Europe, with protests in Dublin and Bonn and sacking of the Belgian embassies in Belgrade and Rome by Yugoslavian students and Italian youths. In Paris, the police were particularly repressive, clubbing and arresting 106 demonstrating African students.

In Africa, students demonstrated their anger in Casablanca, Morocco; Khartoum, Sudan; and Accra, Ghana. "Lumumba believed in his mission," wrote Frantz Fanon, "[he] continued to express Congolese patriotism and African nationalism in their most rigorous and noblest sense."[31] Of course, Fanon was not alone in his respect for Lumumba. Throughout the Congo Crisis, such progressive national leaders as Nehru, Nkrumah, and Toure had insisted that the world recognize only Lumumba's government as the legitimate representative of the Congo, and they were outraged at the news of his murder.[32] Ghanaian president Kwame Nkrumah charged that the United Nations connived to murder Lumumba and particularly attacked Britain, France, and the United States.[33] In a wire to President Eisenhower, President Sekou Toure of Guinea condemned the role of the United States in the Congo. In line with the African condemnations, the Cuban representative criticized the United Nations.[34] In the East, students roared in Colombo, Ceylon; Bombay and New Delhi, India; Karachi, Pakistan; and Malaya, Malaysia. The largest demonstration was reported in China, where one rally, attended by 100,000 in Beijing, was led by the legendary Premier Zhou Enlai.

The UN Incident: Afro-American Nationalists

In the United States, there were demonstrations in Washington, D.C., where a number of students from Howard University were arrested. And in Chicago, black people carried signs saying: "Shame on the West!"[35]

Yet, the most dramatic indication of black outrage was demonstrated in the communications capital of the United States, New York City. On Wednesday evening, February 15, 1961, at the United Nations headquarters in Manhattan, a group of African Americans, the women wearing black veils and men black armbands, shocked Americans when they took their outrage right onto the floor of the Security Council meeting on the Congo Crisis. On several occasions, key officials in U.S. foreign policy circles had indicated that they were against Lumumba and favored the Belgian interests and the dismemberment of the Congo. Thus, while the U.S. Representative Adlai Stevenson was speaking, "about sixty men and women burst into the Security Council Chamber, interrupting the session, and fought with guards in a protest against the United Nations policies in the Congo and the slaying of Patrice Lumumba, former Congo Premier."[36] After the violent clash between demonstrators and the special UN police force, twenty people were treated for injuries by United Nations medical personnel.

There was another contingent of black people protesting outside the UN headquarters, on the north side of 42nd Street. As that contingent marched from First Avenue westward across Manhattan, the group chanted, "Congo, yes! Yankee, no!" That protest met the same kind of repression as the one inside. One group, including a young LeRoi Jones, was beaten and arrested in front of the United Nations.[37] Others were attacked at the corner of Sixth Avenue and 43rd Street by mounted police, seeking to prevent them from taking the demonstration to Times Square.

A mass rally was held in Harlem to protest police repression, but another issue captured national media attention. Some U.S. officials were quick to label the demonstration part of a "worldwide communist plot." The issue of an international communist plot became an obsession, and in that context the *New York Times* sent reporters to Harlem to investigate the social origins of the demonstration. Their findings were published in a series of articles in the week following the UN demonstration.

What they found seems to have surprised them. Essentially, they un-covered that the protest was not run by communists at all but by a new breed of Afro-American nationalists based in Harlem. The initial pub-lished reports of the demonstration made the U.S. charge of a communist plot a bit ridiculous. Those reports made it clear that the black demon-strators barred any support from the American Communist Party.[38] For instance, outside of the UN, Benjamin Davis, the first black man on the New York City Council and a well-known member of the Commu-nist Party (USA), was actually pushed away when he and Paul Robe-son Jr. attempted to join the picket. Clearly, the protesters were not black communists.

George M. Houser, chairman of the Quakers' American Committee for Africa, thought that "the American public did not fully appreciate the intensity of feeling among many [blacks] in relating African struggles for freedom to their own fight against discrimination and prejudice."[39] The protest was the work of a black united front, a diverse group ranging from black nationalists in the tradition of Marcus Garvey to a new breed of black radicals supporting the causes of Robert F. Williams and the Cuban Revolution.

Furthermore, the demonstration chants were not communist slogans. They chanted in a call-and-response form: one part of the line asked, "Who died for the Black Man?" Another chanted, "Lumumba!" Then one asked, "Who died for freedom?" And, the other chanted "Lumumba!" Not all of the chants and slogans were about the Congo Crisis; some ad-dressed the explosive issue of Black identity. At times they sang, "The word Negro has got to go!" Then, they would thunder, "We're Afro-Americans!"

During an interview, Daniel H. Watts made it clear that the demon-strators were not an appendage of any communist organization; but the ranks of the supporters of African liberation were growing. Later Daniel Watts became the editor of the important *Liberator* journal, but in 1961 he was the leader of an organization named On Guard. On Guard was estab-lished in June 1960 and, according to Watts, had "450 members, including chapters in Denver, Chicago, San Francisco, and Houston." About a dozen members of On Guard had gone to the United Nations planning on a quiet demonstration, wearing symbols of mourning for Lumumba, black veils and armbands.

"We are not Communists," insisted Watts. "We are not a Commu-nist affiliation. We have nothing to do with Communists. We are Afro-Americans, fighting for African liberation." Watts described On Guard as a part of the Harlem Writers Guild, led by Rosa Guy. Along with Daniel Watts in the leadership of On Guard was Richard Gibson, the former CBS journalist who invited Jones to Cuba in 1960.[40]

Malcolm X: The Bridge

The assassination of Malcolm X on February 21, 1965, represented a critical turning point in the life of LeRoi Jones. After the death of Malcolm X, Jones left his wife and children in Greenwich Village in order to join the Black Revolution. Further in his identity transformation, Jones married the black actress and dancer Sylvia Robinson of Newark, New Jersey. Symbolizing the depth of Jones's transformation, Hajj Heesham Jaaber, the Islamic priest who buried Malcolm X, renamed LeRoi Jones Ameer Barakat, "Blessed Prince" in Arabic. Subsequently, Maulana Karenga, a leading cultural nationalist from Los Angeles, Africanized the name Ameer Barakat, making it Amiri Baraka in Swahili, and gave Baraka the distinctive title "Imamu," meaning spiritual leader. Amiri Baraka explains:

> Sylvia was named Amina (faithful) after one of Muhammad's wives. Later, under Karenga's influence, I changed my name to Amiri, Bantuizing or Swahilizing the first name and the pronunciation of the last name as well. Barakat in Arabic is pronounced "Body-cot," the Swahili drops the "t" and accents the next-to-last syllable, hence Baraka. Amiri with the rolled "r" is pronounced "Amidi."[41]

Like many other black revolutionaries of that era, Baraka attempted to follow the path outlined by Malcolm X; the most popular themes were those of self-determination, self-respect, and self-defense. For Baraka, Malcolm X embodied the black ethos and the new man produced by revolutionary black consciousness. He sought to flesh out the principles of the new nationalism in several of the most challenging lessons of Malcolm X: the urgency of the modernization of black nationalism, the priority of black cultural revolution, the centrality of the African Revolution, and the necessity of developing a black ideology of self-determination, one reflecting the African American ethos.

Unfortunately, scholars have not placed enough emphasis on Malcolm X's work for the *modernization* of black nationalism. Malcolm X was intensely interested in the use of mass media for black nationality formation, particularly television, radio, and newspapers; he personally initiated the *Muhammad Speaks* newspaper to spread the Nation of Islam movement. Moreover, Malcolm X was the bridge between the old nationalism and the new, developing a secular nationalism in tune with many of the innovations of the civil rights revolution. His agitational slogan "the Ballot or the Bullet" supported the voting rights of African Americans at a time when the old black nationalism rejected the American franchise; Malcolm sought to experiment with the use of group voting in order to gain some degree of political autonomy in Harlem.

Furthermore, in addition to Elijah Muhammad's thrust of *social rehabilitation*, borrowed from the self-reliance program of Booker T. Washington, Malcolm X stressed the need for *ethical reconstruction* and *cultural revitalization* in the African American community.[42] For many, the personal example of Malcolm X's own ethical reconstruction was particularly important. As the most advanced spokesman for the new black ethos and a new common sense, his example of self-discipline and self-transformation was a compelling influence. He outlined his style of self-transformation in a three-step program for change, accessible to anyone, urging a new generation to "wake up, clean up, and stand up." In other words, black leaders and activists in the community had to first of all become politically *conscious* of who they were and the oppressive situation of their people; this was the black consciousness thrust in the Black Revolt. Then they had to raise their standard of ethics and behavior, so that they would be incorruptible in the struggle for black liberation. Thus, Malcolm X insisted that those who wanted to lead the Black Revolution would have to abstain from alcohol and drug abuse, because such pathologies aggravated the already severe social problems in the ghetto, and made such leaders toys in the hands of their ruthless enemies. And finally, they had to be prepared to stand up for equality and justice for black people by any means necessary.[43]

Further, in contrast to the Nation of Islam's tracing the group identity of the black community back to the Asiatic black man, Malcolm increasingly emphasized an African group distinctiveness.[44] It is difficult to say whether this African emphasis was the result of his reflections, especially in the last years of his life, upon his parents' background as followers of Marcus Garvey's Pan-African nationalism; his development within the Harlem nationalist tradition, with its heavy emphasis on African identity; or the close associations that he established with the new generation of African revolutionaries such as Mohammed Babu in Zanzibar. Perhaps in combination, these factors led Malcolm X to transform himself into a bridge between the old nationalism and the New Nationalism.

Moreover, Malcolm X placed a great deal of emphasis on the African Revolution and on the 1955 Bandung Conference of Africans and Asians held in Indonesia, insisting these were models both for forming black united fronts and for breaking Western hegemony over people of color. In the hands of the younger generation, this emphasis manifested itself in the significance they placed on the Third World Revolution.

Stressing the need for African Americans to develop their own revolutionary ideology and organization, Malcolm X urged them to search for philosophical and political approaches rooted in the African Personality. He taught that if black people wanted to be free, they could not be guided by the thinking of their former slave masters: the logic of the oppressor is different from the logic of the oppressed. Significantly, Malcolm X saw black music as the paradigm for the creation of an alternative black ideology of change, because it represented an area of black psychological autonomy:

> He improvises, he creates, it comes from within. It's his soul, it's that soul music. It's the only area on the American scene where the black man has been free to create. And he has mastered it. He has shown that he can come up with something that nobody ever thought of on his horn. . . . Well, likewise he can do the same thing if given intellectual independence. He can come up with a new philosophy. He can come up with a philosophy that nobody has heard of yet. He can invent a society, a social system, an economic system, a political system, that is different from anything that exists or has ever existed anywhere on this earth. He will improvise; he'll bring it from within himself. And this is what you and I want. . . . You and I want to create an organization that will give us so much power we can sit down and do as we please. Once we can sit down and think as we please, speak as we please, and do as we please, we will show people what pleases us. And what pleases us won't always please them. So you've got to get some power before you can be yourself. Do you understand that? You've got to get some power before you can be yourself. Once you get power and you be yourself, why, you're gone, you've got it and gone. You create a new society and make some heaven right here on this earth.[45]

The impact of the New Nationalism on Baraka and the younger writers and artists was quite dramatic. By building a bridge between the old nationalism and the new, Malcolm X helped lay the basis in political culture for a black united front of various classes and social groups that would bond together in the Modern Black Convention Movement. And under his sway the urban black poor were not isolated; instead of middle-class reformers on a mission in the ghetto, the poor would have allies in their struggle for dignity and justice.

These ideas of the new black nationalism had an epic impact on Baraka's generation as it sought to interpret and continue the legacy of Malcolm X. One thing was clear, Malcolm X opened the door so that a new social stratum, the grass roots, would aspire to national leadership in the Black Revolt. They were the kinds of people that former generations had pushed into the background of the movement; for instance, consider the leaders galvanized by this new message in the Black Panthers: Huey P. Newton, Bobby Seale, Eldridge Cleaver, Bobby Hutton, and Fred Hampton. These leaders would not have come to the forefront under the hegemony of the traditional NAACP. Thus, as black people made their own history, according to Malcolm X, the masses at the grassroots level would become the vanguard for black liberation. This became a major theme in the poetry, art, and plays of the Black Arts Movement.

Because of these powerful influences, what began in the Black Arts as a critique of the white establishment's interpretation and evaluation of black music, poetry, and drama, led to a thoroughgoing social challenge to racist and capitalist hegemony over the cultural life of the black community in the Modern Black Convention Movement. This antihegemonic thrust of the Black Arts informed the Modern Black Convention Movement's ideological challenge of the prevailing direction and content of American politics. Thus, in the initial stage, this social movement sought to create autonomous institutions where new interpretations of art and society, running counter to those of the white establishment, could materialize.[46]

Even though the last year of Malcolm X was crisis ridden, he stood as a steadying force for the New Nationalism. He was that sturdy bridge for the younger generation in their journey from the old nationalism to the new. Especially after his break with the Nation of Islam and his call for a broad black united front, many new writers and intellectuals who were not drawn to Islam, sought out Malcolm X's leadership.

Thus, the assassination of Malcolm X on February 21, 1965, was, in the words of Larry Neal, "an awesome psychological setback to the nationalists and civil rights radicals." Neal knew this more than many other writers, because he actually witnessed the events of that day of shame. He was in the audience at the Audubon Ballroom in Upper Manhattan that Sunday as children sat next to their parents and Malcolm X mounted the platform. He writes:

It could have been church. There was such a very diverse grouping of black people; some of the women were matronly, but tricked up real fine in their Sunday clothes. There were many young children there. The sun was shafting through the windows. The audience had quieted down in anticipation of Malcolm; and after what seemed like two or three long minutes Malcolm came out.

Neal heard Malcolm X give the traditional greeting, "As salaam alaikum, brothers and sisters," and the audience answer, "Wa-laikum salaam." But soon that peaceful, sunny, February day was shattered by the bullets of assassins, and, as Neal puts it, "The whole room was a wailing woman. Men cried openly." It was over so quickly; many felt ashamed of themselves. "They felt that they had not done enough," writes Neal, "to support Malcolm while he was alive."

> Hence, they had not protected him, and, somehow, they felt responsible for his assassination. After all, had Malcolm not said that his life was in danger? Had not the man's home been bombed only a week before his assassination? [47]

Such questions haunted many black nationalists as they scattered in a hundred different directions. It was a changing of the guard, compelling new leaders to come to the fore as older leaders faded into the background in disbelief at the brutal murder of Malcolm X. Neal observes that "after Malcolm's death, thousands of heretofore unorganized black students and activists became more radically politicized." [48]

Black Arts Repertory Theater/School

There was an outpouring of expression by artists and writers about the meaning of Malcolm X, the most definitive symbol of the Black Revolution. [49] Two of the most prophetic voices were Ossie Davis, with his bold eulogy "Our Shining Black Prince," and Amiri Baraka (LeRoi Jones), with his fiery song "A Poem for Black Hearts." At the funeral at Faith Temple Church of God on February 27, 1965, Ossie Davis explained, "Malcolm was our manhood, our living, black manhood! This was his meaning to his people. And, in honoring him, we honor the best in ourselves." [50] Further developing the theme of Malcolm X's nobility, Amiri Baraka's poem, more than any other, expressed the combination of adoration, rage, and guilt that fired the minds of his generation. Consider the passionate manifesto he offered black youth:

> For Malcolm's eyes, when they broke
> the face of some dumb white man, For

Malcolm's hands raised to bless us
all black and strong in his image
of ourselves, For Malcolm's words
fire darts, the victor's tireless
thrusts, words hung above the world
change as it may, he said it, and
for this he was killed, for saying
and feeling, and being/change, all
collected hot in his heart, For Malcolm's
heart, raising us above our filthy cities,
for his stride, and his beat, and his address
to the grey monsters of the world, For Malcolm's
pleas for your dignity, black men, for your life,
black man, for the filling of your minds
with righteousness, For all of him dead
and gone and vanished from us, and all of him which
clings to our speech black god of our time.
For all of him, and all of yourself, look up,
black man, quit stuttering and shuffling, look up,
black man, quit whining and stooping, for all of him,
For Great Malcolm a prince of the earth, let nothing in us rest
until we avenge ourselves for his death, stupid animals
that killed him, let us never breathe a pure breath if
we fail, and white men call us faggots till the end of
the earth.[51]

Amiri Baraka's interpretation of Malcolm X's behest did not end with a poem. On February 22, 1965, Baraka held a press conference to announce plans to establish the Black Arts Repertory Theater/School (BARTS) in Harlem. At that point a site had not been chosen, but Baraka explained that the school would offer "both practical and theoretical" schooling in all areas of drama: "Acting, writing, directing, set designing, production, [and] management."[52] While the program was particularly aimed at black youth, the Black Arts also wished to provide a place for professional artists to perform.

Baraka announced that funds for the Black Arts venture would be raised from the proceeds of a March 1, 1965, performance of several plays.[53] By March 28, 1965, a major jazz concert for the benefit of the Black Arts Repertory Theater/School was recorded at the Village Gate. The concert featured such jazz artists as Sun Ra and his Myth-Science Arkestra, Betty

In the 1960s, Amiri Baraka began experimenting with filmmaking in Newark, New Jersey, and produced a documentary about the Black Arts Movement, *Black Spring*. (Courtesy of Baraka family collection)

Carter, John Coltrane, Jimmy Garrison, Elvin Jones, McCoy Tyner, Albert Ayler, Joel Freedman, Lewis Worrell, Donald Ayler, Sonny Murray, Grachun Moncur, Bill Harris, Cecil McBee, Bobby Hutcherson, Reggie Johnson, Virgil Jones, Marion Brown, Roger Blank, and Archie Shepp.[54]

Later that spring Amiri Baraka opened the Black Arts Repertory Theater/School in Harlem in a four-story brownstone at 109 West 130th Street. Harlem found out about the opening of the cultural institution when Sun-Ra and his Myth-Science Arkestra led a parade of writers and artists across 125th Street, with "Albert [Ayler] and his brother Don blowing and Milford [Graves] wailing his drums."[55] They waved the Black Arts flag designed by one of their artists, a black and gold flag with Afrocentric theater masks of comedy and tragedy. At the cultural center, Harold Cruse taught black history; Larry Neal, Askia Muhammad Toure, and Max Stanford came as cultural and political advisors; and such musicians as Sun-Ra, Albert Ayler, and Milford Graves provided regular jazz performances.

At the major rallies the Black Arts held in Harlem on 125th Street and Seventh Avenue, the jazz musicians drew the crowds with their music. Advocating black self-determination, Amiri Baraka proposed that "Harlem secede from the United States."[56] Speaking as the director of the Black Arts at one such rally in front of Harlem's Hotel Theresa, Baraka pleaded for unity: "If you want a new world, Brothers and Sisters, if you want a world where you can all be beautiful human beings, we must throw down our differences and come together as black people." Further, he insisted, "All these groups, organizations, viewpoints, religions, had better come together, agreed on one term, that they are black people, and that they are tired of being weak slaves. We are asking for a unity so strong that it will shake up the world."[57]

That summer the Black Arts ran a very successful program for young people, an expanded project funded by some $44,000 from HARYOU-ACT, the major Harlem antipoverty agency. For eight weeks it taught 400 students black studies and African American drama.[58] Some of the poets who flowered at the Black Arts were Sonia Sanchez, Larry P. Neal, Clarence Reed, Clarence Franklin, Sam Anderson, and Ed Spriggs.[59]

The Harlem Black Arts experiment inspired the development of a national Black Arts Movement and the establishment of some 800 black theaters and cultural centers in the United States. Writers and artists in dozens of cities began to assemble to build alternative institutions modeled after the Harlem Black Arts Repertory Theater/School, blending the Black Arts and Black Power. Between 1966 and 1967, the Black Arts Movement spread quickly through a number of important black arts festivals and conventions. In 1966, Baraka organized a black arts festival in Newark, New Jersey, featuring Stokely Carmichael, the leading proponent of Black Power, and Harold Cruse, the foremost theorist of cultural nationalism; that event was important to the development of Baraka's own cultural troupe, the Spirit House Movers and Players in Newark. The development of Black Arts West in San Francisco drew together Ed Bullins, Jayne Cortez, Marvin X, and Amiri Baraka as well as Eldridge Cleaver of the Black Panther Party. Meanwhile two black arts conventions in Detroit mobilized artists and writers in the Midwest. Dudley Randall reported that perhaps 300 people attended the first Black Arts Convention in Detroit, held June 24–26, 1966, at the Central United Church of Christ. He explained that the scope of the convention "went beyond the arts, for in addition to workshops on literature, music, art, and . . . drama, there were workshops on education, religion, [black] history, and politics." This convention had national influence because people came "from most of the major cities across the nation."[60]

These developments inspired a wave of black arts institutions across the nation: the Free Southern Theater in New Orleans, led by Kalaamu ya Salaam; the Concept East Theater and Broadsides Press in Detroit, led by Dudley Randall; the New Lafayette and the National Black Theater in Harlem, under the direction of Barbara Ann Teer; Imamu Amiri Baraka's Spirit House in Newark; and the Afro-Arts Theater and the Organization of Black American Culture in Chicago, led by Gwendolyn Brooks and Haki Madhubuti (Don L. Lee). The Black Arts Movement inspired Chicago's giant mural *Wall of Respect*, devoted to the new voices of the Black Revolt, which influenced murals in ghettos across the country. A host of new black arts and black studies journals provided vital forums for the development of a new generation of writers and a national Black Arts Movement: *Umbra, Liberator, Black World, Freedomways, Black Scholar, Cricket, Journal of Black Poetry, Black Dialogue, Black America,* and *Soulbook.*[61] By 1968, Larry Neal and Amiri Baraka had edited *Black Fire*, a thick volume of poetry, essays, and drama, which drew national attention to the transformation that was underway among African American writers.

Although the Harlem Black Arts had far-reaching effects on the Black Arts Movement in the United States, the original Black Arts Repertory Theater/School was short-lived. At that point the Black Arts Movement in Harlem remained a small, isolated circle of artists and radicals which had not yet learned how to weave itself into the fabric of the black community. Instead of connecting to the politics of mass mobilization, the Harlem Black Arts revolved around sectarian conflicts within the ranks of religious and cultural nationalism. Harold Cruse warned against the black nationalist temptation of withdrawal from the rest of the world, arguing that the politics of cultural nationalism could not afford to become one that "retreats from social realities of the white power structure under the guise of separatist nationalistic moods."[62] In fact, Cruse urged the Black Arts Movement to avoid the malicious fringe element that threatened to take over the Harlem cultural center, suggesting that the leadership develop a concrete political program that addressed the monumental problems of the ghetto.

Unfortunately, none of that happened; instead a group of nihilistic youth at the BARTS destroyed the program "from the inside." According to Cruse and Baraka, the group "forced out everyone else who would not agree with their mystique." Baraka left in disgust, and later, on the night of March 10, 1966, Larry Neal was shot by two men in Harlem at 130th Street and Seventh Avenue. Even before that violent incident, a demoralized Amiri Baraka had retreated to Newark, New Jersey, one night in late 1965, feeling hopelessly defeated.[63] In Newark, Baraka was haunted by several questions: How had the Harlem Black Arts Repertory Theater/School failed? What was his own responsibility for allowing such youthful fanatics to destroy the Harlem Black Arts program? What kind of leadership and organization could successfully combine culture and politics?

CHAPTER 2

Black Fire

Imamu Amiri Baraka and the Newark Uprising

This letter goes out as a call to young Negro men. A call to form some *highly militant* organization in the United States to combat the rise of Uncle Tomism, shallow minded white liberalism, racism, and ignorance. It is a call to form some kind of formal *resistance* against these peculiarly American evils, and to discredit the members of our own race who are willing or unwilling pawns of these disgusting attitudes. . . . It goes out to all those who recognize in the NAACP, URBAN LEAGUE, and like organizations merely gigantic factories for the manufacture of handkerchiefs to put on our heads . . . or knee pads to put on our knees as they would have us continue to scrape and grovel before the not so invisible dollar hierarchies of this, America, our so called Fatherland.

—Imamu Amiri Baraka, "An Organization of Young Men," an open letter, April 18, 1961

The emergence of Black Power as a mass slogan signaled a fundamental turning point in the modern Afro-American liberation struggle, carrying it to the threshold of a new phase. It marked a basic shift in content and direction of the movement, from civil rights to national liberation, with a corresponding realignment of social forces.

—Harry Haywood, *Black Bolshevik*

Black Power

In 1966, Amiri Baraka began to find his bearings. Speaking for the Student Nonviolent Coordinating Committee (SNCC) in June 1966, Stokely Carmichael introduced the new agitational slogan: "Black Power." Calling for broad political and social experimentation with black liberation and political autonomy, SNCC challenged a new generation of leadership to realize self-determination, self-respect, and self-defense for Black America. Baraka was so elated by that prospect that he immediately went into the streets of Newark's inner city and stamped the Black Power slogan on the walls. He also initiated a new cultural organization, the Spirit House Movers and Players, a repertory group that traveled across the nation performing the new plays and poetry of the Black Arts Movement. Baraka established his new cultural center, the Spirit House, at 33 Stirling Street in the heart of Newark's Central Ward ghetto. When the Spirit House sponsored the Black Arts Cultural Festival in Newark that year, Stokely Carmichael was the keynote speaker.[1]

As the Black Arts Movement spread to other urban areas, Baraka was no longer isolated. Moreover, in the aftermath of the traumatic Watts uprising of 1965, a new generation of political organizations spreading a militant black consciousness emerged, particularly in California. Eager to see the controversial West Coast Black Power experiments firsthand, Amiri Baraka accepted an invitation to teach black studies at San Francisco State College in the spring semester of 1967. Baraka lived at the San Francisco Black House of the Black Arts West, which served as both the cultural center and the residence of Ed Bullins, Marvin X, and Eldridge Cleaver. From San Francisco, in 1967 Baraka traveled to Oakland to examine the remarkable development of the Black Panther Party by two young men, Huey P. Newton and Bobby Seale. For Baraka, the specter of the militant street youth organized by the Black Panthers restored faith in the prospect of effective grassroots political organization. He was even more impressed by the Los Angeles US Organization, created by a young man named Maulana Karenga. Baraka first met Karenga in late 1966; Karenga arrived unannounced at the Spirit House in Newark and initiated their relationship. Initially, Baraka did not know what to think, but after visiting the rapidly growing US Organization, he was convinced that Karenga had developed the most important paradigm for Black Power. Unfortunately, he was also convinced of the illusion of Karenga's infallible leadership.

Returning to Newark in the spring of 1967 with these model leaders and organizations in mind, Baraka was propelled into the political arena by the July 1967 uprising in New Jersey's largest city. As the 1967 National Black Power Conference opened in Newark in the aftermath of one of the most severe rebellions in the United States, Baraka became foremost among the leaders who linked the fate of the black freedom movement to the political momentum generated by the African American urban uprisings of the 1960s. After the uprising and the Black Power Conference, Baraka and his associates founded the United Brothers, an organization of black men and women, to struggle for power in that city where African Americans had grown to over half of the population.

The Black Arts Movement, the ghetto uprisings, and an explosive

African American identity produced a new generation of Black Power organizations and leadership. The fusion between these leaders, organizations, and the intense consciousness of both African American nationality and racial oppression became incredibly powerful in the context of the black urban uprisings of the 1960s. The hundreds of ghetto revolts of the 1960s marked a major turning point in the Black Revolt. During the first wave of unrest in the 1960s, 329 major rebellions unfolded in 257 different cities; after Dr. King's assassination on April 4, 1968, there were another 200 uprisings in 172 cities.[2] In that context, wave after wave of black youth demanding local autonomy were galvanized by the Black Power slogan. Indeed, Manuel Castells notes that Black Power "was not just a slogan. It was the practice of an excluded community that transformed the walls of its prison into the boundaries of its free city."[3] A third wave of youthful activists joined the Black Revolt following 500 racial confrontations in 1969.[4] These hundreds of racial confrontations were the most violent expressions of ethnic conflicts that shaped black consciousness and spread the demand for African American self-determination.

As the uprisings spread from city to city, a new generation of Black Power organizations developed in their wake. Each of these organizations developed a distinct perspective about the meaning of Black Power, and each experimented to test the effectiveness of its approach to black liberation. Despite their differences, at the outset they shared some fundamentals, and their political trajectories established a common pattern. Each organization claimed to be the true heir of Malcolm X; each organization concluded that Black America suffered as an internal colony of the United States; and each demanded black self-determination. Furthermore, many of these groups embraced black nationalism and later incorporated significant elements of Marxism.

In the aftermath of the August 1965 Watts Rebellion in Los Angeles, two rival political styles were generated in California: the *cultural nationalism* of the US Organization and the *revolutionary nationalism* of the Black Panther Party. In Los Angeles, Maulana Karenga, formerly the young student activist Ronald Everett, benefited from the phenomenal spread of the Black Arts Movement as he developed cultural nationalism as the influential political style of the US Organization. Born in Maryland, during his youth Karenga and his family migrated to California where he learned African Studies and several languages, including Swahili, at the University of California, where he earned a masters degree in political science. He founded the US Organization on September 7, 1965. The US Organization insisted that African Americans formed a cultural nation in need of a black cultural revolution as well as Black Power. Influenced by the political ideology and style of Malcolm X and the Nation of Islam, Karenga's organization was named US, "as opposed to *them*." Stressing self-determination and self-reliance in black liberation, the designation "US" has a connotation similar to the Irish nationalist group Sinn Fein, meaning "ourselves alone," the battle cry of the 1916 Easter Uprising.[5]

Early in the development of US Organization, Karenga proposed that African Americans study Swahili. Impressed by Malcolm X's ethical reconstruction in the Nation of Islam, Karenga emphasized the need for a black cultural revolution guiding Black America toward seven principles (*Nguzo Saba*): black unity, self-determination, collective work and responsibility, cooperative economics, the purpose of nation building, creativity, and faith in the ultimate correctness and victory of black liberation. As part of his cultural program, Karenga developed a popular African American holiday, Kwanzaa, to teach the seven principles during a week-long celebration of black heritage. Today Kwanzaa is celebrated by millions of African Americans. As part of its political program, the US Organization organized the Black Congress, an important united front group, embracing many of the new militant organizations in Los Angeles. Karenga's influence spread quickly because of his role in the organization of the National Black Power Conferences between 1966 and 1969. Finally, as part of the US Organization ideological program, Karenga wrote a doctrine for the new black nationalism, which he called *Kawaida*, meaning "tradition and reason."[6]

Karenga met Huey Newton and Bobby Seale in a study circle in the early 1960s. While the US Organization's cultural nationalism emerged in Los Angeles, Newton and Seale developed revolutionary nationalism as the forceful political style of the Black Panther Party in Oakland. Actually, Newton and Seale were not the first Black Panthers; there were earlier groups organized by the Revolutionary Action Movement (RAM) in the aftermath of SNCC's voting rights experiment in Lowndes County, Alabama, led by Stokely Carmichael. In 1965, one year before the Black Power slogan emerged, the independent Lowndes County Freedom Organization stood up to white terror in the Deep South, using a black panther to symbolize its defiance. A number of black activists from northern cities provided material support for self-defense to the Lowndes County Black Panthers and asked Stokely Carmichael if they could form Black Panther organizations in their urban centers.[7] Consequently, Black Panther groups developed in Chicago, New York, and San Francisco. In New York, alongside Eddie Ellis, Ted Wilson, Donald Washington, and Walter Ricks, one of the leaders of the Harlem Panthers was Larry Neal, a co-founder of the Black Arts Repertory Theater/School.[8] In July 1966, with the public endorsement of Stokely Carmichael, the Harlem Party established headquarters at 2409 Seventh Avenue near 140th Street and opened a Malcolm X Liberation School. In September 1966, twelve Panthers were arrested in Harlem during a school boycott, their first direct-action campaign. The *New York Times* estimated their membership at 100. In San Francisco, the Black Panthers were in communication with Robert F. Williams, the exiled leader of RAM, in Cuba.

After the Watts uprising, Newton and Seale began discussing the need for a new kind of organization of their own in Oakland; those exchanges resulted in the founding of the Black Panther Party for Self Defense in October 1966. Although Black Panther organizations emerged in other cities before the birth of the Oakland Panthers, the revolutionary grassroots party established by Huey P. Newton and Bobby Seale quickly developed a militant stance that propelled them into the forefront of the Black Revolt. The definitive political style of the legendary Oakland Black Panther Party soon eclipsed the earlier Panthers in New York and San Francisco.[9] Instead of promoting a new value system in the style of the US Organization, the Black Panthers wrote a ten-point program demanding an end to police brutality and capitalist exploitation as well as the right to full employment, decent housing, meaningful education, military exemption, and black self-determination. The program explained that the "major political objective" was "a United Nations–supervised plebiscite to be held throughout the Black colony in which only Black colonial subjects will be allowed to participate, for the purpose of determining the will of Black people as to their national destiny."[10] Eventually, the debate between Karenga's cultural nationalism and Newton's revolutionary nationalism became a major feature of the ideological struggle over the direction of the Black Power movement.

Parallel processes unfolded following the 1967 Detroit Rebellion; in 1968, the Republic of New Africa and the League of Revolutionary Black Workers emerged. The Republic of New Africa (RNA), led by Imari Abubakari Obadele, demanded land to establish an African American nation in the Deep South.[11] In contrast, the League of Revolutionary Black Workers developed into a black Marxist organization. The League was the culmination of several black revolutionary union insurgencies, particularly in the auto industry—for instance, the Ford Revolutionary Union Movement (FRUM) and the Dodge Revolutionary Union Movement (DRUM). In the 1970s, some of the more radical members of the League of Revolutionary Black Workers founded a Marxist-Leninist organization called the Black Workers Congress (BWC), declaring that African Americans were an oppressed nation in the Black Belt South and demanding the right of self-determination.[12] Thus, in the aftermath of the urban uprisings a new generation of Black Power organizations developed a radical leadership, demanding black self-determination and generating four principal political styles: Marxism, revolutionary nationalism, territorial nationalism, and cultural nationalism.

The Black Revolt in Newark

The most widespread expressions of Black Power in the 1960s were cultural, and the leading figure in the development of the politics of cultural nationalism was Baraka, the prolific poet and playwright. Similar to the Black Panther Party and the League of Revolutionary Black Workers, Baraka's Congress of African People developed from black nationalism to Third World Marxism;[13] however, in Newark, New Jersey, Baraka's movement took a distinct political route through the politics of cultural nationalism.[14]

By the time of the July 1967 uprisings, Baraka had developed a political and cultural appreciation for the principle of self-determination, drawn from his contact with Fidel Castro and the Cuban Revolution and Malcolm X and the Organization of Afro-American Unity; in this sense, black self-determination involved a process of self-emancipation resulting from the development of black consciousness. However, just how that process would unfold in the Black Power era was not clear. Even before the Newark Rebellion Baraka searched for answers to these questions about black liberation: What kind of ideology and organization was suited for black revolution? What blend of nationalism and socialism was right for Black America?[15]

In 1967, while teaching at San Francisco State, he paid close attention to the development of militant organizations in California, attempting to learn where his Harlem experiment had gone wrong. Inspired by the disciplined Panthers and the US Organization, Baraka returned to Newark at the end of the spring semester more confident about building a new Black Power organization based on those West Coast models.

However, upon his return Baraka found the largest city in the nation's most urbanized state already in turmoil around four heated issues, which would result in the uprisings of July 1967: (1) the lack of political representation for the city's black majority; (2) the local government's plans to replace a black community of 20,000 people with the campus of a medical college; (3) the lack of black representation at the Board of Education; and (4) the outrageous acts of white police brutality against black people. Consider these issues in turn. By 1967, more than half the population of Newark was black, but an Italian American political machine headed by Mayor Hugh J. Addonizio had a stranglehold on political power, controlling City Hall, the Newark Housing Authority, the municipal courts, and the police department. According to Chuck Stone, 15 percent of New Jersey's population was Italian American, and some 82,238 members of that ethnic group were concentrated in metropolitan Newark and neighboring communities. Reviewing Italian American political strength in the four areas of Connecticut, Massachusetts, New York, and Newark, New Jersey, in 1970, Stone wrote that "only Newark exemplifies total political control by Italians."[16]

> This area has two Congressmen, Peter W. Rodino of the Tenth Congressional District and Joseph G. Minnish of the Eleventh Congressional District. Both are Italian. Newark has an Italian mayor, Hugh Addonizio, a former Congressman. Italians do more than dominate the city government. They have a stranglehold on it. The mayor's administrative assistant, . . . the police director, the chief magistrate of the municipal court, the president of the city council, the director of public works, the business administrator of the city, and the assistant director of the city's Housing Authority are all Italian.[17]

This white political machine held its power despite the unprecedented white flight from the city. In his study of Newark, Robert Curvin concluded that the racial changes after the Second World War were nothing less than cataclysmic. In 1940, there were some 384,000 whites in Newark, but in 1960 only 265,706.[18] In the space of the seven years after 1960 the city lost another 70,000 white people.[19]

On the other hand, Kenneth Jackson estimates that between 1950 and 1970, some 130,000 black people migrated to Newark.[20] In 1950, African Americans made up 17 percent of the city's population, and in 1960 they were 34.5 percent of Newark's community. By 1970, with 54.2 percent of the city's population, Black Newark was the largest urban concentration of African Americans in New Jersey.[21] In terms of cities with black majorities, Newark ranked among those with the highest percentages, beside Washington, D.C., and Gary, Indiana.[22]

This situation called for strong group leadership; however, there was an extreme and chronic leadership crisis in Black Newark. For decades the civil rights organizations had made little headway in mobilizing the bulk of Newark's black community. Several studies found that most members of Newark's tiny black elite lived in the suburbs and took little interest in the tremendous problems of the inner city.[23]

However, in 1966 a new black leadership rooted in the community was developing alongside the rise of a heated controversy over a proposed inner-city medical school campus slated to uproot a black community; this issue generated unprecedented interest and activity in Black Newark. It became known as the Medical School Crisis; the officials at City Hall and the Newark Housing Authority insisted that some 20,000 black people vacate about 183 acres in the inner city to clear the way for construction of a campus for the proposed New Jersey College of Medicine and Dentistry.[24] Robert Allen notes, "This site was three times larger than had been originally requested. . . . This created bitter resentment in the black community, and residents crowded the planning board hearings for weeks in a futile effort to have the medical school site decision reversed."[25] The Medical School Crisis pulled together the many different classes that remained in the inner city and generated a militant sense of black community identity in conflict with the forces behind the new medical school plans. The medical school was an important part of the plan for growth intended to build a postindustrial economy in Newark. As the struggle developed it became clear that the official white vision for Newark's postindustrial economy excluded the majority of African Americans.

The crisis developed against the background of the decay of Newark's industrial economy. Consider several reports analyzing the situation. Robert Allen observed that Black Newark found itself "trapped in a deteriorating situation." According to Nathan Wright, "Between 1938 and 1944, industries left at such a pace as to represent a loss to the city of Newark of three hundred million dollars in assessed valuation."[26] Robert Curvin reports that during the 1950s, Newark lost 250 manufacturers.[27] These losses developed in the context of increasing suburban investments. Looking at the years between 1954 and 1956 alone, Jon C. Teaford estimates that "roughly 90 percent of the capital committed to the construction of new factories in the New York metropolitan region was invested in suburban areas."[28] The situation worsened throughout the 1960s. By Robert Curvin's count, a total of 1,300 manufacturers left. The total harm to employment between 1958 and 1970 was shocking; Curvin found that Newark "lost 20,056 manufacturing jobs, a loss of 24.2 percent."[29] The trauma of this decline was increased by the fact that the manufacturing sector was where many blacks had made their first employment break-throughs during the 1940s.[30] Thus, Robert Allen reports:

> At the time of the July rebellion, there were some twenty-four thousand unemployed black men within the city limits. According to the city's application for planning funds under the Model Cities Act, Newark had the nation's highest percentage of bad housing, the greatest rate of crime . . . , and the highest rate of venereal disease, maternal mortality, and new cases of tuberculosis. Newark was second in infant mortality, second in birth rate, and seventh in the absolute number of drug addicts. According to the 1960 census, more than half of the adult black population had less than an eighth-grade education.[31]

As the industrial base of Newark's economy disintegrated, the black community pressed for school reform; African Americans believed that the quality of public education in the schools affected the life chances of their children in the job market.

The announcement that the secretary of the Board of Education, Arnold Hess, would retire sparked another struggle between City Hall and the black community. While the black community proposed Wilbur Parker, a black certified public accountant, to replace Arnold Hess, Mayor Hugh J. Addonizio nominated James Callahan, a white high school grad-uate. The struggle over black representation on the Board of Education was just as heated as the Medical School Crisis. Since some 70 percent of the school population was black, the African American community de-manded some representation in the Board's bureaucracy. Moreover, since the standard argument against black appointments had been that they were not qualified, the black community was outraged at Mayor Addoni-zio's rejection of Parker. Wilbur Parker was not only a public accountant, he was also the city's budget director. This conflict was especially impor-tant in view of black middle-class aspirations for upward mobility in the city's bureaucracy. This is the classic shape of the social conflict that gen-erates nationalist movements.[32] Thus, in this heated conflict the black community stepped up its mass mobilization for representation in the ad-ministration of the Board of Education. New organizations and leaders began to appear on the political scene, including a local SNCC chapter led by Phil Hutchings, the Afro-American Association spearheaded by Willie Wright, and the Spirit House directed by Imamu Amiri Baraka.

Several Board of Education meetings were disrupted by protests as this issue became a focal point for the black freedom movement. Robert Allen reports that the standoff between City Hall and the black community "ended in an unsatisfactory stalemate when the outgoing secretary decided to stay on the job for another year." He notes, "This dispute over integrating the city's educational bureaucracy particularly incensed middle-class blacks, who viewed this bureaucracy as a potential vehicle for social mobility."[33] The seeds of one key element of black nationalism are in these failed attempts of the black middle class to integrate the official bureaucracy. This class was educated in the competitive ethic to covet such positions in the system. Once they had been told that they could not enter this world because they were not educated; so they continued their schooling. Now that they were educated, they had to face the ugly fact that white groups would use their political and bureaucratic power to monopolize these positions through racial discrimination. Thus, the "young, gifted, and Black" aspirants were discriminated against despite their educational credentials. This placed the black middle class and the civil rights movement in a classic nationalist dilemma. Caught in this predicament, many in the black middle class contributed to the spread of black cultural nationalism, particularly its political demands for proportional representation in the government. Anthony Smith, the sociologist, explains that in such situations people will opt for nationalism, particularly "where the alternatives of large-scale emigration or proletarian socialist revolution are ruled out, or hard to achieve."[34] Although some historians have insisted that black nationalism is a throwback to a rural peasant mentality, black nationalist movements are generated by the competitive group life of the modern city.[35] Thus, the groundwork for a black nationalist movement had been laid before the 1967 uprising.

The Newark Uprising, July 1967

While the community struggles over the size and location of the medical school and black representation on the Board of Education were important, clearly the most explosive ingredient in this situation was police brutality. The Newark Rebellion began on July 12, 1967; that was the night that fighting erupted in the Central Ward in the Fourth Police Precinct, after some people in the black community caught a glimpse of a black cab driver named John Smith, who was badly beaten, as the police dragged him into the police station. The Fourth Precinct station house, on the corner of 17th Avenue and Livingston Street, faced Hayes Homes, one of the largest public housing projects in the ghetto. Moreover, Robert Allen reports that because of the solidarity of cab drivers, "Smith's arrest was quickly reported by other black cab drivers over their radio. Within a short time word of the arrest had spread throughout black Newark, along with rumors of Smith's beating. A large and angry crowd gathered in front of the Fourth Precinct station house."[36] Hearing about the incident, the leadership of Newark's Congress of Racial Equality (CORE) and other civil rights organizations called for a demonstration to intervene in the police beating. By 1967, CORE had been working on the explosive issue of police brutality for some time. Only 250 of Newark's 1,400-member police force were African Americans. In 1965, CORE had demanded a civilian review board to remedy the community's complaints of racism and police brutality; however, Mayor Addonizio had rejected that demand.[37]

Standing only five-foot-seven, John Smith was not a particularly menacing figure, but the police beat him like an animal. After a police car stopped his taxi, supposedly for a minor traffic violation, the police officers told Smith's passenger, "*Get the hell out!*" Then, Smith was placed under arrest, and, as they drove him to the police station, one officer in the front seat turned around.

"He used his stick on me," Smith recalled, "The cop who was driving told the other one who was hitting me to stop.

"'*No, no, this baby is mine,*' the one who was using the stick said. When we got to the precinct I couldn't walk because he had also kicked me in the groin, and they started to drag me across the pavement. . . .

"'You don't have to drag him like that,' somebody called out. . . .

"'Well, they carried me the rest of the way but once we got to the door they threw me in. There were at least six or eight policemen there who began hitting and kicking at me. They took me to a cell and beat on me some more until I thought it would never stop. They held my head over the toilet and one of them threw water on me[,] from the bowl[,] all over my head. Another hit me on the head with a gun butt and I was also hit with a blunt instrument in the side. Finally they just left me lying there."[38]

But John Smith was not alone. While he was being beaten, the black community was gathering outside, fearing that the worst had happened to

Smith, and demanding to see him. This led to protests the next day. Eventually, the mood in the crowd turned ugly. CORE members attempted to divert the crowd by leading a march on City Hall, but the attention of the black youth in the streets was riveted on the precinct station house. Before long, a hail of bricks, bottles, and Molotov cocktails hit the side of the police station.

After one officer was heard yelling, "How long are we going to wait?"[39] seventy-five riot police, wearing helmets, stormed out of the station house, attacking those demonstrators who remained across the street and clubbing anyone they could get their hands on. Indeed, Robert Allen reports, "The cops beat everyone and anyone with black skin, including a black policeman in civilian clothes and several black newsmen. Cursing and mouthing racial slurs, the club-swinging cops indiscriminately smashed into the throng."[40]

The nonviolent phase of the struggle was over. After laying siege to the Fourth Police Precinct in the Central Ward, black people attacked a mile-long section of the Springfield Avenue shopping area, then headed downtown. The newspaper reported that the weapons they used were bricks and pieces of concrete that they threw at the police.[41]

The night after John Smith had been beaten, so was Imamu Amiri Baraka. Baraka's beating at the hands of the police during the Newark Rebellion took on a national significance, placing him on an important roster of political defendants that included Angela Davis and Huey P. Newton. According to Theodore R. Hudson, "During the height of the confusion and violence, . . . [Amiri Baraka], accountant Charles McCray, and actor Barry Wynn, riding in [Baraka's] Volkswagen bus, were stopped and arrested by police officers at South Seventh Street and South Orange Avenue" in the Central Ward. After they were savagely beaten, they were charged with unlawfully carrying firearms and resisting arrest. Baraka was scarred for life; a photo in *Jet* magazine, showing Baraka in police custody, pictured him handcuffed to a wheelchair, covered in his own blood. He recalls, "I was left in the [hospital] hallway, handcuffed to a wheelchair, completely covered with the drying blood, my head on fire." That is the way his wife, Amina, saw him when she arrived. "The police attributed [Baraka's] wounds," writes Hudson, "to his having been hit on the head by a bottle thrown by some unknown person." Baraka, however, "accused the police of premeditated brutality," and as far as the guns were concerned, "[Baraka] claimed he did not know where they had come from but suspected that the police had 'planted' them."[42]

Reporter Ron Porambo provides this account by Amiri Baraka of his brutal beating that night:

We were told to come out of the camper bus. When I opened the door and stepped down, one detective . . . preached to me, screaming that we were "the black bastards" who'd been shooting at him. I said that we hadn't been shooting at anyone. . . . whereupon he hit me in the face and threw me against the side of the camper. The detective then began to jab me as hard as he could with his pistol in my stomach, asking, "Where are the guns?" I told him that there were no guns. Suddenly it seemed that five or six officers surrounded me and began to beat me. I was hit perhaps five times on top of my head by nightsticks, and when I fell, some of the officers went about methodically trying to break my hands, elbows and shoulders. One officer tried to kick me in the groin and there were many punches thrown. As they beat me they kept calling me "animal" and asking me, "Where are the guns?"[43]

In his own autobiographical account, Baraka adds:

The blood felt hot in my face. I couldn't see, I could only feel the wet hot blood covering my entire head and face and hands and clothes. They were beating me to death. . . . I was being murdered and I knew it. . . . But then I could hear people shouting at them. Voices calling, "You bastards, stop it. Stop it. You're killing him." From the windows black people were shouting at the police. . . . They started throwing things.[44]

The astute Ron Porambo did his own investigation, which turned up a black police officer who said that night he was

standing about thirty feet away when they snatched [Baraka] out of that little truck, knocked him to the ground and began to beat him so viciously that I don't know how that little man is still living today. I started to go over and butt in, but I just knew they were going to kill him from the way they were beating him and I figured they'd just kill me, too. *Man, I was crying.* That was all I could do without committing suicide.[45]

Feeling powerless and humiliated, the unnamed black officer never found his voice; he told Porambo that "he didn't testify at the trial because 'it would have been just another *nigger* telling lies on the whole Newark police force.'"[46] The first trial ended in Baraka's conviction and a prison sentence, but at the end of a second trial that ruling was overturned.

Imamu Amiri Baraka after his release from prison in 1968. (Courtesy of Baraka family collection)

The beatings of John Smith and Imamu Baraka were not isolated experiences; Black Newark was occupied by white troops. Robert Allen explains that, at Mayor Addonizio's request,

> [New Jersey governor Richard J. Hughes sent in] three thousand [National] Guardsmen, called up from the surrounding white suburbs, and five hundred white state troopers . . . "The line between the jungle and the law might as well be drawn here as any place in America," Hughes announced. To his mind the black community was indeed a "jungle" which encroached upon and threatened to destroy so-called white civilization.[47]

Although no one was ever arrested for sniping, the image of the urban guerrilla was a convenient excuse as the troops opened fire on the black community. "The reign of terror," writes Robert Allen, "resulted in the deaths of more than twenty blacks, including six women and two children."[48] A number of these victims were killed in their homes. For instance, Mrs. Eloise Spellman, a widow and mother of eleven children, was killed as she looked out of her tenth floor apartment in Hayes Homes. When she dropped, Mrs. Spellman's daughter caught her mother's body; blood was everywhere. Tom Hayden reports that bullet patterns marked the building from the sixth floor upward.[49]

The "Stop Killer Cops" campaign was popularized with this booklet published by the Congress of African People. (Author's collection)

As far as these white troopers were concerned, black life was worth about a six-pack. One *Life* reporter was talking to William Furr, soon after the young man had stolen some beer. Furr and the reporter were sharing some of that lager when "the police raced up with their sirens off, [and] jumped out of the car with shotguns." The police shot William Furr dead as he fled the scene with beer in his hand.[50]

Similarly, James Rutledge, a 19-year-old, was executed as he lay on the floor in a looted tavern. One witness reports that a trooper shot Rutledge with a rifle "from about three feet away. . . . While Jimmy lay on the floor, the same trooper started to shoot Jimmy some more with the rifle. As he fired . . . he yelled 'Die, you dirty bastard, die you dirty nigger, die, die.'"[51] James Rutledge's head and body were riddled by forty-five bullet holes.

Tom Hayden concludes that the police and the military had engaged in a pattern of "systematic violence, terror, abuse, intimidation, and humiliation" to keep African Americans in a subordinate position. "Clearly the evidence points to a military massacre and suppression in Newark rather than a two-sided war," writes Hayden: "This was not only the conclusion of the Negroes in the ghetto but of private Newark lawyers, professors of constitutional law and representatives of the state American Civil Liberties Union."[52]

National Black Power Conference and the United Brothers

The July 1967 Black Power Conference in Newark was the second National Black Power Conference. One thousand black people attended the conference and debated issues of rebellion and revolution in the shadow of the Newark and Detroit uprisings that summer. Detroit's unrest had been some of the worst in American history. The National Black Power Conferences, mobilized between 1966 and 1969, mark the beginning of the Modern Black Convention Movement. This movement became a center for the development of national black leadership in a number of ways: it created a forum for an ideological struggle over the direction of the Black Revolt; it was a political training ground for new leadership, offering workshops and plenary sessions where young people were exposed to new political perspectives; it nurtured in many local leaders a new identity in a national movement; and it created the political atmosphere for the development of black united fronts.

The 1967 Newark Rebellion catapulted Amiri Baraka into the political arena and paved the way for his new organization, the United Brothers.

On July 20, 1967, only a few days after the smoke had cleared from the Newark insurrection, the already scheduled National Black Power Conference began its proceedings. A number of public officials had pressured the conference chair, Dr. Nathan Wright Jr., to either postpone the sessions or select another city. The decision to go forward with the conference in Newark was a bold act of defiance.

Although Robert Allen argues that the 1967 Black Power Conference marks the end of the radical thrust of the Black Revolt, this summit meeting signaled the beginning of a new phase of the movement. Allen's account of the conference places a great deal of emphasis on the presence of reformist elements and corporate funding. However, whatever the original plans for the conference may have been, the background of urban revolts made this question the key issue on the agenda: Reform or revolution?

The 1967 meeting was the result of a one-day Black Power Planning Conference on September 3, 1966, called by Harlem Rep. Adam Clayton Powell Jr. in Washington, D.C. According to Chuck Stone's account, that planning session was attended by "169 delegates from 37 cities, 18 states and 64 organizations." The 1966 meeting established a Continuations Committee charged with the responsibility for planning the first National Black Power Conference. That committee included five men: Isaiah Robinson and Omar A. Ahmed, both of New York; Chuck Stone of Washington, D.C.; Maulana Karenga of Los Angeles; and Dr. Nathan Wright Jr. of Newark, New Jersey.[53]

It was Dr. Wright's idea to host the conference in Newark, and between 1966 and 1967 a number of meetings were held there to formulate the black congress. It was after one of those meetings that Maulana Karenga went to the Newark headquarters of the Black Arts Movement, the Spirit House, and introduced himself to Amiri Baraka. Baraka and his new wife, Bibi Amina Baraka, lived in the Spirit House, which served as both their home and office. That meeting was probably in 1966, because during the spring semester of 1967 Baraka left Newark to teach black studies at San Francisco State with Nathan Hare and Asa Hilliard. That casual meeting between Baraka and Karenga ultimately grew into a very close political friendship, particularly between 1968 and 1970.

At the Newark Black Power Conference, the key debates revolved around the choice between reform or revolution. Both trends were evident at the sessions. Seeking a representative meeting, the conference drew a body reflecting the diversity within the black community, including both civil rights leaders and black militants. The sessions opened with a press conference on Thursday, attended by Rev. Jesse Jackson and

Maulana Karenga.[54] Calling for a black united front at the meeting, black nationalists like Karenga insisted, "We can all keep our individuality, our differences, and still move in the same direction."[55]

Originally the conveners expected some 400 delegates, but the attendance swelled to more than 1,000 during the four-day conference and included a few scattered representatives from militant groups in Bermuda and Zimbabwe. Some leaders began looking forward to an international Black Power Congress in the near future.

Each of the fourteen workshops held six sessions where position papers were presented over the four days of the conference. The workshops were organized around such issues as the urban crisis, social change, economic development, family, religion, youth, fraternal and civil groups, culture, professionals, black politics, alliances and coalitions, as well as nationalism and internationalism.[56]

While the workshops were substantial, the plenary sessions were electric. At the beginning of one session, Sam Anderson, a young Harlem poet and mathematician, mounted the stage and replaced the U.S. flag with a black nationalist flag. During that session, the conference introduced the new chairman of SNCC, H. Rap Brown. Rap Brown spoke about black liberation in a down-to-earth manner that everyone understood: "If this country doesn't come around, then black people are going to burn it down."[57] He ended his talk by assuring the plenary that he would return after speaking in Cambridge, Maryland, where some "brothers and sisters" needed him.[58] In addition to Brown, the plenary saluted its other new heroes: Robert F. Williams, Muhammad Ali, and Amiri Baraka.[59]

At that meeting, Baraka, still bandaged from the police beating, insisted that what had developed in Newark was "a rebellion of black people for self-determination," then added, "The next time, don't break into liquor stores. Go where you can get something to protect yourself!"[60]

No one at that summit was fiercer than Maulana Karenga. According to one published account, looking over the audience during his speech, Karenga asked, "Any white people here who oppose our demands? Any Negroes who want to stand up for their white masters? *We're giving you a chance to die for your white master!*" The *Life* reporter noted that "no one stood up."[61]

It does not seem that the Black Power Conference had any mellowing effect on the Black Revolt. Nonetheless, Robert Allen's influential account of the first Black Power Conference suggests that the conference's downtown location and $25 registration fee made it an exclusive affair. But, in addition to the account of the tone and content of the meeting already provided, consider the reports published in the *New York Times* and the *Star Ledger*, which agree with Chuck Stone's depiction of the meeting as representing a broad cross-section of the black community, with many thinking about the issues raised by the rebellions.[62]

Writing for the *New York Times*, Thomas A. Johnson reported that the delegates included "representatives of the National Urban League, the Southern Christian Leadership Conference, the National Association for the Advancement of Colored People, the Congress of Racial Equality (CORE) and the Student Nonviolent Coordinating Committee" and that other groups included "such black nationalist organizations as US, from Watts, and Harlem's Mau Mau and the Organization for Afro-American Unity, which was founded by Malcolm X." Furthermore, Johnson observed, "Black Muslims, teachers, laborers, civil servants and two New York City police inspectors are attending the all-Negro meeting."[63]

The reports of fellow *New York Times* reporter Earl Caldwell agreed:

As promised, the conference here has brought together many of the diverse elements from Negro communities across the country. Nationalists, Muslims and Mau Mau sat down with moderates and conservatives in the workshops to help build black power programs for Negroes.

Caldwell quoted one moderate who said that "some of these ideas sound radical, but when you study them they have a lot of validity" and that his understanding of what the black militants were saying was that "the system doesn't work for you so you must change the system."[64]

Perhaps, the most radical sessions of the Black Power Conference took place not downtown but at a church in the Central Ward. One four-hour mass meeting was held at the Mount Zion Baptist Church at the end of the first day's sessions. At that rally, Floyd McKissick, the chairman of National CORE, urged a recall movement to rid City Hall of Mayor Hugh J. Addonizio. Reportedly, Newark's commissioner of human rights, Alfred Black, set the tone for that rally by stating: "*A black man today is either a radical or an Uncle Tom.*" There were three resolutions passed at the rally: first, "to demand the release of persons still in jail after last week's rioting in Newark"; second, "to support the 'right of black people' to revolt when conditions made it necessary"; and third, "to ask the United Nations to investigate Newark under the authority of its charter on colonial territories."[65]

The evidence suggests that rather than either ending or coopting the militant thrust of the Black Power experiment, the National Black Power Conference in 1967, coming on the heels of a wave of urban rebellions in Atlanta, Detroit, and Newark, marked the beginning of the National Modern Black Convention Movement. The call for Black Power and a black united front helped galvanize a new set of organizations in Newark, New Jersey.

A new organizational network was slowly coming together. For instance, a growing circle of women gathered around Amina Baraka to discuss black liberation and African culture as she established the African Free School at the Spirit House in 1967. At first they established an informal group, the United Sisters; later they developed into political activists in the Congress of African People.

Another group that formed in the wake of the 1967 Black Power Conference originated in nearby East Orange; they were known as the Black Community Defense and Development (BCD). Still another group gathered around Amiri Baraka himself and formed a defense committee to help with his trial for gun charges stemming from the rebellion; they joined a core of young men and women doing poetry and drama at the Spirit House.

The turning point came when the United Brothers idea emerged in 1967. That development began when Harold Wilson, a childhood friend of Baraka's, joined with the poet at the Spirit House. Wilson was a community merchant, a retailer who at various times sold groceries, clothing, and furniture. Apparently, during the Newark Rebellion the National Guard had riddled Harold Wilson's Springfield Avenue furniture store with bullets.

With his extensive network of contacts in Newark, Wilson began to mobilize resources and recruit men to form the core of a new political organization; he would become the first elected spokesman for the group.[66] According to oral tradition, John Bugg, a door-to-door salesman, was the first recruit, and it was he who thought of a name for the new organization—the United Brothers.

Probably in November 1967, Amiri Baraka, Harold Wilson, and John Bugg sent a letter to a list of black leaders of Newark, requesting their support in organizing a black convention:

> The United Brothers of Newark would like you to attend the initial meeting of interested citizens coming together to form a steering committee that would issue a call to Black Leaders for a citywide unity meeting.

The meeting to form a steering committee will take place at Abyssinian Baptist Church—W. Kinney Street, 8:00 P.M. Friday, December 8, 1967. You are urged to attend. Don't let your people down!

In Unity,

THE UNITED BROTHERS[67]

More than a dozen men attended the meeting. The call drew Kenneth Gibson, Theodore Pinckney, Donald Tucker, Earl Harris, Harry Wheeler, Junius Williams, Eugene Campbell, Eulius "Honey" Ward, David Barrett, and Russell Bingham. Together they would change the complexion of politics in Newark.

While Eulius Ward was already the chairman of the Central Ward Democratic Party, the United Brothers group was pivotal in the political careers of many of the other men, propelling them to both appointed and elected public offices. Harry Wheeler was appointed the head of Newark's Manpower; Eugene Campbell, superintendent of schools; and Junius Williams, executive director of the Model Cities program. David Barrett was elected president of the United Community Corporation; Donald Tucker, councilman-at-large; Earl Harris, the first black president of the City Council, and Kenneth Gibson, the first black mayor of Newark.

Several of these men joined the black cultural revolution and changed their names, becoming full-time cadres in a growing movement that unfolded first as the United Brothers, then as the Committee For A Unified NewArk, and later as the Congress of African People. LeRoi Jones became Imamu Amiri Baraka, the Spiritual Leader; Harold Wilson, Kasisi Mhisani, a chief community organizer; David Barrett, Kaimu Mtetezi, a key political officer; John Bugg, Kite Safidi, chief economic officer; and Russell Bingham, Baba Mshauri, premier political advisor.[68]

Although at times the United Brothers was perceived as an all-male organization, these men worked alongside a number of dedicated black women at the core of the organization: Shirley Johnson, Linda Wheeler, Rosa Lee Gray, Louise Layton, and Golden E. Johnson, the last of whom eventually became a Newark municipal judge. Furthermore, a number of the women in the United Brothers joined the black cultural revolution, became full-time cadres, and changed their names as well; for example, Jackie Bugg became Muminina Fahamivu, and Carolyn Reed became Safi Mfuasi.[69]

These new leaders envisioned a black united front, an organization of organizers and a political vanguard bold enough to lead the black community in a ruthless struggle for power. As the United Brothers built their ranks and committed themselves to the politics of cultural nationalism, they pledged their families to a lifetime of struggle for black liberation. Thus, when a child was born into that organization, the parents and the community of activists made a secret pledge during a special ritual celebrating that occasion, *Ahadi Ya Akika*. When Ndada Mali was born, her mother, Muminina Asali, and this community of activists swore:

> On this day we commit our child *Mali* to the Black nation forever becoming. We promise to teach her her identity, support her in her purpose and provide her with the direction she needs to build a better place for Black people on this earth.

> Even as our forefathers believed that their children would be placed on a camel [which] would take them to Ahera (paradise)[,] So we commit our children by placing them on this camel[,] Symbolic of our organization which will build that paradise for Blacks on this earth where we can live in peace, walk in dignity and create in confidence.

> And if I fail to keep this commitment may my children denounce me and may my name be forgotten. For Black people must survive in spite of all and anyone for as long as the sun shines and the water flows.[70]

CHAPTER 3

The Ballot or the Bullet?

The Politics of Cultural Nationalism in Newark

Our gospel is black nationalism. We're not trying to threaten the existence of any organization, but we're spreading the gospel of black nationalism. . . . Join any organization that has a gospel that's for the uplift of the black man. . . . *it is our intention to have a black nationalist convention which will consist of delegates from all over the country* who are interested in the political, economic and social philosophy of black nationalism. After these delegates convene, we will hold a seminar, we will hold discussions, we will listen to everyone. *We want to hear new ideas and new solutions and new answers.* And at that time, if we see fit then to form a black nationalist party, we'll form a black nationalist party. If it's necessary to form a black nationalist army, we'll form a black nationalist army. It'll be the ballot or the bullet. It'll be liberty or it'll be death.

—Malcolm X, "The Ballot or the Bullet," in Breitman, *Malcolm X Speaks*

And in that atmosphere, brothers and sisters, you'd be surprised what will come out of the bosom of this black man. I've seen it happen. I've seen black musicians when they'd be jamming. . . . that black musician, he picks up his horn and starts blowing some sounds that he never thought of before. He improvises, he creates, it comes from within. It's his soul, it's that soul music. It's the only area on the American scene where the black man has been free to create. And he has mastered it. He has shown that he can come up with something that nobody ever thought of on his horn. . . . Well, likewise he can do the same thing if given intellectual independence. He can come up with a new philosophy. He can come up with a philosophy that nobody has heard of yet. He can invent a society, a social system, an economic system, a political system, that is different from anything that exists or has ever existed anywhere on this earth. He will improvise; he'll bring it from within himself. And this is what you and I want. . . . You and I want to create an organization that will give us so much power we can sit down and do as we please. Once we can sit down and think as we please, speak as we please, and do as we please, we will show people what pleases us. And what pleases us won't always please them. So you've got to get some power before you can be yourself. Do you understand that? You've got to get some power before you can be yourself. Once you get power and you be yourself, why, you're gone, you've got it and gone. You create a new society and make some heaven right here on this earth.

—Malcolm X, in Breitman, *By Any Means Necessary*

Between 1967 and 1972 the politics of black cultural nationalism crystallized in the Modern Black Convention Movement, and Imamu Amiri Baraka sought to establish Newark's Black Power experiment and its black political conventions as a national prototype for the black liberation movement. In this new paradigm for black liberation, leadership would be accountable to the will of black assemblies; instead of the media, the black conventions would legitimate black leadership. By the 1968 Black Power Conference in Philadelphia, it was clear that the politics of cultural nationalism in Newark was part of a national movement to build a black political party. However, one of the most controversial questions raised in the early stages of that movement concerned the main focus of its political activity: the ballot or the bullet?[1] This chapter shows how black cultural nationalism entered the urban political arena in the midst of violent racial conflict, and how the two most prominent cultural nationalists, Imamu Baraka and Maulana Karenga, assumed leadership of the Modern Black Convention Movement by forging the politics of nationality formation.

During this period several factors contributed to black nationality formation. For one thing, the black nationalists led in the political mobilization of the black community; that helped to shape a new black consciousness of African American nationality.[2] The fact that the black cultural nationalists developed an expressive style of politics, with its own political conventions, aimed at the consolidation of black identity, also enhanced nationality formation.

Furthermore, the politics of cultural nationalism was born in a period of extreme racial conflicts, struggles that penetrated into the urban political arena. One of the basic functions of social conflict is group identity formation and solidarity.[3] If Louis Wirth is correct, nationalities are essentially conflict groups.[4] Such conflicts have helped shape nationality consciousness and ethnic political traditions for African Americans, Irish Americans, and Jewish Americans.[5] The emergence of black politics in Newark, New Jersey, was accompanied by "group trauma," the kind of "collective suffering" that stimulates the development of a collective na-

tionality consciousness. Peter Eisinger, a student of ethnic political traditions in the U.S., notes that at the early stages of nationality formation the
group's development proceeds much faster than the power structure's
willingness to incorporate them into the polity; this renders the group politically invisible, and consequently such emergent groups advocate violent
and/or radical solutions to their problems.[6] This was true of Newark in
the 1960s. In this sense, the dramatic debates between reform or revolution at both the 1967 Black Power Conference and the 1968 Black Political Convention in Newark were a part of the formative stage in the development of black politics. Moreover, those debates were a major indication
that the black community in Newark was not yet incorporated into the political system; this contributed to black nationalism's distinctive global
consciousness and radical potential in American politics—it had not been
absorbed into the ethnic political machine.[7]

Finally, an important indication of nationality formation is the degree
of support that nationalist candidates receive from the black community;
in its election debut, Baraka's United Brothers group was supported by
more than 70 percent of the voters in one black ward and by more than
80 percent in the other. These facts suggest the phenomenal rate of black
nationality formation that unfolded during this period in Newark. Although the United Brothers lost the 1968 elections, the black convention movement and mass mobilization were crucial, formative experiences
for Newark's black political community. In this sense, black nationality
formation gained substantial ground in 1968, setting the stage for major victories in the 1970 municipal elections. Because of these dynamics,
black leaders, with ideologies across the political spectrum, began paying special attention to the Black Power experiment unfolding in Newark,
as that urban center became a key city for the politics of black cultural
nationalism.

Dr. Martin Luther King Jr. Comes to Newark

In the midst of a whirlwind of speaking engagements gathering resources for the Poor People's Campaign, Dr. King arrived in Newark on
March 27, 1968. In the morning he addressed an enthusiastic audience of
1,400 students and teachers at South Side High School, sounding some of
the major themes of Black Power and black consciousness. "Stand up with
dignity and self respect," King told them. For far too long black people
had been ashamed of their race. "Now," declared King, "I'm Black, but
I'm Black and beautiful!"[8]

In the afternoon Dr. King surprised Amiri and Amina Baraka when he arrived at their front door for an impromptu meeting in their home and headquarters, the Spirit House. When the Barakas opened the door, they noticed that Dr. King was trailed by the news media and hundreds of supporters. After King introduced himself, Imamu Baraka invited him upstairs to his office. In spite of the striking contrasts between the political ideologies of these two leaders, the situation in the country was rapidly changing, and King was approaching key proponents of Black Power. In Baraka's office, Dr. King did not appeal for help with the Poor People's Campaign. Instead, he emphasized the importance of a concerted black political strategy. Warning Baraka that the increasing divisions between black leaders were dangerous and "counterproductive," King spoke to the militant writer about the need for a unified African American leadership. The meeting made an impression on Baraka and his organization and signaled the possibility for a broader black united front, one that would include such civil rights organizations as King's Southern Christian Leadership Conference.[9]

That evening Dr. King addressed a packed audience at Newark's Abyssinian Baptist Church at 224 West Kinney Street, in the midst of three of the most densely populated, high-rise public housing projects in the Central Ward. The people in the church responded with a lengthy round of cheers when Dr. King declared, *"The hour has come for Newark, New Jersey to have a Black mayor."*[10]

Tragically, one week later, on April 4, 1968, Dr. King was gunned down in Memphis, Tennessee, by James Earl Ray. That night more than 100 cities exploded with black rebellion, posing the worst domestic threat since the Civil War. Gauging the magnitude of the uprisings, Manuel Castells observes that in the ensuing month "there were 202 violent incidents in 172 cities with 27,000 arrests, 3,500 injured and 43 deaths." That storm of black rage, protesting King's death, represented "the most direct challenge ever posed to the American social order, an order historically based on racial discrimination and ethnic fragmentation among the lower classes."[11]

In the aftermath of Dr. King's assassination, there were more than 200 black urban uprisings, marking a major turning point for the Black Revolt. As the uprisings spread, state troopers, the National Guard, and U.S. Army units attempted to restore control in Memphis, Nashville, Jackson, Birmingham, Raleigh, Baltimore, Harlem, Boston, Pittsburgh, Cincinnati, Youngstown, and Chicago. In Boston, the United Front, including CORE and SNCC, rallied 10,000 black people at White Stadium in Roxbury. With a black nationalist flag flying at half-mast, the front presented twenty-one demands; one called for black control over Roxbury.[12] In Washington, D.C., federal troops surrounded the White House and "manned a machine-gun post on the steps of the Capitol."[13] By the weekend, the *Washington Post* reported that more than 11,500 armed troops were being deployed in and around the nation's capital.[14] Enraged by white hatred and losing faith in the prospects for powerful white liberal allies, the black community could no longer be restrained by the old social controls. Subsequently, diverse political forces in the black America would find new ways to work together against racial oppression.

In the midst of this national upheaval, sections of the civil rights establishment sounded a new theme. They began to look inward and emphasized a common interest that black people felt, whether they were moderates or militants. This caused an important realignment of political forces in the freedom movement, making possible united fronts between black radicals and moderates.

During the national crisis triggered by King's murder, the leader of CORE, Floyd McKissick, refused to attend an emergency meeting with President Johnson at the White House, because he saw that such militants as Stokely Carmichael and H. Rap Brown of SNCC were not in attendance. Similarly, Whitney Young, the head of the moderate, integrationist, and establishment-oriented National Urban League, made a major tactical shift, putting him on the road to a black united front with Imamu Baraka in 1970. At a press conference, Young said that he did not care about how white people felt or how sorry they were; he wanted to know what actions they would take. On the one hand, Young urged the Congress to set the tone with its actions on legislation pending for civil rights, housing, and employment. But on the other hand, he insisted that if nothing was done, "people like me may be revolutionists."

The leader of the Urban League insisted: "*There are no moderates today. Everybody is a militant. The difference is there are builders and burners.*" He explained to reporters, "If you think I am not as angry as Rap Brown, then you misread me. I'm just no fool. I'm not going to give them an excuse to kill all Negroes with all the new weapons and practice they have." Young added that he was no longer a moderate but that he "would not be a stupid revolutionary."[15] Thereafter, Whitney Young became an important participant at the 1968 National Black Power Conference in Philadelphia as well as at the 1970 Congress of African People in Atlanta.[16]

Death Ground

Like the rest of Black America, Amiri and Amina Baraka were stunned and full of woe after King's death. Moreover, the death threats against Imamu Baraka were increasing. As many artists and writers gathered in New York, shocked at King's murder, Baraka's sister Kimako informed the playwright Ed Bullins that "the officials of Newark, the New Jersey state government and the Mafia were vowing to 'kill' LeRoi."[17] Furthermore, in the aftermath of King's death, many black nationalists were alert to the threat that reactionary forces would use the opportunity to terrorize black revolutionaries. Moreover, there was little doubt in the freedom movement that white vigilantes and reactionaries on the police force wanted to unleash armed terror on unarmed black youth.

Consider the police mentality of the time. In *The Second Civil War*, Garry Wills reports that his research on U.S. riot preparations had stunned him; the white racism that he discovered was profound. Wills wondered why the police were obsessed with the use of tanks. He found that the tanks were symbolic of steel gloves for handling black people. In other words, the police actually preferred *not* dealing with blacks; however, if it was necessary, "they want to do it as one manipulates some foreign substance, with gloves on, the thicker the better, gloves of steel." Reviewing a number of urban rebellions for Wills, Major General George M. Gelston, who was a veteran of such street warfare, thought about the strategies he would have used to halt black uprisings. Gelston suggested that in Philadelphia, a military man would have taken control of the highest buildings in the ghetto; in Newark, gas would have nipped them in the bud: "You won't find a greater proponent of gas than I am. We've used it several times in Cambridge [Maryland], with excellent results." Gelston was the military leader who devastated the nonviolent demonstrations led by Gloria Richardson in Cambridge in 1964.[18] Wills reflected that for him the investigation turned into "an odyssey in reverse; one that made me lose, in some measure, my home, the things I had taken for granted, had thought of as familiar and safe."[19] In the aftermath of the racial confrontations in Watts, Detroit, and Newark, the U.S. Army stockpiled weapons for airlifts for the summer and trained SWAT teams at Fort Benning, Georgia. The preparations for repression were also local. The city police forces assembled armored vehicles, helicopters, and high-powered rifles and deployed undercover agents into the ghettos.[20]

With these dangers in mind, some of the black nationalists cautioned black youth.[21] Imamu Baraka and the United Brothers distributed flyers that read:

> Don't be a chump—Be cool—Cool. Support the United Brothers and their black convention . . . Don't riot. Don't do what the man wants you to do. Come together as blacks and support blacks. Take this city by ballot. This is not punking out. This is being smart.[22]

When a *New York Times* reporter asked Baraka why he was out in the Newark streets trying to prevent racial violence, he told him: "We've come to the conclusion that the city is ours anyway; that we can take it with ballots." At the Spirit House, surrounded by posters of such Black Power proponents as Maulana Karenga, Huey P. Newton, and H. Rap Brown, Baraka explained, "We've issued a call for a black convention to pick black candidates for every city office."[23]

Imamu Baraka's black political convention signaled a new stage in black nationality formation, and that new identity and consciousness developed in the context of group conflict: black against white. Increasingly, white racism had become a decisive part of the fabric of Newark's political culture. In the 1968 special election to fill two vacancies on Newark's city council, ethnic politics turned into "an abrasively widening schism between Italians and blacks."[24] By 1968, the violent conflicts that had raged in Newark's workplaces, public schools, and city streets stormed into the political arena when two Italian Americans won seats on the city council: Anthony Giuliano and Anthony Imperiale.

The entrance of these two figures into the political arena signaled the end of any hope of racial moderation or effective white liberalism in Newark during that period. Detective Anthony Giuliano had been a leader in the Policeman's Benevolent Association, which resisted black demands for a civilian police review board to examine charges of police brutality. While Anthony Giuliano left little doubt about his intentions for "law and order," neither did Anthony Imperiale. He was not only the chief of the North Ward vigilantes, arming them and leading white attacks on blacks and Puerto Ricans as his cars patrolled and enforced the ghetto borders, but Imperiale was also making national links with such racists as former governor George Wallace of Alabama. As governor, Wallace had defied a federal court order by refusing to admit two black students to the University of Alabama. In fact, he was infamous for declaring war on black equality: "I draw the line in the dust and toss the gauntlet before the feet

Imamu Amiri Baraka, leader of the Congress of African People, early 1970s.
(Courtesy of the Baraka family collection, photograph by Zachariah Risasi Dais)

of tyranny, and I say, *Segregation now! Segregation tomorrow! Segregation forever!*[25] In New Jersey, Imperiale headed the presidential campaign for Wallace's racist American Independent Party. Newark's black community was alarmed when it heard that the Italian American community had chosen Imperiale and Giuliano as its political representatives.

Race and power had become the most important issues in the Newark political arena. In fact, by 1969 white power was threatening to become white terror against the black and Puerto Rican communities. What Councilman Anthony Imperiale meant by "law and order" became clear during his November 1968 victory statement: *"We're going to support the police, right or wrong!"*[26] Moreover, at a white rally in Newark's North Ward, some vigilantes demonstrated an ominous and perverse version of call and response. When one shouting participant wondered, "Why can't we kill a thousand niggers and about fourteen thousand Puerto Ricans?" another racist answered, "The other way around!"[27]

Ron Porambo, a Newark journalist who investigated these developments, suspected that there may have been some association between Anthony Imperiale's group and the Klan: from prison, J. Robert Jones, Grand Dragon of the North Carolina Ku Klux Klan inquired, "How's Imperiale doing?" Doubtless, the campaign that Anthony Imperiale ran for George Wallace accounts for the 4,000 votes Wallace received in the North Ward.[28]

At any rate, Imperiale did not need any encouragement from the Klan or George Wallace. At times Newark's racial conflict was like that of Alabama and Mississippi. Consider Ron Porambo's accounts of Imperiale's role in the worsening racial confrontations. Imperiale delivered a speech to a white audience of screaming supporters at Vailsburg High School, savaging civil liberties and civil rights and then attacking such black leaders as Dr. Martin Luther King Jr. and Imamu Baraka. Afterward, the huge crowd of whites, intoxicated by Imperiale's racism, attacked nine unsuspecting black Seton Hall College students in the streets of Vailsburg, a small residential enclave in Newark's West Ward.[29] According to Porambo's investigation, Imperiale had turned that audience into a "bloodthirsty mob" rampaging through the streets, with several white people hurling bricks at black youths.

A white priest, Father William Linder, told Porambo that the black students moved toward him and several nuns "for security," and that "Imperiale's little gang was there . . . They circled us in a double row. It was organized, no doubt about it!" Shouting at the white throng from the top of a police vehicle, Sergeant Chester Popek counseled, "Don't behave like animals!" and asked, "Do you really want a thousand against a handful?" Unfortunately, the crowd roared that these odds were just fine, and only some exceptional police action by several white Newark policemen, "who formed a human wall around the college students and three priests and two nuns also under attack, prevented a literal massacre."[30]

At one point, Imperiale announced to another white audience at East Side High School that he would circumvent Governor Hughes's anti-vigilante bill by simply stripping his vigilantes of their uniform army fatigues.[31] Where would this white rage lead? One of Imperiale's political advisors, an attorney named Sam Raffaelo, made this prognosis: "They say all Maddox did in Georgia was wield a pick handle and catapulted himself to the governor's chair. . . . Tony can be mayor of Newark, he can be governor. Tony is sweeping the country, everybody's talking about him."[32] But for Anthony Imperiale, in the aftermath of numerous racial confrontations with blacks and Puerto Ricans, the reward would be a seat in the New Jersey State Senate. Imamu Baraka could only shrug and wryly concede that Imperiale had developed into "an authentic spokesman for his people." However, for Baraka, white repression had become a personal matter.

Consider a few actions by Newark police officer Frank Hunt as indications of a sustained pattern of intimidation against the leaders of the Black Revolt. Regarding the African American children in the community as "black bastards" and "little niggers," Officer Hunt watched the streets in front of the United Brothers headquarters with unequaled zeal. One night he arrested the leader of Baraka's youth department, Kaimu Sonni, only a half hour after his driver's license had expired at midnight. On another occasion, Officer Hunt confronted Baraka, ranting, "I'm gonna take you out before this is over!" He boasted, "I got your picture, I use it for target practice. I'm gonna blow your brains out!" Later, carrying a shotgun, Officer Hunt menaced Baraka, while growling, "Imperiale is gonna clean you people up!"[33] When Baraka scoffed, "Without that shotgun you'd be a punk," Hunt took the poet into custody, charging him with using profanity and resisting arrest. In Newark's justice system, that meant that Baraka was convicted, fined, and sentenced to sixty days in jail.[34] Thus, Baraka's movement was increasingly on "death ground," that situation defined by the ancient Chinese military genius Sun Tzu as one in which the group "survives only if it fights with the courage of desperation."[35]

June 1968: The Newark Black Political Convention

Coming in the aftermath of the assassinations of Dr. Martin Luther King Jr. in April and Robert Kennedy in early June, the 1968 black political convention in Newark represented a major turning point in the Black Revolt, opening a new period of united fronts between black radicals and moderates. Newark's black assembly was chaired by one of the United Brothers, Harry Wheeler, a Newark school teacher and community activist. Wheeler opened the three-day convention on Friday, June 21, by announcing the aims of the summit. As part of the United Brothers drive for political control of the city in 1970, when the positions of mayor and city council would be contested, the convention aimed to win two seats on the Newark City Council in the special November 1968 elections. The 1968 elections would be a dress rehearsal for the 1970 political contests.

C. Gerald Frazer of the *New York Times* writes that "spokesmen for the United Brothers said their immediate aim was to see that [blacks] running for office, whatever their party affiliation, had no competition that might result in a white candidate winning office without his receiving a majority of votes cast."[36] But in order for all that to work, the Newark Black Political Convention had to become an important legitimation process for the leadership of the black community. Thus, it had to be representative in order to claim to be the voice of the community. The Black Convention insisted that its candidates were the "Community Choice." Its candidates ran on a black agenda endorsed by the black assembly.

Harry Wheeler explained that the purpose of the summit was "the development of a platform on important city issues."[37] For the most part, the black agenda was a restatement of the concerns and demands of the grassroots movements in Newark's black community. During a number of workshops where resolutions were discussed in preparation for the political platform, there were heated discussions about the direction of convention policy on urban renewal and housing, social welfare, public health, black youth, tenant organization, education, black politics, and police brutality. To curb police brutality, the convention pushed for a civilian review board; this had long been a demand of CORE and other civil rights forces on that matter.

The most contentious questions surrounded the issue of what political tactics the Newark movement would use to win its demands in the other areas: the ballot or the bullet. Not everyone was convinced that electoral politics was the way forward. Furthermore, some of the militants connected to SNCC questioned whether the United Brothers were representative enough to lead this movement. Since the power to choose leadership was vested in the convention, that issue was settled by the voting process at the plenary sessions that approved the platform and candidates. The most important issue of leadership would be decided by those who worked in the campaign after the convention. In the end, the workshop on politics did agree on a *process*. The black assembly decided that it would endorse only one candidate for each office and that political hopefuls had to attend the convention, submit to its scrutiny, and seek its nomination. By the end of the political deliberations, the convention nominated Theodore Pinckney and Donald Tucker for the two seats on the Newark City Council.[38]

The platform issues were announced in the form of an eight-point program based on the workshop proceedings: (1) city financing, (2) health and welfare, (3) housing and land use, (4) urban education, (5) employment, (6) political fundraising, (7) voter registration, and (8) political organization.[39] Between the June 1968 Black Political Convention in Newark and the March 1972 National Black Political Convention in Gary, Indiana, several major black political assemblies developed important agendas to set priorities for the African American political community. Although these agendas should be essential evidence in any serious debates about the nature and content of the politics of black nationalism, thus far this documentation has not been considered.[40] Since the black assemblies were the broadest expressions of deliberative summits in the black community, neglecting the agendas that were developed is a monumental error. These agendas reveal an African American political community both determined to struggle against the conditions in the ghetto and equally resolved never to surrender to slum death. The proceedings of these black assemblies cast doubt on at least three major assumptions about black nationalism. First, William Julius Wilson and others see the rise of black nationalism as the measure of the breadth and depth of pessimism and despair.[41] Second, Wilson argues that because of pride and denial, black nationalism and black consciousness neglected the issues of poverty and social disorganization in the African American community.[42] Third, Theodore Draper insists that the African American idea of a black nationality in the United States is at best a political mirage and at worst an escapist "fantasy."[43]

However, examination of the black agendas shows they were clearly focused both on identifying the social horrors of poverty and despair in the ghetto and on finding solutions to those shocking conditions. For instance, the participants in the sessions on health and welfare decided to emphasize the establishment of day-care centers, "the rehabilitation and employment of drug addicts, and a complete re-evaluation of the current welfare system." Clearly, they saw no contradiction between expressing black pride and solving the community's serious social problems; for them black self-respect was an important motive for social rehabilitation and social responsibility in their community.[44]

Similarly, in the face of the Newark Housing Authority's aggressive urban renewal plans for the devastating demolition of thousands of units of housing and the horrendous construction of high-rise public housing projects and highways running through the heart of the black ghetto, the black assembly discussed revamping the Newark Housing Authority.[45] The black convention also considered "Black control of the Newark Model Cities program and development of a stand against the construction of any further highways through the city; development of a program for private acquisition of land and de-emphasis of the construction of high-rise apartments." By 1968, the Newark Housing Authority was controlled by the Italian political machine; and during the 1970s, the U.S. Department of Housing and Urban Development (HUD) charged that the agency was controlled by the underworld. The convention agenda makes clear the broad-based concern with these issues, which became the foundation for Baraka's policy emphasis on black control of urban renewal and housing development. Baraka and his planning office, the NJR-32 Project Area Committee, which designed and actually revitalized a 100-acre community in the heart of the ghetto, fought the Newark Housing Authority in a struggle for power.[46] These are plans intended to face the problems in the ghetto; they are not schemes to escape the realities of the United States.

In the face of a school drop-out rate of more than 30 percent, community people in the sessions on urban education demanded reforms, including the "teaching of black history starting at the grade-school level; support of community control of the schools and a more equitable plan for more black administrators in the school system."[47] Although the majority of Newark's pupils were black, the curriculum embodied the concerns of whites. These demands were a reflection in the community of the struggle for black studies and relevant education taking place at the time in colleges and universities. Meanwhile black college students on campuses were demanding that the institutions of higher education provide material support to the school children in the black community.[48]

To provide the black convention movement with broad-based support, the participants decided that political fundraising campaigns should be directed not solely at people in high places but at "every level of the community."[49] Furthermore, these activists did not believe in voter registration without political education, so they considered a "house-to-house voter registration drive to educate the black community to the importance of electing black councilmen and the ultimate goal of a black mayor in 1970."[50] These are not the ideas of a movement paralyzed by pessimism and despair; the politics of cultural nationalism was about increasing the mass mobilization of the black community in the struggle for power.

In line with the concern for mass participation, the black convention movement was concerned about participatory democracy; thus, the nature of the political organization that the black summit considered was decisive for the development of the politics of black nationalism because it placed the black conventions at the center of movement from the beginning. Those at the political sessions decided on the "establishment of a united 'black front' committed to the convention's platform and to work with the convention for the implementation of the points covered in the platform."[51] Thus, the largest body was the representative black assembly, which would establish a black united front to carry out its wishes as expressed specifically in the resolutions of the workshops. It was an interesting proposition, but could it be done? And was that the answer to some of the burning issues of organization, mass mobilization, and party program in the Black Power experiment?

Unity without Uniformity

Speaking on Friday evening to an audience of some 600, Imamu Amiri Baraka called for the "political emergence of the Black man."[52] He told them, "We say we want to govern ourselves. What we want is for black people to control their community."[53]

On Saturday, Maulana Karenga addressed the plenary. Karenga combined a discussion of the immediate work of voter registration and precinct organization, with the invocation of his long range vision of black liberation. Most of his emphasis was on winning black activists over to the process of mobilizing and organizing the black community in the political field; he insisted that they would win leadership in the broader community by winning election victories, rather than by pursuing political theatrics. Explaining the importance and practicality of establishing a black united front in the political arena, Karenga introduced the slogan, "Unity without uniformity." Ultimately he envisioned black politics as part of a cultural revolution involving a process of self-emancipation, creating a new man and a new woman, who would—as the poet Baraka said—"walk tasting the sunshine of life."[54]

By far the most controversial figure to address the Newark Black Political Convention that weekend was the new leader of SNCC, Phil Hutchings. When Hutchings delivered the keynote address on Sunday, the air was charged for a number of reasons. SNCC was the vanguard group in the Black Revolt; Hutchings had been the leading SNCC field organizer in Newark for several years before he replaced H. Rap Brown as the national program secretary. In Newark, SNCC had worked out of the Black Liberation Center on South Orange Avenue before that office was mysteriously bombed one night. On the heels of the increasing radicalization of SNCC, apparent with each successive election of national leaders since Stokely Carmichael in 1966 and H. Rap Brown in 1967, the movement was anxious to hear from Phil Hutchings the political line that had come out of SNCC's private executive sessions in 1968.

Many people in the freedom movement were keen to the ideological debates between the leading revolutionary nationalists associated with the Black Panther Party of Oakland and the foremost cultural nationalists aligned with Karenga's US Organization of Los Angeles. Some were also aware that those debates were degenerating into firefights in the streets between the rival groups on the West Coast. But just where SNCC would side in these disputes was not altogether clear. At one point that year, SNCC's James Forman had acted as a mediator between the Panther Party and the US Organization. To make matters even more complicated, the leaders of SNCC were sending out mixed signals. While H. Rap Brown had criticized certain kinds of cultural nationalism for having more form than substance, Stokely Carmichael had reproached several brands of revolutionary nationalism for emphasizing alliances with whites in the New Left at the expense of a broad black united front. Moreover, there were rumors circulating about negotiations of a merger between SNCC and the Black Panther Party. If the rivalry between the Panthers and US were to break out into a shooting war in Black America's Northeast, what would that mean for Newark's black convention movement? Many people listened to Hutchings on the edges of their seats.

This was Hutchings first major speech as the leader of SNCC, and he raised a number of burning issues to the convention: the SNCC-Panther alliance, the danger of gun cultism, the choice between reform and revolution, and the necessity for a black united front. First, Hutchings led some to believe that a merger between the Panthers and SNCC had been consummated. The audience roared when he explained that "an alliance with the Black Panther party was initiated because 'there was no difference between the Democratic and Republican parties'" and black people needed their own party. He insisted that the black panther would be the symbol for the new party. However, in reality the merger between the Panthers and SNCC was never accomplished; the negotiations had been disastrous. And consequently, party building by organizational mergers would be put off for several years by ideological warfare between the different factions in the Black Power movement. Moreover, concerning the gun cultism that was surfacing in the Black Revolt, Hutchings said, "Guns are no good without political education. You can't just run out into the street and get shot. You need a strategy, a plan to take over."[55]

Most controversial were Hutchings's blunt remarks about reform and revolution, the issue of the ballot or the bullet. Attempting to face the issues squarely, Hutchings could not help but reflect the profound uncertainty of black radicals on the most important strategic question. He was of two minds. On the one hand, he insisted that control of Newark by black people was impossible: "You won't have control of Newark unless you take over the whole country. The honkies still would maintain control over you through the state and federal government." Further, Hutchings told the black assembly that Black Power meant "tearing down capitalism," because it had served as a means of enslaving black people. However, on the other hand, Hutchings said that if there were to be a black takeover that "Newark is the key city." He explained that in terms of white racism that Newark was an "urban Mississippi." "If we can't get black power here," he argued, "we can't get it anywhere." He concluded, "You should get it either with the ballot or the bullet!"[56]

Finally, his call for black solidarity was welcomed by the plenary because it signaled that whatever differences the factions held to, they should not fight each other. Hutchings visualized a black united front, consisting of moderates and militants, with several functions: "It would provide an umbrella of defense, set an example of how well organizing works, create a forum on diverse opinions, and create a national hookup with other communities."[57]

The June 1968 Black Political Convention launched the momentum for Black Power in Newark, bringing the most controversial issues of the Black Revolt into the political arena. While black radicals raised strategic issues before the black convention, they could not provide definitive answers. Thus, like many other urban centers, Newark would have to come to its own answers to these issues through mass mobilization and political experiments. Yet, the first step in Newark's Black Power experiment seemed promising. The black community was forging a black united front of radicals and moderates in the United Brothers and in the black political convention movement. Baraka would report on the early results of this experiment before a national audience at the Black Power Conference in Philadelphia.

The Third National Black Power Conference

Baraka sought to establish Newark's Black Power experiment and the Black Convention Movement as a national paradigm for the black liberation movement. In the midst of the 1968 municipal campaign, Baraka, Maulana Karenga of the Los Angeles US Organization, and the black convention candidates journeyed to Philadelphia,[58] where they joined thousands of other delegates and observers from around the country at the third annual Black Power Conference, held August 29–September 1.[59]

The Continuations Committee of the Black Power Conference anticipated 2,000 black people representing 600 organizations would assemble that Labor Day weekend to discuss strategies for black liberation and to hear such speakers as Maulana Karenga, Stokely Carmichael, H. Rap Brown, Max Stanford, Imamu Baraka, Rep. John Conyers, Jesse Jackson, and Whitney Young.[60] By Friday, the summit had already drawn at least 2,500 people from across the country, in a crowd that overflowed North Philadelphia's Church of the Advocate at 18th and Diamond Streets. By the end of the conference, more than 4,000 had registered.

Rev. Jesse Jackson said the purpose of the summit was to plan "implementation" of the Black Power philosophy that came out of the 1967 Newark Black Power Conference. Chuck Stone, a former aide to Harlem's Adam Clayton Powell, explained the scheduled sessions to the press. The conference would last four days, Thursday through Sunday, with speakers and workshops. There were ten workshops: black women, students and youth, religion and mythology, economics, politics, education, communications, culture, history, and community organization. The subjects of the papers presented ranged from job creation and communications to folklore and nationhood.[61]

The conference drew national attention to Maulana Karenga and his Los Angeles US Organization. While Dr. Nathan Wright remained in the leadership of the National Black Power Conference Continuations Committee, by 1968, Karenga was recognized as its chief organizer and foremost theoretician. In his Friday night speech he told several thousand delegates to the conference that *defense* and *development* were two essentials for black survival. Speaking to an overflow crowd at a school at 17th and Norris Streets, Karenga received a standing ovation as he insisted on a common front: "We must learn to use every black man in this struggle."[62]

For the 4,000 delegates engaged in the four-day discussions of strategy and tactics, the mood was one of "angry militancy, disenchantment with the nation's present political establishment and insistence on black self-determination." The black assembly passed a number of resolutions by unanimous vote, including one calling for the "unilateral and immediate withdrawal of the United States from the war in Vietnam" and another calling for staunch resistance "by draft-age black youth against 'being used as cannon fodder for this racist imperialistic war.'"[63]

The political recommendation that placed party building at the top of the Black Revolt's agenda developed in the workshop led by Rep. John Conyers of Detroit. That Sunday the National Black Power Conference in Philadelphia voted unanimously to work for the establishment of a national black political party to lead black communities in the struggle to control their own space.[64]

The plenary sessions demonstrated that the summit was single-minded in its pursuit of black self-determination; Karenga was "instructed to convene a national constitutional convention for [the] formation of the national black party." Karenga explained that they would win self-determination, either through the established political system or "by any means necessary."[65]

Imamu Baraka received standing ovations when he spoke about the political importance of the Black Power experiment in Newark, New Jersey. He was seeking the Philadelphia summit's endorsement for the United Brothers candidates, Donald Tucker and Ted Pinckney, and for the struggle for power in Newark.[66]

The Committee for a Unified New Ark

The Black Revolt was committed to black political power, and Newark became a key city for that experiment in black liberation. With the endorsement of the Philadelphia summit came a stream of talent and resources to the United Brothers.[67] On the national level, black leaders began paying special attention to the events unfolding in Newark.

As both the theoretician and practitioner of the politics of cultural nationalism, Maulana Karenga spent a great deal of time training Imamu Baraka and helping him organize the United Brothers. As far as the political veterans in the United Brothers were concerned, Karenga was well schooled in political organization. He gave Imamu Baraka training in how to organize precinct work effectively.[68] That was the period of Baraka's apprenticeship under the 24-year-old Karenga, who helped with the planning of the 1968 campaign, raising funds from Newark's black undertakers for a strong and innovative voter registration drive and advising the young United Brothers candidates about how to present themselves to the wider community. One United Brothers candidate, Donald Tucker, reminisces that as a young black militant, he did not want to switch from his African attire in order to campaign for a city council seat election. Ironically, it was Maulana Karenga who convinced him that it would be politically counterproductive to campaign in his dashiki.[69] Instead Karenga advised the candidates to dress so they would appeal to a wider audience and, rather than emphasizing different fashions, to raise political issues. These facts suggest that some writers have been much too eager to stereotype both Karenga and cultural nationalism as impractical. Students of the Black Revolt should not assume that the public rhetoric offered by radicals was the same as the practical advice they provided for organizing actual political mobilization.[70]

At any rate, the United Brothers had to organize black voter registration and the campaign for the special November election. Several groups that had worked together with Baraka on the convention were pulled together by Karenga to establish a campaign organization to coordinate political activities. Karenga felt that the name, the United Brothers, sounded too sinister for the political arena.[71] Thus, for the larger umbrella organization, he proposed a new name: the Committee For A Unified Newark, which was later abbreviated to the Committee For Unified New Ark, known to many as CFUN (C-FUN). Because he was dealing with three distinct political circles in the Newark area with different organizational styles and attitudes, the best Karenga could do was to form a coalition in order to coordinate the campaign. Maintaining their differences, each group conserved its own leadership and structure. The United Brothers came into the structure with their increasing political influence and grassroots organizing; Kasisi Mhisani (Harold Wilson) was elected its first chairman. Imamu Baraka brought the writers and actors in the Spirit House Movers and Players into the new structure; they were responsible for culture and communications during the campaign. A third group, the Black Community Defense and Development (BCD), came from a base of operations in East Orange, New Jersey. This group was led by two men, Balozi Zayd Muhammad and Mfundishi Maasi. While Muhammad had worked at the United Nations, Maasi was a martial arts instructor. The people in BCD styled themselves after the military wing of Karenga's US Organization, the Simba Wachunga (Young Lions). CFUN was headed by a triumvirate: Baraka, Muhammad, and Maasi.

A Black United Front Strategy

After Dr. King's assassination, the leadership of the Black Revolt had to make some difficult choices. Many thought that the movement was on "death ground," on which one must fight or die.[72] In this situation, Baraka began to emphasize taking power with ballots instead of bullets. Similarly, Robert Allen, an investigative journalist, concluded that black leaders had very few viable choices:

"When the Black Panther comes," says Anthony Imperiale, "the White Hunter will be waiting." If black people are not consciously prepared and organized to meet this eventuality, then the genocide which it has become fashionable to denounce will be an all too tangible reality.[73]

To make matters worse, before the Modern Black Convention Movement, Newark's militants were poorly organized and had little support mobilized for their cause. At best, many were impressive speakers, but very few were actually community organizers. In this context, Baraka began to insist that it would take more than rage to dislodge the white grip on political power in Newark; the Black Revolt would have to find a way to unify and mobilize the black community. In an interview with *Ebony*'s David Llorens, Baraka explained that the increasing racial oppression required that black people distinguish between symbolic masculinity and self-defense in order to survive in this new urban situation:

Certain actions may be a necessary form of gaining your manhood, but the point is, if you are then to develop a scientific way to defeat this mother, you have got to get old enough to realize what is necessary. The real work is building, building, building, and training and educating and passing on. The white man ain't gonna fall off because a lot of niggers get mad at him. He ain't gonna die. They had a war in Detroit, man, you know, and there was a lot of bullets and mess flying around here. He can take it.[74]

For the United Brothers the upcoming political contests were battles in a protracted people's war against white racists. Candidly, Baraka explained:

> What you've got to do is get your people together to fight. Your people. . . . The war ain't gonna be on today and off tomorrow. It's going to be years and years . . . It's gonna be generation to generation. It's gonna be people passing on information and passing on ways to kill this bastard off. Nobody decided not to kill him, but face the reality. The two biggest nations in the world, Russia and China, ain't tangling with his ass.[75]

In Baraka's strategy for self-determination for African Americans, it was more important to make alliances with black civil rights organizations than with the white New Left organizations. Thus, he caustically remarked: "better a nationalist is trying to join with the NAACP or join *behind* the NAACP to bring about real change, where possible, than discussing theoretical nationalism in coffee shops, or smoking bush with 'revolutionary' devils."[76] He was especially strident in his criticism of Left groups, particularly the Progressive Labor Party, which condemned all shades of black nationalism:

> "Nationalism is reactionary." That's Progressive Labor talk. Lenin, Trotsky and all that shit to the contrary . . . the people themselves, they will dig this, man. They are not going to be making no damn detentes with hippies or SDS. What we're talking about is building institutions for black people, first, you know.[77]

Baraka's own approach was to abandon the Negro political tradition and to revolutionize black political culture with the politics of cultural nationalism. In *New Day in Babylon*, William Van Deburg makes a key observation for understanding Baraka's sense of the politics of cultural nationalism emphasizing innovation and improvisation:

> Malcolm X once suggested [that] there was no reason why black people's proven ability to create and to improvise musically couldn't be adapted to the formation of new social and political structures. Their music offered essential instruction in mental decolonization and self-definition at least as cogent as any "political" broadside of the day.[78]

Baraka was exploring how African American folk culture, particularly its music, might provide a model for the Black Power experiment and the politics of cultural nationalism.

Peace and Power

That experimentation in black political culture developed in the context of extreme racial and ethnic conflict. The tone of the 1968 political campaign was set by the tenor of the national white political reaction to the Black Revolt; seeking the White House, Richard Nixon developed the Southern Strategy, assuring the South that once elected he would grant them autonomy in racial matters. As he put it: "If I am President, . . . I am not going to owe anything to the black community."[79] Looking forward to a similar kind of neglect of civil rights enforcement in the North, Imperiale and Giuliano employed the "law and order" slogan, the same byword that Richard Nixon and Spiro Agnew used in the presidential race.

CFUN led its "Peace and Power" campaign with a great deal of energy, but the young organization lost the November 5, 1968, election.[80] According to Chuck Stone's analysis, in the two political wards with the major concentrations of the Newark black community, the United Brothers ticket received 73 percent of the votes cast in the South Ward and 86 percent of those cast in the Central Ward.[81] There are at least two different interpretations of that defeat: one offered by Chuck Stone in his important analysis of the emergence of a new black politics, *Black Political Power in America;* the other by Robert Curvin in his dissertation examining the rise of the new politics specifically in Black Newark. While Chuck Stone attributes the United Brothers loss to inadequate black voter registration, Robert Curvin explains the defeat in terms of the crucial difference between number of black votes cast in the November 1968 presidential race and those cast in the city council contest.[82] There are three reasons to believe Robert Curvin's interpretation. First, while Chuck Stone's analysis was part of a national survey of black politics, Robert Curvin was able to observe these developments much more closely as a political scientist focused on the dynamics of black politics in Newark. Second, from that vantage point, Curvin specifically notes that the United Brothers led "a strong voter registration drive." And, third, he explains that nearly half of those voting in the presidential race in the Central Ward and almost 63 percent of those in the South Ward "did not vote at all in council races."[83] In its first campaign the United Brothers and the Committee For Unified NewArk achieved a considerable degree of political hegemony in the black community; however, the national influence of the Democratic Party was much stronger.

Although that first political contest ended in failure for the black community, the 1968 convention, campaign, and election were formative experiences for CFUN. Baraka's movement had taken several steps to advance the Black Power experiment. Black consciousness was developed into a new and explosive force in the elections. Moreover, similar to the way a socialist or labor party contributes to class formation by its leadership and mobilization, a black nationalist party like Baraka's CFUN stimulated *nationality formation* in the political arena.[84] Indeed, the Black Convention's first bid for leadership in the black political wards was dramatic.

To the campaign experts and political veterans, it was perfectly reasonable that the United Brothers convention ticket would lose its first election. After all, that year's campaign was only a dress rehearsal for the real showdown in 1970. But that is not the way youth in the ranks of CFUN saw it; they were nearly shattered. It haunted them: What had they done wrong? To answer that question, they would have to study politics. Karenga helped the organization review its experience in the campaign and provided them with *Kawaida*, his own political doctrine of black nationalism and cultural revolution.[85] For Baraka, he provided some special instructions and readings on leadership and cadre development. Unfortunately, many in CFUN, including Imamu Baraka, became increasingly convinced of the lore of Karenga's infallible guidance.

After the November election colorful posters appeared all over the black community with a message from CFUN, apologizing for losing the election. The signs included both an African proverb provided by Karenga and a new slogan. The proverb introducing the apology read: "To stumble is not to fall, but to go forward faster." The new slogan advised: "Get it together for 1970!"

CHAPTER 4

The Modernization of Cultural Nationalism

The Black and Puerto Rican Convention and the Election of Newark's First Black Mayor

When we say "revolution" we mean the restoration of our national sovereignty as a people, a people, at this point, equipped to set new paths for the development of man. We mean the freeing of ourselves for the development of man. We mean the freeing of ourselves from the bondage of another, alien, people. We are not warring upon our own society among ourselves. These pigs are no kin to us. We are trying to destroy a foreign oppressor. It is not "revolution" but *National Liberation*.
—Imamu Amiri Baraka, *Raise*

Always bear in mind that the people are not fighting for ideas, for the things in anyone's head. They are fighting to win material benefits, to live better and in peace, to see their lives go forward, to guarantee the future of their children.
—Amilcar Cabral, "Tell no lies. Claim no easy victories . . ." in *Revolution in Guinea*

Between 1969 and 1970, a new and distinctive style of expressive politics crystallized in Newark, New Jersey; it was a dynamic movement combining the politics of black nationality formation with the modernization of cultural nationalism. The politics of cultural nationalism mobilized many new social forces, bringing black and Puerto Rican women, youth, workers and veterans to the fore in the struggle for power. Laying the foundation for a black and Puerto Rican alliance was essential for the rise of the Black Power experiment in Newark; together African Americans and Puerto Ricans constituted some 65 percent of the city's population. Galvanized by an alliance of people of color against white racism, the campaign pulled a broad mass of black, Latino, and progressive white voters under the banner of the Black and Puerto Rican Political Convention's

"Community Choice" slate. In the June 16, 1970, election, Kenneth Gibson, the Community Choice candidate for mayor, received some 95 percent of the black vote; Ramon Aneses was appointed the first Puerto Rican deputy mayor of Newark. At the time, the victory was understood as a powerful endorsement of Imamu Baraka's innovative politics of cultural nationalism. Certainly, it is strong evidence of the considerable extent of black nationality formation in the political arena; CFUN had established a hegemonic role in Newark's black political community.

The basic strategy of the politics of black cultural nationalism reflected a radical sense of the urban crisis of the 1960s. The black nationalists of the 1960s viewed the radical liberation parties in the Third World not only as allies but as brothers and sisters in the struggle. Identifying with the battles for self-determination in Africa, Asia, and Latin America, the politics of cultural nationalism proposed a strategy of black liberation involving struggles for regional autonomy in urban centers, in alliance with oppressed people of color in the United States, particularly Puerto Ricans and Mexican Americans. Tactically, this stratagem involved mass social mobilization for black self-government at the municipal level and for proportional representation at higher levels of government. From these semi-autonomous urban enclaves, the African American cultural nationalists sought to accelerate the process of black nationality formation through the rapid spread of independent black economic, institutional, cultural, social, and political development. One of the driving forces of these processes of nationality formation was the increasing degree of conflict between the black communities on the one hand and both the welfare and police bureaucracies on the other; the highest expressions of that conflict were the intrusion of urban renewal plans that threatened the physical existence of many black communities, followed by hundreds of mass urban uprisings.[1] Another important driving force in that process was the collapse of basic government and commercial services in the second ghettos. The cultural nationalist strategy of African American radicals was to develop parallel black institutions in that void left by the urban crisis, thereby emphasizing the failure of the American government and mainstream economy in providing basic services and offering black nationalism and cooperative economics as rational alternatives. Considerations of strategic allies revolved around other communities that experienced similar urban dynamics.

At the heart of the politics of black nationality formation were African Americans experiencing a process of self-emancipation, involving varying degrees of self-definition, collective transformation, and mass mobilization. This black awakening was not a diversion from revolutionary nationalism; it reflected the rising political consciousness of a people mobilized in a life-and-death struggle against white racism and internal colonialism. In contrast to the more narrow versions of black nationalism, paralyzed by dozens of rival sects and dedicated to different levels of secrecy and mysticism, this modernized sense of black nationality expressed a global consciousness that led its proponents not only to identify with the independence movements of Africa, Asia, and Latin America but also to see Newark's Puerto Rican community as a strategic ally against internal colonialism.[2]

Setbacks, Crises, and Reorganization

Although CFUN developed considerable momentum in the 1968 election, everything was placed in jeopardy in 1969; ideological differences between political factions within the Black Power movement degenerated into bloody streetfighting and deadly gunplay. This destructive political trend, particularly in California's leading Black Power organizations, threatened to paralyze Baraka's CFUN and to turn the Black Revolution into a plaything in the hands of the police and the FBI.[3] In 1969, CFUN was rocked by two major crises, which together set the stage for a radical change in the politics of black nationality formation. First, there was the loss of the support of Maulana Karenga, which Imamu Baraka had come to regard as an anchor for the development of CFUN. Second, with the withdrawal of the Black Community Defense and Development from CFUN, CFUN itself unraveled. Paradoxically, this crisis situation set the stage for the flowering of an indigenous grassroots politics of cultural nationalism in Newark, including innovative developments in mass mobilization and community organization and marking a distinctive period in black nationality formation.

The first crisis for CFUN emerged from the fratricidal war between Karenga's US Organization and the Black Panther Party in California. Ironically, only a few years earlier Maulana Karenga, Huey Newton, and Bobby Seale had all been members of the same black student study circle, discovering African American history and culture in the Afro-American Association.[4] Although both the Panthers and US grounded themselves in the ideological works of Frantz Fanon and Mao Zedong, each group emphasized different aspects of those revolutionary theories. While the Black Panthers called people's attention to Mao's statement that "political power grew out of the barrel of a gun," Maulana Karenga argued that it was "suicidal" to take that line of thought out of context. In fact, Maulana Karenga insisted that the Black Revolution needed a cultural revolution first and foremost to win the hearts and minds of black people and that without such a change of mind black liberation was not only impossible but unthinkable. However, the Black Panther Party argued that Karenga's cultural program was a dangerous diversion from revolutionary nationalism and that the radical consciousness necessary for the battle for power would be raised by political education and revolutionary struggle.[5] Former Black Panther chief of staff David Hilliard argues that the cultural nationalists were concerned with the superficial manifestations of African culture, such as clothing and folklore, rather than with Black Revolution.[6] Indeed, at times Newton suggested that cultural nationalism was ideologically linked to a "reactionary nationalism" similar to the notorious Haitian fascism. "Papa Doc in Haiti is an excellent example of reactionary nationalism," argued Newton. "He oppresses the people but he does promote the African culture. He's against anything other than black . . . He merely kicked out the racists and replaced them with himself as the oppressor." Newton concluded that "many of the nationalists in this country seem to desire the same ends."[7]

The most important disagreement between US and the Black Panthers was over the strategic issue of which groups would be allies for black liberation. For revolutionaries, this is a central question. Karenga and US saw white racism as the main enemy and emphasized the need for a black united front between black radicals and moderates. Although US felt that blacks might enter into *temporary* coalitions with some whites around specific tactical issues, the leading cultural nationalists did not consider any white group as the strategic ally of the Black Revolution. By contrast, increasingly the Black Panther Party saw capitalism as the main enemy and believed that white radicals and revolutionaries were important allies in the struggle for black liberation.[8]

Certainly, the strategic issue of allies was one that demanded serious consideration; however, it proved extremely divisive. Indeed, the issue of alliances was one of the major disagreements that caused the split between the Black Panthers and Stokely Carmichael during the attempted merger between the Black Panther Party and SNCC. Carmichael condemned the Panther strategy of an alliance with white radicals.[9] Unfortunately, instead of generating ideological and political discussions about the strategy for black liberation, these controversies resulted in factional fighting and shootouts, which severely retarded the development of the Black Revolt.

On this key issue of strategic alliances, Imamu Baraka remained aligned with Stokely Carmichael and Maulana Karenga. Although in the beginning Baraka had been fascinated by the courage of Huey Newton and Bobby Seale and the revolutionary fervor of the people in the Black Panther Party, he was moving increasingly closer to Maulana Karenga, convinced that the US doctrine was the answer to CFUN's problems in Newark. In fact, Baraka became a leading critic of the Black Panther Party alliance with Abby Hoffman's Yippies, insisting that it was better for the black liberation movement to establish alliances with the NAACP than to join with white radicals.[10] In other words, he argued for the primacy of a black united front—in Garvey's terms, "race first." As far as Baraka was concerned, the Black Revolution was essentially a national liberation struggle; thus, establishing a black united front for black liberation was primary, and building coalitions with liberal and progressive whites was secondary.

As matters worsened, James Forman of SNCC attempted to settle the Panther-US disputes in 1968 with a meeting that included Imamu Baraka, Maulana Karenga, Bobby Seale, and Eldridge Cleaver; that offered only a temporary solution. Forman provides a rare glimpse into those peace negotiations in Los Angeles:

> I accompanied a Panther delegation headed by Bobby and Eldridge to Los Angeles in an effort to resolve some . . . inter-organizational problems. . . . We were met at the airport by a contingent of US members, headed by Ron Karenga. Both Karenga and Seale exchanged cordial greetings and talked . . . LeRoi Jones was arriving at the same time and this was perhaps the last meeting between all these forces at one time. . . . I thought a public statement of unity would reveal to the masses of black people that solidarity within the black struggle was emerging. . . . A series of meetings followed and on Wednesday, February 7, 1968, there was a large gathering at the Black Congress of the diverse elements. A working unity was established that lasted through the rally in Los Angeles on February 18, although it was filled with tension and minor breaks.[11]

Baraka too remembers his own attempts to establish a common front including US, RAM, SNCC, the Republic of New Africa, and the Black Panther Party; yet those efforts also foundered.

Ultimately, what had begun as an important debate between US and the Panthers rapidly degenerated into violent, protracted, and self-destructive duels that ushered in the ruin of two of the leading groups of the Black Revolution. During an interview, Paul Nakawa, who was alternately a member of US in Los Angeles and CFUN in Newark, explained that one source of the conflict was gang rivalry. He observed that the Panthers recruited heavily from one gang territory, the US Organization from another. As far as Nakawa was concerned, the gang preoccupation with such matters as the control of turf colored the ideological dispute and exacerbated the conflict.[12] In his book *Picking Up The Gun*, Earl Anthony makes a similar observation, and in *Spitting in the Wind* he confesses that while acting as an FBI agent provocateur inside the Panther leadership, in establishing the Los Angeles Party, he *intentionally* recruited from the gangs at war with those that had joined Karenga's US Organization. Besides those observations, there are numerous reports that the FBI's Cointelpro program played on the friction between the two political factions.[13] Cointelpro sent phony messages back and forth between the Panthers and US Organization, provoking several shootouts. While such challenges as gang culture and the use of agents provocateurs were very serious problems, there were leadership weaknesses as well. Such traits as youth, inexperience, pride, and inflated egos worked to the detriment of both organizations. Unfortunately, it was only a matter of time before the forces of repression, which had targeted Dr. King and SNCC, would also menace these groups; however, the internal weaknesses made the respite that much shorter.

Hence, after a fateful shootout in California that left two Panthers—Bunchy Carter and John Huggins—dead, the die was cast, and the development of both organizations, US and the Panthers, was ruined. In his autobiography, Amiri Baraka provides this revealing account of the night that Maulana Karenga, who was visiting New York, was notified of the shootout in Los Angeles. There had been an intense struggle between the Panthers and US over the control of Black Studies at UCLA.

Late in 1968 something happened which changed our whole relationship to Karenga and Kawaida. Karenga had come East again for a fund raiser we were giving in Harlem at the Renaissance Ballroom. The place was packed, perhaps a thousand people. We had music and dancers, skits and political speakers. At the height of the program Karenga received a long-distance phone call backstage. I had organized the program and was walking back and forth keeping everything rolling. But I was backstage with him when he got the call. It was something very heavy that went down. Karenga questioned the caller, talking furiously and almost hysterically. What had happened was that there had been a shootout at UCLA, coming out of the sharply intense contradictions between US and the Black Panther Party. Two of the US brothers had shot and killed two of the Panthers, Bunchy Carter and John Huggins.[14]

Apparently, Karenga immediately understood the consequences. At the age of 24, he had reached the summit of his political influence, successfully leading the Black Power Conferences and spreading his influence from coast to coast, but now he would be consumed in deadly firefights with the Black Panthers. From Baraka's account, it is difficult to believe that Karenga had planned that gunplay in Los Angeles; instead, the portrayal is one of a monstrous sense of dread. Baraka writes, "Karenga was frozen by what he had heard on the phone. He was scheduled to speak very shortly and it was obvious he could not."[15] By the end of the street warfare in the 1970s, the US Organization lay in ruins, and Karenga was imprisoned for several years.

Unfortunately, the relationship between Baraka and Karenga had already gone beyond the bounds of healthy admiration; Baraka had become fanatical, almost religious, in his faith in Karenga's leadership and doctrine. Baraka would not allow anyone around him in Newark to question Karenga's authority on any subject. In an interview, Baraka's wife Amina told this writer that on one occasion at home she had made the mistake of referring to Maulana Karenga simply as "Karenga." Angrily, the poet challenged her: how dare she not call Karenga by his title, *"Maulana"*![16]

In line with this, Baraka had the members of CFUN recite the seven principles of Karenga's US Organization several times each day. At the weekly forums known as Soul Sessions, each public speaker in CFUN finished his or her speech with the ritual statement, "If I have said anything of value or beauty, all praise is due to Maulana Karenga, and all mistakes have been mine."[17] Consider the adoration and devotion in this passage of an unpublished manuscript penned by the usually skeptical writer a few years *after* his break with Karenga. Reflecting on the period of Karenga's greatest influence, Baraka recalls that for him his mentor and his doctrine had become everything, literally "a sword, a shield, a pillow of peace."

It was now that the doctrine of Kawaida, Swahili for tradition or custom, was used in an organization context in the East. The seven principles, the Nguzo Saba, the study of Swahili—at first commands, greetings, hours, days, holidays, titles—karate moves, then the language itself, and then the systematic phase-by-phase doctrine in its still-unfolding impressiveness. From the "kitabu" [the book], which is the first seven phases of the doctrine, and then beyond to the mass of digested, organized, systematized correlation and digest of the blackest thinkers of our time recreated into a single point-by-point community-organizing-style reference book. *"A sword, a shield, a pillow of peace," is what the doctrine is purported to be by its creator. It is exactly that.*[18]

Thus, the loss of Karenga as a mentor, advisor, and friend was a severe blow to both Baraka and the young CFUN; however, that was only the first crisis. In Newark, CFUN came apart at the seams—this time, as a result of a political dispute within its own ranks. In contrast to the notoriety of the US-Panther warfare, the rupture of CFUN's organization remains obscure. The split emerged in the top leadership of the organization among the triumvirate of Imamu Baraka, Balozi Zayd Muhammad, and Mfundishi Maasi. *Ebony* magazine's David Llorens provides the most memorable popular portrait of that militant leadership:

> The Organization is directed by a triumvirate: Balozi Zayd, who once worked for the Tanzanian Mission and has traveled widely in Africa, is chairman; Mfundishi Maasi, an ex-Marine who returned his Karate Black Belt, is Master of Martial Arts; and the man who has added many roles to those of poet, playwright, novelist and essayist, Imamu [Amiri] Baraka, completes the trio."[19]

However, in reality, the unity of that triumvirate was extremely brief. After the political defeat in the 1968 elections, Baraka was convinced that the upcoming 1970 political struggles in Newark required an ideologically trained core of black nationalists to lead the broadest possible united front against Mayor Addonizio's rule. Nevertheless, Muhammad and Maasi were against the new emphasis on political education, especially if it meant changing the umbrella structure of CFUN into one unified group or questioning their authority.

The situation came to a head in a flare-up one night when Baraka complained about Maasi pulling some of his martial arts students out of a political education class that the poet was teaching. What followed escalated quickly from heated arguments and physical confrontations to threats of gunplay. With a few words Baraka had challenged the organizational arrangement that had allowed the BCD, the Spirit House, and the United Brothers to maintain their autonomy; that skirmish tore the umbrella structure apart. Ultimately, it took the intervention of Maulana Karenga to avoid bloodshed; in the end, BCD left CFUN in Newark for its own headquarters in East Orange, New Jersey. Karenga sent a few of his cadres to Newark to help Baraka train the remnants of his group to replace the vital security functions of the paramilitary BCD. Baraka explains:

I called Karenga and told him what was happening and he got Balozi and Mfundishi on the phone and told them to back off. But Mfundishi pulled all the BCD people out of the CFUN at that moment. . . . Later Karenga sent a couple of his top people to the East to hang around and make sure that all was well.[20]

Preparing for Mass Mobilization: Identity and Transformation

Although Karenga and US Organization helped as much as they could, understandably in 1969 they had problems of their own. Thus, for the first time, a youthful CFUN was on its own; there was no Maulana Karenga to provide the answers. Political forces throughout the Black Revolt would help, but CFUN had to lead. Relying on its own wits, organization, and development, CFUN built up the black community's organizing and fighting capacity. As a result, CFUN became a very different organization, one focused on awakening the black community in the struggle for political power. The next period witnessed the full-fledged emergence of a new and distinctive style of expressive black politics in Newark; it combined the politics of nationality formation with the modernization of black nationalism. The first steps of that modernization were the introduction of black women as full members of the group and the revision of CFUN's organizational structure.

Following the breach with BCD, women came to the fore within CFUN. Earlier, the women of BCD had established their own unit, the Sisters of Black Culture. Although most of the Sisters of Black Culture left with BCD, a few young women remained; one of them was Malaika Akiba. Daughter of the respected Dr. Edward Verner, Akiba was raised in South Orange, New Jersey, and educated in private schools. This elite family background was one pattern in CFUN; a few of the youthful recruits came from the leading families in Black Newark and its surrounding suburbs. The daughters of both mayoral candidate Kenneth Gibson and the head of Newark's NAACP also joined CFUN during this period of mass mobilization and increasing militancy. As Akiba attended Upsala College in East Orange, she was drawn to black students in the US and BCD organizations who were advocating armed self-defense.[21] After the split in CFUN, Akiba became the second most powerful woman in the organization, second only to Baraka's wife, the founder of the African Free School, Bibi Amina Baraka.

Amina Baraka's study circle, the United Sisters, had been holding discussions and studying African politics and culture at the Spirit House drama center, where they established the African Free School. After the break with BCD, that informal women's circle soon established itself as the leadership of the new women's division of the CFUN. These women felt that CFUN should have been better organized, especially in the administration of its headquarters at 502 High Street. They introduced a number of organizational innovations, including standard operating procedures for many of the regular functions, which once had been conducted haphazardly. The women's division became the largest section of CFUN; that branch included the most original and enthusiastic activists within the organization.

The women's division developed many of its new structures through work, study, and improvisation. The black nationalist organizations that CFUN idealized had little to recommend in terms of either women's equality or the political leadership of women. According to William Sales, even Malcolm X's Organization of Afro-American Unity (OAAU) "had difficulty dealing with the leadership of women."[22] In fact, there was so much tension surrounding that issue that the problems confounded the political activism of women in the group. Furthermore, the women in the OAAU resisted the introduction of the Nation of Islam's conservative practices of gender segregation and women's exclusion into Malcolm's new organization. Fortunately, after leaving the Nation of Islam, Malcolm X eventually abandoned notions of gender exclusion, including the idea "that the women's role was in the home." Indeed, according to Malcolm X, the Black Revolution pivoted on the political consciousness and social development of women. In his own organization, Malcolm not only encouraged the leadership of Lynn Shifflet and Sarah Mitchell but also sought to recruit Maya Angelou from Ghana to help lead the OAAU.[23] Nonetheless, no clear pattern of women's leadership was established for the organizations that claimed Malcolm's legacy.

Unfortunately, too many of the radical disciples of Malcolm X were not revolutionary in that regard: some were either conservative or reactionary on the issue of women's emancipation. In fact, the two models that Amiri Baraka had chosen for his new political organization had nothing revolutionary to contribute in terms of women's leadership. While the Black Panther Party proclaimed its support for women's liberation, its practice was more ambiguous. The autobiographical accounts by Assata Shakur and Elaine Brown underline the contradiction between the public rhetoric of women's liberation and the organizational practice of women's subordination.[24] Indeed, Eldridge Cleaver's emphasis on "pussy power" was an insult to the dignity of black women.[25] Leading the militant cultural nationalist camp, Cleaver's ideological rival Karenga argued that the three "natural" tasks of a black woman were the "inspiration, education and social development of the nation."[26] In practice, in the formative period of the US Organization, far too often the pattern was women's exclusion. Furthermore, Karenga insisted that the essence of femininity was *submission*. Thus, there were major blunders in the radical projects of both the revolutionary and cultural nationalists: while Black Revolution farsightedly envisioned self-emancipation for men, it shortsightedly imagined submission for women.[27]

In that ambiguous conservative context, the women in CFUN began first to experiment with their own ideas and practices about the roles of women in Black Revolution; they were determined to become their own liberators. Seizing the initiative, the Women's Division began fashioning the institutional arrangements necessary for their own political development. That improvisation included new arrangements for the collective organization of housework, meals, and child care, so that women could be fully mobilized for black liberation. That was the first factor that came into play after BCD left.

Second, alongside the women's division, the leadership of the United Brothers took responsibility for the day-to-day operations of the organization. Earlier, the United Brothers had been content to allow the youth in BCD's Young Lions to run CFUN's headquarters on a daily basis, while the adults in the United Brothers directed community-organizing activities in the neighborhoods. But with BCD gone, the organization was in a crisis which required that the United Brothers increase their commitment of time and resources. They raised funds to employ several people on a full-time basis by taxing their own incomes.

One of the first full-time employees was Muminina Salimu, a young dancer and playwright; alongside Amina Baraka, Salimu had been part of the Newark black arts and jazz circles that had developed prior to Imamu Baraka's return to establish the Spirit House. Salimu directed the work of the central office for CFUN as it developed into the headquarters for several local, regional, and national structures: the Newark Black Leadership Council, Congress of African People, National Black Assembly, African Liberation Support Committee, and Black Women's United Front. Representing the new procedures developed by the women's division, Salimu trained the central staff as the organization grew larger and stronger. When observers praised the organizational expertise of CFUN, they were commenting on the work of the women's division.[28]

Self-Transformation

For most of the members of CFUN, joining the Black Revolution reflected a profound process of self-transformation, marked by a name change, personal redefinition, and ethical reconstruction. One of the most remarkable changes was signaled when Russell Bingham, a former professional gambler, became Baba Mshauri. Born in 1898, Russell Bingham was the oldest member of the organization. During the First World War, Bingham joined New York's legendary Black 369th Infantry; after meeting with Paul Robeson, he was convinced that this service would further "the *race*." The white racism he encountered during the war laid the early basis for his black political consciousness. His experiences in Europe were unforgettable; as he was recovering from a wound in the army hospital, Bingham found that the "personnel there was from *Down South*." When he asked one of the white attendants for assistance, he recalls, "he told me that he never waited on a nigger in his life. That was pretty tough, you know, when you are laying in bed after you have been wounded, you know, fighting for your country and have that slammed at you."

As Bingham remembers it, "We had problems in France. We had more problems in France with the *crackers* than we had with Germans, actually. We felt as though . . . some of them, like the Alabama group and the Fifth Marines, they were more enemies to us than the Germans were."[29] At one point in Europe, the marines shot into the barracks of his company:

> They opened the door that night, and told us to put out the lights and then shot in [the] place, shot in our barracks. But we got together and got some ammunition together the next night, when they were riding . . . donkeys. We shot at them, so they moved them out of the camp.[30]

His struggle for black equality continued after the war. In the 1920s, Bingham worked with the NAACP to desegregate movie theaters in both Newark and Elizabeth, New Jersey. During the New Deal, he helped pull black people away from the Republican Party and into the Democratic Party.[31] During the 1950s he helped put together Newark's first black political convention and elect the city's first black city councilman, Irvine Turner. However, in Newark, ethnic politics was intimately associated with the underworld, and Bingham was associated with both of these worlds.

In 1966, when the Medical School issue stirred the black community, Russell Bingham began to feel torn between his allegiance to the Democratic Party, which was pushing the Medical School, and his loyalty to black people. In fact, this issue led to a temporary breach within the ranks of the local Democratic machine. Bingham vowed not to support Mayor Addonizio, the Democrat sponsoring the Medical School, for reelection.[32]

After the Newark Rebellion, Russell Bingham attended the 1967 Black Power Conference, where he met Maulana Karenga. Soon thereafter, Bingham became a founder of the United Brothers and CFUN, as well as the senior political advisor to Imamu Baraka.[33] Signifying the change in his values and his identity, Russell Bingham pledged himself to live by Karenga's seven principles and was reborn Baba Mshauri, literally "the elder counselor." Explaining why he joined Baraka at the age of 69, Baba Mshauri said that he was struck by the seriousness of the organization that Baraka was building and by the sincerity of the youth in the Black Power movement, particularly their dedication and selflessness. "That impressed me," he explained, "because as a rule, when you meet people, especially when [they are] becoming involved in politics, they have some ultimate goal that they want *for themselves*."[34]

Sometimes the radical identity transformation occurred for married couples, like David and Lydia Barrett, as they sacrificed their middle-class status to join the Black Revolution. Both David and Lydia Barrett were active in CORE before they joined CFUN. Lydia Barrett was born in Montclair, New Jersey; she was one of the pioneers alongside Amina Baraka in the United Sisters, CFUN, the Congress of African People, and the Black Women's United Front. David Barrett was born and educated in Newark, New Jersey, earning a master's degree in mathematics from Rutgers University. He left a management position in computers at Lockheed to join the United Brothers; as a leader in the Black Power movement, he was elected the head of the city's antipoverty agency, the United Community Corporation (UCC). In the organization, they lived in a Zulu-styled commune, an *umuzi*. Signifying their transformations, David Barrett became Kaimu Mtetezi, and Lydia Barrett became Muminina Staarabisha.

The name change was only one of many signs of the new black identity; most activists demonstrated their renewal by a change in their political direction. While nearly every segment of the urban black community contributed to the upsurge of the Black Revolt, high school youth and college students filled the ranks of most of the rising Black Power organizations in Newark.

Young black people mobilized themselves along new lines, created innovative organizations, and developed bold leadership. For instance, among black teenagers, Pat Green and Cliff Carter established the Black

Baba Mshauri, holding the Barakas' son Ras, with Saidi Komozi in Newark, 1974. (Courtesy of the Baraka family collection, photograph by Zachariah Risasi Dais)

Youth Organization (BYO) and the Chad School in Newark. Pat Green was raised in the Central Ward's Rose Terrace public housing projects and drew members from that area. Green began organizing black youth while he was still in high school, but Cliff Carter returned to Newark after attending Stanford University. He attracted a college-aged membership, a number from the South Ward, where he had attended Weequahic High School. BYO was perhaps the first citywide black youth group, and it drew support from the suburbs surrounding Newark, where students were starved for talk of black liberation and discussions of black history. Urban centers like Newark, where the Black Revolt flowered, became intellectual centers for black teenagers. The organizational emphasis of the Chad School was on independent black education, and the ideological focus was on Pan-Africanism; they were in touch with the Malcolm X Liberation University and the Student Organization Black Unity (SOBU) in North Carolina.

During the summer of 1968, Cliff Carter debated the black Central Ward councilman Irvine Turner at the inner-city Jones Street YMCA.

The debate, which drew nearly 100 black youths, indicated the dynamics of ideological struggle in the black community at the time. First Cliff Carter spoke for BYO. He articulated the themes of Black Power: the right of self-determination, self-respect, and the need for building independent black institutions in Newark. In that whole process, he explained, black youths were the main force. It was a riveting presentation. When the moderator turned to introduce the Honorable Councilman Turner's remarks, youthful snickers broke into open laughter; immediately the moderator realized why the young people were amused: Turner, the timeworn politico, was slumbering on the dais.

Black nationality formation was particularly pronounced in the youth mobilizations in Newark. Traditional Negro politics could no longer be taken seriously with new political forces on the scene. Young people had attended the Newark Black Power Conference and seen H. Rap Brown. For those black youth the choice was clear; they found Negro politics not only shabby and threadbare but hopelessly decadent. As far as the younger, more educated generation was concerned, if the Negro political bosses were not outright agents for the white political machines, they were so personally corrupt that they had lost any fascination for youngsters. They were not planning to rely on the old system of Negro patronage for a few picayune positions; they felt that they had other choices. They mobilized and organized themselves in increasingly large numbers, especially in the high schools.

That is where Larry Hamm developed his political consciousness. Later the first student on the Newark Board of Education, Hamm knew little or nothing about black consciousness before he heard Imamu Amiri Baraka speak at Arts High School. There Hamm had learned from his white teachers to fear Baraka: "The white teachers really had bad opinions of him. The Black teachers—I don't think they had an opinion at all! They rarely really expressed their opinions about anything, *but the white people, you could hear them talking.*"[35] Hamm recalled:

I expected to see this, like, fire-breathing Black giant, you know, this man who . . . would literally make you tremble just to look at him. I tiptoed down there, and there was this little man down there, you know, he couldn't have been more than about five feet, six or seven. He was very thin. . . . He had on these strange-looking clothes, and he was speaking at the podium, and he had these *two big dudes* on either side, you know. I guess they were watching the audience to make sure that none of us were going to do anything to hurt this man. And, . . . he didn't look like he could harm anybody. *But boy, when you heard him talk, you knew that this was a man to be reckoned with. . . .* That was my first [time] hearing, I guess, what you would call a race leader speak.[36]

Later, Hamm would organize a high school student movement that eclipsed the BYO, the formidable New Ark Student Federation. They used the designation "New Ark," as Hamm explained it, "to be in tune with the New Ark and Black culture and everything that was going on at the time."[37] The mass mobilization of the New Ark Student Federation reveals the kinds of black nationality formation that unfolded among African American youth: the students were ready for action. On some occasions, the New Ark Student Federation used its organization to launch mass demonstrations at the Board of Education by pulling thousands of black students out of high schools with militant chants. Here is an account by Larry Hamm of how they mobilized for a march on one of those days:

> We would go over to Weequahic High School, and we would call out, literally call out, all the students from Weequahic High School, and they would come out because we had an organization. We had representatives of the New Ark Student Federation in every school in the city, and they would pre-arrange that all the students were going to walk out at 11 o'clock. And I would be up there at 11 o'clock and all the students would walk out. And we would march from Weequahic High School to South Side High School. . . . The students of South Side saw these thousands of students from Weequahic coming, and they were at the windows, waving, you know, saying, *"we are ready."* And they would come out and we would march those [thousands] over to Arts High and get those 500. And we would march over to Central [High School], and get a thousand more. The Black students at East Side would march up from East Side and meet us at the Board of Education. *People would say that they could hear us coming before we got there—that's how many of us there were.*[38]

The new sense of black identity and power spread into the workplace with dramatic results. For instance, at the Ford auto plant in Mahwah, New Jersey, 500 black workers shut down production for three days after a white foreman called one of them a "black bastard." They lost no time establishing a new group, the United Brothers of Mahwah, akin to the Detroit League of Revolutionary Black Workers; with their uncompromising organization, they did not hesitate to fight racism on the shop floor, even if it meant struggling against both the company and the union leadership.

They resisted both Ford and UAW appeals for an end to their wildcat strike until the white foreman was removed from the Mahwah plant. The United Brothers of Mahwah claimed to represent all 1,700 African American workers in that plant.[39] Their leader was Wilbur Haddock, who would head the insurgent workers' delegations in the Black Convention Movement. Unlike Detroit's League of Revolutionary Black Workers, the United Brothers at Mahwah was not the leading force in Newark's Black Revolt. This may be explained by one important difference between the two groups. With the workplace located in or adjacent to the black community in Detroit, the League spread quickly. It led struggles against racism both in the workplace and in the community. Soon there were a number of groups at various workplaces, for example, the Dodge Revolutionary Union Movement (DRUM), the Eldon Avenue Revolutionary Union Movement (ELRUM), and the Ford Revolutionary Union Movement (FRUM). They merged and established the League of Revolutionary Black Workers, with a newsletter called *The Inner City Voice*.[40] In contrast, by 1970 most of Newark's industrial base was gone, and many black workers found jobs outside of the city, intensifying the split between their activities as workers and their undertakings as members of Newark's black political community.[41]

Perhaps because of their life experiences, the workers who joined Baraka's organization in Newark demonstrated far more race consciousness than class consciousness. One of the men recruited by Kasisi Mhisani, chairman of the United Brothers, was Saidi Nguvu, a young army veteran from Mississippi who was working in Newark as a machinist. Protesting southern racial injustice, Nguvu reports that in his county in Mississippi "only black people [were] drafted," adding that "the thing about it was when I got drafted I was married with two kids." In the Mississippi Delta, Nguvu had been a sharecropper. He started in the fields early in life: "I can't remember not working."[42] But he did remember playing ball in his youth with James Chaney—the young black civil rights worker murdered during Freedom Summer by white racists, along with Andrew Goodman and Michael Schwerner. Nguvu was well aware of racist terror long before that incident. Thinking about his early experiences with white racism, he recalls the impact of the 1955 murder of Emmett Till on his development:

> I think that the thing that really drove it home was the lynching of Emmett Till. I remember vividly that day because my aunt came to me and said that if you don't straighten up this is what's going to happen to

you. When I look back I understand why she said that because I was always like a non-conformist, kind of rebellious. I didn't pay deference to white people. . . . I didn't like the idea of farming. Doing all the chores for white people. White people standing over you. So I resented that, and I always let my feelings be known, verbally or some form of physical expression, whether facial or things like that. They were always scared for me.[43]

But the hegemony of white supremacy was not always broached in violent terms; the fiction of black inferiority was instilled in children as a part of "common sense," a deadly strand of the fabric of everyday life:

I remember we were at the train station one day and I wanted some water. So I went to the fountain and this just happened to be the one for whites. My grandfather said that I couldn't drink out of that so I had to drink out of the one marked "colored." So then I asked him, I said, "All the water tasted the same to me, so what's the difference in the water?" So, you know, this was the thing that always got me in trouble, because I always questioned things. . . . That's why every summer I got out of school basically they would send me up North.[44]

Upon returning from the service, Nguvu had to leave Mississippi hastily after a racial confrontation. Nguvu told this author that after serving his country overseas he just could not take racial indignity any more. He explained:

I couldn't go back. I couldn't handle it, you know what I mean. I remember when I went back there, the first confrontation I had was with the insurance man that came there to collect some money from my mother for her insurance policy and she told him she didn't have no money—to come back. I'm sitting right there and he's going to get nasty. . . . I jumped up and said, "*Wait a minute this is my mother you're talking to!*" And, I proceeded to knock him off the porch, you know. And he left. I didn't see him no more, but my mother got scared cause I attacked this white man. . . . Me and my mother are very close. I wouldn't let nobody disrespect her—*not with me standing there.*[45]

A number of the black militants who fled Mississippi migrated to northern cities such as Chicago, New York, Philadelphia, Jersey City, and Newark. While Nguvu was in the service, his wife had moved north to live with her sister in Newark; and after leaving Mississippi, he followed her.[46] In Newark, Nguvu was working in an employment training program when he first encountered the United Brothers; the experience would change his life.[47] Occasionally, the program invited speakers. There was one from the Nation of Islam, but the group that caught Nguvu's attention was the United Brothers:

> I was gonna be a machinist . . . While I was in that trade school, a brother named Mhisani, Harold Wilson, . . . came in one day. He wore a dashiki and had his head shaven. He came over to me and talked to me and told me that I should come to Soul Session and think about joining the organization.[48]

The Soul Sessions were weekly meetings on Sunday evenings during which the organization and its allies congregated and celebrated at CFUN's headquarters at 502 High Street. The program alternated between music and speakers. It featured several black nationalist lessons as well as cultural presentations by members of CFUN. At times the Simba Wachunga (Young Lions) performed the South African boot dance or the Zulu dance; on special occasions the Malaika singers moved the congregation with songs by Miriam Makeba. At the end of the program, Imamu Baraka delivered the keynote speech. Afterwards the folding chairs were put aside, and the men and women danced to the music from a juke box, with the men in one line and the women in another line. One by one each couple joined at the beginning of the lineup, and then danced through the center lane. They repeated this into the night. Nguvu was recruited immediately after one of these Sunday meetings: "I remember my first Soul Session. Matter of fact, I was real impressed. The first Soul Session, I joined the organization." At the time Nguvu joined Baraka's organization he noted that, "They had a lot of sisters" in the group, "more sisters than there was brothers!"

Moreover, Nguvu recalls the impact of the first speech he heard by Imamu Baraka at the Soul Session, one emphasizing the need for members with a new value system:

> Imamu Baraka made a speech; *I never will forget it*. It was dealing with morality, like cleaning up your lifestyle—drinking and smoking and all this type of stuff. The *new man*, an alternative *value system*. The speech was so strong and so convincing that I remember when I walked out from the Soul Session—because I was smoking cigarettes at that time—I remember that I got a block away from the place, I threw my cigarettes away. *I never smoked a day since*. That was the impact it had on me.[49]

Holding up Baraka's booklet *A Black Value System*, the Malaika, women of the Newark Congress of African People, stand outside headquarters, Hekalu Mwalimu (Temple of the Teacher), in 1972. (Photograph by Sura Wa Taifa, from author's collection)

Nguvu was one of a number of veterans who joined the movement; like him, some had served in the army, but others like Baraka had enlisted in the air force. These veterans were an important stabilizing force in, what was for the most part, a youth movement.

Attracted by the rising tide of mass political mobilization in Newark, CFUN was becoming national in its membership, as young people left schools and careers in other regions of the country to join the organization. For instance, Muminina Furaha left the San Francisco Black Arts West to help establish the Spirit House Movers and Players. Furaha was a breathtaking actress, who sang in the Malaika Singers and taught in the African Free School. Moreover, college graduates joined CFUN in large numbers. The principal of the African Free School, Muminina Jalia, came to CFUN from Dayton, Ohio, after graduating from Kalamazoo College. Similarly, Jaribu Hill, of Cleveland, Ohio, joined the organization after graduating from Central State. While Malaika Kimya and Ndada

Super Simba Boot Dancers in Harlem in the early 1970s, a youth cultural group developed by Baraka's Newark Congress of African People. The boot dance comes from South Africa. (Photograph by Sura Wa Taifa, from author's collection)

Chekesha came to CFUN from Dickinson College, Malaika Nadra and Muminina Karimu were recruited from Rutgers University. In many cases, new members were recruited by black students at their schools.[50] Many of these women became part of the mainstay of the organization.

Departments and Institutions

With the demands of mass mobilization and communications, CFUN was reorganized into social divisions and departments. There were several social divisions: one for the women, the Malaika (Good Spirits); another for men, the Saidi (Lords); one for young males (ages 16 to 21), the Simba (Lions); another for the boys, the Super Simba (under 16 years old), and yet another for little children of both genders, the Watoto (Children).

As new recruits began to flood CFUN during the 1969–1970 political mobilization, the organization was divided into several departments: Communications (Habari), Economics (Uchumi), Security (Usalamu), Community Organization (Jamii), Education (Elimu), and Politics (Siasa). Furthermore, the organization established a network of institutions, pro-

Baraka's cultural group, The Advanced Workers, around 1976. (Postcard in author's collection, photograph by Zachariah Risasi Dais)

grams, and business operations: the Spirit House Movers and Players, for drama; the African Free School, for early childhood education; Jihad Productions, for book publication; *Black New Ark* newspaper, for local communications; *Unity and Struggle* newspaper, for national communications; Nyumba ya Ujamaa, for the sale of books and clothing; Duka Ujamaa, for the cooperative sale of groceries; Events, Inc., for public relations; Proposals, for development grants; and Kawaida Towers and the R-32 Project Area Committee, for urban planning and community development.

With political victories, Siasa (Politics) established the Political School of Kawaida to train activists from different cities. Similarly, as the African Free School gained a national reputation, the women's division established the Teacher Training Institute, preparing black instructors from across the country. The women in the organization were faced with the additional burden of family responsibilities; however, they were determined to take part in the political work of the movement. Thus, in Newark black women developed institutions to collectivize both housework and child rearing. For example, they institutionalized a collective kitchen (Chakula Ujamaa), where every family ate; a sewing collective (Ushoni Ujamaa), which tailored African attire; and the 24-hour nursery at the African Free School. While some aspects of the structure were developed based on trial and error, other aspects of women's participation were based on the study

Two of the Baraka children, Ras (above) and Shani (opposite), taken at the African Free School in 1972. (Courtesy of the Baraka family collection, photograph by Zachariah Risasi Dais of Sura Wa Taifa)

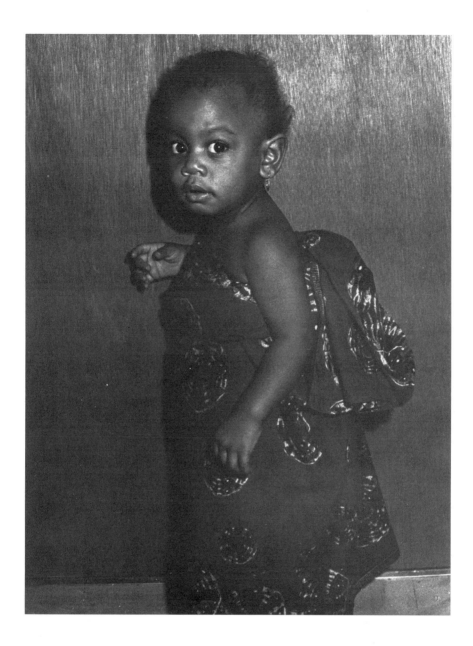

of Third World liberation movements and African social organizations that emphasized communalism.[51]

In short, the break with BCD modernized the organization, and those developments ended the infancy of CFUN. With these many changes, a marked difference developed between CFUN and the US Organization; there was very little parallel in the Los Angeles US Organization to political role of the women's division in CFUN.[52]

Obalaji Baraka, oldest son of Amiri and Amina, selling *Unity and Struggle* newspaper to unidentified African woman. (Courtesy of Baraka family collection)

Mutual Defense Pact with the Young Lords

While CFUN improved its organizational capacity for mass mobilization, it also enhanced its political alignment by establishing an alliance with the radicals and progressives in the Puerto Rican community. During the period of police and vigilante actions against the black community, the Puerto Rican community was pressured by Imperiale's armed men, patrolling "the line" between the Puerto Rican and Italian neighborhoods with shotguns protruding from the windows of their vehicles. After a number of conflicts, one Puerto Rican group, the Young Lords, signed a mutual defense pact with CFUN against white terror. The Young Lords were noted for their national alliance with the Black Panther Party; however, with the situation as it was in Newark, the Young Lords decided to establish a treaty with CFUN's cultural nationalism on the local level.

In fact, one of the leaders of Newark's Young Lords had worked with

Imamu Baraka in the Black Arts Movement, the gifted Felipe Luciano of the Last Poets. The Last Poets was a group of Harlem blacks and Puerto Ricans that emerged in the fire of the Black Revolt. Their name indicated their stance on the Black Revolution: they were the *last* poets before the conflagration; after them there would be no others. Reading poetry at an outdoor rally before an audience of thousands at the 1968 Black Power Conference in Philadelphia, the Last Poets created a riveting lyrical style, capturing not only the rhythm and language but the urban ethos developed by black and Puerto Rican youths in the streets.[53] As Imamu Baraka explained: The Last Poets—"Felipe, . . . Gylan Kain and David Nelson had extended the form of the ensemble poetry performance that we had worked with in the Spirit House."[54] They became one of the most popular groups springing from the Black Arts Movement, with many recorded poems. In the North, especially around the New York metropolitan area, black youth recited those poems in the streets during the 1960s in the same manner in which youth perform contemporary rap music.

When Felipe Luciano moved to Newark, New Jersey, the idea of an important alliance between blacks and Puerto Ricans in Newark became possible. In his autobiography, Baraka recalls:

> Felipe Luciano, the first national chairman [of the Young Lords], was an old friend of mine.
>
> We had that special connection that cultural workers have. . . . Despite the fact that the Lords were heavily influenced by the Panthers, Felipe and I remained friends and our ties with the Newark Lords remained so strong despite the anti-cultural nationalist bias that must have informed the national organization. The Newark captain, Ramon Rivera, and I got very tight . . . and so the planning of the Black and Puerto Rican Convention went forward.[55]

The mutual defense pact between CFUN and the Young Lords set in motion the dynamics that led to the alliance which took form in the 1969 Black and Puerto Rican Convention. Later, during the 1970 drive for black and Puerto Rican power in Newark, New York's former Bronx borough president Herman Badillo would come to New Jersey to campaign for the Community Choice slate.[56] In return, mayoral candidate Kenneth Gibson would campaign in New York City for Badillo, who sought a congressional seat.[57] For CFUN this alliance was not simply a tactic, but a serious matter; the alliance grew before, during, and after the 1970 elections. CFUN would stand beside the Young Lords after the election in

1970, when the Puerto Rican community groaned under the burden of continuous police brutality; and the Young Lords would be a reliable ally to CFUN during the worst of times.

The Black and Puerto Rican Convention

With CFUN's increasing solidarity with the Puerto Rican community, the situation was ripe to change the Black Convention into a Black and Puerto Rican Political Convention in November 1969. Baraka was convinced by 1969 that change in Newark would come only through the mass mobilization of the black community, and that such mobilization would come only by developing the broadest possible black and Puerto Rican united front.

While the Young Lords were mobilizing young Latinos in Newark's North Ward, one indication of the spread of the black community's increasing determination to struggle against racism was the grassroots mobilization that led to the recall of South Ward councilman Lee Bernstein and the election of the insurgent black leader Rev. Horace Sharper on March 4, 1969. The strong 1968 United Brothers race, their single-minded, year-long voter registration drive, and the recall victory demonstrated that African Americans unquestionably had become the foremost political group not only in the Central but now in the South Ward.[58]

The 1969 steering committee for the Black and Puerto Rican Political Convention was far broader than the group that had sponsored the 1968 black assembly. The United Brothers were still the core of that leadership, but the chairman of the Newark Convention Planning Committee was Robert Curvin, the head of CORE and at that time a political science professor at Rutgers University in Newark. Joining Curvin at the head of the expanding new steering committee were James A. Pawley, the executive director of the Essex County Urban League, and Ruth McClain, associate director of the Newark Urban Coalition. Ruth McClain managed the 27-member credentials committee for the convention.

Tactically, the 1969 Black and Puerto Rican Convention was called simply to prepare for victory in the 1970 elections by narrowing the field of candidates competing for the black and Puerto Rican vote. But strategically, the Newark Convention Movement aimed to establish itself as the sole legitimate process for the selection of black elected leadership.

Even before the Black and Puerto Rican Convention could commence, its attempt at hegemony over the black vote was challenged by three black figures. Instead of supporting the black and Puerto Rican summit, Willie

Wright, the head of the black nationalist Afro-American Association, broke with the planning committee and publicized his own idea of holding a black primary; however, that project promptly disintegrated. Second, the black New Jersey assemblyman George C. Richardson announced that he was entering the 1970 race for mayor and refusing to participate in the Black and Puerto Rican Convention. Richardson had led an earlier challenge to the Newark machine at the head of the United Freedom Party. From the very outset the struggle for black legitimacy was not confined to Newark, New Jersey. George Richardson boasted an endorsement from Cleveland's Carl B. Stokes, who in 1967 became the first black mayor of a major city in the United States. Third, another candidate for the mayor's seat, Harry Wheeler, broke ranks with the Black and Puerto Rican Convention by announcing that he would run in the election. Harry Wheeler had been the chairman of the 1968 Newark Black Political Convention, a member of the United Brothers steering committee, and then a coordinator of a program for the U.S. Department of Health, Education and Welfare. After a year's absence, while serving in that government position in Washington, D.C., Wheeler calculated that he had no chance of winning the convention nomination. However, if Wheeler had not remained in Washington so long during the year leading up the convention, he might have placed himself within striking distance of the nomination.[59]

With the announcements of their own candidacies in the weeks before the black and Puerto Rican summit, both Wheeler and Richardson openly challenged the legitimacy of the convention process and the credibility of all the leaders and organizations it represented. All the opposition leaders, including Mayor Addonizio's camp, charged that the convention process did not actually represent the will of the community, and further that it was racist.

Responding to the challenge that they were not the voice of the community, the Newark Convention Planning Committee announced the opening of the Newark Black and Puerto Rican Political Convention at Clinton Place Junior High School in the South Ward for the weekend of November 14–16, 1969. They outlined the highlights of the summit. On Friday, November 14, the delegates would be addressed by Atlanta's Georgia state Rep. Julian Bond, Chicago's humorist Dick Gregory, and Newark's Imamu Baraka. On Saturday various candidates would present themselves to the assembly, and delegates would have three voting machines at their disposal to select one candidate for each position on the 1970 ballot. Saturday evening the winners would address the plenary session and share that moment with the keynote speaker, Richard Hatcher, the black mayor of Gary, Indiana.

That black and Latino movement put together the broadest possible common front of leaders from the African American and Puerto Rican communities. The civil rights community and black and Puerto Rican moderates were represented at every level of the summit. Presiding over the general sessions were such chairs as Gustav Heningburg, president of the Greater Newark Urban Coalition; Hilda Hidalgo, chair of ASPIRA, an Hispanic organization; and Sally Carroll, president of the Newark chapter of the NAACP.[60] Robert Curvin announced that some of the other leading figures in the joint effort were Mae Cooke, president of the Newark section of the National Federation of Negro Women's Clubs; Jennie Diaz, a member of the Rutgers Student Puerto Rican Organization; Sidney Snead, a representative of the Rutgers Black Alumni Association; Rev. Ralph Stephens, a member of Newark's Metropolitan Ecumenical Ministry; Dr. Edward Verner, a member of the North Jersey Medical Association; Robert Mathis of the United Brothers; and John Bugg of CFUN.

Robert Curvin explained that it was "the first time the blacks are joining forces with the Puerto Ricans to develop a platform, candidates and plan of action."[61] He reported that Blacks were 52 percent of Newark's population, while Puerto Ricans accounted for another 10 percent.

Moreover, each black and Hispanic organization was entitled to three voting delegates. The area's black and Puerto Rican elected officials were invited as voting delegates as well. Further, there were some seventy-five "selected individuals not affiliated with any organization but nevertheless influential in their neighborhoods," including such personalities as Dr. Harold Ashby, the first black president of the Newark Board of Education, and Newark municipal judge William Walls.[62] Robert Curvin argued that virtually every nonwhite faction in the city was represented except "the clique that is already receiving crumbs from the city."[63]

The convention preparations were characteristically extensive and exhaustive. For screening voting delegates, the black assembly retained the American Arbitration Association to run the elections. All delegates were provided information packets filled with quick-reference briefing materials on the functions of municipal government and the positions developed by the assembly's commissions on economics, city finance, land and housing, schools, law enforcement, health, welfare and employment. Further publicizing the proceedings, WNJR radio broadcast the summit. The *Star Ledger* reported that "to insure instant communications, the committee had Bell Telephone install a switchboard at the school," as well as fourteen phones throughout the building. Moreover, to facilitate the heavy work schedule, the planners arranged the provision of food by a caterer and the transportation of guests by a fleet of cars. Finally, child care was provided, with free milk for the children.[64]

The black attorney Ray Brown was the keynote speaker that Friday. Ray Brown had been a member of the New Jersey Governor's Select Commission on Civil Disorders, a former president of the Jersey City NAACP chapter, and Imamu Baraka's defense lawyer when he appealed the weapons conviction stemming from the 1967 Newark Rebellion. Addressing the jam-packed opening plenary of 500 delegates and observers, Brown explained, "We must rescue the inner city the whites are abandoning. . . . Recognizing the forces of reaction that are building up in the nation, you are taking action long overdue!"[65]

On the first evening the meeting discussed the specter of Newark's urban crisis: a black unemployment rate of 11.5 percent, contrasting with a 6 percent rate for whites; a median household income of only $3,839 for black and Puerto Rican families, compared to $6,858 for white families; a shortage of 10,000 pupil stations and a drop-out rate of 32 percent in the school system; the highest maternal mortality and venereal disease rate in the country; as well as the highest rate of new tuberculosis cases for all cities; a drug crisis ranking seventh and an air pollution problem ranking ninth in the nation; and a housing crisis that involved more than 75 percent of the city's old and rapidly aging structures.[66] Thus the challenge before the Modern Black Convention Movement was to develop the kind of politics that would address the horrors of the urban crisis, the demands of the urban social movement, the development of black and Puerto Rican unity, and the requirements of Black Power.

Boasting the colorful spectrum of a rainbow as the emblem of their alliance, the black and Puerto Rican candidates of the Community Choice ticket were Ramon Aneses, Theodore Pinckney, Donald Tucker, and Earl Harris—seeking four at-large seats on the city council; Al Oliver, Rev. Dennis Westbrooks, and Sharpe James—running for the three council seats representing the East, Central, and South Wards, respectively; and Kenneth A. Gibson, running for mayor.

The Campaign: New Ark Fund

From the outset there were at least two perspectives on running the campaign: *competitive* politics vs. *expressive* politics. From the vantage point of competitive politics, with Mayor Addonizio under federal indictment for corruption and extortion, the key issue in 1970 was good government. From that perspective, the 1970 election would be won by standard six-week campaigns for each candidate, based on their individual resources and the assumption that the black vote was necessary but not sufficient to win the race. Its watchword was moderation. Thus, from that perspective, the white vote was increasingly key, so the campaigns would have to tone down the emphasis on black identity. This was the logic of the competitive strategy for the 1970 campaign, and Kenneth A. Gibson was the reform candidate.[67]

In contrast, Imamu Baraka and CFUN expounded another political logic, that of an expressive strategy for the campaign that would arouse a collective black and Puerto Rican identity, stress progressive platform principles and even controversial issues, and register and mobilize new black and Puerto Rican voters. This camp did not believe that the white vote was key to the election; instead it felt that blacks and Puerto Ricans had to be convinced that they were their own liberators. In line with the expressive thrust of this politics of nationality formation, CFUN began its campaign for political power within days after the November 1969 Black and Puerto Rican Convention. The grassroots organizations began mobilizing alongside CFUN for the whole Community Choice team and its political agenda, months ahead of the individual candidates.

Imamu Baraka wanted to experiment with some of the lessons from the Black Arts Movement in this mobilization and, in one sense, he handled the campaign as a director might guide a play to its climax. CFUN designated its independent campaign effort the "New Ark Fund." One of the first tasks of the New Ark Fund was to identify the campaign as a national priority in the Black Revolt. Then the New Ark Fund brought a national consciousness to the communities of Newark, New Jersey, by parading trusted symbols of antiracist black, Puerto Rican, and white leadership through their neighborhoods to stir interest in the race. Baraka thought that Newark's black community would not move unless its age-old feelings of isolation were transformed to those of national community.

Though the campaign picked up steam over time, it began with such small but spirited turnouts as the Manhattan fundraiser for the New Ark Fund at Town Hall. As Imamu Baraka and James Baldwin read their works, a black and white audience, filling about half the seats in Town Hall, cheered, applauded, and shouted, "Tell the truth!" At one point during that reading Baldwin remarked, "This country is in desperate trouble because it still believes it is a white country in a white world."[68]

Left to right: Newark mayor Kenneth Gibson, Central Ward councilman Dennis Westbrooks, Detroit minister Albert Cleage of the Church of the Black Madonna, and Imamu Baraka in 1970. (Courtesy of the Baraka family collection, photograph by Zachariah Risasi Dais)

"We want to set an example in Newark," declared Baraka, "because the cities will be black, and whites will have to come to the mature understanding that no matter how they'd like to see it happen, blacks will determine the way it will happen." He added, "We want to get control of the space where 300,000 black people live, not only for us to live in, to work and to play in, but for our ideas and the development of concepts that are of benefit to us as a people with a peculiar ethos."[69]

Baraka and the Spirit House raised funds for the campaign with their poetry readings and dramatic performances. In that effort many other writers and artists helped, notably John Killens, Haki Madhubuti (Don L. Lee), and James Baldwin. On tour on college campuses reading his poetry, Madhubuti implored black students to make the journey to Newark and get involved in the campaign as a part of the struggle for Black Power. At one conference at Dickinson College in Carlisle, some 500 black students from across Pennsylvania met to found the Congress of African Students. Madhubuti lectured and read poetry, explaining the importance of black

Imamu Amiri Baraka speaking at Newark City Hall in the early 1970s.
(Courtesy of the Baraka family collection, photograph by Zachariah Risasi Dais)

identity, purpose, and direction for black youth. The Spirit House read poetry and performed a skit, then Baraka lectured on the national significance of the struggle in Newark. In the aftermath, students organized transportation on weekends so that they could work in the Newark elections, canvassing neighborhoods. A few students organized vans to travel the distance from Chicago to Newark.[70]

In their bid for national attention in the Black Revolt, Imamu Baraka and Kenneth Gibson journeyed to Chicago to meet with Jesse Jackson and Carl Stokes about endorsements and support for the race. There, at Jackson's Operation Breadbasket, both Jackson and Stokes were amused to find Gibson out of step with the contemporary black appearance and militant ethos. They remarked that if Gibson was going to win an election in a major northeastern urban center, "*he was going to have to slick up a bit.*"[71] In other words, they did not think that Gibson was in step with the tempo of the new black urban politics. For instance, they were taken aback at first when they saw that, despite coming from Newark, Gibson kept his hair in a by-then outmoded, close-cut Julius Caesar or Quo Vadis style during a period when most black men wore the universal and obligatory Afro. Jackson expressed his amusement on stage at a huge public rally. And Baraka recalls that in a style era of cuffless slacks:

> Gibson . . . showed with a suit with cuffed pants and a short haircut. Jackson [reacted] publicly to Gibson's lack of big-city slickness. Jesse said to his huge Breadbasket audience, "We gon have to slick bro Gibson up a bit. He gon have to grow some hair and get rid of these old-fashion shoes . . ." The audience loved it. I'm not sure about Gibson.[72]

Despite that amusement at Gibson's expense, it was clear that Jackson understood the importance of the Newark elections; he helped put together the network contacts for the stream of celebrities and entertainers who endorsed the Community Choice slate.

For the first election in May and the runoff in June 1970, Baraka organized a flood of endorsements through the New Ark Fund. Entertainers, celebrities, and elected officials came to Newark to support the Community Choice slate. Baraka notes that they "preached to the masses of black people that what was happening in their city was important, not only within that city but across the country."[73]

The public endorsements streamed in from Georgia state representative Julian Bond, Gary mayor Richard Hatcher, East Orange mayor William S. Hart, Manhattan borough president Percy Sutton, South Dakota senator George McGovern, New York gubernatorial hopeful Howard Samuels, Manhattan congressional candidate Herman Badillo, and U.S. Representatives Shirley Chisholm of New York and John Conyers of Michigan. Also, Harlem's legendary congressman Adam Clayton Powell Jr. campaigned in the poorest districts of Newark's Central Ward for several days, stirring the masses with lectures on the importance of Black Power and the benefits of *audacious* politics.

The entertainers rushed in from around the country to help stimulate interest in the Community's Choice. Helping to raise funds to pay for the campaign, the stars addressed various segments of the black community by their own diversity: Leontyne Price, Ossie Davis and Ruby Dee, Sammy Davis Jr., Dustin Hoffman, the Temptations, Chuck Jackson, Herbie Hancock, Max Roach, Harry Belafonte, James Brown and Stevie Wonder. Stevie Wonder electrified large crowds as he campaigned for the slate. Then Harry Belafonte led a jubilant march around Newark in what reporters described as the biggest black political street demonstration in the city's history. At one point the crowd, standing seven abreast, stretched about a half mile from City Hall to Military Park. It was an outpouring of support for the Community's Choice. They chanted, "Right On! Right On!" and shouted, "Addonizio got busted cause he couldn't be trusted!"[74]

Harry Belafonte read a message of encouragement from Coretta Scott King. There was a spontaneous outpouring of ordinary people on that march: "mothers carried their small children and bystanders such as postmen and office workers simply changed their direction and joined in the midday march from City Hall."[75] Harry Belafonte told hundreds of people at a rally, "I'm here because I don't want to see another black child lying bloody in the street here in Newark. There'll be no more rioting in this city."[76] He stressed the international significance that black people placed on the race: "Ken Gibson is the property of black people around the world. His destiny . . . is our destiny."[77]

Coretta Scott King could not attend the Newark rally, but she did attend a mass rally in Atlanta, which drew some 10,000 people. She was joined by Senator George S. McGovern and Rev. Ralph David Abernathy of SCLC. Both McGovern and Abernathy would endorse Kenneth Gibson in Newark. Rev. Abernathy explained, "Today we are marching against repression and tomorrow we are going to get registered to vote against repression." He said that they would use those registered votes to sweep racist politicians and political hustlers out of office. Abernathy called for the defeat of a number of politicians on his "ten most wanted list," including President Nixon, Spiro Agnew, Gov. Ronald Reagan, Gov. Lester Maddox, and Newark's mayor Hugh Addonizio.[78]

Events came almost daily as the campaign reached its climax in May 1970. Dick Gregory spoke to the masses of black people at church rallies, stressing the seriousness of the campaign and the need for a new kind of black politician—a statesman. And at a rally in Weequahic Park, with the comedian Flip Wilson as the master of ceremony, Rev. Jesse Jackson gave the keynote speech, and the actor Dustin Hoffman offered his warm endorsement.

In anticipation of his appearance, the New Ark Fund played James Brown's hit "Say it loud: I'm Black and I'm Proud," from the squadron of sound cars covering the neighborhood streets, hoping to raise the spirits of people trapped in the ghetto. On the day of the James Brown tour through Newark for the Community's Choice, two of the black opposition candidates confronted Brown at the airport, urging him not to endorse the convention slate.[79] But Brown persisted, and as usual his performance stirred the people. That night Brown displayed his special power by gliding across the stage before a packed audience at Newark's Symphony Hall, singing for people to *get involved!*"

During the same month Bill Cosby also packed Newark's Symphony Hall for the New Ark Fund, and after seeing what was unfolding in Newark, Cosby even purchased a number of billboards for the campaign, emblazoned with his own message: "Bill Cosby says vote for Gibson and the Community's Choice."[80]

In the last days of the campaign, Jesse Jackson came to Newark again, this time with his rhythmic and mellow Operation Breadbasket band. There he could observe the New Ark Fund's innovations in mass political education. It set up trucks with television monitors of videotaped speeches by the candidates to run throughout the neighborhoods; such monitors were also situated in the front windows of the campaign headquarters. Other monitors showed the new registrants how to use the voting machines.

Certainly, the campaign literature drew a great deal of attention. Imamu Baraka boasts, "These were bright, rainbowed posters that filled you with inspiration and concrete hope just seeing them. (We used all seven colors of the spectrum, tuning in to everybody's wavelength.)"[81] By far the most controversial voter registration and political education poster was the colorful reproduction of a *Life* photo of the little black boy, lying in a pool of his own blood, shot down by white police during the 1967 Newark Rebellion. Imamu Baraka recalls:

Our signs were everywhere, in color, right out of *Time* Magazine; a little kid, laid out in the street, shot down by Officer Scarpone . . . , with Scarpone standing over the little dead brother, lighting a cigar. There was controversy even over the posters. This technicolor poster was pushing voter registration, caption: *"Don't let this happen again — vote."*[82]

Then the campaign's steering committee received reports that Mayor Addonizio's political machine was paying off a number of people to express skepticism about a black victory on election day. One candidate, Earl Harris, suggested a slogan that was broadcast with music from the fleet of sound cars: *You can take the man's money, but vote for the brothers.* Nevertheless, as rumors mounted of an Addonizio plot to steal the election, Imamu Baraka, speaking at a rally of hundreds of black students on the eve of the election, reemphasized Malcolm X's theme, "the ballot or the bullet," insisting that if black people were to win the election only to have it stolen, they would seize power *by any means necessary.*

A Great Victory

On election day, May 12, 1970, the struggle for power was fierce. Even in the heart of the black community, Addonizio's machine committed numerous violations of the voting procedures. In some instances, Addonizio's people attempted to get inside the booths with voters, select the Addonizio slate, and then pull the lever down for them. As black students and grassroots volunteers protested such blatant violations, officials looked the other way. Whenever possible, the politicos attempted to demoralize new voters by simply challenging their credentials. The New Ark Fund had a fleet of cars standing ready to transport voters to file appeals. But the voters kept coming, no matter what.

By far the worst violations were concentrated in the North Ward. At the heavily Puerto Rican and black public housing project, Columbus Homes, black women organizers mobilizing the vote called CFUN's headquarters to alert them to a crisis: Imperiale's men had positioned themselves in front of the polls and would not let voters enter. After a standoff between the North Ward vigilante squads and CFUN's Simba Wachunga (Young Lions), the door to the polls was cleared and black and Puerto Rican voters flooded out of the projects to cast their ballots.

In the May 12, 1970, election the Modern Convention Movement demonstrated its leadership over the black and Puerto Rican constituency when the Community Choice ticket won an astounding victory, with nearly every member of the team placing ahead of the opposition. In the at-large races for city council, Theodore Pinckney, Donald Tucker, and Earl Harris headed a pack of other candidates, with Ramon Aneses placing fifth; however, the vote was divided by so many political hopefuls that no one achieved the required plurality and thus the contest was forced into a runoff. Indeed, the Community Choice slate did so well that CFUN was suspicious later during the June 16, 1970, runoff when only one of the four at-large candidates, Earl Harris, was finally elected to the City Council. Imamu Baraka explained several reasons for those feelings of skepticism:

> The results of this first councilmanic race, more than anything else, helped convince us that the runoff was tampered with, as far as the Tucker-Pinckney candidacy was concerned. Earl Harris led all councilmanic candidates with 26,073, then Tucker with 25,608 and Pinckney with 24,998. Giuliano, with 21,847, came in fourth, and then Aneses with 18,448. Bontempo with 11,113; Villani with 13,555, were in the dust. However in the runoff, Giuliano got 44,807; Bontempo 42,809; Villani 42,470, and Harris 42,166! . . . And even the night of that election early final results announced Pinckney and Tucker as winners along with Harris.[83]

In other words, on June 16, Bontempo and Villani received about *four times* their May 12 votes; with *increases* of about 20,000 per candidate.

Similarly, a runoff was required in the mayor's race. On May 12, Kenneth Gibson headed the pack of seven candidates, with 43 percent of the vote (37,859), and Mayor Hugh Addonizio came in second (with 18,212). The two black opposition candidates drew the lowest number of votes: George Richardson, with only 2,038, and Harry Wheeler, placing dead last with 146. Wheeler actually quit the race at the last minute and endorsed Gibson. The Black and Puerto Rican Convention had won that first major power contest.

In the South and Central Wards, the Community Choice drive swept Sharpe James and Rev. Dennis Westbrooks into office. In the South Ward, James defeated Rev. Horace Sharper, who had just won that seat in the March 1969 recall election bid against Lee Bernstein. For Rev. Sharper the decision to boycott the Black and Puerto Rican Convention meant political suicide, and thereafter he would join George Richardson, railing against the Modern Black Convention Movement with rare devotion.

In the Central Ward race, Westbrooks defeated the incumbent since 1954, Irvine Turner, the first Negro to win a seat on the City Council. Rev. Westbrooks earned a reputation as a most fervent supporter of the Modern Black Convention Movement. Taking the African name Mjumbe (the representative), he spoke for the poorest of the poor in the inner city.

In the runoff race between Mayor Addonizio and Kenneth Gibson, Addonizio decided to campaign openly on the race issue. He consistently stated that whites had to fight to hold onto what was *theirs* and insisted that the key issue was white political power. Robert Curvin reminds us that the racial strategy adopted by Addonizio was the same one that helped the white Los Angeles mayor Sam Yorty defeat the black candidate, Tom Bradley, in 1969.[84] "Police Director Spina," writes Curvin, "campaigned for the Mayor, telling voters that the election boiled down to an issue of 'Black versus white.'"[85]

Newark mayor Addonizio explained the realities of power to his white audiences in terms that would have been familiar in a white settler's colony in Africa: "You all know what is involved here. Everything you hold sacred—your homes, your families and your jobs. We cannot let the leaders of race hatred take control of our city. You all know what I'm talking about."[86]

It was a chilling reminder of the dynamics of race relations as explained by James W. Vander Zanden: the oppressed group is "the source of the dominant group's advantages."[87] In this unequal power relationship, an important aspect of the dominant group's identity is its entitlement to such advantages as the ownership of choice property, control of preferred sections of the city, the exclusive right to high status jobs, occupations, professions, schools, churches, and recreation facilities, and supremacy in the political arena; and privileges over scarce public goods and services are viewed by so many as part of the exclusively white birthright.[88]

If the key issue in the power struggle was black versus white, one wonders where Mayor Addonizio's political ally, the black councilman at-large Calvin West, fit into that equation.[89] West was part of Addonizio's "Peace and Progress" campaign slate; under indictment at the time, his own dubious slogan read: RE-ELECT WEST – HE STOOD THE TEST. Wherever Councilman West fit in that formula, it must have been just a bit uncomfortable, as it may have been for the fifty black ministers who endorsed Mayor Addonizio.[90] But it seems that one of those ministers, Rev. Levin West (no relation to Councilman West), felt no discomfort, even as he urged the North Ward community to fight back against what he perceived as an anti-Italian conspiracy at work in the federal indictments against Newark officials. Despite his own emphasis on race in the campaign, the Addonizio camp boldly attacked the Black and Puerto Rican Convention process, and especially Imamu Baraka and CFUN, as racist. Indeed, Addonizio went so far that he made the mistake of campaigning against Imamu Baraka rather than Kenneth Gibson, projecting CFUN's black nationalism as a key issue in the campaign.[91]

But Mayor Addonizio was under a great deal of pressure, perpetually in court defending himself and his associates against a long list of federal indictments for mob-related corruption and extortion—charges for which he was eventually convicted after the election. As the Addonizio camp grew more somber, the black community felt more strength and self-confidence.

On June 16, 1970, Hugh Addonizio lost the election with 43,086 votes, and Kenneth Gibson won with 55,097. The voter turnout reached an unprecedented 73 percent of the electorate.[92] Some 7,000 white voters felt uncomfortable with Addonizio on election day, casting their ballots for Gibson alongside some 48,000 black and Puerto Rican voters. Thus, with the solid support of 19 out of every 20 black votes, Kenneth A. Gibson broke a major color bar in the power structure by becoming the first black mayor of a major eastern seaboard city.

That night the contrasts between the black and Italian American reactions were striking. After speeches by Jesse Jackson and Imamu Baraka at CFUN's headquarters at 502 High Street, black people marched downtown and danced in the streets. It was a time of jubilation for the black community. However, at Mayor Addonizio's campaign headquarters in Thomm's Restaurant, the media encountered violent white rage first hand. When it became clear that Addonizio was losing the election, an angry crowd surged at one news crew, punching two cameramen and smashing their equipment. The police restored order, and Anthony Imperiale made an ambiguous speech.

When someone at Thomm's shouted, "Kill the nigger!" City Councilman Imperiale responded, "Just a minute. Would you advocate the death of an innocent person? I refuse to be a part of advocating violence against innocent people." However, when the crowd settled down, he told them, "I saw voters intimidated by the Black Panthers. I'm ashamed of the judicial system. I'm ashamed of the FBI. I'm ashamed of law enforcement. They have surrendered themselves to the activists. . . . When does the President of the United States find the guts to fight Communism?"[93]

Meanwhile at the Community Choice celebrations at the downtown Terrace Ballroom, Rev. Jesse Jackson told some 1,000 people: "What you saw here three years ago [the 1967 Newark Rebellion] were people running from genocide to suicide. What you see now is people talking about a tomorrow which we are going to control."[94]

Black self-determination was the fruit of the Black Power experiment in Newark; it reflected the political consciousness of masses of African American and Puerto Rican people mobilized in a life-and-death struggle against white racism and internal colonialism. This black awakening was not a diversion into narrow nationalism; it expressed a global conscious-

Left to right: Bibi Amina and Imamu Amiri Baraka at the inauguration of
Kenneth Gibson, the first black mayor of Newark, in 1970. (Photograph by the
Congress of African People's Sura Wa Taifa, author's collection)

ness of Third World liberation, which sought progressive white cooperation but *not* white liberal permission in the fight for equality. In his unsuccessful bid for reelection, Mayor Addonizio made the mistake of campaigning against Imamu Baraka's black nationalism; thus, he located both
the democratic ideology of cultural nationalism and the radical agitational
slogan of Black Power in the spotlight of a major political campaign, making them topics of intense consideration and heated discussion from the
classroom to the bar room. Furthermore, the extensive degree of African
American nationality formation that was mobilized by this campaign
would have been impossible without Baraka's modernization of the expressive politics of black cultural nationalism. The dynamics of the Modern Black Convention Movement pulled Baraka and CFUN away from
the magnetism of sectarian politics and toward the power of mass mobilization and social movement. In the year between the November 1968
municipal election and the November 1969 Black and Puerto Rican Political Convention, Baraka unleashed the politics of cultural nationalism
from the narrow confines of the small-circle sectarianism that had long

ago relegated much of black nationalism to obscurity. Once black cultural nationalism escaped these narrow sectarian confines and embraced the Modern Black Convention Movement, the politics of nationality formation flowered in the 1970 elections. These mass political mobilizations forged a black consciousness of African American nationality and made Baraka's black convention movement one of the leading paradigms of Black Power in the United States. Emboldened by these successes, Baraka attempted to transform this local model of nationality formation into a national movement.

Part II
Zenith
and
Decline

CHAPTER 5

It's Nation Time

Building a National Black Political Community

SOS

Calling black people
Calling all black people, man woman child
Wherever you are, calling you, urgent, come in
Black people, come in, wherever you are, urgent, calling
you, calling all black people
calling all black people, come in, black people, come
on in.
—LeRoi Jones, *Black Magic*

THE NATION IS LIKE OURSELVES

The nation is like our selves, together
seen in our various scenes, sets where ever we are
what ever we are doing, is what the nation
is
doing
or
not doing
is what the nation
is
being
or
not being . . .
—Amiri Baraka, *It's Nation Time*

The period between 1970 and 1974 was the zenith for the politics of black cultural nationalism. The development of the scope of the dynamics of nationality formation from the local political arena to the national political stage marks the most important phase of the politics of cultural nationalism as well as the birth of a black national political community. The genesis of that political community was supported by the rapid emergence of the Modern Black Convention Movement in the form of four national organizations: the Congress of African People, the African Liberation Support Committee, the Black Women's United Front, and the National Black Assembly. The Modern Black Convention Movement emerged as a national structure that embraced the growing tensions between the reality of black diversity and the calls for African American unity. The black convention constructed its own democratic process of *agenda building* around the principle of proportional representation, articulating the numerous viewpoints within the black community and giving each perspective due weight in decision making. In essence, agenda building was a counterhegemonic strategy that meant changing the political discourse on local and national issues. Instead of black communities passively awaiting whatever political candidates might decide were the pressing issues in the next election, black assemblies took the initiative in their own hands to determine and define the issues they felt were most important, speaking in a language that they clearly understood. In these circumstances, Imamu Baraka proposed that the politics of cultural nationalism would win the fight for hegemony over the black community.

The Founding of the Congress of African People

Imamu Amiri Baraka emerged from the Newark Black Power experience convinced that African Americans would have to fashion their own ideology in order to liberate themselves from racial oppression in America. Emphasizing the importance of a black cultural revolution to win the minds of black people, Baraka insisted specifically on a psychological separation "away from assimilation or brainwashing or subjugation by the mind of the white nation." In this regard he was concerned that too many black revolutionaries, who studied the classical political works of Marxism, were doing so uncritically. He charged that they were so hypnotized by these European writings that they did not keep in mind the vastly different circumstances that distinguished the situation of the European working class from that of African Americans in the United States. For Baraka, the black experience was the basis for the development of a new political ideology, and that experience had been a history of internal colonialism, a racial oppression distinct from class oppression. Therefore, he was convinced that in the United States the black revolutionary struggle was for national liberation from internal colonialism and that it was not a direct fight for socialism.

Nevertheless, increasingly in the 1970s, Baraka suggested that the struggle for black liberation unfolded in stages: the first stage was for national liberation, and the second stage was for social transformation, involving some form of socialism. Furthermore, although Baraka argued that the Black Power experiments in Newark in the fight against internal colonialism suggested a paradigm for the national movement, the international dimensions of his politics became more pronounced as he rose to leadership in the national black political arena. Baraka suggested three anticolonial African models for the politics of cultural nationalism, combining national liberation and socialism: Amilcar Cabral's Partido Africano da Independencia da Guine e Cabo Verde (PAIGC), which was leading the fight against Portuguese colonialism in the West African territories of Guinea-Bissau and the Cape Verde Islands; Sekou Toure's Democratic Party of Guinea (PDG) in West Africa, which had led a successful radical movement against French colonialism in the 1950s; and Mwalimu Julius Nyerere's Tanzanian African Nationalist Union (TANU), which led the independence initiative in East Africa.[1] Baraka came of age during the formative years of Third World independence, the decade between the 1949 Chinese Revolution and the 1959 Cuban Revolution. These international developments left an indelible mark on his cultural nationalism. In 1961, when Baraka was arrested at the United Nations, protesting the murder of Patrice Lumumba, the premier of the Congo, the African Americans actively supporting African liberation represented only a handful of the activists inspired by the independence movements in such African nations as the Congo, Egypt, Ghana, Nigeria, and Guinea.[2] However, by 1970, black nationalism's African liberation support efforts represented the sentiments of millions of African Americans who grew up during the triumph of freedom movements from Tanganyika to Algeria. The road traveled by Nyerere's TANU in Tanganyika had been peaceful, but the path taken by revolutionaries in Zanzibar and Algeria had been bloody. By the 1970s, most of the liberation movements in Africa were involved in some phase of armed warfare against white colonialism.[3] At that time, black nationalists in America led a determined national community in the support of African liberation movements, targeting South African domination in South-West Africa (Namibia); Portuguese colonialism in Angola, Mozambique, and Guinea-Bissau; and white minority rule in both Rhodesia (Zimbabwe) and South Africa. By 1975, these African liberation movements had defeated Portuguese colonialism in Angola, Mozambique and Guinea-Bissau, and subdued white minority rule in Zimbabwe. Inspired by African ideals of nation building and liberation, the central theme of Imamu Baraka's politics of cultural nationalism became *black self-determination.*

As 3,000 black people met in Atlanta, Georgia, on Labor Day weekend in 1970 to found the Congress of African People, both black self-determination and Pan-Africanism were central themes.[4] While the Atlanta Pan-African summit was aimed at black people in the African diaspora, the gathering also embraced other oppressed peoples in the spirit of the Bandung Conference. According to Arnold Pinkney,

> The first Congress of African Peoples attracted . . . delegates from around the world, including Afro-American integrationists and separationists; peoples of African descent from the Caribbean and South America; Africans from independent nations and colonies; oppressed minorities from other continents, including Australian aborigines; and observers from the Mexican American, Puerto Rican, and Japanese communities. The purpose of the Congress was the establishment of unity among peoples of African descent throughout the world and the development of political, economic, and social institutions to liberate blacks from oppression.[5]

It's Nation Time!

The Congress of African People in Atlanta, Georgia, was the successor to the annual National Black Power Conferences held between 1966 and 1968. The 1969 Black Power Conference in Bermuda had been a disaster; that government banned many of the militant leaders from attending the international gathering. In the aftermath of that catastrophe, a number of Black Power leaders, particularly those associated with gathering support for Imamu Baraka in the 1970 Newark election, began discussing how to rescue those annual meetings. That group decided that one of the weaknesses of the movement was that there was no organizational structure to follow through on the radical resolutions reached at those summits. Establishing a broad, working federation of black nationalists was one of the central goals of the Congress of African People in Atlanta.

The Congress of African People marked a turning point in the Black Revolt in several regards. That summit signaled the introduction of the leading black nationalists into the national black political community that was just taking shape. The Atlanta Congress also represented a temporary end to the political exclusion of black nationalists from the dynamics of the

Imamu Amiri Baraka at the founding meeting of the Congress of African People in Atlanta in 1970. (Courtesy of Amiri Baraka, photograph by Sura Wa Taifa, poster in author's collection)

national black political arena. In line with this, that first Congress represented an unprecedented degree of unity in the Black Revolt, drawing as it did both civil rights and black nationalist leaders. Moreover, the widespread unity of black nationalists at the Atlanta gathering was unprecedented. Finally, the Congress of African People signaled an important early step in the formation of a national black political community.

Considering the goal of establishing a federation of nationalists, the widespread unity of that political camp in Atlanta was encouraging. The congress drew together for the first time such figures from the fragmented black nationalist camp as the widow of Malcolm X, Betty Shabazz; the national representative of Elijah Muhammad, Louis Farrakhan of the Nation of Islam; a spokesman for Stokely Carmichael, Howard Fuller (Owusu Sadaukai) of Malcolm X Liberation University and the Student Organization for Black Unity (SOBU); Imari Abubakari Obadele of the Republic of New Africa (RNA), and Imamu Baraka of CFUN.

The Atlanta Congress was also encouraging because the black nationalists had never before attracted so many black elected officials and civil rights leaders to a Pan-African summit; the range of participants included such black elected officials and political figures as gubernatorial candidate John Cashin of the National Democratic Party of Alabama, Julian Bond of the Georgia legislature, Mayor Richard Hatcher of Gary, Indiana, and Mayor Kenneth Gibson of Newark, New Jersey; and such civil rights leaders as Rev. Jesse Jackson of People United for Self-Help (PUSH), Rev. Ralph Abernathy of SCLC, and Whitney Young Jr. of the National Urban League. The list of international representatives included Roosevelt Douglas of the Organization of a Black People's Union (OBPU), addressing the problems of black people in Canada and the West Indies; Raymond Mbala, speaking for one of the liberation groups in Angola; Evelyn Kawanza, voicing the concerns of the people of Zimbabwe fighting the Rhodesian government; and Ambassador El Hajj Abdoulaye Toure, the Guinean representative to the United States.

In a major departure from the traditional competition and feuding of these factions in the Black Revolt, the Congress of African People (CAP) called for working coalitions between black nationalist and civil rights organizations around concrete programs for the development of the black community. The Pan-African summit elected as its first chairman a 27-year-old Harvard instructor in Afro-American Studies, Heyward Henry, who was also the chairman of the National Black Caucus in the Unitarian-Universalist Church.[6] Symbolizing the pivotal role that the Congress of African People would attempt to play as a bridge between the various wings of the black freedom movement, Henry embraced Minister Louis Farrakhan on his right and Whitney Young on his left, holding their hands aloft in a gesture of unity. That marked the beginning of a brief period of hegemony in the Black Revolt for the black cultural nationalists.[7] During that period, the Congress of African People named the slogans, thus the banners read: "It's Nation Time."

Paradoxically, as Baraka's CFUN publicly launched the Congress of African People, secretly his organization and Maulana Karenga's US Organization had decimated their political alliance. Unfortunately, in order to usher in a new phase of the Modern Black Convention Movement and to protect that black assembly from the warfare that had plunged the US Organization into the abyss, Baraka found it necessary to break with Karenga. As much as Baraka admired Karenga, he understood that the Modern Black Convention Movement was essential to the further development of the politics of cultural nationalism. The rupture between the Congress of African People and the US Organization remains obscure; it is one of the strangest developments in the history of the Black Revolt.

Consider the facts. During the period leading up to the founding of the Congress of African People, Karenga was increasingly estranged from the new momentum. At the same time, Baraka was receiving indications that something had gone seriously wrong with the US Organization in Los Angeles. There were reports that the war between the US Organization and the Black Panther Party had paralyzed the work of Karenga's group, leaving it more and more isolated from the black community and weakened by a "foxhole" mentality. Even worse, there were stories that the strain of the constant bloodshed had impaired Karenga's judgment. Former members of the US Organization began to arrive in Newark, declaring to Baraka that Karenga was losing his wits and that he was increasingly paranoid about police agents and was tormenting members of his own organization. And matters worsened. On the eve of the Congress of African People, Karenga sent orders to Baraka to abandon the summit. That order put Baraka in a precarious situation. Theoretically, Maulana Karenga was the ranking leader of the national Kawaida movement, and Karenga had promoted Baraka to the rank of *imamu*, or spiritual leader, of that structure in Newark, just as he had designated Imamu Sukumu in San Diego. However, in fact, Imamu Baraka and CFUN had developed considerable autonomy at the head of the Modern Black Convention Movement in Newark. That movement had dynamics of its own, and those dynamics had ushered in a new group of leaders who had no organizational allegiance to Karenga. Thus, Baraka had to choose between his loyalty to Karenga and his devotion to the Modern Black Convention Movement. Apparently, he did not want to make a choice: he believed in Karenga's doctrine and actively promoted the Seven Principles throughout the country, arguing that it was the ethical foundation for the politics of cultural nationalism. However, Baraka disobeyed Karenga's direct order to scrap the summit meeting, and that set the stage for a political and organizational break between the two foremost proponents of cultural nationalism.

At any rate, on the weekend of the Congress, Karenga sent several of his men from Los Angeles to Atlanta to intimidate Baraka's leadership. Ominously, Karenga's men carried briefcases ostensibly filled with firearms— briefcases with concealed weapons had become a nefarious trademark of the US Organization. That raised the possibility of another tragic shootout within the ranks of the Black Revolt, the probability that the chaos that had consumed the Black Power movement on the West Coast would spread to the East Coast. Fortunately, even after several confrontations, there was no bloodshed in Atlanta. Although there was no shooting, behind the scenes Baraka called CFUN together in Atlanta to announce the formal split between his group and the US Organization. In the rift, the BCD leadership of Balozi Zayd Muhammad and Mfudishi Maasi stood with the Congress of African People. Moreover, the San Diego leader Imamu Sukumu also broke with Karenga, standing with the Congress. Two years later, at the Second International Congress of African People in San Diego, once again members of the US Organization arrived at the summit to menace the new leadership. Again, there were confrontations, and bloodshed was narrowly avoided. But, for obvious reasons, Baraka and Karenga grew apart.

Meanwhile, on May 26, 1971, a Los Angeles Superior Court jury found Maulana Karenga and two other members of US guilty of "torturing [Deborah Jones], once a member of his organization." According to the *Herald Dispatch*, Ms. Jones testified in court that she and another member of the US Organization, Ms. Gill Davis, had been "beaten with an electrical cord and a baton." To make matters worse, Karenga's estranged wife, Haiba Karenga, testified "that she heard screams coming from the garage where her husband and the co-defendants were holding the two women hostages." However, there were a number of inconsistencies in the testimony, including the fact that initially Ms. Jones did not name Maulana Karenga in those charges until a "grand jury theft charge pending against her was dismissed." Thus, Karenga maintained his innocence, and his attorney argued that the state had encouraged Ms. Jones to make false accusations against his client. Nonetheless, such was the debacle of the US Organization in 1970. After several years in prison, Karenga made a remarkable comeback. The details of Baraka's political break with Karenga's US Organization remained obscure until the 1980s when the poet published the first edition of his autobiography. Although this was one of the most bizarre developments in the Black Revolt, Baraka did not allow that awesome personal and political setback to endanger the success of the Congress of African People in Atlanta. By 1970, CFUN had developed more than enough independence, confidence, and experience to lead a national movement.[8]

In keeping with the new collective leadership of the Congress, the Pan-African gathering held eleven workshops to determine the character of black programs for the 1970s. These sessions were led by an impressive array of scholars, writers, and activists: religion coordinated by Rev. James Cone and Bill Land, history by John Henrik Clarke and Yosef Ben-Jochannan, creativity by Larry Neal, education by Preston Wilcox, black technology by Ken Cave, community organization by Lou Gothard, law and justice by Raymond Brown, communications by Tony Brown and Lou House, economics by Robert S. Browne and Dunbar S. McLaurin, social organization by Bibi Amina Baraka, and political liberation by Imamu Amiri Baraka. These workshops were established as ongoing work councils, and in the national movement their leaders were charged with the implementation of key items in the resolutions; the resolutions were the beginning of a "Black Agenda" for the 1970s. As the chair of the Political Liberation Work Council, Baraka began to play a new role in the development of a national black political community as a national spokesman for black nationalism.

With its new emphasis on Pan-Africanism, the Congress of African People set the stage for the next developments, African Liberation Day and the African Liberation Support Committee (ALSC). A generation of black political leaders forged its identity in the politics of black revolution and African liberation. It would become knowledgeable of the struggles against racism and colonialism in Southern Africa during the 1970s and assume what it considered its international responsibility to end white minority rule. The Congress of African People resolved to raise funds for combat boots to send to the liberation forces fighting in Africa and to help establish an "African Liberation Front" to work with "the various national liberation fronts throughout Africa, the Caribbean, South and Central America as well as the U.S.A."[9] To express its solidarity, the summit sent greetings to the Organization of African Unity in Addis Ababa and to the Non-Alignment Conference in Zambia.

The participants felt that without an effective black national political presence to influence foreign policy, CAP could not realize its aims for African liberation. Thus, in line with the resolutions of the 1968 Black Power Conference in Philadelphia, the Atlanta Pan-African summit mandated the formation of a black political party. The resolutions outlined the procedures necessary for party building. In the urban areas where there were large concentrations of black people, CAP resolved to work on black voter registration; to mobilize, organize, and politicize the black community; to run black and Puerto Rican candidates; to make alliances with other people of color; and to establish Third World relations.[10] One of the first steps in this process laid the groundwork for the first National Black Political Convention at Gary, Indiana, and the establishment of the National Black Assembly, the largest black pre-party formation in the history of the United States.

Significantly, that Pan-African summit decided to federate the groups attending the National Black Power Conferences into a new organization, the Congress of African People (CAP). The summit committed itself to the development of a process of forging a common political program; creating one umbrella political organization, the "prototype" for a black party; establishing a communications network for the movement; and pooling and increasing the various resources necessary for black liberation and Pan-Africanism.[11] In line with this goal, CAP resolved to either establish its offices in the black communities represented at the summit or "use existing community organizations as CAP oriented structures."[12] There were, in fact, more than 200 local organizations represented at the summit.[13] While at least forty cities were represented at the Atlanta Congress, the new organization planned to focus on about thirty urban areas with major black population centers, ranging from Newark (138,035), Pittsburgh (100,692), Gary (69,123), and Boston (63,165) to New York (1,087,931) and Chicago (812,647).[14]

The Congress of African People galvanized many of the local leaders and organizations into a new generation of men and women who would become national leaders in the Modern Black Convention Movement. In the 1970s, the Congress of African People had an extensive national organization that reached at least twenty-five urban black population concentrations, with a branch in San Diego, California, led by Imamu Sukumu; one in Wilmington, Delaware, led by Mwanafunzi Rahsaan and Cheo Kamau Opio; another in Washington, D.C., led by Mumba Kali; headquarters in Chicago, Illinois, founded by Mwalimu Haki Madhubuti (Don L. Lee); one each in South Bend, Gary, and Elkhart, Indiana, led by Kaimu Dadisi Muata, Fano Mahiri, and Malik Nyerere, respectively, and another in Indianapolis; a branch in Baltimore, Maryland, headed by Abdul Malik Shabaka; an office in Boston, Massachusetts, led by Heyward Henry; an organization in Detroit, Michigan, founded by Pili Sababu; another organization in St. Louis, Missouri, led by Kalimu Endesha; at least four in New Jersey—in Camden, East Orange, Jersey City, and Newark—headed by Poppy Sharp and Weusi Msafiri, Balozi Zayd Muhammad, Ndugu Kabili, and Imamu Baraka, respectively; four in New York State, led by Dalila Kudura in Albany, Cheo Simba in the Bronx, Bill Land in Manhattan, and the largest one by Jitu Weusi at "The East," a black cultural center in Brooklyn; one in Cleveland, Ohio, led by Sababa Akili, and another in Oberlin, Ohio, headed by Frank Satterwhite at Nairobi College; two in Pennsylvania—Philadelphia CAP, led by Mjenzi Kazana (Richard Traylor) and Maisha Ongoza, and the Pittsburgh organization by Kiongozi Sala Udin; finally, in Texas, the Houston CAP office was headed by Cheo Omowale Lutuli.[15]

While the debate over the best path to black liberation was necessary, the new stance at the Congress of African People insisted that a black united front was to be established for common defense against repression and for the development of community programs. CAP argued that the continuation of the shooting war between revolutionary nationalists and cultural nationalists was *impermissible*. Thus, the Political Liberation Workshop led by Imamu Baraka specifically called for an alliance between cultural nationalists and the Black Left: "In the case of the U.S.A. specifically the congress should establish a Black National Liberation Front, and set up a body to consolidate the Congress of African Peoples with all the various Black revolutionary movements in the U.S.A. including the League of Revolutionary Black Workers, the Black Panther [Party], and the Republic of New Africa."[16]

Although the shooting war came to a close, several distinct positions on the solution to black liberation remained. Imamu Baraka asserted CFUN's ideological influence over the youthful organization in his outline of the various positions within the black liberation movement. His arguments established the main political orientation for the new organization.

Baraka insisted that black people had to fashion their own unique ideological and political program because the situation in the United States, especially for African Americans, was singular:

The United States is not China nor nineteenth-century Russia, nor even Cuba or Vietnam. It is the most highly industrialized nation ever to exist, a place where the slaves ride in Cadillacs and worship their slave master's image, as God. American power over Africans around the world must be broken before the other colonial powers are completely broken. Also, it should never be forgotten that we are a different people, want a different nation, than our slavemasters.[17]

While the situation in the U.S. was distinct, Baraka did *not* want the black nationalists to ignore international developments; instead he argued that the African liberation movements had set important examples of nationality formation with their broad-based united fronts against colonialism and their reorganization of national life in the liberated areas:

> Newark, New Ark, the nationalist sees as the creation of a base, as example, upon which one aspect of the entire Black nation can be built. We will build schools or transform present curriculum to teach National Liberation. We will create agencies to teach community organizing, national & local politics, and send brothers all over the country to re-create the model. We will nationalize the city's institutions as if it were liberated territory in Zimbabwe or Angola. There are nations of less than 300,000 people.[18]

While calling for a common front with the different varieties of black nationalism, Baraka did not hesitate to critique the old nationalism and to reinterpret Garveyism according to the New Nationalism. He criticized both the program of a Black Zionist return to Africa and the notion of an immediate seizure of five states in the South. First he addressed his remarks to those in the workshop who insisted, as did the Republic of New Africa, on seizing several states in the Black Belt South:

> The South may be the great strategic battleground of the African in America perhaps; it has the food, and space, to allow a people to survive, against great odds, but whatever we would do with the people, with ourselves, actually, we must first organize. And if the struggle is raised, and of such a nature that we must all go into the South, or that we migrate constantly because of the mounting pressures that force people to that realization, then it will still be a raised level of political consciousness that permits that move.[19]

Pragmatically, he argued against immediate repatriation:

> We feel that Repatriation people must understand, and to a certain extent the Separation (meaning to remove to Africa or another part of the U.S.) people, that Black people, ca. 1970, ain't going anywhere. It is very difficult, as you well know, to get them to go up the street to a meeting.[20]

Baraka wanted to shift the emphasis of the teachings of Marcus Garvey from the establishment of the land base in Africa by African Americans to political and cultural solidarity with Pan-Africanism, African Socialism, and the liberation movements. This, he insisted, was the way to end the domination and humiliation of Africans all over the world:

> But "Back to Africa" for certain, in all the ways we can reestablish contact, since we understand our connection Racially, Historically, Culturally, Politically, and Emotionally. . . . Garvey's thought is best interpreted as a movement to recreate the power of the African state . . . To create Africa as a unified power base to demand respect for Black people the world over. This is Pan-Africanism, because wherever we are we have a commonality based on our common struggle.[21]

Rather than repatriation to the Black Belt South or to the African continent, Baraka insisted on a black cultural revolution, one separating the hearts and minds of African Americans from white hegemony. He outlined the case for revolutionary cultural nationalism this way:

> In the meantime we must separate the mind, win the mind, wage the revolution to win the Black man's mind so we will begin to move *together* as a people conscious that we are a people, struggling for national liberation. Separation must come *mentally* before any physical movement can begin. Separation away from assimilation or brainwashing or subjugation by the mind of the white nation. And that separation from white control must be a prerequisite for the mental and emotional trip "Back to Africa," i.e., [the] realization that we are an African people (meaning Black of a common color culture and consciousness. And whether we call ourselves Arabs, Saudis, Sudanese, Ethiopians, Egyptians, Kamites, Hamitic, we have only said Black a number of different ways).[22]

Thus, unlike Marcus Garvey and the Universal Negro Improvement Association (UNIA), the Congress of African People never considered emigration to Africa.

After the summit in Atlanta, Baraka and CFUN would never be the same. With the founding of the Congress of African People, CFUN became Newark CAP, the program office of that organization and the headquarters for the *national* Modern Black Convention Movement. Increasingly, in discussions with the African liberation movements of Angola, Mozambique, Guinea-Bissau, and Zimbabwe, the African radicals asked: *if the Congress of African People is truly revolutionary, why is it not socialist?* In that international context, CAP began to take ideological issues more seriously, and ultimately it would reassess its views on race and class in the struggle for black liberation. In these circumstances, the ideological and

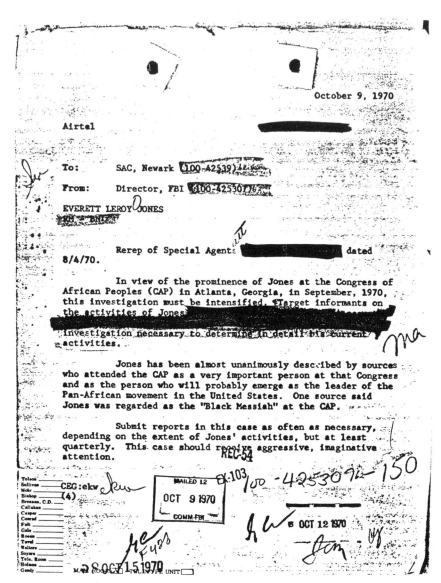

October 9, 1970

Airtel

To: SAC, Newark (100-A2539)

From: Director, FBI (100-425307

EVERETT LEROY JONES

          Rerep of Special Agent ▮▮▮▮▮▮▮▮▮ dated
8/4/70.

          In view of the prominence of Jones at the Congress of
African Peoples (CAP) in Atlanta, Georgia, in September, 1970,
this investigation must be intensified. Target informants on
the activities of Jones

investigation necessary to determine in detail his current
activities.

          Jones has been almost unanimously described by sources
who attended the CAP as a very important person at that Congress
and as the person who will probably emerge as the leader of the
Pan-African movement in the United States. One source said
Jones was regarded as the "Black Messiah" at the CAP.

          Submit reports in this case as often as necessary,
depending on the extent of Jones' activities, but at least
quarterly. This case should receive aggressive, imaginative
attention.

A 1970 FBI memorandum targeting Baraka as a "Black Messiah" leading a "Pan-African movement." (Courtesy of Amiri Baraka)

political dialogue between the cultural nationalists and the Black Left called for in the resolutions set the stage for several of the leading cultural nationalist organizations to move rapidly to the left. At the head of the Modern Black Convention Movement, Baraka's organization would chart its own unique road from black nationalism through Pan-Africanism to socialism.

African Liberation Day

One major step in the radicalization of the Congress of African People was the development of the African Liberation Support Committee (ALSC); African Liberation Day signaled CAP's deepening involvement in international politics. The CAP resolutions condemning white colonialism in Black Africa reflected a new initiative among the top leaders of the black nationalist movement to strengthen their direct ties with the African liberation movements at the very same time that President Nixon increased his support of white colonial regimes. By 1972, fifteen former State Department officials, including two undersecretaries of state and twelve ambassadors of the Kennedy and Johnson administrations, denounced President Richard Nixon for expanding contacts and communications with South Africa and Rhodesia. They also condemned Nixon's increase in aid to stimulate trade with Portuguese colonialism in Angola and Mozambique, saying that Nixon's measures conveyed "a sense of collaboration" and that they retarded "the eventual independence of black Africans."[23] Some of those who signed that statement included Undersecretaries W. Averell Harriman and Chester Bowles and Ambassadors Mercer Cook and Franklin Williams.

By that time, the black nationalist community had already taken its own political initiative. The idea for African Liberation Day developed in the mind of Milwaukee-born Owusu Sadaukai during the period between the 1970 Atlanta Congress of African Peoples and the 1972 National Black Political Convention. Owusu Sadaukai (Howard Fuller) had been closely associated with SNCC and Stokely Carmichael, following Carmichael as he developed his emphasis on Pan-Africanism in the late 1960s and at times acting as his official spokesman. Much of this work was done in association with an organization headquartered in North Carolina, the Student Organization for Black Unity (SOBU), which involved a number of SNCC veterans. Sadaukai developed extensive contacts with foundations, and when the emphasis of the Black Revolt changed to institutional development, he founded Malcolm X Liberation University in Greensboro, North Carolina.

In 1971, Sadaukai visited Africa, talking to leaders of the struggles against Portuguese colonialism in Guinea-Bissau, Mozambique, and Angola.[24] On his return to America, Sadaukai elaborated on plans for political education and community mobilization, which would culminate in a national demonstration on May 25, the anniversary of the founding of the Organization of African Unity (OAU). By a January 1972 meeting at

Newark Congress of African People demonstration against Portuguese attack on Guinea. (Courtesy of the Baraka family collection, photograph by Zachariah Risasi Dais)

Malcolm X Liberation University, Sadaukai's idea had become "African Liberation Day," to be held on the Saturday closest to May 25th, the day the OAU had established for demonstrating international solidarity with African liberation struggles. Thus, the planning for African Liberation Day began, targeting the efforts for May 27, 1972, a day on which African

Americans would demonstrate their support for the end of colonialism in Africa.[25]

Malcolm X Liberation University and SOBU provided the beginning of a network for such a political statement, but Sadaukai wanted to enlist the support of the various black nationalists around the nation to make African Liberation Day a major event. SOBU contacted CAP leaders early in those talks, and the major Pan-Africanists agreed to give African Liberation Day (ALD) 1972 their full support. The Congress of African People used its political contacts to enlist support among black elected officials.

On May 25, 1972, black leaders met at Howard University in Washington, D.C., for two days before African Liberation Day at the African American National Conference on Africa to hammer out a new approach to foreign policy. At that meeting the chairman of the Black Congressional Caucus, Louis Stokes of Ohio, told the delegates, "It is time to make America live up to her 200-year commitment to freedom and self-determination."[26]

The chairman of the African American National Conference on Africa was Michigan Representative Charles C. Diggs Jr., who was also the head of a congressional subcommittee on Africa. The conference extended the African American criticism of U.S. foreign policy in Africa, drawing special attention to President Nixon's diplomatic support of white minority regimes in Southern Africa. Generally, the speakers criticized the United States, Britain, and France for the support given to those white colonial rulers. At the end of those sessions they decided to establish a new national organization, the African Liberation Support Committee (ALSC). Before the birth of the TransAfrica organization, the ALSC was one of the most important forces for African liberation in African American history.

The ALSC was for the 1970s what the Council on African Affairs, led by Paul Robeson and W. E. B. Du Bois, had been in the 1940s. The ALSC mobilized an unprecedented degree of grassroots support for African liberation movements. "Assembled by local branches of the ALSC," explains St. Clair Drake, "participants came from all over the United States."[27] Drake adds:

> Over 10,000 Afro-Americans demonstrated against Portuguese colonial oppression in Angola, Mozambique and Guinea-Bissau; called for majority rule in Rhodesia [Zimbabwe] and South Africa; and pledged financial and political support to the liberation movements in southern Africa. One goal was to influence American policy toward Africa, and it was significant that Congressman Diggs not only agreed to address the

rally, but he promised to continue to fight for freedom and justice in Africa. Nothing like this had happened since the days of the Council.[28]

Black people from the Midwest, South, and Northeast began to gather in Washington, D.C., early on Saturday, May 27, 1972, for African Liberation Day. Generally, teenagers at the march wore African symbols; specifically, the youth organized by the Congress of African People were dressed uniformly in black and green. The new branches of CAP were demonstrating the effectiveness of their organizational efforts by bringing large delegations of community people, including their teenage members wearing green CAP sweatshirts. As the CAP youth lined up city by city, the representation from Chicago, South Bend, Pittsburgh, Philadelphia, Brooklyn, the Bronx, Wilmington, Delaware, and Washington, D.C., was impressive. Teenagers from Newark's African Free School had the honor of carrying the African Liberation Day banner at the head of the march. Other young people carried banners and signs saying "Arm Yourself or Harm Yourself" and "Black People Must Unify." And some carried signs saying "Africa for the Africans" and "We Are An African People."

Not to be outdone by the youth, on the front line of the march was the revered elder Queen Mother Moore, 74 years old, an activist in the movement since the days of Marcus Garvey in Harlem. Also on the front line were U.S. Delegate Walter Fauntroy of Washington, D.C., George Wiley of the National Welfare Rights Organization, humorist Dick Gregory of Chicago, Roy Innis of Harlem CORE, and poets Haki R. Madhubuti and Imamu Amiri Baraka of the Congress of African People. One journalist, who apparently had not witnessed the new black consciousness displayed at the Atlanta Congress of African People, noted that the march "differed from recent demonstrations here as well as from civil rights marches not only in its all-black composition, but in its strong black nationalist tone."[29]

There were various estimates of the numbers of demonstrators at the first African Liberation Day in Washington, D.C. The *Washington Post* reported that the turnout "far exceeded the 3,000 predicted by metropolitan police, but fell within the 10,000 to 15,000 persons predicted by march organizers."[30] According to the *New York Times* the "police" estimate was somewhere between 8,000 to 10,000; but the African Liberation Day Coordinating Committee consistently reported that some 30,000 marched on Washington, D.C., and that another 30,000 demonstrated at the other rallies in San Francisco, Toronto, and Dominica, Antigua, and Grenada in the West Indies as well.[31] In any event, the *Washington Post* reported that the march on the nation's capitol was the largest black demonstration "in

Imamu Amiri Baraka (left) and Bibi Amina Baraka in a park in Washington, D.C., at the African Liberation Day march in May 1972. (Courtesy of the Baraka family collection, photograph by Zachariah Risasi Dais)

recent Washington history . . . to show black support here for African guerrilla groups and to denounce United States policy in Africa."[32] Dick Gregory admired the demonstration, calling it "the greatest moment for liberation in the history of black folk in America," because unlike with the civil rights marches, black people had rallied in such numbers without support from the white news media.[33]

The march route was typical of that period of black mobilization and struggle; the organizers knew how to rally the community. Although the demonstration stopped in front of several of the official missions to draw attention to the African Liberation Support Committee's criticism of the U.S., Portugal, and South Africa, for the most part it paraded through the black community to take its message to the people and to draw even greater numbers to the rally. The *Washington Post* reported that "some of the marchers beat conga drums as they marched through the city, and the caravan was headed by a truck featuring conga players from Friendship House in Southeast Washington."[34] They began at 11:30 A.M., parading down 16th Street Northwest from Malcolm X Park (Meridian Hill Park) at 16th and Euclid Streets Northwest toward Embassy Row. When the marchers wound through Rock Creek Park toward the State Department and Lumumba Square,[35] sections of the group broke off to hear speakers denounce colonialist governments and business investors in front of the Rhodesian information center, the South African and Portuguese embassies, and the State Department.

After about two and a half hours, the march ended with a rally as the throng gathered on the grounds of Lumumba Square. Looking out over thousands of activists, the speakers expressed their determination as they voiced opposition to racism, colonialism, and imperialism and called for liberation and revolution. The master of ceremonies, Washington's Walter Fauntroy, introduced U.S. Representative Charles Diggs. Standing in front of a black nationalist flag, dressed in a purple dashiki, Diggs told the gathering, "We are sounding a warning that no longer will the movement for justice stop at the water's edge."

SNCC veteran Cleveland Sellers read a message from Stokely Carmichael, who was out of the country, calling for African Americans to take "a revolutionary posture" toward "colonialism and imperialism." Carmichael called for a black political party and the "total liberation and unification of Africa under scientific socialism." Meanwhile, the presence of the Black Panther Party at the African Liberation Day rally signaled a new period of unity among African Americans. Indeed, surrounded by five bodyguards, the minister of information of the Black Panther Party, Elaine Brown, called for unity and urged "an end to divisions among blacks."

Representing the Congress of African People, the gifted young poet Haki Madhubuti read a moving Pan-African poem to the huge gathering seated in the grass, and Imamu Baraka spoke at length about the need for the organization of a party for black liberation and African revolution, one

Left to right: Tanzanian minister of economic development Abdulrahman Babu, Baraka associate Naibu Mchochezi, Imamu Baraka, and unidentified Zanzibar dignitary in early 1970s. (Courtesy of the Baraka family collection, photograph by Zachariah Risasi Dais)

strong enough to carry those struggles through to the end. Madhubuti and Baraka were very warmly received, but perhaps the most stirring words that day were delivered by the initiator of the whole project, Owusu Sadaukai.

The gathering held on to each word as Sadaukai reminded them of Frederick Douglass's philosophy of reform: "There is no progress without struggle. . . . Find out just what people will submit to, and you have found out the exact amount of injustice and wrong which will be imposed upon them; and these will continue till they are resisted with either words or blows, or with both." The rally reached a crescendo when thousands stood in unison, joining Sadaukai as he chanted the watchwords of the new period: "*We are an African people.*"

On that resounding note, the African Liberation Support Committee (ALSC) was launched as one of the most important mass organizations in the country and the most influential among African Americans on U.S. foreign policy. Throughout the 1970s there were annual African Liberation Days, but none would ever match the claim of 60,000 participants made for the 1972 activities. ALSC developed a diverse regional leadership, chaired internationally by Dawolu Gene Locke in Houston. The Caribbean section was chaired by Tim Hector; the South by Owusu Sadaukai in Durham, North Carolina; the Midwest by Haki R. Madhubuti; and the East by Imamu Baraka. These regional leaders were members of the ALSC Executive Committee, along with such at-large figures as Nelson Johnson and Abdul Alkalimat.

Ironically, the ALSC, originally conceived to support the fight against white supremacy in southern Africa, would have a profound impact on the black freedom movement in the U.S., pushing it increasingly to the left.

Black Women's United Front

While the emergence of ALSC placed foreign policy at the top of the developing black national political agenda, the establishment of the Black Women's United Front signaled that African American women, particularly black nationalist women, demanded full equality in the black national political arena. The Black Women's United Front (BWUF) was called for in July 1974 at the International Afrikan Women's Conference, initiated by Bibi Amina Baraka and the Social Organization Council of the Congress of African People. It was an historic meeting, coming on the heels of the May 1974 ALSC Conference in Washington, D.C., and the June 1974 Sixth Pan-African Congress in Dar Es Salaam, Tanzania, both of which were redefining Pan-Africanism with socialism in mind.

That combination of Pan-Africanism and socialism had already radicalized the Women's Division of the Congress of African People, which had been steeled in the struggle for gender equality beginning with the Committee For Unified NewArk. Paradoxically, while CFUN was publicly endorsing the conservative notion that the submissiveness of black women was "natural," in 1971 inside that organization the Women's Division launched a determined struggle against the introduction of polygamous practices. As a stream of former US Organization members arrived in Newark to join CFUN, secretly a few of them began to invoke the traditional African concepts of polygamy for the manipulative and vulgar purposes of American adultery and sexual exploitation.[36] That kind of sexual exploitation was always a danger in the Black Revolt, but the menace was heightened by extremely naïve understandings of Africa. Both Amina and Amiri Baraka denounced the introduction of those practices in CFUN; at one point in 1971 in the internal *CFUN Newsletter* Imamu Baraka's editorial warned the men that the women were revolutionary comrades deserving nothing less than full respect and that in that organization it was impermissible to treat women otherwise. Before long, a few of the high-ranking former US members resigned, charging that Baraka was a "revisionist" of the doctrine. That battle against polygamy became a protracted one as CFUN became the political headquarters and exemplar for the national CAP organization, projecting a monogamous family ideal. As these tensions became both national and ideological, the battle against polygamy grew into the struggle against male chauvinism; all of that culminated in the more general fight for gender equality within both the Congress of African People and the Modern Black Convention Movement. Ultimately, within CAP, male chauvinism became an offense punishable by both denunciation and demotion. Those protracted struggles produced the women's leadership that developed the ideas within CAP for the 1974 Afrikan Women's Conference.

Over 700 black people went to Newark in July 1974 to discuss the conditions necessary for the liberation of black women. They talked about ways in which they might draw the broadest possible range of black women together: women in the workplace and students in the schools, as well as mothers on welfare, those in prison, and even some in other women's organizations. The delegates from some twenty-eight states decided that a new organization was needed to deal with the concerns of black women on a consistent basis.

The official task force established to put the new organization on its feet represented seven groups: the All African Peoples Revolutionary Party (AAPRP), National Welfare Rights Organization (NWRO), Black Workers Congress (BWC), Pan African Students of America (PASOA), Youth Organization of Black Unity (YOBU), Ethiopian Students, and the Congress of African People. The national BWUF was founded at a Detroit summit on January 25, 1975, attended by 500 women and men who expressed their determination to defeat what they thought were the triple barriers to the liberation of black women: racism, capitalism, and imperialism.[37] Signaling the radical fervor of the black women mobilizing that gathering, the poster calling for the Detroit meeting declared its slogan: the "abolition of every possibility of oppression & exploitation."[38]

Nonetheless, these women faced some sobering ideological barriers to full equality. Indicative of the situation of black women in the freedom movement, the BWUF fought two initial battles. First, some black activists questioned the necessity of having an independent organization led by black nationalist women. Second, even more activists disagreed with

The Malaika cultural group performs a dance about women in the wars of African liberation, on stage in Newark in the 1970s. (Photograph by Sura Wa Taifa, poster in author's collection)

the proposal to make antisexism one of the political principles of the BWUF.

By the Second Assembly of the BWUF in Atlanta, Georgia, on October 25, 1975, the fledgling organization adopted three principles of unity: "Anti-Racism, Anti-Imperialism and Anti-Capitalism." However, at that point, the principle of antisexism remained too controversial for adoption without risking a split in the young organization. To make matters even more complicated, the BWUF wanted to place its emphasis on the problems of working women; there was a great deal of concern that the new organization distinguish itself from "bourgeois Feminism."[39] That conference assigned to the Detroit BWUF local the responsibility to draft a detailed platform on antisexism. Thus, the Atlanta summit began an important debate about the merits of political work against sexism within the ranks of the black freedom movement.

In a major departure from past black nationalist practice, the BWUF decided to endorse the December 1975 National Fight Back Conference sponsored by the Marxist-Leninist organization, the October League. They also determined to support the Defense Committee for Cheryl S. Todd and Dessie X. Woods, as a blow against the crime of raping black women. Ms. Woods was the black woman inmate who killed a prison guard to stop him from raping her; defense committees sprang up all across the country. They concluded that the emphasis on the right of a woman to self-defense, especially against rape, was of such importance that they made it into a national program of the BWUF.

The BWUF aimed to draw even more black women into the struggle for black liberation by addressing the issues that were of immediate concern. That Atlanta summit was followed by a number of assemblies in other cities. Local chapters, in some cases acting as regional centers, were established in the Bronx and Albany, New York; Newark, New Jersey; St. Louis, Missouri; Pittsburgh, Pennsylvania; Detroit, Michigan; South Bend, Indiana; Washington, D.C.; Columbia, South Carolina; and Baltimore, Maryland.[40]

Raising the political consciousness of women and men about the triple oppression of black women was another concern of the BWUF. In its developing analysis, imperialism oppressed black women on the basis of their race, class, and gender. The BWUF educational programs had an important impact on modern black nationalism. It reminded many nationalist leaders that in the nineteenth century, black nationalism had stood in the vanguard of the fight for the political equality of black women; while women could not participate in much of the black convention movement, they played leading roles in the historic 1854 Cleveland black nationalist convention.[41] Furthermore, leading cultural nationalists such as Amiri Baraka, Haki Madhubuti, and Maulana Karenga began to repudiate sexism and male chauvinism in Black America. By 1975, Karenga endorsed the defense of Joanne Little, who was on trial in Wake County, North Carolina, in a case parallel to that of Dessie X. Woods, insisting that actually the African American people were on trial: "We sit at the same defense table, hear the same lies the system has assembled to take her life and deny her right to defend herself against rape and all the psycho-cultural assumptions and violence it represents." As far as Karenga was concerned, the real issues in the Joanne Little case spoke "to the right of women everywhere to be free from sexual abuse, oppression and exploitation and [it raised] the question, and simultaneously [reaffirmed] the right, of an oppressed people and each of its members to resist its oppression everywhere and on all levels of life and struggle." In fact, Karenga's argument for the support of Little demonstrates the degree to which cultural nationalists took seriously the issues raised by black women in the struggle such as those in the BWUF:

> We must do this first because she is our sister in nation and struggle, because she is one of us, sharing the same history and oppression and because we know in awful and agonizing detail the history of our oppression and exploitation and the many ways it's been executed, especially against our sisters, mothers and daughters. It is thus a clear choice between the word of a sister against that of the system which oppresses and exploits us daily. There is no third choice; we either support our sister or the system, her truth or the organized and institutionalized lies of the oppressor.[42]

For the Newark Congress of African People, the recognition of the leadership of women was long overdue. In one sense, the BWUF was a new beginning, signaling the fact that the women in CAP would be partners in struggle with black men, but they would no longer tolerate anything less than equal status in the Black Revolt. They welcomed men in the meetings because they wanted progressive black men involved in the struggle to liberate black women. In the fight for women's equality, they asked men for their cooperation but *not* for their permission.

The Gary Convention

While the mobilization of specific sectors of Black America around the issues of antisexism and anticolonialism was essential to black nationality formation, the most prominent step in that process was the National Black Political Convention in Gary, Indiana, which pulled together 12,000 African American leaders in 1972. The Gary convention was the culmination of a number of processes unleashed by the tumult of the Black Revolt of the 1960s; these uprisings stirred all the basic social, economic, and political segments of the black community to express their particular perspectives, concerns, and aspirations. That period witnessed the increased differentiation of African Americans and the formation of black organizations and caucuses in nearly every area of American life. One consequence of this broad and complex insurgency was that each social group left its special imprint on the Black Revolt, and this new portrait of African American diversity baffled many black leaders.

In that confusing situation, there would be no new national leadership linked to the masses until a national black political community developed.

But, how would that community embrace such divergence without anarchy? The answers to this question crystallized in the Modern Black Convention Movement, which attempted to embrace the tension between diversity and unity within the national black community between 1972 and 1975. That social movement constructed its own democratic process of agenda building around the principle of proportional representation, voicing the numerous viewpoints within the black community and giving each perspective due weight in decision making.[43] The new process of agenda building and the mass mobilization for the Gary convention demonstrated the extent of the Modern Black Convention Movement's appeal. The Gary convention drew an estimated 1,800 black elected officials within an assembly estimated at somewhere between 8,000 to 12,000 black people.

At first the most influential black elected officials and leaders of the civil rights establishment were reluctant to hold the National Black Political Assembly to determine a black political agenda for the 1972 presidential elections. Instead, they preferred small and exclusive meetings of the black elite to establish themselves as the patronage referees for the emerging national black political community; with this vehicle they would bargain for political patronage with the Democratic Party. Thus, rather than attending a Black Leadership Unity Conference organized by the Congress of African People at Howard University in June 1971 in Washington, D.C., Jesse Jackson called exclusive meetings in Chicago and Cleveland, involving Mayor Carl Stokes, Congressman John Conyers, and John Cashin. These meetings undermined the Black Leadership Unity Conference, which was attended by only two major political figures, Newark's mayor Kenneth Gibson and the former New York state legislator Basil Patterson. The participation of civil rights organizations was waning also; only two representatives attended, one from the National Urban League and one from a local chapter of the NAACP.

In response to this split in leadership, a number of the black nationalists were reluctant to pursue a black united front strategy for the 1972 national elections; a spirit of pessimism permeated the meeting. However, in response to that pessimism, the Congress of African People initiated a mass political dynamic which led to the Gary convention, drawing together black nationalists and black elected officials. Several summit meetings were decisive in this initiative, particularly the Black Political Convention held at "The East" in Brooklyn, New York, on the July 4th weekend of 1971. "The East" was the popular black cultural and educational center established in Bedford-Stuyvesant by the controversial educator Jitu Weusi (Les Campbell), who had been a teacher in the hotly contested, community-controlled schools in New York.

The convention at "The East" drew a formidable assembly of black nationalists. The Washington, D.C., Black United Front sent Rev. Douglass Moore. Later, after defeating U.S. Rep. Walter Fauntroy in the black convention election, Moore would go to the Gary convention as the head of the important Washington delegation. Philadelphia's African People's Party (APP) sent Saludin Muhammad and Muhammad Ahmed,[44] both of whom had a great deal of influence in the nationalist movement. For the most part, the meeting was attended by black political activists who wanted to formulate a strategy for 1972; they came from such communities as Roxbury, Massachusetts; Brooklyn, Manhattan, Queens, the Bronx, and Syracuse, New York; Montclair, East Orange, and Newark, New Jersey; Philadelphia and Pittsburgh, Pennsylvania; Alexandria, Virginia; Washington, D.C.; Durham, North Carolina; and Cleveland, Ohio.

Strategy and Tactics

The conference served as a dress rehearsal for a gathering like the National Black Political Convention in 1972. Imamu Baraka was determined to dispel the pessimism that had surrounded the Washington summit and to regain the party-building momentum. His new plan was not simply a matter of putting the black nationalist house in order; Baraka's idea for establishing a national black political community advanced a stratagem for modernizing black nationalism and revitalizing African American political culture, arguing that everything rested on training a new leadership and developing new strategy and tactics.

For CAP, the centerpiece of the "East" Conference was a position paper developed by Baraka, *Strategy and Tactics of a Pan-African Nationalist Party*, which provided an overview of their plans. Baraka argued for the importance of modernizing black nationalism and revitalizing black political culture. Then he proposed several immediate organizational and political priorities for African Americans: (1) developing political cadre organizations; (2) creating circles of operational unity with black elected officials and civil rights leaders; (3) establishing a broad united front of black nationalists and Pan-Africanists on the regional and national levels; (4) building an African Nationalist Party; (5) organizing a national voter registration drive; and, (6) holding a national political convention and running their own black candidates in 1972.

Black nationalists, insisted Baraka, had to run candidates "from district leaders through to president," for several reasons. First, a presidential campaign on a separate party line would help black nationalists run for public offices ranging from seats on local school boards to those in the U.S. Congress. Newark CAP was already making preparations for a new black congressional seat; they had initiated a legal challenge to New Jersey's political map, with a redistricting plan of their own. Baraka's position paper explained that they should enter the race for president "because it is the only way to qualify for an entire line on state wide tickets."

Second, he thought that running for president might attract some respected black political figures into the nationalist political camp. There were a number of such people discussing the possibility, ranging from Carl Stokes to Shirley Chisholm. While Baraka proposed this stratagem, he was never uncritical of the purposes of some of these figures. In his estimation, the black presidential hopefuls of 1972 were "mainstream American Negro political figures . . . already hypnotized by the glamour of a fantasy hegemony as *quote* Serious Black Presidential Candidates *unquote*." More to the point, Baraka insisted that some of these public figures were using a fake black presidential dynamic to mask their real attempts to establish themselves as national patronage referees. In Baraka's words, they were "in many cases simply hoping to transform this rather whimsical title into some forms of goods and services by being designated as chief of some establishment-Negro-sometime-going-for-Black power-brokerage." For these reasons, Baraka urged that it was essential for the black nationalists to intervene in the 1972 political arena, so that black people would not mobilize themselves only to discover they had been betrayed; such a gigantic betrayal could demobilize the black community with distrust for years to come.

Baraka pointed to the state maneuver of Alabama's John Cashin as an example of the tactics he was proposing for the 1972 national elections:

Just as John Cashin ran for Governor of Alabama not because he actually thought that was accomplishable, but because by so doing he could provide the impetus to take control over the elective offices that the community actually could take and could control. And finally whatever we leave uninfluenced by Nationalism will be white controlled.[45]

But the heart of Baraka's argument was his third point, that the political training of cadre was essential to this whole gambit in the political arena:

Important to any movement we can make as a people . . . is the selection and training . . . of the cadre. The Committed. The Dedicated. Those of us who move out of a clear sense of Identity—African[;] Purpose—Restore Our People To Their Traditional Greatness[;] Direction—Black Nationalism.[46]

These cadre were the agents for the cultural and political revitalization of African American people, necessary, in CAP's vision of politics, to heal the historic wounds of white supremacy.[47]

Placing these trained political activists at the center of his new strategy, Baraka contended that without such cadre forming an inner circle of politically conscious "brothers and sisters," the movement for black liberation was impossible. "If the so[-]called inner circle is confused, drugged, or basically jive, like successive waves from some heavy weight's initial impact, [the] entire circumference of that dynamic will be equally faulty and weak." Placing his emphasis on the *ethical reconstruction* of the black nationalist, Baraka insisted that these cadre would have to be held to a higher code, "a value system superior to the one that enslaves our community." Without this new code, black nationalists would not be able to continue to fight the *protracted* struggle for black liberation: "This is basically how the cadre can survive, emotionally, intellectually, or morally."[48]

Self-Criticism

Baraka's ruthless self-criticism of the ideological and political weaknesses within the ranks of the black nationalists was second only to his harsh words for white opponents. He was especially critical of nationalists who were "drunk with the rhetoric of revolution": "We should not make any statements we cannot back up, in ways that our community can see and understand. Words are not immediate change. Crackers killed in revolutionary sentences are walking around killing us in the real streets." Instead of revolutionary rhetoric, he argued, black people wanted actual social changes in their lives:

We must learn to build houses, and how to acquire the land necessary to build houses. We can write revolutionary slogans in the lobbies of those buildings if we like, as part of our educational programs, or paint pictures of revolutionary heroes on the fronts of those buildings and in the hallways if we want to, but we must learn to build those buildings and get hold of the political power necessary to effect this dynamic, now.[49]

Basing his views on his experience in Newark's urban social movement, Baraka insisted:

> The most revolutionary Africans as far as the community will be concerned will be those who can deliver goods and services. Who can actually build health centers and hospitals, who can actually build housing, who can actually run and create schools, and transform the present educational processes.[50]

By 1971, the ideas of social change and these cadre were integral to Baraka's concept of revitalization:

> We recreate ourselves as African Men in the last part of the twentieth century. We recreate ourselves as African Philosophers, African Historians, African Politicians, African Economists, African Artists, African Soldiers, African Scientists, not of any past era, not in any far away land, but here and now.[51]

While the rhetoric of revitalization was important, the follow-through was decisive. Professor of political science Ronald Walters recalls that after the "East" convention there were preparatory sessions at Howard University "at which policy experts discussed a range of issues such as political empowerment, economic development, human resources, environmental development, international relations, rural development, and communications."[52] These sessions prepared the outline for the National Black Agenda developed by the Gary convention.

The Eastern Regional Congress of African People

While the Washington parley stressed the importance of building a black party and the Brooklyn convention underscored the value of creating cadre, on the Labor Day weekend of 1971 the Northeast Regional Conference of the Congress of African People in Newark, New Jersey, emphasized the strategic and practical significance of a national black political convention. Rather than specifically focusing attention on plans to build a black political party, at the regional conference CAP highlighted the practical benefits of establishing a national political organization. When asked about working in the Democratic Party, Heyward Henry, the chairman of CAP, said only, "We are discussing the whole range of political options open to black people." Thus, Heyward Henry gingerly focused the media attention away from talk of a break with the Democratic Party and toward the discussion of a 1972 national political convention.[53]

The Northeast Regional CAP gathering of about a thousand black people used the political developments in Newark as a paradigm for Black Power. The *New York Times* reported that "the 1,000 delegates from 15 states [studied] the anatomy of successful black political campaigns, including that of Mayor Kenneth A. Gibson of Newark, as well as successful organizing techniques, in 11 workshops conducted at the West Kinney Junior High School." At the press conference, Imamu Baraka said that Newark would be used as a case study for the Black Power experiment, focusing on such black united front organizations as the "Black Leadership Conference, an organization of divergent black community leaders who meet weekly to discuss city affairs with city officials."[54] The *Times* report continued, "Mr. Baraka, chairman of the Committee for a Unified Newark, which functions as the Congress of African Peoples chapter here, said these and other techniques that had worked successfully would 'be presented for study, analysis and modifications by each of the 11 workshops.'"[55]

Building a broad black united front was more than an idea discussed in the workshops, it was an important feature of the Newark conference itself. CAP's developing alliance with civil rights organizations drew the Urban League's eastern regional director, Alexander Allen, to the meeting. Mr. Allen explained that the situation in the freedom movement had changed:

> There was a time when we felt that black liberation could come with blacks working one by one to improve their own individual situations. But now we realize that liberation for blacks will come only on a group basis. We must develop joint strategies.[56]

Thus, CAP had revived the momentum for building a black united front and sponsoring a broad-based national black political convention.

Northlake Summit

Despite these successful summit meetings, the influential political figures meeting with Jesse Jackson remained aloof from this broader process of agenda building. Mayor Richard Hatcher of Gary, Indiana, decided to intervene in this situation. Hatcher and Baraka had been working together for some time, struggling for black political equality. In fact, Hatcher had intervened in Newark to support the 1969 Black and Puerto Rican Political Convention when it was under attack by local black politicians. Furthermore, Hatcher had spoken at the Atlanta Congress of

African People.[57] Then, Hatcher and CAP leaders closed ranks in the struggle for proportional representation inside the National Democratic Party, demanding a proportional share of the 1972 convention delegates and the $6 million presidential campaign fund for black voter registration.

They brought that unity and momentum into the September 24, 1971, summit in Northlake, Illinois. The Northlake summit was called by Hatcher to discuss a black electoral stratagem for 1972. The summit boasted an impressive list of cosponsors: Charles Diggs, Coretta Scott King, Jesse Jackson, Julian Bond, Imamu Baraka, and Willie Brown. (Although Brown, then California state representative and future mayor of San Francisco, cosponsored the gathering, he did not attend.) In Manning Marable's assessment, the Northlake conference was "probably the only instance between 1965 and 1983 when representatives of virtually every major tendency of the black movement sat down together in the same room."[58] Key leaders from three sectors of the black community were in attendance: civil rights leaders, black politicians, and black nationalists. From the civil rights community, there were Andrew Young (SCLC), Vernon Jordan (Urban League), Rev. Jesse Jackson (PUSH), and Coretta Scott King. From the ranks of those civil rights leaders who had become elected officials, there were such figures as Georgia State Representative Julian Bond (SNCC) and U.S. Delegate Walter Fauntroy (SCLC). The leading black elected officials in attendance were U.S. Representatives Charles Diggs and John Conyers of Michigan and Augustus Hawkins of California, as well as the host, Mayor Hatcher. Other key political figures were Barbara Jordan, a Texas state legislator; Maynard Jackson, who would become the mayor of Atlanta; and Percy Sutton, who would become New York's Manhattan borough president.[59] Also represented was the National Welfare Rights Organization, by its leader George Wiley, the former CORE activist. Roy Innis spoke for both Harlem CORE and a number of black nationalists concerned with the busing issue. Then there were political experts such as James Gibson and Antonio Harrison. Meanwhile, Baraka and other CAP leaders represented the political agenda of the new nationalists.

Baraka's journal of these developments provides the most detailed description of the process. In it, he reports that there were a number of different perspectives at the parley, and several specific strategies:

The content of the meeting was hopeful but confused. The main proposals advanced were: Julian Bond's idea that Black people should run as favorite sons from various states, so as to bring blocs of Black delegates to the Democratic National Convention; Julian stated very forcefully in his paper that a Black party was not the answer at this time. Percy Sutton advanced the idea of a Black person running for President of the United States "to nationalize the Black vote" and give the national Black community greater bargaining power on consolidated demands.[60]

Before the Northlake Conference, the idea of a black presidential candidate had been presented by U.S. Rep. John Conyers and former Cleveland mayor Carl Stokes.

The most likely candidate for a black presidential strategy in 1972 would have been Brooklyn's U.S. Representative Shirley Chisholm, the first black woman in the history of the U.S. Congress. By the end of 1971, however, it became apparent that these professional politicians, most of whom were men, would not support her presidential candidacy; and when Chisholm distanced herself from the Modern Black Convention Movement, she lost that opportunity to press her position before the national black political community in 1972. One might speculate that at a national political convention of grassroots leadership, Chisholm would have been irresistible. Baraka begged Chisholm to attend the Gary convention, but it seems that Chisholm was not interested in any particular accountability to the Modern Black Convention Movement.[61]

In her own defense, Chisholm later said that even if she had "had the time," she might not have attended the Gary convention "because of all the negative reports" she had heard in regard to her presidential candidacy. "I didn't intend to present myself in front of a group of people who were just going to slash me right and left when I saw myself moving in an entirely different direction." She added:

> The fact of the matter is many of them were very upset because they felt I should have come to them and discussed my potential candidacy before I went out there and made the announcement. But the fact of the matter is that black men are no different from white men or no different from yellow men or whatever color they may be. I knew that they would not give support to my candidacy, although people had raised some money and I had some very good support among the female population of this country and the Hispanic population.

Chisholm felt that some of the leaders at Gary would have "laughed" at her bid for the presidency.[62] Although Chisholm's distrust of black men was definitely justified, especially by her treatment in the Congressional Black Caucus, her decision to shun the Gary convention might suggest that she trusted the *white* men in the Democratic Party more than the *black* men in the National Black Political Convention.

At any rate, for the nationalists, the presidential candidate was not the central issue. Until late 1971, all of the black nationalist gatherings had stressed the priority of *party building;* they wanted an independent and, in some cases, a revolutionary black political party. However, at the North-lake Conference, CAP maneuvered, as it had at the Northeast Regional meeting, by arguing instead for both the utility and the urgency of a National Black Convention. CAP's leadership had come to understand, after a series of public and private meetings, that the idea of a black political party was premature if they wanted the support of black elected officials in 1972. Yet CAP had developed a number of options that might lead to a black political party, and the political convention was at the top of that agenda.

But what would such a convention try to achieve? In his journal, Baraka explains:

> The convention would try to bring all the tribes of Black people in America together to talk about our political priorities. Certainly about 1972, and what an American Presidential year meant to the national Black community; but also what kind of continuing priorities should be sounded for Black people. And, as always, we hoped that there would be some talk of a continuing mechanism, some structure upon which to build what we still feel is the absolute *sine qua non* of Black political movement, i.e., a permanent structure, or party.[63]

In addition to this organizational dimension, politically CAP thought that by pressing the immediate demands for black equality publicly to the Democratic Party, they would hasten the day when blacks left the ranks of the Democrats in numbers large enough to establish a broadly based black political party of their own.

Key to that strategy was to have an unprecedented number of black leaders at all levels involved in dual tactics: (1) fashioning a "Black Agenda" of demands on the outside; and (2) demanding concessions from the Democratic Party on the inside. CAP wanted thousands of black leaders to see the other face of the Democratic Party, the face that Baraka and Hatcher had seen in their struggle for proportionate representation at the 1972 Democratic National Convention. But it was impossible for CAP to complete that gambit, which might take some time, without a national organization that would coordinate black demands and hold national leaders accountable in power negotiations. If CAP was wrong about the Democratic Party, then blacks would have more power in that political organization. But if CAP was right, then the Democrats and their Negro brokers would expose themselves before the black community, paving the ground for the development of a black political party between 1972 and 1976. That was the logic behind the new nationalist proposal at the Northlake parley.

National Conference of Black Elected Officials

A number of the black leaders at Northlake seemed receptive to the idea of a black political convention, but as was the case with earlier summits, the procedures for further discussion and implementation of that approach broke down soon after the meeting because there was no legitimate ongoing structure. Actually, the decisive summit meeting was the first National Conference of Black Elected Officials, sponsored in November 1971 by the Congressional Black Caucus. A private meeting of key black leaders at that gathering established both the decision and the procedures for a black political convention.

The Washington, D.C., meeting, on the weekend of November 18–20, 1971, involved black elected officials at the municipal, county, and state levels from across the country. One panel discussion at that conference focused on a "Black Strategy" for 1972; the panelists included Richard Hatcher, Charles Diggs, Percy Sutton, Imamu Baraka, and Coretta Scott King. Coretta King's paper sounded a theme very similar to the points that were explored by Dr. Martin Luther King Jr. on the eve of his assassination. (In addition to the March 27, 1968, meeting between King and Baraka mentioned earlier, a few days later Dr. King also met with Representative John Conyers and Mayor Richard Hatcher to develop a national political strategy. In June of that year these same leaders joined with Stokely Carmichael, Floyd McKissick, Sidney Poitier, Harry Belafonte, Andrew Young, Hosea Williams, and Rev. Ralph David Abernathy to establish the National Committee of Inquiry, some 200 strong, to "evaluate the Presidential candidates" and make voting recommendations to the national black community.[64]) At any rate, prepared with the assistance of Tony Harrison, a brilliant young Alabama political activist, Mrs. King's position paper was entitled "The Transformation of the Civil Rights Movement into a Political Movement."[65]

The question that riveted the attention of many conferees concerned a black national strategy for the presidential elections. By November 1971, the matter had gone beyond the exclusive control of the black establishment in its small private meeting; it had become a mass question that would be either answered or tabled in public, not in private, and in either case black leaders would be held accountable.

By the Washington conference in November 1971, the development and execution of any unified "Black Strategy" for 1972 was problematic. After almost a year of discussions with the black political establishment, not one binding decision had been made on this broader question. Even worse, the process was amorphous; when workable plans were proposed and agreements were reached, there was no mechanism for carrying out a decision. Without an organization, none of the leadership could be held accountable; worst of all, the public never knew the substance of those summit meetings.

Imamu Baraka used that panel discussion to press once again the case for a national black political convention, where issues could be debated openly and decided democratically. Baraka pleaded for a unified strategy; however, clearly this was the last chance for the proposal: if black politicians were not involved, if they refused to enter these strategic discussions, then the black nationalists would call their own mini-convention without them.

But at the very last moment, at the Washington conference, there was a break in this impasse. By happenstance, Shirley Chisholm decided to attack publicly the Congressional Black Caucus for its lack of political nerve; they had ignored her daring bid for the Democratic nomination. At a hectic plenary session, U.S. Rep. Ron Dellums supported her criticism, also crying foul on the issue of gender discrimination. All this unfolded before an audience of hundreds of black elected officials drawn from across the United States. It seemed the Black Congressional Caucus had to do something. If it could not agree to Chisholm's presidential maneuver, then what leadership would the Caucus provide for developing a "Black Strategy" for 1972?

In a small conference room, away from the public discussion, key political figures including Richard Hatcher, Jesse Jackson, and Imamu Baraka met with Charles Diggs and the Black Congressional Caucus. The Caucus had been backed into a corner; it had to show some leadership and some political backbone. Once again, Baraka pressed his case for a political convention; this time, with the support of Diggs, Hatcher, and Jackson, he won the backing of the other leaders.

At the end of the weekend, the Congressional Black Caucus issued a press release calling for a national black political convention. In December, another summit of these black leaders decided the convention site,

Gary, Indiana, and its leadership, a triumvirate: Richard Hatcher, Charles Diggs, and Imamu Baraka. By January, at Howard University, a session of scholars, intellectuals, and political experts began drafting the framework for the envisioned National Black Agenda. And, in a matter of weeks thereafter, the massive political mobilization for the Gary convention took its place in history.

In the following weeks, the Congress of African People became a national headquarters for organizers across the country as requests for information poured into Newark. The prophetic call to the Gary convention was distributed widely in Black America:

> The challenge is thrown to us here in Gary. It is the challenge to consolidate and organize our own black role as the vanguard in the struggle for a new society. To accept that challenge is to move to independent black politics. There can be no equivocation on that issue. History leaves us no other choice. White politics has not and cannot bring the changes we need.[66]

Galvanized by Gary's call, the mobilization that led to the national convention came from hundreds of community leaders and local black elected officials who had decided that the time had come for the black community to become the master of its own destiny.

Grassroots Mobilization and Agenda Building

The black nationalists and national black leadership played crucial roles in preparations for the National Black Political Convention held in Gary, Indiana, on the weekend of March 10–12, 1972, but the grass roots were the mainstay of the Gary convention. Black communities across the country organized themselves along new lines, and that process unleashed an unprecedented tide of black political energy around the development of a national black political agenda.

Agenda building, as Ronald W. Walters called it in *Black Presidential Politics in America*, was a key element in the Modern Black Convention Movement. Agenda building stressed mutual respect among the various leaders of the black community for their different concerns and emphasized the principle of proportional representation. But at a deeper level agenda building meant that in the Modern Black Convention Movement the priorities would come from *below*. And this process struck a powerful blow at the hegemony of the two-party system in determining issues for the black community. The Modern Black Convention Movement took the *initiative* out of the hands of the Democratic Party leadership and their brokers. Instead that initiative would rest with grassroots leaders in the black community. The agenda they would set was rooted in demands of the urban social movement that gripped big-city politics.

Agenda building allowed those local demands to develop into a coherent national platform for social change and black development. This process unfolded in a matter of weeks in a number of states with large black urban concentrations. In those cities this social movement provided a window into the changing composition and mood of black leadership. No longer was the emphasis on the "civility" of the Negro establishment; these new leaders spoke to White America in a harsh language born of the Black Revolt.[67]

Not only did the language of black politics change, but the composition of the membership of this movement reflected the increasing participation of black women. For instance, the *New York Times* reported on the work of the controversial New York Black Political Convention. That state's gathering, held in Brooklyn's Bellrose Ballroom, elected 339 delegates, half of them black women. At the meeting the steering committee adopted a platform emphasizing black self-determination. Their resolutions expressed concerns ranging from reparations to land use, education, and social welfare reform. In addition to calling for quality public education and free higher education, the New York Black Assembly proposed that the aid to dependent families for impoverished people be established at a minimum of $10,000.[68] These were the various concerns of the urban social movements in New York. In the day-to-day struggles in the community for economic relief, better schooling for their children, and decent housing for their families, black women at the grass roots were the main force of the Modern Black Convention Movement.[69]

The newspapers did not focus on these aspects of the changing composition of black leadership; instead, they emphasized the controversial move of the New York delegation when its spokesman barred white reporters and news crews from covering convention meetings. As the controversy grew in anticipation of the national coverage at the Gary convention, where thousands of white newsmen and media crews had planned to converge to cover that event, the *New York Times* registered its protest of that racially exclusive policy. Underneath the emotional reaction of the New York delegates to the presence of white news reporters was the well-established racially exclusive pattern of the national media, many of which employed no black reporters, editors, or technical staff.[70]

In New Jersey, the Essex County Black Political Convention was not without its own brand of controversy. While several hundred black people from Montclair, East Orange, Orange, and Newark met inside Newark's West Kinney Junior High School on the weekend of January 14–16, 1972, outside about fifteen black people registered their opposition to the movement. The picketers were led by Rev. Horace P. Sharper, who expressed alarm at concessions won by community struggles from the Newark Board of Education, especially one that supported display of the symbols of black liberation in the public schools.[71] Specifically, the protest was opposed to a resolution passed by the Newark School Board to fly black liberation flags at all schools and classrooms where blacks were in the majority and the city's decisions to rename some streets and schools for such black leaders as Harriet Tubman, Dr. Martin Luther King Jr., Marcus Garvey, and Malcolm X.[72] In one case, Newark CAP had proposed that the city's Arts High School be renamed after John Coltrane, the musical genius, and in another case that a school be named after W. E. B. Du Bois, the intellectual titan. At the bottom of the protest was that group's outrage over the fact that Baraka and the Modern Black Convention Movement were successfully turning Newark into a showplace for black nationalism and black liberation.

Although the black community had been excluded from the workings of the Essex County and Newark political machines, it participated en masse at the black assemblies convened in their own neighborhoods. What would the poor in the black community demand when mobilized and organized? What would they say when voicing their own concerns? At the Essex County Political Convention, the Black Agenda emphasized the immediate and pressing issues of the community struggles in New Jersey's urban centers: police brutality, inequalities in health care, a social crisis for black youth, public education that lacked dignity and equality, and unequal economic and political arrangements between the black and Puerto Rican urban centers and the white suburbs.

The Essex County Black Agenda proposed a number of alternatives to the urban crisis, most of which involved the restructuring of power relations. If the black community was to become the master of its own house, then it had to have control over urban renewal in terms of the funding and the redesign of urban spaces. For instance, in the housing workshop of that convention, the community—including tenant leaders, advocacy planners, construction workers, small contractors, and church developers—discussed the impact of the urban crisis and urban renewal on their communities, and developed some guidelines for alternative community developments: affordable housing; centers of culture, education, communications, and commerce in their neighborhoods; and community-inspired career training and economic development. First the resolutions of such workshops were gathered from a consensus of the views articulated there and then fashioned into agenda items, dominated by a grassroots perspective, that they felt would benefit the maximum number of black people in that area. These resolutions were developed from the bottom up, in the sense that the initiative remained in the hands of those representing the poor and working people in the immediate neighborhoods. Those resolutions also benefited from the technical assistance of small contractors and advocacy planners. In the case of such advocacy planners as the Project Area Committee (PAC) in the Central Ward of Newark, the community had direct control over its work through mass meetings.

But the redefinition of urban space in Newark was not simply a technical issue, it was an immensely *political* question. As people became involved in planning community spaces that were wholesome for their families, they began to challenge the role of the black community in the urban social order as the designated ghetto and slum. They felt that if they had the power, they would not design their neighborhoods to be ghettos and slums but rather community spaces where they could nurture their children. Why were there no parks for their children in the Central Ward? Why had the city built nothing but overcrowded high-rises with public housing funds? Who owned the private property in the Central Ward? Such questions were at the heart of Newark's urban social movement. The black assembly wanted to expand the areas controlled by such community-based advocacy planning agencies as the Project Area Committee, which seized the initiative from the Newark Housing Authority for planning a nearly 100-acre urban renewal site.

The same process was applied to alternative schools, health centers, youth programs, and child care agencies. In other words, this agenda-building process meant changing the political discourse on local and national issues. Rather than those black communities passively awaiting whatever political candidates might decide were the pressing issues in the next election, these black assemblies took the initiative in their own hands to determine and define the issues they felt were most important, speaking in a language that they well understood.[73]

"The Impossible Dream"

The Essex County gathering heard U.S. Delegate Walter Fauntroy of Washington, D.C., deliver a keynote address, which ended literally on a musical note, as he sang "The Impossible Dream." In New Brunswick a few weeks later, the New Jersey State Black Political Convention listened to New York's Basil Patterson, an astute politician who was instrumental in pulling together the Gary convention. The New Jersey State Black Political Convention drew delegations from such black communities as those in Jersey City, Elizabeth, Willingboro, Trenton, and Camden, as well as those from Essex County. After fashioning their local Black Agendas into a platform for the state, these community leaders and elected officials listened as Basil Patterson emphasized the importance of black people charting their own destiny in the political arena, free of control and coercion from powerful white interests. Like those in dozens of other states, these delegates were headed for Gary to announce their new leadership and direction to the world.

In their plans to make the New Jersey delegation as representative as possible, the conventions also raised funds, so that no delegates would be passed over for financial reasons. That way tenant and welfare rights leaders could represent themselves directly. Sidney Poitier and Harry Belafonte, stars of the movie *Buck and the Preacher*, donated some of the receipts from the movie's Newark premier to the New Jersey delegation. With the monies raised, the New Jersey Black Assembly chartered an airplane and reserved a floor in a Gary motel, where they planned their convention tactics.

The National Black Agenda, which was fashioned at Gary, represented the will of hundreds of black communities. Agenda building was a unique process of creating broad-based black united fronts and representative leadership grounded in democratic political principles rather than in the undemocratic dynamics of tokenism between white political overlords and their Negro agents in the black community. The results were unprecedented for black politics. In North Carolina, grassroots organizations also mobilized themselves for the Gary convention. As Ben Chavis recalled:

Our preparation to go to Gary, Indiana, for the convention was enormous. First of all, we had a statewide convention ourselves, in North Carolina. Thousands of people attended. And, of course we sent delegates from across the state of North Carolina to Gary. Some went by bus, some went by car, some went by plane. We drove up. And all the way up, we were thinking about what we were going to see when we arrived in Gary.[74]

On another level too, activists like Chavis reflected on the road to Gary and the course of the Black Revolt:

It was a good notion to go to Gary, Indiana, when we all knew we're not going to a funeral. I had gotten tired of going to funerals. . . . I have to emphasize King's assassination was a tragic blow to the movement. So four years later, March of '72, for us to be gathering up our wherewithal to go to Gary, Indiana—hey, that was a good shot in the arm for the movement. Because it meant that somehow the various forces, all these local struggles, survived that repression. Somehow we survived the grief that we all had from Dr. King's loss. And somehow we were making a statement that we were going to pick up that baton and run with it again in the 1970s.[75]

In the usually divisive setting of black politics, agenda building produced a platform that represented the culmination of months of feverish preconvention organizing, organizing that resulted in community and black nationalist groups coupling with politicians as convention delegates. With its emphasis on mutual respect and proportional representation, most perspectives in the black community found a place in the platform of this social movement.

However, not all perspectives were represented at the Gary convention. Within the Michigan state delegation, a black United Auto Workers caucus sounded a sour note with its exodus from the summit meeting over a voting technicality; however, the denunciation and boycott of the Gary convention by the National Association for the Advancement of Colored People was far more ominous. The NAACP circulated a memo at the Gary convention, directed especially to the large number of veteran NAACP members in attendance, that severely attacked the legitimacy of the convention. The memo argued that

the draft preamble is rooted in the concept of separate nationhood for black Americans. It calls for withdrawal from the American political process on the theory that this is white politics. It proclaims the doctrine of racial superiority in that it holds that only persons of African descent are capable of spearheading movement toward desirable change in society.[76]

Coming from the executive office of Roy Wilkins's assistant, John A. Morsell, the charge that the Black Agenda was rooted in black nationalism and that its rhetoric was "that of revolution rather than of reform" announced that the Modern Black Convention Movement had formidable opponents on the outside of the national gathering.[77]

While the division between black nationalists and the civil rights establishment still carried considerable weight, the events triggered by the Gary convention revealed that by 1972 that rift was no longer the central and exclusive conflict in the black national community. The foregoing discussion has emphasized the common front that began to emerge in the Black Revolt as early as 1968 in the aftermath of Dr. King's assassination; that common front was increasingly evident in Baraka's politics of cultural nationalism from then on. Furthermore, most of the authors of the Gary Convention Call, especially Walter Fauntroy and Richard Newhouse, were neither black nationalists nor revolutionaries. Considering that Fauntroy, formerly Dr. King's assistant in SCLC, was the U.S. Delegate representing Washington, D.C., and that Newhouse was a state senator representing Illinois, the NAACP's warning must be viewed as simply a lashing out at the Gary convention. At the national executive level of the NAACP, the tactic of alienating and isolating any currents of black political autonomy had been a pattern evident since the first stirrings of the black awakening, when SNCC proposed the slogan "Black Power." Rather than join in the process of discussions in the black national community, the NAACP chose to hold itself aloof and to isolate those leading the black assembly by calling them separatists, extremists, and revolutionaries aiming to withdraw from the political process. Since most of the Gary delegates had been searching for new ways to achieve meaningful black equality, they resented that NAACP posture.

Considering the unprecedented number of black delegates at the 1972 Democratic National Convention in Miami, including the formidable number of Gary convention delegates who became delegates to the Miami Convention, the NAACP charge was misleading; rather than leading to a "withdrawal from the American political process," Gary led instead to a new intensity of struggle for black equality and proportional representation within the American political arena. Ironically, after the Gary convention, Imamu Baraka and CAP found themselves increasingly in situations in which they were defending the equal rights of the black community against white segregationist forces.

Understanding the paradoxes that arose during that transitional period is key to developing an appreciation of the fabric of the new political culture unfolding in the Modern Black Convention Movement, a culture that interwove the concerns for self-determination with those for equality, autonomy with proportional representation, and social rehabilitation with cultural revolution. Thus, the division between black nationalists and civil rights advocates must be applied with greater caution during that period; the distinctions drawn from the early 1960s were problematic for 1972; and for historical analysis today, they simply will not do. In other words, the lines between forces in the freedom movement of the 1970s were increasingly more complex. While battles between integrationists and nationalists were beginning to wilt, another battle was budding. The struggle that was coming to the forefront at Gary was nominally between grassroots community leaders and black elected officials. Specifically, a line emerged between, on the one hand, rising black leaders, accountable to the group politics of the black community, and on the other hand, black public figures and professional politicians, retreating to the habitual politics of individualism, brokerage, and clientage.

In contrast to the Modern Black Convention Movement's search for a Black Agenda rooted in the politics of proportional representation, both broker and patron-client politics were based on the premise of a handful of blacks shaping either "personalized links with influential whites" or small group links with powerful white factions. In both cases, such blacks became the agents of these white power interests within the black political arena for purposes as varied as those powerful concerns.[78] Later, as black people attempted to implement the independent agenda developed at Gary, they realized that these black political brokers and clients increasingly represented a Trojan horse inside the walls of the insurgent black convention movement.

A National Political Community

The Gary convention opened on Friday, March 10, 1972, under the leadership of three co-conveners: Imamu Baraka of CAP, Mayor Hatcher of Gary, and U.S. Rep. Diggs of the Congressional Black Caucus. Thousands of black people arrived at Gary's West Side High School that weekend to hear a list of speakers that included Bobby Seale, chairman of the Black Panther Party; Minister Louis Farrakhan of the Nation of Islam; U.S. Rep. Walter Fauntroy; and Rev. Jesse Jackson.[79] Looking at the workings of the Gary convention, Ronald Walters observed:

> Baraka is not only a man, he is himself a movement with an effective organization. His people are simple in taste, elegant in their black dress, yet dedicated and hard working; in a real sense they held together the

staff work of the Convention in places where committees need skills and long hours of devotion to tasks.[80]

The Congress of African People had built a strong national organization since its founding in 1970; assembling its cadre from across the nation, the cultural nationalists were able to function as the backbone of the Gary convention.

By Friday night, delegates were packed into Gary's hotels, assembled by states so they could caucus around their floor tactics and state resolutions. Still, delegates met people from other states and regions at the convention, exchanged information and experiences, and found that what they had thought were local issues of schools, housing, social welfare, and health care were actually the national issues of modern Black America. Most delegates were excited to meet each other for the first time and to begin to feel their collective strength as they created a national movement and the sense of a national political culture.[81]

When the delegates reached Gary, the air was electric. Ben Chavis recalled "a sense of pride, just to be there. To know that we'd made it out of those local struggles around the country to come into this convention to express the aspirations of the people we left back home."[82] A *New York Times* reporter interviewing the delegates captured some of that mood; he found "enthusiasm and a near-universal anxiousness to maintain a 'network' or a 'conduit' aimed at keeping the geographically and philosophically diverse black communities in contact with one another."[83]

Some delegates spoke of the Gary convention in historic terms, evoking meaning for black people that dated back to the enslavement of Africans. Representing the United Citizens Party of South Carolina, attorney John Roy Harper, the party's founder, called the convention "the most significant event to happen to black people since 1619, when our ancestors were first brought to the colonies as slaves."[84]

For many, the development of a national, autonomous, political community was a key step in any real development of a new black politics. One black Republican state legislator, Michael K. Ross of Washington state, emphasized that "the importance to us . . . is that we have a conduit to plug into to keep up with the national political thought of black people." And Barbara Jordan, the influential Democratic Texas state senator, explained that building a black political community was also an important advance on the state level. "The ongoing structure," Jordan said, "will give blacks in Texas this vehicle for communicating with others." Thus, these concerns were not partisan; both black Republicans and Democrats agreed that the development of an autonomous and structured African American political community was essential.[85]

The beginning of such a political community was assembled in Gary that weekend. In line with the national convention's theme, "Unity without uniformity," the delegates represented much of the breadth of the Black Revolt. Mayor Hatcher recalled that the diversity and intensity of that assembly was striking and electric:

> The colorful dashikis and other African garb that some of them wore, mixing with three-piece suits and so forth. It was just an incredible sight to behold. There was this wonderful sense that we had truly come together as a people, and a warm feeling of brotherhood and sisterhood that I'm not sure we've been able to duplicate since. But it was certainly there, and there was a kind of electricity in the air, and it was clear that people were there about very serious business, and really saw this as a meeting that would have a long-term, long-range impact on the lives of Black Americans.[86]

Similarly, the *New York Times* observed:

> The diversity of attitudes at the convention was reflected in the wide variations in the appearance of the delegates. Some wore Afro hair styles, beards and multicolored scarves. Others had short hair and wore business suits. But the leaders were confident that the sessions would achieve their goal—defined by Imamu Amiri Baraka, the playwright formerly known as LeRoi Jones, as "the unification of the black people."[87]

That diversity was not limited to the Republican and Democratic state representatives already mentioned; it embraced black Democrats and Republicans at the national level. In addition to Democratic U.S. Representatives John Conyers, Ronald Dellums, and Charles Diggs, at least two prominent black Republican members in the Nixon administration attended the Gary convention: Robert Brown and Samuel C. Jackson. In his comments to the press, Brown, a Nixon aide, toyed with the notion that an autonomous black vote might be used to the Republicans' advantage. He told news media that it did not appear that blacks "would put all their eggs in one basket [the Democratic party] this year." When asked why, he replied, "They're too smart." But Brown was not the most prominent Republican at the convention; the highest ranking black official in the Nixon administration, general assistant secretary of Housing and Urban Development Samuel C. Jackson, served as a platform committee chairman of the Gary convention. When the press reached him, Jackson boasted, "There are black Republicans on each committee."

Thus, the unification and mobilization of the national black community had immediate political implications, which were cast in a more independent light by U.S. Rep. Charles Diggs as he commented on the new interest in black politics by the white power structures:

> I don't think there is any question about the recognition of this convention. The major political forces and personalities have already provided ample evidence that from the White House to various statehouses and courthouses around the country they are fully cognizant of the implications of this movement, are nervous about it and obviously see this as a new criteria for approval in the political arena.[88]

Clearly that weekend Congressman Diggs lacked no enthusiasm for the Modern Black Convention Movement. As a founder of the Congressional Black Caucus and one of the three co-conveners of the Gary summit, Diggs was selected to chair the crucial general sessions on Saturday, the first day of the National Black Political Convention. However, a major problem developed with Diggs as the leader because he was acquainted with neither the grassroots language of that new political culture nor its insurgent sense of order. The Black Revolt had generated its own leadership, a new generation that had emerged out of the streetfighting and community struggles of urban Black America; those militants spoke the rebellious idiom and understood the grassroots sense of decorum in the mass conventions.

With Diggs at the helm, the situation became tense that Saturday, as the number of black people attending the assembly soared from the 4,000 counted early Friday to estimates ranging from 10,000 to 12,000 on Saturday. Anyone facing that massive gathering would have had difficulty maintaining order, but during those hectic Saturday plenary sessions Diggs added to the obvious difficulties of the new assemblage by infuriating leader after leader, state by state, with his style of leadership.

One problem was that Diggs attempted to apply Robert's Rules of Order in a heavy-handed fashion, inappropriate to the grassroots dynamics of the Modern Black Convention Movement. On the surface, people were angered whenever Diggs rather abruptly cut off their elected state leaders, who were struggling to formulate their presentations and floor motions. At one point, Diggs misread a voice vote at the end of a long discussion, and the mood of the assembly turned ugly. The deeper problem, however, was that Diggs could sense only anarchy looking at that huge assembly and that he failed to give community, municipal, county, and state leadership due respect. The heart of the unity built in the mobilization for Gary was mutual consideration.

By the end of the Saturday general sessions, a number of states were threatening to leave Gary before the critical Sunday plenary. If delegates had left en masse before the Sunday session at which they established a new organization, a national black assembly that weekend would be known as the nadir rather than the zenith of black nationalism. Fortunately, the burning issue of a black political party, raised by Mayor Hatcher and Rev. Jesse Jackson on Saturday night, held most people's attention for the evening.

A Black Political Party?

By Saturday night the attendance at the convention reached its high point, and every speaker was emboldened by that huge national black assembly. Mayor Hatcher recalled,

> That morning I still had some concern that not very many people would show up. Well, the truly wonderful thing was when I got to the hall, and came from behind the stage and out onto the platform, I saw a veritable sea of faces. It was probably one of the most glorious moments of my life when I walked out and saw all these black people of every color, every hue, every shade.[89]

The vitality of that unprecedented grassroots mobilization had charged the atmosphere, and no leader would openly defend the broker and client politics that transformed black leaders into tokens in the "hip pocket" of either the Republican or the Democratic Party. The evening program included such legendary leaders as Bobby Seale, a founder of the Black Panther Party. Seale was warmly received, and many were glad that he had survived the police repression that had slaughtered some of the best leaders of that generation; the murder of Fred Hampton by the Chicago police was in the forefront of everyone's mind. But the controversy that evening was not generated by the Black Panther Party but rather by the burning questions raised by Rev. Jackson and Mayor Hatcher.

In light of Hatcher's struggles for equality inside the National Democratic Party, the militant tone in his keynote address was not surprising. Hatcher had argued for black equality using the principle of proportional representation inside the party: if blacks were 20 percent of the national Democratic vote in 1968, then they deserved 20 percent of the delegates to the national convention and of its resources in 1972. Because of the pressures applied to the Democratic Party by a new generation of maverick black Democrats, the party conceded to increase the number of black delegates at its 1972 National Convention in Miami and to select Yvonne Braithwaite Burke as the convention's co-chair.[90] Thus, Hatcher symbolized the political vitality and black pride of his generation of maverick elected officials.

But Hatcher also voiced the frustrations of progressive black elected officials, who were trying to change the conditions in America's major cities during the nation's worst urban crisis and receiving very little help from national leaders during the Nixon years. The black assembly roared during Hatcher's keynote address when he thundered: "We demand the eradication of heroin from the ghetto, now eating away the vitals of Black youth. Black people know that white society would never tolerate it in such epidemic proportions in suburbia."[91]

He also received unanimous applause when he declared,

This convention signals the end of hip-pocket politics. We ain't in nobody's hip pocket no more. We say to the two American political parties this is their last chance. They have had too many already. These are not idle threats. Only senile fools would think so. The choice is theirs. . . . I, for one, am willing to give the two major political parties one more chance in the year 1972. But if they fail us, a not unlikely prospect, we must then seriously probe the possibility of a third party movement in this country.[92]

However, the black assembly was cool to Hatcher's suggestion of an alliance that included white people. After centuries of hostility, conflict, manipulation, and betrayal, many black people were suspicious of white allies. Thus, there was great anticipation as Hatcher explained that a third-party movement would take from the Democrats not only African Americans but other peoples of color—the Chicanos, Puerto Ricans, the Native Americans, the Asian Americans. But the assembly offered Hatcher a chorus of "No's" rejecting his suggestion that "we shall also take with us the best of white America."[93]

Speaking after Mayor Hatcher, Rev. Jesse Jackson sensed the nationalist mood of the assembly on this issue and took the challenge a step further with his remarks on a third-party movement. Since 1970 it had been evident that in some ways Jackson was moving closer to the black nationalist camp. An eyewitness to the vitality and mobilizing power of Baraka's politics of cultural nationalism, Rev. Jackson had been prominently involved both in the Pan-Africanist Atlanta Congress of African People and in the Newark elections, where he allied himself with Baraka and the Committee For A Unified NewArk.[94] By 1971, Jackson had been involved in a number of strategic meetings that looked at the possibility of an independent, black third party.[95]

Rev. Jesse Jackson opened the address with his usual greeting, borrowed from the New Ark, by asking, "What time is it?" and in response the assembly thundered, "It's Nation Time!" In retrospect Jesse Jackson recalled,

> I had drawn much of the strength of Nationtime from a poem written by LeRoi Jones, Amiri Baraka at that time. The sense of people saying, "What's happening?" . . . Say, . . . "It's Nationtime, it's time to come together. It's time to organize politically. . . . It's time for blacks to enter into the equation, it is indeed, whether you're in California or Mississippi, it is Nationtime."[96]

That Saturday night in Gary, Jackson electrified the assemblage when he declared, "We must form a black political party."[97] "Nationhood is the politics of multiple options," he argued, "One of those options must be a black political party."[98] He explained, "Without the option of a black political party, we are doomed to remain in the hip pocket of the Democratic party and in the rumble seat of the Republican party."[99]

The difference between the stands taken by Mayor Hatcher and Rev. Jackson toward the Democratic Party heated up the debate on the floor of the Gary convention, and it also drew a great deal of media attention. The media reported that this encounter between Jackson and Hatcher was the main threat to unity at the convention. No doubt, the speeches did generate a great deal of controversy. But that evening Jackson played down the differences that emerged; and within weeks Jackson endorsed George McGovern as the Democratic candidate for president of the United States.

However, the real threat to the unity and success of the assembly went undetected by the media. That was the immediate threat that delegates, insulted by Congressman Diggs at the plenary session, would leave en masse for home and boycott the decisive Sunday sessions. For the Congress of African People, that prospect spelled disaster; without an organizational structure, legitimized by the political convention, no new mass movement would be initiated.

Congress of African People leaders spent all night building a working agenda in the state caucuses. They were making necessary assurances to each state that its most important agenda items would be heard in the limited time that was left on Sunday. Alabama was the most hectic caucus that Baraka approached. At one point during the negotiations with the Alabama caucus, in a provocative move, John Cashin accused Baraka of being an "agent" for the Republican Party; understandably, Baraka was livid.[100] Nevertheless, by working at it all night, CAP found enough common ground for solutions to most of the procedural difficulties that had frustrated Saturday's plenary session. The next day, the media, unaware of that unrelenting work, would focus exclusively on the forcefulness of Baraka's *personality*.

Imamu Baraka, Grassroots Parliamentarian

Early Sunday morning CAP leaders met with more than twenty nationally known political figures in special sessions to further refine the day's procedures, so that they could air the pressing issues brought by state caucuses from various regions of the nation. Imamu Amiri Baraka was the chairman of Sunday's often tumultuous plenary session. Without the benefit of a night's sleep, at first he stood there slumping over the podium, short and thin with slightly stooped shoulders, looking incredibly tired. Major political leaders had failed to calm that sea of humanity, and now they passed the baton on to a prophetic poet to move the agenda. Because of the mistakes on Saturday, a two-day agenda of work had to be packed into one.

But as the rhythm of the sessions began, and it seemed that the evening's work had paid off, Baraka came to life in the role of parliamentarian. With a new surge of energy from the massive assembly of black people, he sped up the proceedings by keeping controversies within the state caucuses rather than on the general floor, which would have tied up the flow of the plenary sessions.

Reporters who had not covered the development of the Modern Black Convention Movement were not used to Baraka in this role. They were also surprised by the language of the new political culture. The reporters often felt they had to assume the role of translators between black culture and white America. Consider this *New York Times* report:

Mr. Baraka, who was wearing a [Kaunda] suit, spoke often in an impassioned manner and moved easily from the language of the parliamentarian to that of the urban slums. He often delighted his listeners, especially during tense periods, with colloquialisms. . . . At one point he found it difficult to end a five-minute recess. He told the group, "Hey y'all, come on—that's a long five minutes, even for bloods." Bloods is often used as a synonym for blacks among black people.[101]

Generally, the media noted that Baraka had emerged as the leader of this insurgent black united front. The *New York Times* reported:

Many here believe that Mr. Baraka's handling of himself and the convention could project him as the new black folk hero. His private self came out: he laughed and joked at news conferences and while chairing the meeting. He dropped the stern, serious expression that most Americans associate with him. He seemed relaxed and worked tirelessly with blacks of political persuasions ranging from the National Association for the Advancement of Colored People to the ultra-nationalist.[102]

However, those involved in the Modern Black Convention Movement between 1968 and 1972 were not surprised by Baraka's leadership at the Gary convention. Both nationalists and civil rights figures recognized Baraka in this role. Florence Tate, a black nationalist from Washington, remarked, "This isn't a new Imamu Baraka. It is just another stage of his development. From LeRoi in the Village and Harlem, to the name change and to Newark, he is merely catching black people where they are rather than imposing his ideology." Her analysis of Baraka's tactics was perceptive. She said, "I don't think, as some other nationalists do, that he has compromised himself. He is moving to help black people to get into the system so they can realize that once they get in they will see that it is no good for them."[103]

In contrast to the perceptions of the national office of the NAACP, which condemned the Gary convention beforehand, many civil rights figures praised Baraka's politics of cultural nationalism. According to Rev. Albert Sampson of Chicago, a former aide to Rev. Dr. Martin Luther King Jr., "Ever since he gave up trying to explain black problems to whites through his activities and writings, and turned to a black nationalist approach, Mr. Baraka has been consistently for black unity through the system."[104] For the most part Imamu Baraka was not seen as a tyrant. Rev. Sampson explained, "What white America doesn't understand is that Imamu does not want to control anyone. . . . He is like Shakespeare, he wants to write the scenario; but he is not interested in acting in the play, he wants to move on."[105]

Baraka's leadership at Gary was part of the assembly's statement of unprecedented unity. A number of civil rights leaders, including Coretta Scott King, raised their clenched fists in a Black Power salute during the

Black National Anthem and joined the assembly as it roared, "It's Nation Time!"

Although Coretta Scott King had met Betty Shabazz, the widow of Malcolm X, before the Gary convention, she recalled that they had never before spent as much time together as they did there. "I think the fact that we were there together, at least presented some semblance of unity. I think that sent a message to . . . the American people—black people and white people alike. . . . I think it was a very forward step to bring the black community and black leadership together in a kind of family relationship. . . . I don't think we've attempted anything since then of that magnitude."[106] Betty Shabazz was pleased "that the organizers had the correct sensibility to have the conference" and felt that it was "a good thing when people come together and discuss their own agenda." Although some critics thought that the Gary convention failed because it did not establish a third political party, Shabazz spoke for many when she said, "No. It didn't fail. Because people came together and crystallized their thinking."[107]

On Sunday, Baraka convinced the convention to accept a proposal to create an ongoing structure, naming fifty state chairs plus a chair from the District of Columbia as a steering committee to see that the plans growing out of the convention were implemented. Within weeks, the steering committee fashioned a new national organization, the National Black Political Assembly, which most members shortened to the National Black Assembly (NBA).

The National Black Assembly generated a "National Black Agenda," a 55-page document that changed the political discourse for the black community on a number of local, regional, and national concerns. Changing that discourse constituted a major breach in the hegemony of the two-party system over black politics. Knowing the history of political candidates' taking black votes for granted, the NBA aimed for accountability. Thus, the agenda contained model pledges that black communities across the nation would use in the political arena, seeking to make the elected officials accountable to the black community. Hence, the commitment for black candidates required a candidate seeking the approval of the Modern Black Convention Movement to make the following pledge:

> As I campaign, and if I am elected, I will conduct the daily affairs and decision making of my activity, and/or office, so as to reflect the actual, explicit desires and concerns of the Black Community beyond question. In this manner I will constantly act out my accountability to the manifest interests of the Black Community, as revealed, at present,

through the National Black Political Convention and whatever instrument(s) this Convention will establish as a means of follow-through.[108]

Newsweek voiced surprise that the National Black Assembly was approved "with little debate," especially since its members aimed to become the "chief brokerage operation for dealing with the white-power political institutions."[109]

The national concerns in the agenda were divided into these seven basic areas: economics, human development, communications, rural development, environmental protection, political empowerment, and international policy.

First, the black agenda insisted that "the economic impoverishment of the Black community in America is clearly traceable to the historic enslavement of our people and to the racist discrimination to which we have been subjected since 'emancipation.' Indeed, much of the unprecedented economic wealth and power of American capitalism has obviously been built upon this exploitation of Black people." At Gary, the delegates called for a number of reform measures, such as reparations in the form of land, capital, and cash; the establishment of a Black United Fund; the institution of a "Buy Black" campaign, combined with a national black consumer protection commission; where there were racist unions, the founding of parallel black unions; the application of pressure on white churches, corporations, and institutions to make meaningful investments in black communities; and the "exploration of alternative forms of economic organization and development of a system that promotes self-reliance, cooperative economics, and people ownership and control of [the] means of production and distribution of goods." The agenda emphasized that there would be no full economic development for blacks "without radical transformation of the economic system which has so clearly exploited us these many years."[110]

It argued, second, that "in every phase of our history in America, the Human Development of the Black community has been seriously impeded" and that the black community "did not control the instruments and institutions of [its] social, cultural and educational development." The summit proclaimed, "We have been—and are now—a *colony*, living in the midst of a society committed to values other than the development of the human spirit."[111]

Third, the workshops had given communications a great deal of consideration. The agenda spoke of the crucial role of black-controlled media:

From the beginning, those who enslaved us understood that by controlling communications they could control our minds. Over the years, as the white communications forces continued to tell the world lies about us, the Black newspaper became our primary agent of communications. From its inception in 1827, it kept us informed about ourselves, because we owned it.

With such concerns in mind, the assembly was determined to struggle for the control of "television and radio outlets." "Of the approximately 355 Black-programmed radio stations in America," the agenda noted, "345 are owned by whites, some of whom have become millionaires through the exploitation of the Black public. At this stage, there are no Black-owned television stations in the country." However, the agenda aimed to make sure that "no cable television comes into our communities unless we control it."[112]

Fourth, the agenda discussed the historic problems of the South. "Rural Blacks have historically been subjected to the lash of Southern oppression and terror. We live under a political and economic system which limits rights of political and economic participation, and circumscribes our capacity for growth and development." It protested that "Government policy and practice [have] historically sought to repress our self-determination, manage and control our rate of progress, and often deny our very existence. *Our material environment is characterized by the worst the American social system has to offer*" [my emphasis]. Similar to the powerless urban ghettos, black rural communities observed:

> Our housing is poor and structurally unsound and we control none of the housing production process. We are mainly tenants rather than owners. Even the land we toiled for centuries has seldom been ours to own, control, or pass on to our heirs. Health services, when they are available, are of low quality, high cost and outside the control of our communities.[113]

Fifth, the agenda set the pace for the issues of environmental racism:

> The critical impact of the environmental pollutants—noise, air, solid waste, sewage, rodents and pests, and lead poisoning—on Black inner-city residents has not yet been fully recognized. So far, the major thrust of the ecology movement has been directed toward environmental issues that do not adequately protect the health and life of Black urban dwellers.

The agenda insisted that the environmental logic for black people was the following: "The major consequence of the present policies and practices of industrial plants, slumlords, and governmental agencies is [that] the powerful pollute, while the powerless suffer the atrocities of the pollution."[114]

Sixth, the foreign policy of the United States was key to the concerns of the Gary agenda on "International Policy and Black People." The black assembly stated its global interests this way:

Because the history and culture of Black people is fundamentally related to our African birthright, we are concerned about the movement of colonized African countries from subjugation to independence and from neo-colonized states to fully independent ones.

While it attacked Western imperialism, headed by the U.S., for its policies on the African continent in Azania [South Africa], Zimbabwe, Namibia, Angola, Mozambique, and Guinea-Bissau, the summit also criticized it "in Vietnam, the Middle East, the Caribbean and other places in the Third and Pan-African World."[115]

Seventh, the agenda pointed out that none of these areas of concern could be changed without organization, mobilization, and political power. Taking an historical perspective, it declared, "The bondage of Black people in America has been sanctioned and perpetuated by the American political system—for the American political system is one of politics dedicated to the preservation of white power." Thus, for the Black Agenda, "The plight of Black people is the result of the workings of the American system. Our political agenda then must transcend this system; it must speak boldly and without reservation to the problems of Black people in the '70s." The agenda urged that "the National Black Political Convention should create a structure to be called the National Black Assembly and an election process to that body to continue permanently after the National Black Political Convention." It called for the National Black Assembly "to organize and mobilize . . . a community-based movement toward amassing the needed resources and power to achieve full Black empowerment"; to "study reapportionment and redistricting and develop and implement strategies for striking down gerrymandering by whites designed to destroy Black political power."[116]

Finally, the agenda also addressed the specific problem of the political status of the District of Columbia:

The nearly 800,000 residents of our Nation's Capital have that dual distinction of being the only citizens of our nation who are by law denied the right to self-government (the last colony) and the only major city in this country with a 72 per cent Black population. These two facts are not unrelated.[117]

Although historians have barely acknowledged the Modern Black Convention Movement, the Gary convention generated a great deal of press coverage and controversy. The black press was not only sympathetic but actually identified with the efforts of the Gary convention, and its coverage of the dynamics before and after that huge assembly was considerable. In a March 18, 1972, editorial titled "The experiment in Gary," the *Amsterdam News* gave an especially insightful assessment of the National Black Political Convention and its prospects. It stated that the Gary convention "must be viewed as an experiment, a test and a trial—20th Century Blacks wrestling with the difficult questions of power, unity and co-operation." The editorial was ambivalent about the results of that experiment in Gary, stating that it was an important first step, revealing both the worst and the best of black politics. "At the worst, there was a viciousness, division, and jealousy; rhetoric rather than hard-working reality; confusion, disorganization and poor planning; a massive distrust represented by the failure to unite behind a single candidate or a unified national platform." On the other hand, it pointed out, "it was certainly the most representative national convention or conference ever held by Black Americans." Moreover, said the editor, "For the first time in more than 50 years, Black people from across the nation gathered together in Gary to deal with the most basic survival issues in these most oppressive times in modern history." Thus, much of the turmoil at the plenary sessions reflected the fact that "every possible viewpoint, every possible ideology, every possible category of Black American was represented."[118]

"This accounted not only for the widely varied opinions, the rancor and the divisiveness; but also for the richness and the warmth that somehow managed to cloak the convention," the editorial continued. "It was Black people trying to get it together, with all of our weakness and all of our strengths out front." In terms of those strengths, the editorial offered this summary assessment:

At the best, there was a general sense of commitment to the eventual betterment of the condition of Black Americans; highly emotional responses to Rev. Jesse Jackson and Gary Mayor Richard Hatcher; a great deal of real productivity within a 24-hour period; and the beginnings of political power movements that will have local implications in New York and elsewhere for years to come.

The editor concluded ominously, saying, "The Gary Convention was a beginning, we say, a soulful new beginning as we modern Blacks begin to seriously wrestle with crucial political issues in our own way, attempting to get ourselves together before our time runs out."[119]

Imamu Baraka and the Modern Black Convention Movement

These developments between 1970 and 1974 consolidated the standing of Baraka as a pivotal leader of the black national community. His climb to that rank was tied directly to the flowering of the Modern Black Convention Movement. So dramatic was his rise in the black national political arena that the *New York Times* could not fail to notice that "most convention officials acknowledged that . . . the 38-year-old Newark native's influence predominated during the convention" and that "no one else had the organization or the strength that he had."[120] In the same vein, Vincent Harding noted Baraka's "tough-minded and powerful presence, based in a highly disciplined, Newark-based black nationalist organization, was the central force in the convention's leadership."[121]

While for Harding the National Black Political Convention embodied the "watershed" between the Black Revolt of the 1960s and the political movement of the 1970s, for Manning Marable "Gary represented, in retrospect, the zenith not only of black nationalism, but of the entire black movement during the Second Reconstruction."[122] Certainly, the Gary convention was an unprecedented gathering of black people that surpassed all other indigenous efforts in the Black Convention Movement, particularly on the critical issue of fusion. Most of the earlier summit meetings were simply elite gatherings that failed to establish any connection with the masses of black people.[123] The Modern Black Convention Movement was a radical departure in this regard, representing the grassroots ethos of the Black Power movement. Even the important Negro Sanhedrin of the 1920s did not reflect such a degree of fusion between the leadership and the grass roots; thus, the Gary convention and the founding of the National Black Assembly were historic events.

The National Black Assembly elected U.S. Rep. Charles Diggs as its president, Mayor Richard Hatcher its chairman, and Imamu Amiri Baraka its secretary-general. Clearly, the Gary convention and the National Black Agenda reflected bold strokes; they represented black nationality formation unfolding at the center of the African American political arena. In the next chapter, we examine what happened when the leadership of this movement attempted to carry out the will of the National Black Assembly.

CHAPTER 6

Hard Facts

Kawaida Towers and the Dilemma of Cultural Nationalism in Black America

We had all been in the rain together until yesterday. Then a handful of us—the smart and the lucky and hardly ever the best—had scrambled for the one shelter our former rulers left, and had taken it over and barricaded themselves in. And from within they sought to persuade the rest through numerous loudspeakers, that the first phase of the struggle had been won and that the next phase—the extension of our house—was even more important and called for new and original tactics; it required that all argument should cease and the whole people speak with one voice and that any more dissent and argument outside the door of the shelter would subvert and bring down the whole house.

—Chinua Achebe, *A Man of the People*

Social movements ultimately fail, at least in [the] minds of many committed participants. As radicals and revolutionaries have discovered throughout history, even the most successful movements generate aspirations that cannot be fulfilled.

—Clayborne Carson, "Civil Rights Reform and the Black Freedom Struggle"

San Diego General Assembly

By the Second International Assembly of the Congress of African People in San Diego on Labor Day 1972, CAP was the most formidable black nationalist organization in the country. Its branches were spreading in various regions of the country, and in the process CAP had been instrumental in developing several new national organizations: the National Black Assembly, the African Liberation Support Committee, and the Black Women's United Front. At the center of all these developments was CAP's national program office in Newark and its leader, Imamu Baraka.

After two years of service, the terms had expired for CAP's first national officers: Heyward Henry, chair; Mjenzi Kazana (Richard Traylor of Philadelphia), finance; Roosevelt Brown, program; and Sonny Carson, public relations. As a result of the San Diego summit, the national leadership was reorganized along the lines of an executive committee (EXCO) and ministries. The EXCO consisted of three at-large positions, some regional coordinators, and eight work council leaders. While Heyward Henry, Frank Satterwhite, and Bill Land held the at-large executive positions, Jitu Weusi of "The East" in Brooklyn, Haki Madhubuti of the Institute for Positive Education in Chicago, and Imamu Sukumu of NIA (Swahili for "purpose") in San Diego, led the northeastern, midwestern, and western regions, respectively. At the same time, the leadership and its work councils took the initiative in CAP's major areas of concern: Jitu Weusi led Education (Elimu); Charles Poppy Sharp, Economics (Uchumi); Imamu Sukumu, Community Organizing (Jamii); Balozi Zayd Muhammad, International Affairs; Mjenzi Kazana, Finance; Haki Madhubuti, Communications (Habari); Imamu Amiri Baraka, Politics (Siasa); and the first woman on the EXCO, Bibi Amina Baraka, Social Organization (Jamaa).

In the election of the second national chair, Imamu Baraka's leadership in the mobilization for the National Black Political Assembly and for African Liberation Day was a major consideration. Furthermore, Baraka led in the development of a number of institutional "prototypes" that would serve as models for other branches of CAP. Many leaders of the new branches were trained in Newark at the Political School of Kawaida. Consequently, at the second general assembly of the Congress of African People, with black nationalism at its zenith, Baraka was elected its national chairman. As the chair, Baraka began fashioning the loose federation structure into a new national vanguard organization, drawing from his own reading of the experience of CFUN as well as those of African liberation movements.

In the early 1970s, the Congress of African People was at the summit of its hegemony in the Black Revolt. It all rested on the foundation of a unique political alignment forged by the Modern Black Convention Movement, embracing the Black Arts Movement, the Black Power movement, black nationalists, Pan-Africanists, and even sections of the black radicals to its Left and black moderates to its Right. Baraka's NewArk was much more than a simple geographic designation; it represented an urban vision and a shared covenant among diverse sections of the black community.[1] While the mainstay of CAP's mass support was its leadership in the Modern Black Convention Movement, its ideological and spiritual main-

Imamu Amiri Baraka (left) and Hoyt Fuller, founder and editor of the pivotal
journal *Black World*, around the time of the Sixth Pan-African Congress in 1974.
(Courtesy of the Baraka family collection, photograph by Zachariah Risasi Dais)

stay was its faith in the power of black consciousness. When that vision
was shattered and that social covenant abandoned, the foundation for the
Modern Black Convention Movement as a black united front no longer
existed. Faith in the black *will* for self determination was at the heart of the
politics of black cultural nationalism and its Black Power experiments dur-

ing the 1960s and 1970s. In his major manifesto of that period, *A Black Value System*, Baraka argues:

> In order to free ourselves, and this may come as a shock to many "hip negroes," we are going to have to do it ourselves! For ourselves. . . . If you cannot have faith in *blackness*, in the black mind and the black man to find a way out of this slavery, you are full of despair, or else emotionally committed to white people.[2]

Describing the nature of that faith, Baraka insists that, "*Imani* is faith— Faith in your leaders, teachers, parents,—but first faith in blackness—that it will win."

> Simple faith, like church people say and that's what we want—hardrock emotional faith in what we're doing. The same way your grandmamma used to weep and wring her hands believing in Jeez-us, that deep deep connection with the purest energy, that is what the Nationalist must have. Can you understand this? . . . That we must believe in Nationalism. We must believe in the justness of our struggle and the certainty of our victory. *No matter how long this might take.* There is no time. Only change.[3]

By 1974, however, those political circumstances had changed quite dramatically; that vision was shattered and CAP's faith in its own experience was profoundly shaken. The crisis began as the Newark black community was expanding beyond the traditional ghetto boundaries of the Central and South Wards; this disturbed elements in the local white power structure, and white leaders in the North Ward mobilized their community into a series of violent attacks on African Americans. As the situation deteriorated, this racial violence spread to the white neighborhoods of Vailsburg and Irvington; Vailsburg was a white enclave of Newark's West Ward, and Irvington was the white suburb directly adjacent to Vailsburg. In 1973, there was a strong white backlash to the entrance of a few black students to the Vailsburg and Irvington high schools. These racial conflicts sent the high schools in both Newark and Irvington into a state of crisis. White students attacked black students at both Irvington and Vailsburg high schools, and then at Barringer High School in the predominately white North Ward of Newark. Near Barringer in the North Ward, another blast that fueled this crisis was the violence that exploded as white mobs began to beat the black construction workers building Imamu Baraka's sixteen-story apartment complex, Kawaida Towers.

Even before that worsening crisis, Mayor Gibson began a containment policy to confine the Modern Black Convention Movement's expanding political power; Newark's 1971 antipoverty election was the first open test of strength between forces within the convention movement. After a year of experience with the city's first black mayor, a number of vocal grass-roots organizations and churches in the convention movement became increasingly anxious for Baraka to openly confront and criticize Gibson for his lack of struggle against the old guard and white racism; they demanded that Baraka take leadership. When the black convention forces ran Baraka's popular lieutenant, Kaimu Mtetezi (David Barrett), for the presidency of Newark's antipoverty agency, the United Community Corporation (UCC), Mayor Gibson secretly established a bipartisan alliance, including both remnants of Addonizio's political machine as well as former members of the United Brothers. Both Gibson and Eulius "Honey" Ward, who had been founding members of the United Brothers, sought to contain the popular power unleashed by Baraka's conventions. They allied themselves with Larrie Stalks, who, along with her defeated and convicted brother Calvin West, was a member of the Addonizio machine; Stalks represented a wing of the old guard political machine that still had a base in the Essex County Democratic Party. Mayor Gibson had run his 1970 campaign on the pledge that he was a reformer who would clean out the corrupt machine forces from the political arena. However, if Gibson was to defeat Baraka and undermine the legitimacy of the Modern Black Convention Movement, he had to rely on forces outside of the community and to portray Baraka as a racial extremist beyond the bounds of reason.

The *New York Times* explained the grounds for Mayor Gibson's new political alliance:

> They reportedly argued that by opposing Mr. [Baraka] the Mayor would be given new access to the minority white voters in the 1974 election with the position that he, as a moderate black mayor, was the only one who could prevent a complete take-over by black militants bent on driving the remaining whites out of the city.[4]

In that first major test of strength, Baraka's forces crushed Gibson's slate in the 1971 election. Kaimu Mtetezi was elected president of the UCC, defeating the Gibson slate by a 2:1 margin. Furthermore, after the Gary convention in 1972, CAP fashioned a new congressional district in Essex County and united the black community behind East Orange mayor William Hart's unsuccessful bid for a seat in the U.S. Congress. Clearly, Baraka's political strength was not shrinking; it was expanding.

However, in the midst of the Kawaida Towers racial crisis, the containment strategy against Baraka and the Modern Black Convention Movement was much more effective. If legal democratic elections failed to defeat Baraka, then extralegal violence and betrayal would be used to devastate him. It was precisely during this worsening crisis that Mayor Gibson and other key black officials that CAP had helped elect and appoint abandoned the black community to the tender mercies of the white vigilantes. Not only did they refuse to defend the black community during this period of racial turmoil, but powerful black elected officials also attacked the very legitimacy of the Modern Black Convention Movement. Ultimately, when black city councilmen emerged as allies of white agents of repression—destroying the urban vision of a New Ark—CAP's confidence in its own nationalist strategy was shattered. Experiencing a profound crisis in faith, Imamu Baraka and the Congress of African People began to consider the theories of socialism more seriously, and at the end of that process they embraced Marxism. These developments and that ideological transformation are the subject of this chapter. Ironically, these tragic events began when Imamu Baraka and the Congress of African People were at the pinnacle of their success. The dynamics of black cultural nationalism had never been stronger than in 1972.

An Urban Vision: The New Ark

Imamu Baraka's emphases on institutional development and on transforming the ghetto into a "New Ark" were more than just poetic and rhetorical. The vision of the New Ark was sustained in part by Newark CAP's plans for housing and economic development. In 1970 some of CAP's community organizers helped to mobilize a large Central Ward neighborhood to challenge the Newark Housing Authority's plan to build more high-rise public housing; the government designated that area urban renewal site NJR-32. Working with CAP, that Central Ward community decided to establish a Project Area Committee by applying HUD provisions that stipulated that such neighborhoods had the right to a voice in the urban renewal process. This community decided that a voice, without a hand in the planning of the new community, meant very little. Thus, it incorporated the NJR-32 Project Area Committee (PAC), presented a proposal to the Newark Housing Authority (NHA) and HUD, and demanded the establishment of a site office to redesign the development of the nearly 100-acre neighborhood.

The community organizer who led that work was Sultani Mhisani (Harold Wilson), a founding member of the United Brothers. CAP pro-

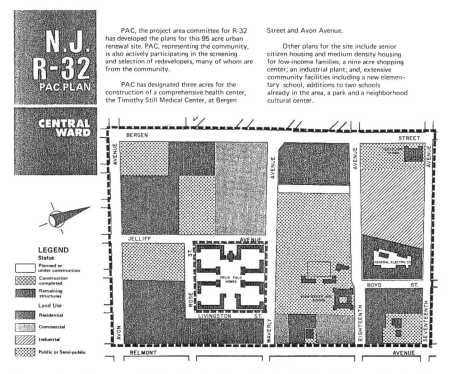

PAC, the project area committee for R-32 has developed the plans for this 95 acre urban renewal site. PAC, representing the community, is also actively participating in the screening and selection of redevelopers, many of whom are from the community.

PAC has designated three acres for the construction of a comprehensive health center, the Timothy Still Medical Center, at Bergen Street and Avon Avenue.

Other plans for the site include senior citizen housing and medium density housing for low-income families; a nine-acre shopping center; an industrial plant; and, extensive community facilities including a new elementary school, additions to two schools already in the area, a park and a neighborhood cultural center.

Alternative urban renewal site plan developed by Amiri Baraka's organization for the redevelopment of Newark's inner city. (Author's collection)

vided extensive resources to that community. Its economic department worked on the proposal for a planning office. Once the PAC office was established, it brought an architect on staff, Earl Coombs (Majenzi Kuumba). Coombs was a young man who had worked with Baraka before, at first in Greenwich Village and then in the Harlem Black Arts. In those earlier days Baraka and Coombs had discussed the development of a neo-traditional or neo-African aesthetic in architecture. By the 1970s, this unique combination of people, circumstances, and aesthetic concerns provided an opportunity for Baraka to flesh out the urban vision of the New Ark.

The New Ark vision concentrated the whole spectrum of Newark CAP's institutional and business development into a plan. In 1972, in its internal documents CAP explained:

> The creation of [PAC] as an institution made many other institutional developments possible. The technical skills of architects and draftsmen committed to the development of African people rather than America and American money, made possible the development of Hekalu

Mwalimu, which houses [the] African Free School, an electronics training program for young Africans, Jihad Publishing Company, African Free School Food Franchise, and Chakula Ujamaa; a new [African Free School] Social Development center being renovated; and, an architectural design of Kawaida Towers, an apartment building which will house some 210 families.[5]

In other words, this institutionalized planning had enabled Newark CAP to design and rehabilitate an abandoned Masonic Temple at 13 Belmont Avenue in the Central Ward near Springfield Avenue. That abandoned building became Hekalu Mwalimu (Swahili for "Temple of the Teacher"), named in honor of President Mwalimu Nyerere of Tanzania, and it served as a community center, housing CAP's programs for education, career training, communications, and youth programs. In addition, Hekalu Mwalimu was the site of CAP's cafeteria for cooperative eating, Chakulu Ujamaa. (Rather than each household cooking daily meals, Newark CAP dined collectively; and each employed adult paid a few dollars each week for the purchase and cooking of the food as well as for the employment of the head cook.)

Furthermore, CAP wrote a proposal to Newark's antipoverty agency, the United Community Corporation (UCC), to operate the City-Wide Youth Communications program in Hekalu Mwalimu. This program taught black and Puerto Rican youth skills in electronic communications by providing career training and hands-on experience in running their own television and radio mini-studio in the community. There the writers, directors, actors, and graphic artists from the Spirit House Movers and Players taught script writing, television direction, acting, and set design to black and Puerto Rican youth in order to drive a wedge into white resistance to the employment of people of color in mass media. Moreover, black freedom movement photographers and filmmakers, including Doug Harris, came to Newark as consultants to teach youth how to film with video equipment. The program trained dozens of youths in the 1970s.

Few documents have survived from this planning experiment, but the following passages provide a revealing glimpse of the New Ark strategy. In a rare CAP manual designed to be instructive for all branches of the national organization, the mission of NJR-32 and its views on the urban renewal process were explained bluntly:

> Traditionally, urban renewal is another arm of white supremacy, where the Black community is uprooted at the whim of white people, so that whites can build institutions to re-establish control of areas which have

grown "too Black." Their dispersal of our communities intends to break up the social organization which exists, potential political power, and to impose development plans which suit the values and interests of white people. Community needs are disregarded traditionally, while even the small gains which our people have made to put ourselves back together, are dissipated.

[PAC] is a broad based popular movement of Africans in the Central Ward of NewArk, revolting against the traditional urban renewal process. It has become the most successful model for community control of land in NewArk and one of the strongest voices in housing in the city. It is a black nationalist alternative to the white supremacist policy of urban renewal.

The popular struggle in our community for control of 100 acres of land in the heart of the city involved everyone from African housewives to African doctors; we were able to organize and rally the mass of people around the question of land, because they were able to see it as directly related to their future. . . . Through constant and dynamic action, we asserted [PAC] as the legal representative of popular will of our people with the power to veto any development in our land which did not meet [PAC] approval."[6]

But, clearly CAP wanted much more than veto power over urban renewal. It insisted that "the power of veto as a community organization is not enough. Our aim is to transform reality so that African people can get the maximum amount of social[,] economic and political self-determination over our lives." In other words, CAP viewed its planning function as one of *social transformation*. One clue to the direction of that planning was Imamu Baraka's admiration of the Tanzanian President Nyerere and his socialist vision of *Ujamaa*, African communalism. Thus, for CAP, the NJR-32 PAC program was the matrix for its urban vision, the New Ark, the first attempt to flesh out what the Black Power experiment could mean for a new community life in a "liberated zone."

Those plans included housing development, particularly low-rise and low-income units with five and six bedrooms for large families, as well as an elderly complex; commercial development of cooperative businesses within a shopping mall; a multipurpose center with family counseling, educational facilities, housing relocation services, and a theater; a park and recreation complex; a hotel for conferences and conventions; and institutional spaces, especially a communications center for a cable television studio, a radio station, and finally, a medical center located next to the elderly housing development.[7] That same internal CAP document explains the key elements of the *Ujamaa* vision:

> The [PAC] plan provides for the development and expansion of Revolutionary Nationalist institutions and the development of a microcosm of the policies of Ujamaa, i.e., the beginning of the control of the means of providing goods and services on these 100 acres, planned economic development and social development around the needs of our community, and popular control of all political processes which affect our lives.[8]

Joining Earl Coombs on the Kawaida community development team were attorney Raymond Brown and housing consultant Alvin Gershen. Brown had served on Gov. Hughes's special panel investigating New Jersey's 1967 civil disorders. Developing a profound respect for Imamu Baraka's creativity and sincerity, Brown did a great deal to help PAC and the other housing development initiatives of the Congress of African People. Brown was also active in the Modern Black Convention Movement, addressing the 1969 Black and Puerto Rican Convention and heading the legal workshop at the founding Congress of CAP in 1970. It was Brown who introduced Baraka to Gershen, one of the best housing consultants in New Jersey.

Gershen was a committed Jewish liberal, with an office on State Street in the state capitol, Trenton. Gershen, Brown, and Baraka began to establish a development team, thinking that it would begin with the NJR-32 urban renewal tract, and then spin off other developments.

While the development of NJR-32 was delayed by the extraordinary red tape at the Newark Housing Authority, Gershen discovered a piece of private property in Newark that was ready for development, a plot of land on the corner of Lincoln Avenue and Delavan Street in the North Ward. If the exact location did not seem important in the beginning, that locus in the predominately Italian American North Ward was crucial as it later became the scene of some of the worst racial confrontations in Newark's recent history.[9] Gershen had been the consultant for the development of Paulus Hook, a 23-story Jersey City apartment building, and he felt that with some modifications those same architectural plans could be used on the Newark site.

Kawaida Towers apartment building was designed with a basement and first-floor plan providing for a 300-seat theater with lighting, projection, and dressing rooms; a lounge, woodshop, hobby shop, day care center, and public kitchen; and rooms for art display, reading, and arts and crafts.[10] For

CAP, it was a minor idea at first, only one building housing about 200 families—while the more serious plans in the Central Ward's NJR-32 involved several hundred housing units, a shopping center, and the development of a whole community.

As Baraka and Coombs discussed the project, they conceived of it as an interesting test of some of their ideas about community planning and housing amenities. It would also be a good exercise, providing a project around which a professional development team could form: architects, engineers, planners, housing consultants, and real estate lawyers. While Coombs went to work on the old plans for Paulus Hook, looking for space to develop amenities, Baraka worked with Gershen to pull together the development team for Kawaida Towers.

Because of the severe pattern of racial exclusion in the city, the black community in Newark could draw upon very few professional resources of its own; many of the professionals raised in black Newark had left for other cities where they could find suitable opportunities. Baraka worked on plans to team a few black people with white experts as a step toward developing an autonomous African American development team. Earl Coombs was paired with a white architectural firm, Bottelli and Martins; a young lawyer in Ray Brown's office, Thomas R. Ashley, with a senior white real estate lawyer; a young college graduate, Vernon Clash, with Gershen's firm; and small black subcontractors like the Benjamin Bannaker Company with the white general contractor Bruno Lucarelli Jr. According to those plans, at the end of the process the black personnel would have the required experience, track records, professional licenses, and bonding capacities necessary to allow them to develop their own projects. This was done with the specific aim of forming a team prepared to build a community on the NJR-32 site in the Central Ward, and the general aim of developing communities in a number of other CAP cities.

Kawaida Towers was put together in record time. Speed was part of its strategy for success; too many housing plans in Newark had already died on the drawing board. Kawaida Towers broke ground without ceremony in July 1972. The Congress of African People's urban planning commitment indicated the relationship between black politics and social development that the group sought to introduce through the National Black Assembly. Later, in the National Black Assembly, it was resolved that black communities in general would develop PACs to redesign sections of the major cities. However, everything rested on the success of the first two projects in Newark: NJR-32 and Kawaida Towers.

Kawaida on Trial

Ironically, CAP's dilemma began on the most auspicious of all occasions: October 12, 1972, the day of the ceremonial groundbreaking at Kawaida Towers. That sixteen-story housing development represented one hopeful possibility: that if black people gained political power and used that power for social and economic development the U.S. might avoid protracted racial strife in America's city trenches. The groundbreaking announcement stressed that Kawaida represented a new experiment in interracial cooperation between black and white leadership. The Temple of Kawaida sent out a press release emphasizing the "mix and match" concept; this concept, it explained, "represents perhaps the most unique feature of Kawaida Towers. It results from the determination of [the] Temple [of] Kawaida and Baraka to give blacks the greatest possible control over their own institutions—in this case, housing."[11]

That announcement concluded with this optimistic statement, which suggests how important that particular housing development was for the Congress of African People:

> The 38-year-old Baraka refers to Newark as "New Ark," which reflects his conviction that the city can be made to lead the rebirth of all of the nation's cities. He views Kawaida Towers as one of the most important steps to be taken toward that rebirth.[12]

The public version of the "mix and match" approach concerned the development of black leadership in terms of architects, contractors, housing consultants, and managers; but the private realities of that formula involved political power, access to it, and mutual concessions. Everything about Kawaida Towers was strategic. The plans for Kawaida Towers had been bought from a successful development in Jersey City, which had already passed every state approval. In fact, the original architectural plans were award-winning. The choice of the general contractor, Bruno Lucarelli Jr., had a great deal to do with his political connections with the popular North Ward councilman-at-large Ralph Vallani. Vallani had grown senile, and very few people could communicate with him, but Lucarelli felt that he could win the support of Vallani and, with that, the Italian political support necessary for the project to secure enough votes for tax abatement. Without those votes, no development like Kawaida Towers or the NJR-32 community could happen under the housing finance programs of HUD and the New Jersey Housing Finance Agency (NJHFA).

Thus, while the public knew little about Kawaida Towers before October 1972, the powerful Italian politicians in the North Ward already knew of that project in intimate detail. Apparently, they had agreed that Newark needed some degree of racial cooperation, at least on such basic issues as housing. No new housing was being built in Newark, and the rise of corporate structures downtown mocked the residential stagnation of that city. Something had to be done, and in 1972 the only group that had figured out a way for black development to proceed was Imamu Baraka's development team. Consequently, in September 1971 the Newark City Council approved a resolution, introduced by North Ward councilman Frank Megaro, for Kawaida Towers's tax abatement.

On a number of occasions during that period, Baraka told the head of his housing development department emphatically, "*We have to live with these people.*" The Italian community, not the downtown corporate leadership, was viewed as the most important white group with which the black community had to find common ground. And wherever there were common goals that could be sought, objectives that were mutually beneficial and equitable for both communities, then privately Newark CAP would go the extra mile. At one meeting early in 1972, Baraka asked Bruno Lucarelli if he knew how to contact Anthony Imperiale, saying that if there were any construction jobs that Lucarelli could offer Imperiale's people, it should be done. Baraka wanted to make certain that among the white workers at Kawaida Towers, the North Ward community was well represented.

In brief, the major political leaders of the North Ward's Italian community—Councilman Ralph Vallani, Councilman Frank Megaro, and Assemblyman Anthony Imperiale—knew about Kawaida Towers in advance of the groundbreaking announcement. However, no one anticipated what Stephen Adubato, a professor at Rutgers University, would do at the groundbreaking.

When all the television cameras had gathered for a groundbreaking shot demonstrating the new era of racial cooperation, Adubato upstaged the whole ceremony. He drew some of the cameras away with his press statement that posed two questions: Why was this project called Kawaida Towers? Why not Garibaldi Towers? With those questions, Adubato triggered a power struggle among the leaders in the North Ward, raising these issues: Who was responsible for this *betrayal* of the white community? Who were the genuine white leaders? How could the old guard leadership have cooperated with an Imamu Baraka? Was new leadership needed? The political careers of a number of Italian political figures would rise and fall on how they responded to Adubato's challenge. Meanwhile, Adubato used the situation to construct a platform of high visibility for his own political career.

For most of those politicians, silence was the wisest policy, because it could be documented quite easily that they had worked for the development of Kawaida Towers; but Imperiale's link to the project was so private and obscure that he could afford to maneuver to his advantage. He decided to take the initiative and picket the housing development.

On November 9, 1972, the picketing began. At first, most picketers were white, off-duty policemen and policemen's wives, many not actually from Newark but from suburban communities. Moreover, Robert Curvin writes, "White police officials appeared at rallies in the North Ward to encourage the demonstrators. The president of the Patrolmen's Benevolent Association urged his members to join the protest and vowed at one meeting, 'If Kawaida Towers is built, my blood will be on its doorstep.'"[13] In other words, the picketing was staged largely by forces among the police. But when that image of whites picketing against Imamu Baraka was shown on television, the new development drew hundreds more white picketers, who vented their resentment of the Congress of African People specifically and black development generally. They were able to stop the construction work, which at that point was nearly completing the foundation. Baraka made several press statements asking that there be no black protest at Kawaida Towers in the North Ward, and that everyone allow the law to handle the situation.

But, step by step, the situation degenerated, and Mayor Gibson offered no leadership, preferring instead to fade as far as possible into the background. The situation quickly got out of hand. The picket leaders developed a unique strategy. They would threaten that blood would run in the streets, and then petition the courts to stop the construction because of the danger of bloodshed. *It worked.*

On November 13, 1972, Judge Irwin Kimmelman called for a seven-day moratorium so that the situation could cool off. The picket leaders understood that as a victory; they had stopped the construction. In court the plaintiffs, Anthony Imperiale and John Cervase, fabricated technical objections about the height of the apartment building and the legality of its tax abatement to disguise the racist objection; the justice system was the only actor that seemed blind to the real intent of the lawsuit. During the case, Imperiale and Cervase charged vaguely that there was something technically wrong with the project and that specifically it had violated the zoning ordinance by building a high-rise in a low-rise residential neighborhood. That first suit initiated a four-year court battle, in which charge after charge against the development was fabricated by the Imperiale-Cervase legal counsel and then defeated one by one by the Kawaida Towers legal defense, Irving Vogelman.

Vogelman was the law partner of Raymond Brown. Physically smaller in stature than even Baraka, Vogelman was a giant in court, and he defeated Imperiale and Cervase at each and every turn. Actually, it was a test of will, because Imperiale and Cervase had no case. Every government body that had approved the project had already checked the zoning ordinances for compliance. The Kawaida development teams knew from the outset that they would win that gambit in court, because the original plans for a 23-story building had been cut down to sixteen stories so that it would fit the prevailing zoning for that neighborhood. But the howling hypocrisy of the case, and especially of its being handled as if that charge was credible, is revealed in the fact that anyone standing on the construction site and looking one block west could see the row of fifteen- and sixteen-story apartment buildings on Mt. Prospect Avenue. In this context, it is interesting that when the television stations aired the footage of Kawaida Towers they never showed those high-rise apartments on Mt. Prospect Avenue; and for those who were unfamiliar with that particular neighborhood—the vast majority of viewers—the news gave some public credibility to the position that the Imperiale and Cervase case had a legitimate "leg to stand on."

Then, on November 20, Judge Kimmelman made a preliminary decision that the project was in fact legal and that it met all the necessary legal requirements. Nevertheless, on November 21, the Newark City Council revealed how far the white racist leadership would take the struggle against the Congress of African People. That was the day the City Council voted to rescind the tax abatement for Kawaida Towers and to retain a lawyer to fight the development in court. Within a few days, white mobs stopped black laborers from entering the gate.

The most interesting episode was never reported. Each morning, members of Newark CAP visited the labor unions. They paid particular attention to the only black-led union, the laborers Local 699 led by James Brown. The first morning Brown invited CAP to speak to the workers about volunteering for work at Kawaida Towers. And suddenly four brave black men stepped forward; one of them was Blanton Jones. Jones was the first black worker at the site; he later described the nature of the white opposition that black labor met at Kawaida Towers to a bewildered board of inquiry that had been called together by the National Black Assembly's

Law and Justice Committee. This NBA committee established a board of inquiry in 1973, composed of Congressman Parren Mitchell; New York City civil rights activist Leon Modeste; Hulbert James of the National Welfare Rights Organization; Preston Wilcox, the Harlem educator of AFRAM Associates; and Irv Joyner of the Commission for Racial Justice.[14] Testifying before the board, Jones explained that he was a member of the laborers Local 699 who lived in Newark. He had been "unemployed for about a year" before the start of the Kawaida Towers project and he needed the work badly. "I had to work! I pay $187 a month plus lights and gas, water. The lights are cut off now."

Jones gave that public hearing some idea of what black workers were up against:

I started to work with Kawaida Towers the Monday after Thanksgiving. . . . I went in that Monday and [it] *was just like going to Korea in '50.* Met all kinds of force. . . . Imperiale saw us turn the corner and said *'here they come, stop them.'* . . . I was the only worker that got in that morning. No work was done that day.

On another day they tried again. Jones testified:

There were 200 pickets, mostly women. We were trying to get the water hose, meaning [we would have to] come on the outside of the fence and bring the water hose on Delavan Street. I was pulling the hose and the police told them to break the hose down. We would have done better with no policemen at all. *Everyday you didn't know whether you would get back home or not.*

The members of the NBA panel reviewing the case had difficulty believing what they were hearing; it was too crude and too ridiculous. How could it happen that way in America? They asked Jones, "On the day you went to work Imperiale saw the workers and told the crowd to stop them from going in?"

Jones answered, "He said, *'Here they are, stop them.'* He was in front."

Next they asked, "What do you think were the reasons behind Imperiale?"

Jones replied, "I think he's a racist, because he called us *nigger*—asks about your wife, [your] mother."

"He does that?"

"The pickets, the women."

"Who is Imperiale?"

"He is the Assemblyman."

"And he is leading people to break the law?"

"That is what he's been breaking ever since November."

Most news accounts confirm Jones's testimony. For instance, on January 6, 1973, the *Asbury Park Press* reported, "A group of protesters opposed to the controversial Kawaida Towers housing project yelled racial epithets at five Negro laborers who crossed a picket line at the construction site yesterday."[15]

The epithets, "Nigger go home!" and "Go back to the jungle!" were accompanied by the placards the white protesters carried portraying black people as monkeys and Baraka as a monkey wearing an African hat.

Finally, Jones made a plea for political leadership: "I think leadership is the biggest thing. It's just like being in the service, if there's no one to lead. We have to get together!"[16]

Rather than providing leadership, Mayor Gibson preferred "invisibility" in the crisis at Kawaida Towers—definitely a hard act to perform at City Hall. However, leadership came from the community. Each night CAP leaders visited the construction workers at home and encouraged them and their families; each morning they spoke to the laborers at Local 699; and each weekend rallies in the black community hailed those four men as heroes.

A number of forces denounced the violence at Kawaida Towers, and called for both justice and reconciliation. Chief among them was a subcommittee of the North Newark Clergy Group, headed by Rev. Frank Gibson Jr. of the Newark Presbytery, Rev. Howard Day of the Montgomery Presbyterian Church, Rev. John Fibelkorn of the Redeemer Lutheran Church, Rev. George W. Freyberger of the Shepherd of the City Lutheran Church, Rev. Emanuel Morino of the Spanish Congregation of the Mt. Zion Baptist Church, Rev. Kim Neilsen of the Christ Reformed Church, Rev. Alphonso Roman of the Metropolitan Ecumenical Ministry, and Rev. Granville A. Seward of the Mount Zion Baptist Church.

Scores of black labor and professional groups supported Kawaida Towers, including the National Black Social Workers Association and the National Black Assembly. Significantly, the Fight Back and Black Economic Survival groups in Harlem and Brooklyn were very supportive. They were prepared to send progressive black, Latino, and white trade unionists to build Kawaida Towers. During the National Black Assembly's public hearing on Kawaida Towers, an Italian American trade unionist, Bill Carlotti from Fight Back, testified that their 2,000 members, "the vast majority of whom are Black and Spanish speaking, in all trades" stood ready to build Kawaida Towers once order was restored.

Linking Italian independence with African cooperation, Carlotti told the panel that he was concerned that some people were associating the good name of Giuseppe Garibaldi with Anthony Imperiale, and that Garibaldi was a liberator and not an oppressor: "I heard the name Garibaldi mentioned a couple of times. . . . Garibaldi led the revolution in Italy and one of the chief generals in that revolution was an African named Akidi."[17]

In an editorial broadcast, WNBC-TV expressed its support of Kawaida Towers:

> No one in Newark seriously questions the need for housing in that city. Yet North Ward residents, led by Assemblymen Anthony Imperiale and Frank Megaro, are resisting the high rise apartment called Kawaida Towers, a low income housing project sponsored by Temple Kawaida and Black Nationalist Imamu Baraka.
>
> Those against the project are trying to use any and almost all means to block it—from keeping workers out, encouraging unions to disobey contracts, rescinding prior legislation, to introducing ex post facto laws.
>
> To us, it boils down to politics. Mr. Imperiale and Mr. Megaro are trying to trade on the white community's dislike for what Mr. Baraka stands for. So they're blocking much-needed housing and inflaming the community. That is irresponsible and should be stopped. If they're worried about black discrimination against whites in the project, they will have recourse to anti-discrimination laws. That's what equal justice under the law is all about.
>
> The Kawaida Towers' sponsors and the North Ward politicos should sit down and make peace. If they can't do that face to face, then suitable stand-ins should be found.
>
> The building should proceed.[18]

As WNBC said, it boiled down to politics; more precisely, however, it was the politics of American apartheid, involving the caste arrangements, both violent and institutional, that kept African Americans locked behind the walls of the second ghetto in the U.S. And the North Ward politicos were not the only ones involved. After conferring with Anthony Imperiale, the Teamsters, Carpenters, and Electricians unions agreed not to cross the North Ward picket line. CAP demanded that Nixon's labor secretary, Peter Brennan, look into the situation. Not only had white labor union leaders broken their contracts with Bruno Lucarelli of B.J. Builders by not coming to work but Kawaida Towers also charged that the Carpenters Union had violated international union rules by refusing black workers from a New York local permits to work at Kawaida Towers. Further, Kawaida Towers wanted Brennan to look into the charge that "on one occasion a Business Agent from the Electrical Workers approached a Black Electrical [foreman] willing to go to Kawaida Towers and told him that he would never work anywhere else again."[19]

Kawaida Towers also demanded that the Justice Department look into the matter, but the department maintained that it was not clear that any black rights had been violated. Privately, black Republicans close to the White House suggested that some action might come from the Justice Department if Imamu Baraka might consider an endorsement of President Nixon. Thus, black citizenship rights would not be enforced on their legal merit but in the light of political considerations.

In the meantime, on November 27, 1972, the Temple of Kawaida issued a detailed press statement listing its grievances, expressing its frustrations and criticizing Newark's law enforcement of court decisions. That day a North Ward white mob physically prevented black workers from entering the gates to work on Kawaida Towers; the leaders of the Temple of Kawaida demanded police protection. The press release charged:

Today all pretense of law enforcement broke down and the mob, either through police unwillingness to stop them, or a gross inefficiency that must border on actual criminality, took control.

The reason we question the meaning of mob rule at [the] Kawaida Towers site, is that it is obvious that the police department is not functioning at any level that is acceptable to responsible elements in the community. The exploitation of this situation by the Imperiales, Adubatos, Megaros, each feverishly trying to out bigot the others would be laughable if it were not so serious in its implications. We recognize the high percent of ethnic whites on the police department who identify with the white North Ward community, even though many of them do not live in NewArk. We have photographs of the many white policemen who have actually been a part of the mob, illegally obstructing workers from entering the site. We would imagine these policemen are off duty, or that picketing *is* their duty. We have photographs of white policemen acting as Anthony Imperiale's bodyguards, at the site, and at the New-Ark City Council. . . .

John Redden [the Newark police director] has taken an oath to enforce the laws of this municipality, he should uphold that oath, or *resign*. The oath is not meant to be enforced against Black people and Puerto Ricans only. But apparently Redden's racist police believe it is. The lack of police law enforcement at the site of Kawaida Towers is a clear violation of the civil rights of Kawaida Towers, Inc., the members of the Temple of Kawaida, as well as the other citizens of NewArk who want to see Kawaida Towers built. . . . today's display of criminal anarchy, aided and abetted by NewArk policemen, is open defiance of the courts and the Mayor of the City of NewArk, and the progressive citizens of this city.[20]

Rather than arrest white picketers who had beaten black people in the North Ward, police director Redden chose to resign, charging that it had been Baraka's fault for triggering the crisis. However, Redden also criticized the business community for its silence as the public order of the city unraveled. According to the *New York Times*, "Mr. Redden said he might reconsider [his resignation] if responsible community elements broke their longstanding silence and moved to ease tensions in the city."[21]

A few days before announcing his resignation, Redden had blamed Mayor Kenneth Gibson and the city council "for permitting the controversy and . . . unnamed community leaders for increasing it." These unnamed "self-serving" community leaders, Redden charged, had caused blacks and whites in Newark to be "at each others throats."[22] Specifically, Redden insisted that the Temple of Kawaida had planned to create the polarization by locating Kawaida Towers in the North Ward "to provide confrontation under the guise of providing housing."[23] Unfortunately, in important ways, Redden supported the contentions of the leaders of the North Ward opposition to Kawaida Towers; furthermore his resignation was a component part of the benign neglect and institutionalized lawlessness that protects American apartheid.

Newark CAP responded: "We have seen a so[-]called liberal white police director so frustrated by having to enforce the law against whites that he had to resign."[24] It argued that Redden could not enforce the law when it was a case of black legal rights against white perpetrators.

At any rate, the Temple of Kawaida had restrained the black community from protesting at Kawaida Towers, holding rallies in the Central Ward instead. This policy of restraint was designed to avoid confrontations and violence at the site of the housing development. When the Marxist-Leninist Progressive Labor Party announced a demonstration against racism at the Kawaida Towers site, Baraka urged black people not to participate in that action. He complained:

No member of the P.L.P. or S.D.S. has consulted with Kawaida Towers Inc. or the Temple of Kawaida. The apparent need for confrontation is a sign to us of incorrect political evaluation or opportunism based on the same kind of racism which is expressed in another way by the Imperiales. . . . One thing that the Temple of Kawaida insists on as our second principle is the right of self-determination and this is to define ourselves, name ourselves and speak for ourselves, instead of being defined and spoken for by others. . . . Let the P.L.P. and S.D.S. begin to understand that we must determine for ourselves how to wage our own struggle.[25]

As soon as Redden announced his resignation, CAP led community forces to demand a black police director, one who would enforce the law. While the city council stalled on the appointment of a new police director, Councilman Michael Bottone actually suggested that the post of police director should be abolished because it was too "political." But the *New York Times* observed that "the proposal appears aimed at blocking Mayor Gibson from naming a black police director, something the Council members see happening if Mr. Redden's resignation is accepted."[26]

In an interview, Frank Megaro, the North Ward councilman who originally sponsored the tax abatement resolution for Kawaida Towers, told the *New York Times* that "his political future depends on whether he can help kill the apartment building project."[27] Megaro had a great deal at stake; he was both North Ward councilman and a state assemblyman. He pushed himself to the forefront of the demonstrators against Kawaida Towers, but that was not enough.

Megaro, who had studied law at the University of Richmond, told a reporter that "he would not have voted for a tax abatement grant to the project 'if I had known LeRoi Jones was behind it.'"[28] When the reporter asked Megaro if he had not seen any connection between Kawaida Towers and Baraka's Temple of Kawaida, the public official said, "You know how it is with corporate names these days. . . . They're always looking for something different. I have a friend who set up a corporation out of parts of his three kids' first names."[29]

However, the tax abatement had remained before the City Council for consideration for months. It first appeared on the City Council agenda on August 4, 1971. "Action was deferred twice," reported the *New York Times*, "first on [August] 4 by Mr. Megaro, and again on [September] 1 at the request of Council President Louis M. Turco." It is difficult to believe that Mr. Megaro, who sponsored the resolution, knew nothing about the sponsor. At any rate, the application had received as much attention as any other project.[30]

The North Ward leaders insisted that they were not racists. However, if these politicos were not racists, then why were race and the specific identity of the sponsor the key issues, rather than the technical features of the development? During the same interview, Megaro explained why he had not questioned the Kawaida Towers application for tax abatement; he said the project did not demand further scrutiny because Italian Americans were involved in it:

> He said he had been told by William Walls, the city Corporation Counsel, that the sponsors included Raymond Brown, a Jersey City lawyer, and Alvin E. Gershen, an urban planner.
>
> "He also told me," Mr. Megaro continued, "that some *paisans*—I don't like to use the term—were involved; Lucarelli the builder and Bottelli, the architect."[31]

Finally, on March 7, 1973, Mayor Gibson agreed to intervene. At a meeting in his office at City Hall attended by representatives of the Justice Department and the FBI, Gibson met with Imamu Baraka and Anthony Imperiale. Imperiale was late for the meeting. But when he walked in the door, Mayor Gibson ran over and embraced him, asking, "Tony, what can I do for you?"[32]

It looked bad for Kawaida Towers. At a meeting before the Justice Department, the FBI, and the mayor, Imperiale explained that he was not really concerned about those issues of zoning that had been raised in court, but he wanted the mayor or someone to help transfer the ownership of the development to a white group in the North Ward so that they could complete the construction. Mayor Gibson apologized to Imperiale, "I'm sorry, Tony—legally, I can't do that." For Kawaida Towers representatives, the accommodation was stunning.[33]

This idea that the Temple of Kawaida should bring the grist to the mill for white developers and politicos was repeated on several occasions during that period. It was a replay of the classic mobster movie, where the Mafia cows the prizefighter into throwing the championship fight; it makes him an offer that he dare not refuse. In other words, some felt that powerful whites who had not applied for mortgage commitments were entitled to take over millions of dollars in such investments secured by the Temple of Kawaida. Bluntly, it was white over black.

From that point on, the city unraveled into a state of near racial anarchy, engulfing the city council, the schools, and the black enclaves in the North Ward. City council meetings were paralyzed by the struggle of the black community to replace the resigned white police director, Redden, with the city's first black police director, Edward Kerr. The city council refused to appoint a black person to the job permanently, however Officer Kerr was appointed to the job on a temporary basis several times after massive demonstrations at the City Council meetings.

During the month of March 1973, CAP led the black community to test the union's professed principle of not crossing community picket lines. Between March 19 and March 26, they picketed the medical school construction under way in the Central Ward and witnessed the same unions, who could not cross a white community picket in the North Ward, cross a black one daily in the Central Ward.

One night a white mob attacked a small black enclave in another community in the North Ward, beating up black people and throwing garbage cans through their windows. There was no response from police officials and even the city's black director of human rights could only stand by and shake his head. Of course, attacking a black community in the 1970s, even a small enclave surrounded by white people, was risky business. The police charged that one black youth shot and killed a white man invading his home.[34]

At this same time, the high schools in Newark and Irvington were in a state of crisis because of the strong white backlash to the entrance of a few black students to the Vailsburg and Irvington high schools. The black community was expanding beyond the traditional ghetto boundaries, which disturbed the white power structure at Kawaida Towers and in the high schools. White students attacked black students in a suburb bordering Newark's West Ward at Irvington High School, and then in the North Ward of Newark at Barringer High School. During that period, one black student activist was found gunned down after he went jogging one morning.[35]

CAP worked with the Newark NAACP to support the students and parents, demanding adequate police protection for their children. At night there were massive workshops in which hundreds of parents and students discussed how the students could stay together, who they could call when attacked, and what kind of a system could be established for adults to intervene when such incidents occurred. Quietly, groups of black students began training in self-defense methods that were appropriate to mob and police attacks. Some students even studied the tactics of Latin American freedom movements, where students made good use of black pepper against the horses of attacking mounted police. In a word, it was a desperate situation.

But the pace of white terror outstripped all those efforts. At Barringer High School, when black and white students fought each other, the Newark mounted police attacked several hundred black school children. The children were herded by the mounted police and then trapped between the high school and the iron fences of Branch Brook park. The best that several Black Panthers and CAP members could do was to lead the children away from that military confrontation and withdraw to a huge garage nearby on Seventh Avenue. From there they called for help, and Baraka arranged for several buses to deliver the children to their homes until CAP could talk to their parents about what they wanted to do next.

The black students were agitated, and they decided to boycott the schools. For some time, each morning they would assemble by the hundreds in the North Ward at Kawaida Towers to witness and encourage the four black workers as they walked through a wall of angry white protesters. It was a standoff.

In 1973, several mysterious shotgun blasts were fired during the night into CAP's headquarters at 502 High Street and at the African Free School baby nursery on Clinton Avenue. The shotgun blast at 502 High Street went through the front window and blew a huge hole in the first floor ceiling. Fortunately, no one was hit by either blast. But, taken together, these developments destroyed the basis for CAP's optimism for black development with white cooperation in Newark.

In an interview, Newark CAP member Saidi Nguvu explained that the obstruction of the Kawaida Towers development was a severe psychological blow:

> The content was going to be black and we were going to be able to do things that other administrations were not doing. For example, eradicating the housing problem; building structures, Kawaida Towers, the R-32 plan.
>
> *We actually had plans.* We had housing sites planned. *We had a lot of potential.* That's why they came down on us so hard and had to stop us. It was real successful because I remember the thing with Kawaida Towers—that it was right. Everything we did was right. *We had followed the law and everything was right; but they refused to build it and they actually physically attacked us.*
>
> That's when my whole philosophy changed. My whole outlook changed from the goals and aspirations of the organization in terms of what we can do. That's when the reality struck me that the power structure was still the power structure and that we were still subordinate. We

were no . . . closer to realizing our goals than [when] we first started. That was really a big psychological blow to me, that it happened like that. *That was the beginning of the end from that point, when we weren't able to do that.*[36]

Thus, the Kawaida Towers development in the North Ward was being destroyed by the same powerful dynamics of American apartheid that contained black people in the worst neighborhoods and turned black communities into ghettos. However, the confrontations at Kawaida Towers made the institutional forces behind ghetto formation more visible than ever before, thus informing the development of black consciousness.

No Way Out

Moreover, CAP charged that after winning each and every legal encounter in court, the Temple of Kawaida lost the original Kawaida Towers design as the NJHFA began to voice the demands of the white mob, albeit more subtly in administrative language. If the violent mob said the building was too tall, then the NJHFA said the apartment building had to be pared down because of inflationary construction costs—which had escalated while the project languished in court between 1972 and 1975. According to one estimate, the original 1972 Kawaida Towers costing $6.4 million would have been built at a price of more than $10 million in 1975. Then the NJHFA proposed cost-cutting measures that effectively eliminated all the amenities that Kawaida Towers had offered to enhance apartment living; next, there was a proposal to eliminate all the balconies from the design.[37] Meanwhile the development team was experiencing internal conflicts as the crisis continued. Since some of these proposals were coming from the contractor, Bruno Lucarelli, the Kawaida Towers board began to question the uncomfortable similarities between his proposals and those of Anthony Imperiale. The crushing blow came when the NJHFA decided that it was not feasible to have any two-bedroom apartments in the building. *Thus, the rents were to be higher, the apartments were to be smaller, and the building would have no amenities.*[38] As far as CAP was concerned, the building no longer served its constituency, which desperately needed decent and livable units for families with low and moderate incomes. (One irony of this last development is the contradictory logic that was applied to Kawaida developments. On the one hand, money was no object as the city rejected the $10 million in mortgage funds brought to Newark by Kawaida; but on the other hand, there was no additional funding available to finance the embattled Kawaida Towers that was already under construction.)

However, in a last-ditch effort, Baraka pressed Robert Notte, the head of the Newark Housing Authority, pointing to the ominously escalating black unrest triggered by the standoff at Kawaida Towers. Notte arranged a meeting with Baraka and another Kawaida Towers board representative in New York City at the jazz club, the Cookery. At the meeting Notte made the Kawaida Towers board an illuminating offer: if Baraka withdrew from Kawaida Towers in the North Ward, then Kawaida Community Development would receive twice the funding to build housing in the ghetto on the NJR-32 site. Since Robert Notte was the executive director of the NHA, the Kawaida board representatives wanted to know how he held the power to make a deal involving funds from the New Jersey Housing Finance Agency, which was the agency under which Kawaida Towers was subsidized. Only a few weeks earlier when Baraka had pressed Notte to talk to the powers in the North Ward Italian American community to resolve the issue of Kawaida Towers, Notte had protested that he had no power in such matters; now suddenly he had the authority to negotiate a $10 million transfer of funds in order to maintain residential segregation. Ultimately, rather than submit to the white supremacist stance that black people had no right to build Kawaida Towers in the North Ward, Baraka rejected the offer. Anything less would have been an accommodation to American apartheid and a betrayal of the rights and aspirations of African Americans for full equality.

The NJR-32 Project Area Committee

Meanwhile, despite the racial turmoil attempting to enforce the boundaries of the ghetto, the determination of the NJR-32 PAC was yielding some results in the Central Ward. PAC was able to convince Warner-Lambert to open a temporary medical facility on the corner of Bergen Street and Avon Avenue, right next to the future site of a senior citizens apartment building. Placing the emphasis on preventive rather than crisis health care, a free examination facility was to conduct a survey to find out the kinds of medical problems that were frequent in that community so that the permanent medical center could plan the proper health programs.

The PAC senior citizens committee was the most active and militant in that community. When CAP explained the red tape at the Newark Housing Authority and urban renewal, the elderly complained that they had been waiting all their lives and that at that bureaucratic pace they would never live to see any change.

But in the wake of the confrontations at Kawaida Towers, several housing projects that had been delayed on the drawing board since the late 1960s were suddenly approved by the New Jersey Housing Finance Agency. Some cynically wondered how that could have happened so quickly, and if it had anything to do with diverting people's attention from the standoff at Kawaida Towers.

Moreover, the NHA was ready to build a senior citizens building in the NJR-32 neighborhood, and seed monies were ready for a park design in that area. The community was involved in the planning of those two projects in the following manner. The senior citizens demanded a bus to tour elderly housing developments in other communities so they could compare and contrast the key features of their designs. The PAC architect, Earl Coombs, had been asking them to consider what they liked and disliked about the proposed NHA design for that senior citizen apartment building. After a number of tours and a few mass PAC meetings, the senior citizens noted their preferences. For instance, they knew they did not like the buildings with long corridors; those made them feel like they were in prisons. They opted instead for a V-shaped building with two shorter wings. Earl Coombs designed the first floor with many of the same kind of amenities for the elderly that were featured in Kawaida Towers. That project was a success.

In terms of the park, which was provisionally named Nat Turner Park, Earl Coombs found a Philadelphia park designer who had experience with parks in Africa. Once the program for the park was decided, the designers could go to work; but Baraka and Coombs felt the program had to come from the people in that community. An extensive survey was conducted by PAC, asking residents what they wanted to see in their park. The results showed that the community was divided into two camps about the nature of the park they wanted, split along the lines of the demography of the residents. The elderly wanted a quiet park with clusters of trees and benches where they could talk to each other and share some time together, and they also insisted on board games that they could play in peace and quiet. The youth wanted a recreational park with baseball, football, and basketball.

Baraka and Coombs went to work with the survey results to develop a program that would reconcile the conflicting views. They proposed that Nat Turner Park take advantage of a natural slope on the site. At the top of the hill, which was near the urban renewal parcels planned for new housing, they would have seating and quiet recreation for the elderly. From there they could look down at the children playing their spirited games at the other end of the park. On the slope of the hill there would be seating for an open-air theater. HUD issued seed money to PAC to develop architectural plans for the park.

Much of the planning for NJR-32 had gone as far as it could go without mortgage commitments. A team of architects and structural engineers had been assembled in Newark, and they developed prototypes for some low-rise, neo-African housing in the Central Ward; many of its apartments were designed with four and five bedrooms, so that they were suitable for the large families in that community. The Temple of Kawaida and Pilgrim Baptist church agreed to be cosponsors of the housing development in NJR-32; the two organizations had developed a close relationship in Newark's Modern Black Convention Movement. Although the Temple of Kawaida secured the earliest mortgage commitments, ultimately it was the Pilgrim Baptist Church's Frederick Douglass Homes that were actually built.

Betrayal: From Crisis to Catastrophe

By 1974, the Temple of Kawaida had received mortgage commitments of more than $20 million to build low-rise housing in NJR-32; and, after extensive negotiations with private and public sources, there was more on the way. However, while the poor people in the Project Area Committee and in the Modern Black Convention Movement were elaborating their vision of the New Ark and while Baraka and the Temple of Kawaida were luring investments into the Central Ward, a group of Italian American and Negro politicos were scheming to destroy the NJR-32 PAC and its urban vision.

Significantly, in the 1974 elections one of the earliest convention candidates, Earl Harris, became the first black president of the Newark City Council. Thus, by 1974, Newark had a black mayor and a black president of the city council, both of whom had begun their careers though the Modern Black Convention Movement. These should have been optimum political conditions for black social and economic development. By 1974, CAP did not expect any community development to come out of City Hall because the politicos were entranced by the downtown corporate development; yet CAP thought that development was possible if the politicians would just stay out of the way. In fact, several of the black developers and investors that came to CAP explained that they had been shut out by Mayor Gibson and the city council.

In the case of Earl Harris, Newark CAP had a long connection with his political career, beginning with its strong support for his candidacy at the

Black and Puerto Rican Convention in 1969. The elder, Baba Mshauri, recalls that although Harris had been a member of the United Brothers Steering Committee, privately he felt he could not run for city council because he had no money. But Baraka and the United Brothers decided to support his campaign financially, and Harris agreed to run. Mshauri recalls:

> I asked Earl—I said, "Earl, why don't you get out there and run?" And his answer was, "I can't afford it. I owe a lot of money from my prior election and I am broke." And I told him—I said, "Well, we are going to financially support our candidate." And he said, "Okay." He agreed to run.[39]

But when Harris announced that he was a candidate on the convention slate for City Council in 1969, Mayor Hugh Addonizio decided to publicly humiliate him, by having Harris arrested in broad daylight for overdue parking fines on High Street. According to Mshauri, even the police officers apologized to Harris, saying that the orders had come directly from the mayor. Mshauri and the United Brothers decided to use their organizational funds to secure Harris's release. Ultimately, Earl Harris became one of the successful candidates in the 1970 drive for black political power. During that campaign he canvassed the poorest neighborhoods in the black community and promised that if they supported him that he would rid the city of racism, poverty, and drugs. Certainly, many thought, here was a man of the people.

Five years later, in 1974, Earl Harris became the president of the city council. When the Temple of Kawaida secured another $10 million in HUD mortgage commitments for 258 housing units in the Central Ward NJR-32 area, the state knew Kawaida's development team could produce results; the only requirement left was the tax abatement from the city of Newark.

In his autobiography, Baraka recalls that the executive director of the Newark Housing Authority insisted that since the Central Ward land was prepared for development the Temple of Kawaida should agree to *front* the development for the underworld, acting as a *buffer* between the mob and the black community. Baraka writes that Mayor Gibson demurred:

> At the Housing Authority, the son-in-law of a Mafioso was the director. He took me into the conference room one afternoon and told me frankly. You take this architect, this consultant, and this construction firm and you go forward tomorrow, otherwise nothing. I told him all

that was cool but how could I tell black people that I've been struggling for black development and then tell them these are the people who're going to make a profit off this development? Gibson would do nothing but burp when he was told of these things.[40]

Thus, while the Temple of Kawaida knew that some white opposition would be orchestrated as it began to develop the Central Ward housing, the exact public scenario that the underworld would use to take away those tens of millions designated for black development was still unknown. Bit by bit, it learned the shape of the conspiracy. While privately the Temple of Kawaida was being threatened by the mob, publicly, rather than white councilmen leading the charge against the Central Ward development, there would be two black councilmen in the van of the opposition. The project was funded with federal and state guaranteed loans; the only aspect of this development that had to come through the Newark City Council was the application for tax abatement.

Tax abatement was crucial for the development. In the case of the tax relief for the Temple of Kawaida, that policy meant that the nonprofit group would pay the city a set rate for services in lieu of an unpredictable rate for taxes over the life of the mortgage. This policy became standard for the HUD housing program; otherwise, with unpredictable taxes, those mortgage guarantees would never have been feasible.

Mayor Gibson's office sent the tax abatement resolution to the city council for its approval, and then one of the ugliest and strangest episodes in Newark's black political history unfolded. Two black city councilmen joined with white city councilmen to oppose tax abatement for the NJR-32 development in the Central Ward: Jesse Allen, a former community organizer for the Students for a Democratic Society (SDS) project, the Newark Community Union Project (NCUP); and Earl Harris, formerly of the Newark Black and Puerto Rican Convention.

Apparently, a number of the old guard black politicos had been involved in negotiations with the Newark Housing Authority, suggesting that if they blocked CAP from developing the land in the Central Ward, then several of that old guard would be named the sponsors for housing development with full Italian American political backing in Newark. Thus, it seemed that if the Newark Housing Authority could not convince the Temple of Kawaida to front the mob's development, it would find other black clients to act as buffers.

Both Allen and Harris made some bizarre statements against the Central Ward housing. Allen claimed that Newark needed no more housing!

It is difficult to believe that Allen actually made that statement—in a city with the worst housing crisis in America. And it is even harder to believe that he was ignorant enough to repeat it—but he was.

Harris used another set of tactics that reveals the depth of his involvement in that obstruction of black community development. Quietly, the year before the Temple of Kawaida's application to the city for tax abatement, Earl Harris instructed the city clerk to send the following letter, dated October 16, 1974, to Patricia Q. Sheehan, a commissioner at the New Jersey Department of Community Affairs, and William L. Johnston, executive director of the New Jersey Housing Finance Agency:[41]

> The Newark Municipal Council has been advised that the Temple of Kawaida is seeking governmental approval and financing for low and moderate income, medium density housing for projects located within the Central Ward Urban Renewal Project in the City of Newark (N.J.R-32).
>
> The Newark Municipal Council has directed me to inform you that they are not disposed at this time to grant tax abatement for the above cited projects.
>
> Very truly yours
Frank D'Ascensio
City Clerk[42]

Next, Harris announced publicly that he had *discovered* that Imamu Baraka was a racial extremist, charged that Baraka was a dictator, and insisted that the Temple of Kawaida must never be allowed to build another development in Newark. He insisted that Newark was on the verge of a housing *renaissance*. As the *New York Times* reported, Harris told them that "the next few years would see 'one of the greatest renaissances in construction of needed housing in the city by men of good will and good faith, but not by those who seek to destroy, polarize and divide the city.'"[43] Harris argued that now he was the president of the City Council, a representative of "all the people," and implied that Baraka and CAP were to be purged from the public arena. Thus, Harris insisted that "the Council stood ready 'to grant a tax abatement to any legitimate sponsor, other than Mr. Baraka.'"[44]

Showdown at City Hall

According to *Unity and Struggle*, reports that Mayor Kenneth Gibson and Earl Harris would betray the Kawaida development thrust began to surface in 1974. CAP accused both men of participating in a crude shakedown with the mob. In *Unity and Struggle,* CAP charged that "these people want to get payoffs if they allow housing to be built" and that "the City Council wrote the State a letter saying it is opposed to the construction of two story town houses for low and moderate income people on the vacant lots that scar Belmont Avenue." It argued that 1975 was the beginning of government cutbacks in the housing development programs and that Newark would lose millions of dollars of that kind of mortgage finance, with subsidies for moderate- and low-income families, forever:

> Without the City's crucial approval of tax abatement for these town houses, the State will not release the $10 million scheduled to construct 250 apartments this winter. Tax abatement means that non-profit housing projects do not pay tax, so that the rents can remain low enough for low and moderate income family living. Tax abatement is the key to the struggle of the people against City Hall resistance to the needs of the people, which is coming to a head November 20th, at the City Council meeting.[45]

Three meetings showed the character of the government repression that Harris would marshal against the Kawaida development plans. When a score of tenants from the NJR-32 community approached the first city council meeting to discuss tax abatement for the project, the director of PAC was detained without charges by the police until the council meeting was over.

In response, CAP called for a massive protest at the November 20, 1975, city council meeting, taking banners that read: "Bagman Earl Harris Takes It From The Top!" The *Unity and Struggle* report of the meeting ran as follows:

> Council President Earl Harris created a police state in a tense city council meeting, when he was confronted by a mass of angry people united in a struggle to construct housing on the vacant lots in the Central Ward, . . . which has been embattled over the housing crisis and without decent housing, for the last decade.
>
> Harris was challenged by a host of people who asked questions about his illegal financial dealings with big time developers, and the suffering it is causing the people of Newark to feed the vices of this infamous black political pimp. Harris refused to answer any questions about his irregular political dealings, and when he was asked detailed questions about his rejection of the tax abatement necessary to construct housing for low-income families in the Central Ward, he resorted to calling in

the city's tactical squad to intimidate the people Harris was supposedly elected to represent. When people would not be silenced by this display of fascist police tactics, Harris had police drag a dozen people out of the council meeting because they would not submit to the increasing exploitation that is carried on by the city council under Earl Harris everyday.[46]

Not only did Harris order mass arrests in that city council meeting but he made a ruling, later defeated by the courts, that no speaker before the city council could harshly criticize any of the councilmen during council sessions. Indeed, it was illegal now to call any member of the city council a crook. This helped set the stage for the final showdown between Earl Harris and Newark CAP.

Next, on January 7, 1975, Mayor Gibson sent two letters to the city council, recommending tax abatement for each of the two housing projects sponsored by the Kawaida Community Development corporation. He explained, "I find that the proposed project meets a pressing need for housing in the City and hereby confer my approval for the granting of tax abatement."[47] With that statement, Gibson effectively washed his hands of the matter; he knew what would happen next.

The showdown between Newark CAP and the Newark City Council came on February 5, 1975, the date that the council voted against tax abatement for the Temple of Kawaida housing developments in NJR-32. That vote meant the state and federal mortgage commitments that the Congress of African People had secured, along with the associated investments in community development, would be lost to Newark. The city council meeting was scheduled for 1 P.M. on Wednesday, while most people supporting the development were at work, so CAP made a point of showing up at the meeting in full strength, and this time Amiri Baraka was one of the scheduled speakers.

As the council meeting began, Earl Harris announced pointedly, "Decorum is the order of the day and slanderous remarks directed at any member of the council will not be tolerated. If you cause any disturbance, I will order you hauled out and arrested."[48]

The council chambers were tense. Everyone knew that Baraka and CAP had gone through a dramatic political transformation, proclaiming themselves socialists. Baraka had developed a new and stinging critique of internal colonialism in Newark, charging that many of the black politicians created by the Modern Black Convention Movement had become neocolonial agents for white racism. In a speech that ended in his arrest,

Baraka reviewed the history of Newark's Black Revolt and the reasons why the black united front that took power in 1970 had disintegrated. The audience was riveted as Baraka charged that instead of black power, it had seen "black faces animated by white desires." According to Baraka, black people had been double-crossed by Earl Harris and Mayor Gibson on countless occasions. Baraka raised a number of questions about their leadership: How had black people's homes been burned, and how had black people been beaten by mobs with impunity in a city with a black executive? Why was there a boom in downtown development, with new office buildings and universities flourishing, while neither housing nor schools were developing for the black community? What *real* difference had a black mayor and black president of the city council made?

Further, Baraka accused the big corporations of playing a parasitic role in the city. He also insisted that many of the problems were linked to the increasing class formation within the black community and a growing gap that had removed one class of black people from the rest of the black community.

But the problems did not stop with City Hall and the corporations; Baraka argued that more black faces in high places at the Newark Housing Authority meant nothing for the masses if they remained trapped in public housing, i.e., "public dungeons," where they faced the "horror" of Newark as a "giant slum."

Since these black public officials had been unaccountable to the black community, they had caused the breakdown of the black united front, the basis for the Modern Black Convention Movement. He charged again that the black politicos had become "degenerate Negroes," who had used the offices created for them by the grass roots for "their own self aggrandizement and individual profit."[49]

Then Baraka insisted that Earl Harris had not only betrayed the cause of black people, but had sold his *soul* to the mob. He explained how "he had spent three years putting together 'a complete package' for the project" in the NJR-32 PAC community, and now it would all be lost because of the corruption and betrayal of Earl Harris.[50] "When Baraka spoke," reported the *Star Ledger*, "he lambasted the council, charging the body was 'more oppressive than your predecessors,' and urging them to 'justify your attempts to block housing in areas where it is needed most.'" Moreover, "he called upon Councilmen Harris, James, Jesse Allen and Anthony Carrino—whom he called 'cafone,' Italian slang for low-class—to explain their actions. Harris admonished him to adhere to the stated rules, and ordered the arrest after Baraka uttered a profanity."[51]

Earl Harris was visibly stunned by Baraka's remarks. When the "angered Harris ordered the black socialist leader jailed," Amina Baraka rushed to the podium, insisting, "You are all unfair and have no reason to arrest him."[52] Then Harris had her and five other members of CAP arrested.

While the Barakas and several of their comrades were booked in the police station, the Newark City Council voted 7–1 to reject tax abatement for Kawaida Community Development. The lone dissenting vote was cast by South Ward councilman Sharpe James, who would become the next mayor. Councilman James argued that "the overriding important issue before us is the question of more or less housing for the city as opposed to our political differences."[53]

Harris assured "those present that the Newark Housing Authority has indicated construction of housing will begin on the Central Ward tracts within a few months. But its future will not be dictated by the angry Kawaida ideology."[54]

Following his release, Amiri Baraka said, "We're not guilty of anything, we're just protesting the fact that no housing is being built in the Central Ward."[55] Given these political circumstances the Central Ward NJR-32 community development became hopelessly entangled in bureaucratic red tape and legal malaise.[56]

Black Power Experiment Concludes

In his study of black politics in Newark, Robert Curvin wonders about the sincerity of the reasons given by Earl Harris and Mayor Gibson for their abandonment of the Kawaida developments. He asks, "Can one really believe their stated reasons for abandoning Baraka, since they joined with him at a time when he was more militant and much less willing to compromise?"[57] According to Curvin, by 1974 "Baraka and [CAP] showed increasing signs of accommodation and willingness to work within the system. Baraka had begun to make stronger efforts to allay fears of a Black takeover while still insisting on Black advancement." In line with this, Curvin cites the use of white contractors and professionals on the Kawaida project as "a manifestation of increased sophistication" and "an effort to accommodate to political exigencies."[58]

At any rate, the Black Power experiment in Newark was over. Within a few months the funding for Kawaida Towers, Kawaida Community Development, the Project Area Committee, and the African Free School was withdrawn, and those programs were dismantled. The Newark Housing

Authority had the buildings that housed the PAC office, CAP's theater and television studio training program, the headquarters of the National Black Assembly and the African Liberation Support Committee, and classrooms for the African Free School demolished. In 1976, the New Jersey Housing Finance Agency buried the $1.5 million foundation of Kawaida Towers.

While these local developments laid the basis for the radicalization of Imamu Baraka's politics of cultural nationalism, they also weakened the political stronghold that gave authority to his projection as a black national leader. The Modern Black Convention Movement began to experience serious political and ideological divisions in 1974. As the 1976 national elections approached, the rift within the National Black Assembly leadership became even more intense. On the one hand, a number of black elected officials shifted from an allegiance to independent politics toward loyalty to the Democratic Party; on the other hand, Baraka's Congress of African People shifted from nationalism to national communism. In the national political arena, the Congress of African People examined the results of the Black Power experiment and charged that it had died at the hands of traitorous black elected officials. In Baraka's analysis, internal colonialism, when faced with the challenge of Black Power, had changed into neocolonialism.[59] In November 1975, Elijah Muhammad, founder of the Nation of Islam, died; in December 1975, Amiri Baraka resigned his position as the general secretary of the National Black Assembly. By 1976, both the African Liberation Support Committee and the Black Women's United Front were in disarray resulting from sectarian conflicts. Ultimately, Amiri Baraka repudiated black nationalism. Because Baraka's journey toward cultural nationalism had been paradigmatic in the development of the Black Revolt, his rejection of nationalism marked one of the most definitive points in the conclusion of that phase of Black Power.

Conclusion

Winter in America

Come, then, comrades; it would be as well to decide at once to change our ways. We must shake off the heavy darkness in which we were plunged, and leave it behind. . . . We must leave our dreams and abandon our old beliefs and friendships of the time before life began. Let us waste no time in sterile litanies and nauseating mimicry. . . . the European game has finally ended; we must find something different. We today can do everything, so long as we do not imitate Europe, so long as we are not obsessed by the desire to catch up with Europe.
—Frantz Fanon, *The Wretched of the Earth*

Individual leaders can project ideologies of many kinds and color them with the hues of their own personal aspirations which very often obscure the very fundamental issues which are of crucial interest to the people for whom the leaders speak. Then historians come along and completely forget or overlook what the basic issues were for the people in the mass, and center their attention on the personal characteristics of the leaders.
—Harold Cruse, *Rebellion or Revolution?*

The Short Twentieth Century ended in problems, for which nobody had, or even claimed to have, solutions.
—Eric Hobsbawm, *The Age of Extremes*

The Modern Black Convention Movement

By way of conclusion, let me summarize several of the key propositions of this argument about the dynamics of black nationality formation and provide a few suggestions for those attempting to solve the current crisis of leadership, program, and policy.

One of the most important political experiments of the Black Power movement was the Modern Black Convention Movement. Before the black assemblies, the politics of cultural nationalism was confined to small circles of students, artists, and intellectuals; in terms of black nationality formation, it remained a head without a body. However, between 1965 and 1970, hundreds of black urban uprisings galvanized a new generation in the struggle for black liberation. The massive tumult of the ghetto revolts set the stage for the fusion between the nationalism of small circles of radical artists and intellectuals and the grassroots nationalism of the broad urban masses; out of that explosive mix came a new generation of militant Black Power organizations, demanding self-determination, self-respect, and self-defense. In the midst of the uprisings, the politics of black cultural nationalism and the Modern Black Convention Movement took form, unleashing the dynamics of African American nationality formation. In the midst of those turbulent struggles, the members of CFUN forged the slogan "It's Nation Time!" Then, Amiri Baraka set it to music.[1]

In summary, the foundation for the Modern Black Convention Movement was twofold: the black united front and the black and Puerto Rican alliance. The first principle was the broad and vital black united front developed by Baraka's repertory group, the Spirit House Movers and Players, and his political organs, the United Brothers and the Committee For A Unified NewArk; hundreds of community organizations, trade unions, block clubs, student associations, and circles of artists and intellectuals gathered at mass assemblies to fashion an independent black political agenda. The black agenda was distinguished from a multitude of other conference resolutions because the grassroots ultimatum of that movement was not simply rhetoric, it was *a plan of action*. The 1968 Black Political Convention produced a stratagem for Black Power and ran candidates for municipal office, galvanizing the black community behind the politics of black nationality formation. The 1969 Black and Puerto Rican Convention established a common agenda between those two communities and ran a slate of candidates that won the municipal elections in June 1970.

Alongside the black united front at the foundation of the Modern Black Convention Movement in Newark, New Jersey, was the black and Puerto Rican alliance in the struggle for municipal power. Beginning with a mutual defense pact between CFUN and the Young Lords, it flowered into the November 1969 Black and Puerto Rican Political Convention. That alliance endured through the crisis at Kawaida Towers, during which the veterans of the Young Lords Party were reliable allies against the threat of white terror. The black united front and the black and Puerto Rican

Amiri Baraka reading poetry. (Courtesy of the Baraka family collection, photograph by Zachariah Risasi Dais)

alliance at the local level served as a strong base for a national movement.

During the 1970s, the dynamics of the Modern Black Convention Movement unfolded to fashion a black national political community. The politics of black cultural nationalism fostered numerous national organizations, including the Congress of African People, the Black Women's United Front, the African Liberation Support Committee, and the

Amiri Baraka at the National Black Assembly in 1975. (Author's collection)

National Black Assembly. At each black assembly African Americans embraced their diversity, consolidated a sense of political community, celebrated their solidarity, and charted their future as a nation within a nation.

One of the mainstays of the Modern Black Convention Movement was the Congress of African People. Baraka's organization took steps to implement the key resolutions of the black assemblies between summit meetings. From all around the country, the Congress of African People attracted a dedicated core of members who practiced the customs and values of black cultural nationalism. CAP had an extensive national organization, reaching at least twenty-five cities with black population concentrations. It trained young men and women to lead its organizational branches; employing their own initiative, they responded to local conditions and fashioned schools, cooperatives, institutions, associations, and networks in order to flesh out the Black Power program of self-determination, self-respect, and self-defense.

The Modern Black Convention Movement spread black nationalism in the major urban centers of America in a number of ways. Much of its political mobilization centered on the demand for regional autonomy through elected officials. One centerpiece of its community agitation was the "Stop Killer Cops" program, which organized black people to resist police brutality. Because of the profound educational crisis in the ghetto,

Right to left: Amina Baraka, Jalia Woods (back row), and Taalamu Holiday with other New Jersey delegates at a National Black Assembly meeting, 1975. (Author's collection)

one of the most popular institutional solutions proposed by the movement was the African Free School. The institutional development of the Modern Black Convention Movement embraced the Black Arts Movement. In addition to drama and poetry, the Black Arts Movement developed local radio and television programs and national publishing companies and newspapers in order to spread the politics of cultural nationalism. The most popular black nationalist ritual developed was the Kwanzaa celebration, organized around the seven principles.

If the measure of an effective nationalist movement is that it hastens the process of turning a specific population into a *nationality*, then the Modern Black Convention Movement played an outstanding role in the Black Power insurgency. According to Anthony D. Smith, strong nationalist movements develop four essential components: a dedicated hard core imbued with the new nationalist values and tastes; an array of institutions and organizations; a set of clearly articulated myths and rituals; and a fairly broad diffusion in the cities. By these criteria, the politics of black cultural nationalism played a critical role in nationality formation between 1966 and 1976.

The Modern Black Convention Movement was an essential component of the Black Power movement, which included the cultural, political, and economic programs proposed and developed by the Black Arts Movement, the Black Panther Party, the US Organization, the Republic of New Africa, the Revolutionary Action Movement, the Nation of Islam, the Organization of Afro-American Unity, and the League of Revolutionary Black Workers. Together these cultural and political formations galvanized millions of black people in the broadest movement in African American history: high school and college youth organized black student unions; professors and educators created black studies programs; athletes mobilized protests against poverty and racism; workers fashioned militant unions; welfare mothers demanded power and dignity; soldiers resisted army discipline; and during prison uprisings such as Attica, politically conscious inmates saluted Malcolm X and George Jackson.[2] Since the Black Revolt was so thoroughgoing and the black cultural revolution was so unprecedented, it is difficult to understand how these developments could be trivialized by serious scholars. Perhaps the answer is threefold: (1) as the politics of liberation, Black Power raised the most profound aspirations for emancipation, which were at that time unattainable; (2) an unfinished revolution by an oppressed nationality is the most difficult phenomenon to assess; and (3) the conservative counterrevolution has been devastating.

While the Black Revolt produced some of the most creative and vital experiments in the politics of liberation in America, a glance at the conditions in today's black ghetto immediately demonstrates that Black Power did not liberate African Americans from the yoke of poverty and oppression. The people of African descent have been the most humiliated people in modern world history; many of the political forces and economic institutions that enslaved, conquered, and colonized them flourished for centuries. Thus, if it is earnest, black liberation—the process of emancipating people of African descent from racial oppression—will be a *protracted* and extremely complex struggle.

Consequently, the critical question cannot be whether or not Baraka's Modern Black Convention Movement—or, for that matter, Marcus Garvey's Universal Negro Improvement Association or Malcolm X's Organization of Afro-American Unity—liberated black people; the more relevant issue is whether or not these movements accelerated the processes of nationality formation and black liberation, whether or not those organizations and institutions hastened the death of racial oppression and internal colonialism. Once Ali Mazrui wrote that "the distinctiveness of the fate of black people is that they have been the most humiliated in recent times. . . . The restoration of black dignity is almost the ultimate measure of racial equality."[3] Since a crucial part of racial oppression was the humiliation inherent in slavery and colonialism, then psychological liberation, ethical reconstruction, and cultural revolution remain essential components of the process of black liberation. By that measure, the Black Power era was a golden age in the sustained quest for black freedom and for the abolition of racial oppression.[4]

A Nation within a Nation

The Black Power movement focused national attention on the key problem of the black community, the ghetto. In the twentieth century, African Americans were urbanized and modernized in a very separate manner, which laid the modern foundations for a distinct black national political community. In the ghetto, Black America further developed into one of America's most distinct language communities.[5] As African Americans migrated to northern urban industrial centers in unprecedented numbers and raised their level of education, urban, bureaucratic ethnic boundaries combined with white racism to exclude a rising group of educated black Americans. The members of this emerging black intelligentsia increasingly sought to establish parallel institutions where they might find appropriate positions. Consequently, the pace of black nationality development accelerated as African Americans were urbanized.

In other words, black nationalism is engendered by the nature of urban bureaucratic competition and conflict in a multiethnic capitalist society.[6] In the schools, another dimension of black nationality formation, the conflict between U.S. *bureaucratic nationalism* and black *romantic nationalism*, is expressed in the contemporary demands for African-centered education and multiculturalism.[7] Black college students are drawn to black nationalism in response to the demand that they fit into bureaucratic slots in American society; they resent the implication that blacks must become "white" in order to *make it* in America. Rather than conform to fit into those notches, many of those youth bolster the forces of black cultural nationalism.

During the Black Power era, the politics of cultural nationalism took advantage of that momentum to accelerate the processes of black nationality formation in several ways. For one thing, it fashioned a strategy of black liberation that demanded regional autonomy in urban centers. Second, it forged coalitions with sympathetic whites. Third, it established alliances with oppressed peoples of color in the United States, particularly Puerto Ricans and Mexican Americans; these were the earliest "Rainbow

Coalitions." Fourth, the agitation against incidents of police brutality and against the failure of government services dramatized the conflict between the municipal bureaucracies and the black community.

Some scholars consider the Black Power appraisal of the situation of the black ghetto in America an expression of pessimism. While it is true that Black Power proponents found racial integration into white America implausible, they made a sober assessment of the urban crisis for Black America. The size and segregation of the black ghetto has reached unprecedented dimensions; today there are more than 10 million African Americans living in fourteen cities that have segregated black populations of at least 200,000: Atlanta, Baltimore, Chicago, Cleveland, Dallas, Detroit, Houston, Los Angeles, Memphis, New Orleans, New York, Philadelphia, St. Louis, and Washington, D.C.[8] Neither of the major political parties proposes a solution to American apartheid; desegregation is off the national political agenda.

The Black Power movement was confident about the capacity of African Americans to solve their own problems—and rightly so. Rather than black communities passively awaiting whatever some political candidate might deem were the pressing issues in the next election, the black conventions seized the initiative in their own hands in order to determine and define the pressing concerns which they felt were most important, speaking in a language that they well understood. In that process, they began to identify and distinguish the immediate, intermediate, and long-range interests and goals of the black national community. That is why those black assemblies represented such an unprecedented and effective political presence: they were not only militant but they fashioned their own agendas.

However, the Black Power movement underestimated the extent to which the problems of Black America are a component part of the dynamics of the political economy of the United States. As blacks and Puerto Ricans migrated to urban industrial centers like Newark, the metropolis was in the midst of a postindustrial transformation. Once they sought streets paved with promise for those who labored hard in factories; now many of them languish unemployed in the shadow of opulent corporate centers, still haunted by the horror of poverty and the violence of despair.

Benign Neglect

While Black America was trapped in the ghetto, the federal urban policies of the New Deal and the Great Society and the postindustrial investment strategies of the corporate world combined forces to shower their bounty on white suburbs. While offering African American urban centers "benign neglect," an unprecedented combination of both public and private investments in the segregated suburbs fashioned the modern structures of American apartheid. This is the contemporary face of internal colonialism; Jonathan Kozol exposed its savage inequalities. While upper-class and middle-class white communities invest a great deal in their public and private schools, libraries, cultural centers, theaters, museums, and shopping malls for their youth, the children of the black and Puerto Rican ghettos are subjected to shocking poverty and despair. The walls of racism, hatred, and indifference surrounding them ensure their exclusion from the great wealth of American society.

When cultural, intellectual, and financial resources were concentrated in American cities, the white upper class and the middle class fled most of those urban centers without so much as a clue about solving urban poverty. In *Safeguarding the Public Health: Newark 1895–1918*, Stuart Galishoff points out that "the 1890 U.S. Census found that Newark had become the 'nation's unhealthiest city.' . . . Clearly Newark had these chronic social problems before the first significant wave of black migrants reached that city during the First World War. . . . [This] suggests that the major elements in the city's chronic problems were first structural, not racial."[9] Consequently, many of the formidable social and economic problems of the urban centers were inherited by black people. Consider the grotesque logic: suburban whites have abandoned the cities and then assigned blacks and Latinos the awesome responsibility for healing urban decay.

Honest people know better. Jonathan Kozol makes it clear that the appalling inequalities in the American school system make a mockery of equal opportunity and democracy. Thomas Philpott reminds us that black ghettos have existed for a century and that, like slavery, they will not fade away; internal colonialism must be abolished. Douglas Massey and Nancy Denton emphasize the role of American apartheid in the making of the underclass.[10]

In the face of these problems, clearly the Black Power emphasis on cultural, political, and economic autonomy was not enough. In fact, black leadership must be extremely careful to distinguish for itself the contemporary aims of black self-determination. As Manuel Castells explains, with its politics of liberation Black America sought to transform "the walls of its prison into the boundaries of its free city."[11] However, the power structure's pattern of response was to *mimic* self-determination by placing black faces in high places, reducing the dream of liberated urban zones to the reality of inner-city Bantustans.

The serious leadership in Black America must address these contemporary issues precisely, whether that leadership is moderate or radical, nationalist or Marxist; preaching and rhetoric are no substitutes for the answers. These vicious problems cry out for analyses, policies, programs, actions, and solutions. Consider, for instance, schooling, employment, and welfare. In the inner city, the crux of the problems of bad schooling, unemployment, and welfare is *poverty;* any "political" program that results in leaving people impoverished is not a solution but simply another diversion. The key problem in the black community, where parents are trying to make a better life for their children, is that the schools simply reproduce (and sometimes exacerbate) the inequalities in the occupational and societal structures. That system treats students differently based on their racial status, class origins, and gender. To put the matter bluntly, the children of wealthy CEOs and upper managers are cultivated to become the next generation of the upper class as well as high-status professionals. In addition to enjoying institutional endowments and large financial investments, that upper-class education involves such features as greater student participation, less direct supervision, more student electives, and a value system that stresses *internalized* standards of control.[12]

However, too many of the children of the oppressed are trained to take their place at the bottom of the postindustrial ladder, in the low-paying service sector of the economy or, even worse, in the ranks of the permanently unemployed and in the prisons. Their schooling features institutions that are more regimented and that place emphasis on strict rules and repressive behavioral controls. No wonder many children in the working class do not like school.[13]

The most reactionary sectors of the business class want to perpetuate the kinds of education that fit certain groups of people to work for the lowest wages: those are the groups that fall in the lowest sector of the working class, many of them women and people of color. Increasingly, there is an expanding bottom layer of the social pyramid, filled with unemployed youth; their schooling is more and more like detention, and they are being prepared to do some *real time* later, in prison.

In sum, there is one kind of education for the CEOs who make roughly $5,000 per hour and another kind for the lowest-level employees, who make $5 per hour. That is only one plank of the agenda set by the reactionaries from above. Unfortunately, too many liberals and moderates who witness what is happening to those children watch in a posture of political paralysis.

But what are some current alternatives? What would the agenda look like if it surged from below? First, we need the type of schooling that will educate people to struggle against that vicious system. Second, we need the kinds of institutions that will produce an alternative agenda, an order of priorities from below, including decent employment and dignified and affordable housing, child care, and health care. Third, at the bottom of such a process of grassroots agenda building are people in struggle, working step by step in mutual respect toward common understandings of social, political, cultural, and economic emancipation. In essence, that process is about making oppressed groups into the self-conscious agents of their own liberation. And I think that is what our schools should be about, teaching people all the thinking, study, and research skills, so that they might develop their own agendas together from below. That kind of education would also teach them how to work together to resist the disastrous imperatives of racism, sexism, and capitalism.

Part of that process of developing oppressed groups into the self-conscious agents of their own liberation is placing the development of alternative values and structures at the center of the struggle against this oppressive system. In the battles for multicultural education, one of the fundamental aims must be that youth do not use each other as the scapegoats for the aggression and frustration generated by capitalist exploitation and social exclusion. One learns of the contemporary, explosive dangers of such displaced aggression in Jay MacLeod's excellent ethnography *Ain't No Makin' It*, which examines the lives of impoverished youth groups that have been denied access to both employment and dignity. The postindustrial economy has denied many inner-city youths the rites of passage that are markers of adulthood in industrial societies, particularly a decent job and the income to establish a household. MacLeod captures the appalling specter of these frustrated young white men replacing those lost rites of passage with such counterrevolutionary rituals as racial and ethnic conflict, violence against women, and prison terms as the new markers of manhood.

What can be done? In this history of Baraka's Congress of African People, there are many examples of the community's generating alternative rituals and progressive standards of both manhood and womanhood in the postindustrial economy—for example, Sunday Soul Sessions, naming ceremonies, promotion rituals, Kwanzaa, and the organization of youth by age groups. The overarching strategy was to provide an alternative value system that bound oppressed peoples together with new identity, purpose, and direction. Today, new social movements must help inner-city youths in developing meaningful alternative rituals of adulthood and in struggling for progressive values that facilitate their coming together in the fight for radical democracy, economic justice, community development, and personal dignity.

Similarly, if public officials are serious about reforming the ills of welfare, they must focus on assisting impoverished households in nurturing children. One way of fashioning a nourishing environment for raising children in the ghetto would be to help impoverished mothers develop cooperative child care industries. Sending mothers to classes to learn the fundamentals of nutrition, health, early childhood education, and cooperative economics would help save a generation of children. Meaningful careers and socially necessary jobs would be provided if both public policy and community organization were to focus upon the requirements of child development. Children in poverty need the same love, attention, and resources as any other children. Far too much of today's public policy is aimed at humiliating those mothers; in such an atmosphere, their children will never know the essential advantages of personal dignity and self-respect.

One lesson to learn from a history of the Black Power era is that creative experimentation with organizations, programs, and institutions is a way forward. Another lesson from that period is that African Americans have a great storehouse of creative energy and that urban youth have tremendous untapped potential that is essential to the regeneration of Black America. When college students, artists, and intellectuals intervene on the side of the grass roots, a great deal is possible. And, as I have suggested, there is a great deal to be learned from past experiments in black self-determination.

Black United Front

Finally, excluding actual traitors, nearly every group in black America has contributed to the African American quest for liberation from racial oppression. For black liberation to close the door to the participation and contribution of black people with different ideologies or religions is to destroy the possibility of ending the urban catastrophe faced by all. Furthermore, while the ideological interchange between the cultural nationalists and the revolutionary nationalists was legitimate, the violent warfare between those two factions amounted to a level of irresponsibility bordering upon treason. It turned the black liberation movement into a plaything in the hands of the police. That is why the FBI Cointelpro sought to expand the fratricidal bloodbath from coast to coast; that program understood that it would spell death for the aspirations of Black Power. The same criticism applies to the debate between the black Marxists and nationalists. It must never be permitted to happen again—the first time *tragedy*, the next time *farce*.[14]

Of course, each party—Muslim, nationalist, or socialist—has legitimate areas of concern about maintaining purity of doctrine, and in any black united front those legitimate concerns must be respected. But Black America is much bigger than any one political party and ideological perspective; it is larger than any one religion or class; its problems are more severe and its fate is more autonomous than that of any ethnic group in the U.S. At more than 30 million people, African Americans are one of the great nationalities in the world today; and it is not unusual for a large nationality such as Black America to encompass several constituent classes, numerous political philosophies, and more than one religion. In the modern world, those large nationalities that have not matured to embrace a reasonable measure of diversity are doomed to disaster.

Although for many proponents of either Marxism or nationalism *any* mixture of socialist and black consciousness is a heresy, for African Americans as a nationality it is essential to recognize that in the twentieth century key elements of each of those ideological perspectives have been necessary. In his last year, Malcolm X was attempting to fashion a political and ideological mixture suitable for black liberation in the U.S. Stressing the need for African Americans to develop their own revolutionary ideology and organization, Malcolm X urged them to search for philosophical, economic, and political approaches rooted in the African Personality. If black people wanted to be free, he argued, they could not be guided by the thinking of their former slave masters: they had to understand that the logic of the oppressor is different from the logic of the oppressed. For Malcolm, the creativity and improvisation of black music was a clear paradigm for revolutionaries. In line with that, in the 1960s most of the leading Black Power organizations braved charges of ideological heresy as they developed political philosophies that were amalgams of various proportions of socialism and nationalism. African Americans will have to continue to draw upon the best knowledge in the world in order to achieve their formidable goals of self-emancipation, political liberation, and socioeconomic development. Those lessons come in different ideological and political packages, and black leadership must use good judgment in choosing the insight and information that is necessary to navigate the road to freedom.

Since African Americans have always suffered from a lethal combination of racism and capitalism, of racial oppression and class exploitation, on most occasions Black America requires an ideological and political arsenal that includes elements of both nationalism and Marxism; the emphasis of black leadership must change according to the nature of the period. During eras of intense group conflict in American society, African Americans will have to draw upon a profound understanding of the dynamics of nationalism, national consciousness, and nationality formation. Because of the dynamics of group competition and the ethos arising from such clashes and hostility, there will probably be periods when progressive allies are scarce. No matter what the situation, African Americans must survive those periods. But during times of powerful capitalist antagonism in the U.S., Black America would be wise to draw upon a rich knowledge of Marxism, political economy, class consciousness, and class formation. During those junctures, there should be a much greater potential for progressive allies—because of the dynamics of business accumulation, increasing unemployment, public policy shifting the weight of economic crisis onto the backs of broad sections of the American people, and the populist spirit that emanates from such conflicts. Still, due to the historic character and complexity of Black America, at no time can the emphasis of serious leadership be purely Marxist or nationalist without doing serious damage to the black national community. In other words, sectarianism is the enemy of black liberation and the fight for equality.

An Oppressed Nationality

Alongside the oppressed people of South Africa and those of Northern Ireland, who have suffered from internal colonialism for centuries, the African Americans are one of the world's great peoples: *they deserve better leadership.*[15] Black America is one of the largest nationalities in the United States; it is not a class, but rather a national community with several classes. African Americans have distinct national interests in both domestic and foreign policy; those issues and concerns were articulated at the 1972 Gary Convention in seven major areas: human development, economics, communications and culture, rural development, environmental protection, politics, and international policy. Black leadership must have a profound understanding of those interests; otherwise it is unconsciously or consciously serving some other group's interests. African American socialists who aspire to lead Black America must understand those simple truths or forfeit any claim to group leadership. Similarly, African American nationalists who aim to lead Black America must recognize the menace of class exploitation within the black community or renounce the privilege to group leadership. National leadership cannot lower its sights to petty sectarian interests; that leadership is an honor and a responsibility that requires national vision.

In *The Crisis of the Negro Intellectual*, Harold Cruse suggests that black intellectuals and leaders must draw upon the rich experiences of both black nationalists and socialists in order to grasp the complexity of the African American situation. The specificity of a liberation theory for Black America should be based on the African American experience in the fight for freedom. Fashioning such a theory and practice is something that each group of people must do for itself. In line with this, the critique that Harold Cruse makes of black intellectuals and radical theorists of the Garvey era is applicable to those of the Black Power generation as well:

> The Negro intellectuals and radical theorists of the 1920s and 1930s did not, themselves, fight for intellectual clarity. They were unable to create a new black revolutionary synthesis of what was applicable from Garveyism (especially economic nationalism), and what they had learned from Marxism that was valid. . . . They could have laid down the foundation for a new school of revolutionary ideas, which, if developed, could have maintained a programmatic continuity between the issues and events of the 1920s and the Negro movements of the 1950s and 1960s. And the young Negro intellectuals of today would probably not be facing a theoretical and intellectual vacuum.[16]

If we are to fill this great vacuum, the Black Power generation and the Hip Hop generation must do this intellectual and political work *together* on a foundation of self-criticism and mutual respect.

One generation ago, millions of Africans suffered under the humiliation and exploitation of colonialism; black people in the African Liberation Support Committee played an important role in supporting the independence struggles of Angola, Mozambique, Guinea-Bissau, and Zimbabwe. That support was part of an international plan to isolate South African apartheid so that it would be overthrown. Those victories did not fall from the sky; they required both an elaborate strategy and a protracted struggle.

And that successful stratagem illuminates what African American leadership and mobilization can do. Frederick Douglass taught black people that "if there is no struggle, there is no progress":

> Find out just what people will submit to, and you have found out the exact amount of injustice and wrong which will be imposed upon them; and these will continue till they are resisted with either words or blows, or with both.[17]

The great people whose ancestors and their allies arose in moral outrage to destroy U.S. slavery will certainly rise again and again until internal colonialism and American apartheid are vanquished.

Notes

The abbreviation KWOF refers to Komozi Woodard's office files at Sarah Lawrence College in Bronxville, New York.

PREFACE

1. Harris, *Jones/Baraka Reader*, xvii.
2. Quoted in ibid., xviii.
3. "Maya Angelou Interviews Amiri Baraka," in Reilly, *Conversations with Baraka*, 261.
4. Lacey, *To Raise, Destroy, and Create*, vii.
5. Ibid., viii.
6. Sollors, *Amiri Baraka/LeRoi Jones*, 1.
7. Lacey, *To Raise, Destroy, and Create*, viii.
8. Sollors, *Amiri Baraka/LeRoi Jones*, 1–2.
9. Ibid., 1.
10. Cruse, *Crisis of the Negro Intellectual*, 355.
11. Lewis, *When Harlem Was in Vogue*; Huggins, *Harlem Renaissance*; J. Anderson, *This Was Harlem*.
12. Harris, *Jones/Baraka Reader*, xvii.
13. Breitman, *By Any Means Necessary*, 63–64; Baraka, *Raise*.
14. Hutchinson, "Cultural Nationalism and Moral Regeneration," 122.
15. Van Deburg, *New Day in Babylon*.
16. Katznelson, *City Trenches*; Castells, *The City and the Grassroots*.

INTRODUCTION

1. Draper, *Rediscovery of Black Nationalism*; W. J. Wilson, *Power, Racism, and Privilege*, 97, 113–14; McAdams, *Political Process and the Development of Black Insurgency*, 108; "Introduction," in Bracey, Meier, and Rudwick, *Black Nationalism in America*, liii.
2. Allen, *Black Awakening in Capitalist America*, chap. 4; Newton, "Huey Newton Talks to the Movement," 50–51.
3. Eisinger, "Ethnic Conflict, Community Building, and the Emergence of Ethnic Political Traditions in the U.S."; Gordon, *Assimilation in American Life*; see debate in Bracey, Meier, and Rudwick, *Black Nationalism in America*, liii.
4. Carson, *In Struggle*, 287; Sitkoff, *Struggle for Black Equality*.
5. Blauner, *Racial Oppression in America*; Ira Katznelson, "Introduction to the Phoenix Edition," in Katznelson, *Black Men, White Cities*.
6. Haywood, *Negro Liberation*; Cruse, *Rebellion or Revolution?*; Cruse, *Crisis of the Negro Intellectual*.
7. For contrast, see earlier ideas in Frazier, *Race and Culture Contacts*; Haywood, *Negro Liberation*.
8. A. D. Smith, *Nationalism in the Twentieth Century*, chap. 7.
9. Gellner, *Thought and Change*; Gellner, *Nations and Nationalism*; Frederick Barth, "Introduction," in Barth, *Ethnic Groups and Boundaries*.

10. Levine, *Black Culture and Black Consciousness*, 152–53; Yinger, *Ethnicity*, 307–9; Fasold and Labov et al., "Are Black and White Vernaculars Diverging?"; Van Deburg, *New Day in Babylon*, 219–20; Massey and Denton, *American Apartheid*, 162–63.

11. Instead of assimilation, acculturation more accurately describes the process: viz., Gordon, *Assimilation in American Life*.

12. E. Franklin Frazier, "Garvey: A Mass Leader," in Clarke, *Marcus Garvey and the Vision of Africa*, 236–41; Park and Burgess, *The City*; W. J. Wilson, *Power, Racism, and Privilege*, 97, 113–14; McAdams, *Political Process and the Development of Black Insurgency*, 108; Patterson, "Going Separate Ways," 43. For critique of Park and Burgess, see Zunz, *Changing Face of Inequality*, 42–43; Karenga, "Afro-American Nationalism."

13. A. D. Smith, *Nationalism in the Twentieth Century*, 166–83.

14. Eisinger, "Ethnic Conflict"; Bayor, *Neighbors in Conflict*.

15. Wirth, "Types of Nationalism," 724.

16. Eisinger, "Ethnic Conflict," 17–18.

17. Haywood, *Negro Liberation*, 168–69.

18. A. D. Smith, "Nationalism," 26.

19. Heberle, *Social Movements*, 13.

20. Symmons-Symnolewicz, *Nationalist Movements*, 41.

21. A. D. Smith, "Nationalism," 46; Symmons-Symnolewicz, *Nationalist Movements*.

22. A. D. Smith, *Nationalist Movements*, 6, 9; see also Symmons-Symnolewicz, *Nationalist Movements*.

23. Symmons-Symnolewicz, *Nationalist Movements*, vii.

24. Haywood, "Remarks on the Chicano Question," in Haywood Files, KWOF; Haywood, *Negro Liberation*.

25. Moses, *Golden Age of Black Nationalism*; Miller, *Search for a Black Nationality*; Lynch, "Pan-Negro Nationalism"; Bell, *Search for a Place*; Stuckey, *Ideological Origins of Black Nationalism*.

26. Haywood, *Negro Liberation*; Haywood, *Black Bolshevik*, 227–35.

27. Stuckey, *Slave Culture*; Stuckey, *Going Through the Storm*; Levine, *Black Culture and Black Consciousness*; Wood, *Black Majority*; Gutman, *Black Family*; Genovese, *Roll, Jordan, Roll*.

28. Jordan, "American Chiaroscuro," 185–200; Jordan, *White Over Black*; Omi and Winant, *Racial Formation*; Winant, *Racial Conditions*; Roediger, *Wages of Whiteness*; Roediger, *Towards the Abolition of Whiteness*; F. J. Davis, *Who Is Black?*

29. Ira Berlin, *Slaves Without Masters*.

30. E. Foner, *Reconstruction*, 102; Holt, *Black over White*, 70; Williamson, *After Slavery*, 364–66; Williamson, *New People*, 61–84.

31. Horton, *Free People of Color*; Du Bois, *Philadelphia Negro*; Katzman, *Before the Ghetto*; Lee, *Think Black*; Lee, *Black Pride*.

32. Levine, *Black Culture and Black Consciousness*, 53.

33. Ibid., 4.

34. For the radicalism, see Harding, *There Is a River*; Stuckey, *Ideological Origins of Black Nationalism*; Stuckey, *Slave Culture*; Stuckey, *Going Through the Storm*; McAdoo, *Pre–Civil War Black Nationalism*; for the conservatism, see Moses, *Golden Age of Black Nationalism*; Moses, *Alexander Crummell*.

35. Aptheker, *Documentary History of the Negro People*, 70–71.

36. Bracey, Meier, and Rudwick, *Black Nationalism in America*, 46.

37 Aptheker, *Afro-American History*, 112.

38. Aptheker, *Documentary History of the Negro People*, 71.

39. Litwack, *North of Slavery*, 73, 100; Wade, "The Negro in Cincinnati," 56; Woodson, "The Negroes in Cincinnati," 7.

40. Litwack, *North of Slavery*, 73–74; Pierson, *Tocqueville and Beaumont in America*, 565. Further attempts to expel blacks are reported in Woodson, *A Century of Negro Migration*.

41. Litwack, *North of Slavery*, 70.

42. Ibid., 69–70.

43. Aptheker, *Afro-American History*, 11.

44. P. S. Foner, *Frederick Douglass*, 52–53.

45. Aptheker, *Documentary History of the Negro People*, 232.

46. Patterson, *Slavery and Social Death*.

47. Berlin, *Slaves Without Masters*, 51–52.

48. Nash, *Forging Freedom*, 79, 83, 80.

49. McAdoo, *Pre–Civil War Black Nationalism*; Aptheker, *Documentary History of the Negro People*, vol. 1.

50. P. S. Foner, *Life and Writing of Frederick Douglass*, 2:246.

51. Aptheker, *Afro-American History*, 112.

52. Fredrickson, *Black Image in the White Mind*, 61, 130–31; Van den Berghe, *Race and Racism*, 18; Hoetink, *Two Variants in Caribbean Race Relations*; Hoetink, "National Identity and Somatic Norm Image," 29–44; Hoetink, "National Identity, Culture, and Race in the Caribbean."

53. Du Bois, *Black Reconstruction*, 149; Wesley, "Lincoln's Plan for Colonizing the Emancipated Negro," 1, 20; George Fredrickson, *Arrogance of Race*, 69, 70, 72.

54. Du Bois, *Black Reconstruction*, 149; Wesley, "Lincoln's Plan for Colonizing the Emancipated Negro," 1, 7–21.

55. Fredrickson, *Black Image in the White Mind*, 175, chap. 5 passim.

56. Litwack, *Been in the Storm So Long*, 400–401; Aptheker, *Documentary History of the Negro People*, 1:496.

57. Ibid.

58. Fredrickson, *Black Image in the White Mind*, 175.

59. Ibid., 177.

60. E. Foner, *Nothing But Freedom*.

61. Painter, "Martin R. Delany," 149–72.

62. E. Foner, *Nothing But Freedom*, 94–95, 97–99.

63. Raines, *My Soul Is Rested*, 249.

64. Gillette, *Retreat from Reconstruction*, xi.

65. Du Bois, *Black Reconstruction*; Perman, *Road to Redemption*.

66. Painter, *Exodusters*, 86.

67. Ibid.; Grossman, *Land of Hope*, 23–26.

68. Blauner, *Racial Oppression in America*; Hechter, *Internal Colonialism*; Katznelson, *Black Men, White Cities*; Katznelson, *City Trenches*.

69. Sitkoff, *New Deal for Blacks*, 3–4; Logan, *The Negro in American Life and Thought*; Woodward, *Strange Career of Jim Crow*; Dittmer, *Black Georgia in the Progressive Era*.

70. Sitkoff, *New Deal for Blacks*.

71. Brundage, *Lynching in the New South*, 8.

72. Sitkoff, *New Deal for Blacks*, 19–20.

73. Lynch, *Edward Wilmot Blyden*, chap. 4; Blyden, *Christianity, Islam and the Negro Race*; Henriksen, "African Intellectual Influences on Black Americans."

74. Redkey, *Black Exodus*; Dittmer, *Black Georgia in the Progressive Era*; Dittmer, "Education of Henry McNeal Turner," 253–74.

75. Padmore, *Pan-Africanism or Communism*, 83–148; Du Bois, *World and Africa*.

76. James, *Holding Aloft the Banner of Ethiopia*, 355–58.

77. Haywood, *Black Bolshevik*; Allen, *Reluctant Reformers*.

78. Meier, *Negro Thought in America*, 140.

79. Harrison, *The Negro and the Nation*, 7.

80. Harrison, *When Africa Awakes*; Harrison, *The Negro and the Nation*; Perry, "Hubert Henry Harrison"; Samuels, "Five Afro-Caribbean Voices in American Culture."

81. Huggins, *Harlem Renaissance*, 18.

82. Kusmer, *A Ghetto Takes Shape*, 234.

83. Ibid., 283; Price, "Afro-American Community of Newark," 45.

84. In his introduction to *The Crusader* (xxx), Hill indicates Sons of Africa as forerunner and IRB as prototype.

85. League of Struggle for Negro Rights, *Equality, Land and Freedom: A Program for Negro Liberation*, 7, in Haywood Files, KWOF.

86. Sitkoff, *New Deal for Blacks*, 179.

87. Ibid., 180; Naison, *Communists in Harlem*; Haywood, *Black Bolshevik*.

88. Sitkoff, *New Deal for Blacks*, 181.

89. Ibid., 182.

90. Ibid., 183.

91. Ibid., 188.

92. Paul Robeson, "I Want to Be African," and "I Don't Want to Be White," in P. S. Foner, *Paul Robeson Speaks*, 92.

93. Haywood, *Black Bolshevik*, 459.

94. Sitkoff, *New Deal for Blacks*, 112.

95. Harris, *The Harder We Run*, 119.

96. For critical assessments of New Deal liberalism, politics, and policies, see Kirby, *Black Americans in the Roosevelt Era*; Weiss, *Farewell to the Party of Lincoln*; Mollenkopf, *Contested City*; Katz, *In the Shadow of the Poorhouse*, 244–45.

97. A. R. Hirsch, "Black Ghettos," 109–13; Massey and Denton, *American Apartheid*.

98. Moses, *Golden Age of Black Nationalism*.

99. Arnold Hirsch, "Epilogue: Chicago and the Nation," in A. R. Hirsch, *Making the Second Ghetto*, 259–75.

100. A. R. Hirsch, "Black Ghettos," 110.

101. Kusmer, *A Ghetto Takes Shape*, 230.

102. Haywood interview.

103. Kusmer, *A Ghetto Takes Shape*, 231.

104. Ibid., 234.

105. Woodard, "Making of the New Ark."

106. Harvey, *The Urban Experience*, 119.

107. Jones, *Home*, 103–4.

108. B. Anderson, *Imagined Communities*.

109. Van Deburg, *New Day in Babylon*, 205.

110. Baraka and Baraka, *The Music*.

111. Jones, *Blues People*, 101–2.

112. Five meanings of color are discussed in Katznelson, *Black Men, White Cities*, 39, and M. G. Smith, *Plural Society in the British West Indies*, 60–66: phenotypical, genealogical, associational, cultural/behavioral, and structural.

113. Clark, *Dark Ghetto*; C. Brown, *Manchild in the Promised Land*.

114. Bloom, *Class, Race, and the Civil Rights Movement*, 189; Newton, *Revolutionary Suicide*, 14–15.

115. Jones, *Home*, 94.

116. Ibid., 94–95.

117. Harris, *The Harder We Run*, 105.

118. Ibid. I owe this insight about the NIRA to Ira Katznelson, "Reinventing Liberalism: Bidding the New Deal Goodbye," KWOF; for documentation, see Wolters, *Negroes and the Great Depression*, chap. 6.

119. Garvin interview. Moreover, Vicki Garvin and Maya Angelou helped arrange for Malcolm X's introduction to African, Asian, and Latin American diplomats in Ghana in 1964.

120. Thompson, *National Negro Labor Council*.

121. Ibid., 23, 27; *"Get on Board the Freedom Train,"* in KWOF.

122. Thompson, *National Negro Labor Council*, 65.

123. Ibid., 66; Ward and Bingham interviews.

124. Curvin, "Persistent Minority," 30–34.

125. Elliott Rudwick, "W. E. B. Du Bois: Protagonist of the Afro-American Protest," in Franklin and Meier, *Black Leaders of the Twentieth Century*, 82.

126. Cesaire, *Letter to Maurice Thorez*, 11.

127. Sitkoff, *Struggle for Black Equality*, 25; Burk, *Eisenhower Administration and Black Civil Rights*.

128. Chafe, *The Unfinished Journey*, 158.

129. For instance, see Dittmer, *Local People*, 53–89.

130. Sitkoff, *Black Struggle for Equality*, 52.

131. Payne, *I've Got the Light of Freedom*; Dittmer, *Local People*.

132. Author's interviews on the Steptoe farm in McComb, Mississippi, summer 1991.

133. Carson, *In Struggle*, 108, 117.

134. Weisbort, *Freedom Bound*, 225.

135. Gregory Nelson Hite is developing crucial research on the role of the Catholic church in the Selma movement; see his "The Hottest Places in Hell: Catholic Participation in the Selma Voting Rights Campaign, 1962–1965."

136. Sitkoff, *Struggle for Black Equality*, 201.

137. Sellers, *River of No Return*, 155.

138. Carmichael and Hamilton, *Black Power*, vii–viii.

139. Sellers, *River of No Return*, 187.

140. Johnson, *Peasant Nationalism and Communist Power*; Rusinow, *Yugoslav Experiment*; Mace, *Communism and the Dilemmas of National Liberation*.

CHAPTER ONE

1. Baraka, *Autobiography of LeRoi Jones*; Baraka, *African Congress*; Pinkney, *Red, Black and Green*; Sollors, *Amiri Baraka/LeRoi Jones*.

2. Newark CAP had different names at each step in its development, beginning with the United Brothers in 1967.

3. Pinkney, *Red, Black and Green*; Curvin, "Persistent Minority"; Marable, *Race, Reform and Rebellion*, 138; Walters, *Black Presidential*.

4. Hutchinson, *Dynamics of Cultural Nationalism*; Pierce, "Roots of the Rainbow Coalition"; Bell, *Survey of the Negro Convention Movement*; Pease and Pease, *They Who Would Be Free*; McAdoo, *Pre–Civil War Black Nationalism*; Klingman, "National Negro Convention Movement."

5. Allen, *Black Awakening in Capitalist America*; Bloom, *Class, Race and the Civil Rights Movement*; Omi and Winant, *Racial Formation*.

6. Van Deburg, "Introduction: A Black Power Paradigm," in *New Day in Babylon*.

7. Compare with John H. Clarke's "Introduction," in Clarke, *Malcolm X*, xxii.

8. Johnson, *Peasant Nationalism and Communist Power*, 25–26.

9. B. Anderson, *Imagined Communities*.

10. Hutchinson, "Cultural Nationalism and Moral Regeneration," 123.

11. Harris, *Jones/Baraka Reader*, xxxi.

12. For the romantic ethnic nationalist reaction to bureaucratic nationalism, see A. D. Smith, *Nationalism in the Twentieth Century*, 166–79.

13. Cabral, *Return to the Source*.

14. Cruse, *Crisis of the Negro Intellectual*, 356.

15. Baraka, *Autobiography of LeRoi Jones* (1984), 163.

16. For three accounts of this trip, see LeRoi Jones, "Cuba Libre," in *Home*; Clarke, "Journey to the Sierra Maestra," 32–35; and Cruse, *Crisis of the Negro Intellectual*.

17. Cruse, *Crisis of the Negro Intellectual*, 357.

18. Ibid.

19. Ibid.

20. Ngugi wa Thiong'o, *Writing Against Neocolonialism*, 1.

21. LeRoi Jones, "Letter to Jules Feiffer," in *Home*, 66.

22. Ibid., 65.

23. Ibid.

24. Ibid., 66.

25. This account of Lumumba's personal history is based on Rajeshwar Dayal's *Mission for Hammerskjöld: The Congo Crisis*.

26. Roger Anstey, "Belgian Rule in the Congo and the Aspirations of the 'Evolué' Class," in Gann and Duignan, *Colonialism in Africa, 1870–1960*, 194–225.

27. *New York Times*, July 28, 1960, 3.

28. Ibid., July 25, 1960, 2.

29. Clarke, "New Afro-American Nationalism," 286.

30. Ibid., 285.

31. Frantz Fanon, "Lumumba's Death: Could We Do Otherwise?" in *Toward the African Revolution*, 193.

32. *New York Times*, November 28, 1960, 1.

33. Ibid., February 15, 1961, 1.

34. Ibid., February 14, 1961, 1.

35. Ibid., February 16, 1961, 11.

36. Ibid., 1.

37. Amiri Baraka interview.

38. *New York Times*, February 16, 1961, 10.

39. Ibid., 11.

40. Later Richard Gibson was the author of an important work, *African Liberation Movements*.

41. Baraka, *Autobiography of LeRoi Jones*, 266–67.

42. Compare with William Toll's interpretation of the debate between Booker T. Washington and W. E. B. Du Bois in *The Resurgence of Race*.

43. See Malcolm X, *Autobiography of Malcolm X*; and Maulana Karenga, "Malcolm X: His Life and Legacy," a lecture delivered on May 21, 1989, at Temple University's Ritter Hall in Philadelphia, Pa., distributed by the National Association of Kawaida Organizations, Philadelphia chapter.

44. See C. Eric Lincoln's *Black Muslims in America* for background on the Asiatic black man.

45. Breitman, *By Any Means Necessary*, 63–64.

46. Goodwyn, *The Populist Moment*, xviii.

47. Neal, "New Space," 26.

48. Ibid., 27–28.

49. Compare with Maulana Karenga, "Malcolm X: His Life and Legacy," a lecture delivered on May 21, 1989.

50. Ossie Davis, "Our Shining Black Prince," in Clarke, *Malcolm X*, xii.

51. LeRoi Jones, "A Poem for Black Hearts," in *Black Magic*, 112.

52. "School and Theater Planned in Harlem by LeRoi Jones," *New York Times*, February 23, 1965, 40; Baraka, *Autobiography of LeRoi Jones*, 205.

53. Ibid.

54. LeRoi Jones, "New Black Music: A Concert in Benefit of the Black Arts Repertory Theater/School Live," in *Black Music*, 172–76.

55. Neal, "Social Background of the Black Arts Movement," 18; Baraka, *Autobiography of LeRoi Jones*, 205.

56. James W. Sullivan, "The Negro 'National Consciousness' of LeRoi Jones," *New York Herald Tribune*, October 31, 1965, in Amiri Baraka clippings, James Weldon Johnson Papers, Box No. B231, Beinecke Library, Yale University.

57. LeRoi Jones, "blackhope," in *Home*, 236–37.

58. *New York Times*, March 19, 1966, 27.

59. Baraka, *Autobiography of LeRoi Jones*, 215.

60. Randall, "Report on the Black Arts Convention," 54; Randall, "Second Annual Black Arts Convention," 42.

61. Neal, "The Black Contribution to American Letters," 777.

62. Cruse, *Crisis of the Negro Intellectual*, 439.

63. Ibid., 440; Woodard, "Making of the New Ark," 62–63.

CHAPTER TWO

1. Baraka, *Autobiography of LeRoi Jones*; Amiri Baraka Collection, Moorland-Spingarn Research Center, Howard University; Baraka interview.

2. Feagin and Hahn, *Ghetto Revolts*, 105–8.

3. Castells, *City and the Grassroots*, 54.

4. Feagin and Hahn, *Ghetto Revolts*, 105–8.

5. Karenga interview.

6. Mtumi and Halisi, *Quotable Karenga*; Halisi, *Kitabu*; Baraka, "Kawaida, The Doctrine of Maulana Karenga," Baraka Files, KWOF.

7. Ture/Carmichael interview.

8. *New York Times*, September 13, 1966, 1, 38; August 26, 1966, 17; September 3, 1966, 10; September 14, 1966, 1, 36.

9. On the Harlem Panthers, see ibid.

10. Carson et al., *Eyes on the Prize Civil Rights Reader*, 346–47.

11. Baraka, *African Congress*, 157–66; Pinkney, *Red, Black and Green*, 125–26; Hall, *Black Separatism*, 219–24.

12. Geschwender, *Class, Race, and Worker Insurgency*.

13. Harris, *Jones/Baraka Reader*.

14. Hutchinson, *Dynamics of Cultural Nationalism*.

15. Mohammed Babu reports that in January 1965 Malcolm X, Baraka, Babu, and representatives of SNCC debated the primacy of race or class all night at the Teresa Hotel.

16. Stone, *Black Political Power in America*, 125.

17. Ibid.

18. N. Wright, *Ready to Riot*, 12.

19. National Advisory Commission on Civil Disorders, *Report*, 30.

20. Jackson and Jackson, "Black Experience in Newark."

21. Marable, *Race, Reform and Rebellion*, 136.

22. Woodard, "Making of the New Ark," 83.

23. Wolak, "A Political Study of the Negro in Newark, New Jersey"; Kaplan, *Urban Renewal Politics*, 155–56.

24. Woodard, "Making of the New Ark," 93; Curvin, "Persistent Minority," 61.

25. Allen, *Black Awakening*, 131.

26. N. Wright, *Ready to Riot*, 14.

27. Curvin, "Persistent Minority," 20–21.

28. Teaford, *Twentieth-Century American City*, 107; see also Woodard, "Making of the New Ark," 72.

29. Curvin, "Persistent Minority," 20–21.

30. Woodard, "Making of the New Ark," 73.

31. Allen, *Black Awakening*, 129–30.

32. A. D. Smith, "Nationalism," 88.

33. Allen, *Black Awakening*, 131.

34. A. D. Smith, "'Ideas' and 'Structure' in the Formation of Independence Ideals," 28.

35. See, for instance, Cronon, *Black Moses;* Frazier, "Garvey as a Mass Leader," 118–22.

36. Allen, *Black Awakening,* 130.

37. Ibid.

38. Porambo, *No Cause for Indictment,* 101.

39. "New Violence in Newark: Stores Burned and Looted," *Star Ledger,* July 14, 1967, 1.

40. Allen, *Black Awakening,* 132.

41. "New Violence in Newark: Stores Burned and Looted," *Star Ledger,* July 14, 1967, 1.

42. Theodore R. Hudson, "The Trial of LeRoi Jones," in Benston, *Imamu Amiri Baraka (LeRoi Jones),* 49–50.

43. Porambo, *No Cause for Indictment,* 34.

44. Baraka, *Autobiography of LeRoi Jones,* 262.

45. Porambo, *No Cause for Indictment,* 34–35.

46. Ibid., 35.

47. Allen, *Black Awakening,* 134.

48. Ibid.

49. Hayden, *Rebellion in Newark,* 83.

50. Ibid., 51.

51. Ibid., 52.

52. Ibid., 53.

53. Stone, "National Conference on Black Power," 193.

54. *New York Times,* July 21, 1967, 1.

55. Earl Caldwell, "Two Police Inspectors from Here Among the Newark Delegates," *New York Times,* July 22, 1967, 11.

56. Stone, "National Conference on Black Power," 193.

57. *Life,* July 28, 1967, 26.

58. H. Rap Brown never returned because of the rebellion in which he was wounded at Cambridge. See picture of Brown's arrest in *Life,* August 4, 1967, 28.

59. *New York Times,* July 22, 1967, 1.

60. *Life,* July 28, 1967, 26.

61. Ibid.

62. Stone, "National Conference on Black Power," 189–98.

63. Thomas A. Johnson, "McKissick Holds End of Violence Is Up to Whites: CORE Leader at Meeting on Black Power Warns of Further Rioting," *New York Times,* July 22, 1967, 1.

64. Earl Caldwell, "Two Police Inspectors from Here Among the Newark Delegates," *New York Times,* July 22, 1967, 11.

65. *New York Times,* July 22, 1967, 11.

66. Harold Wilson was once a Muslim; then his name was Hassan.

67. Baraka, "Creation of the New Ark," Baraka Files, KWOF, 71.

68. In Swahili, "Baba" means father or elder, and in this case "Mshauri" took the meaning of counselor.

69. List of United Brothers members, Amiri Baraka Collection, Box 17, Moorland-Spingarn Research Center, Howard University.

70. "Ahadi Ya Akika" in the "Ritual Celebrating the Birth of Our Children," in "Customs and Concepts of the Committee for Unified NewArk," KWOF.

CHAPTER THREE

1. Eisinger, "Ethnic Conflict."

2. Przeworski and Sprague, *Paper Stones;* Omi and Winant, *Racial Formation.*

3. Coser, *Functions of Social Conflict;* Himes, "Functions of Racial Conflict."

4. Wirth, "Types of Nationalism," 724.

5. Eisinger, "Ethnic Conflict"; Bayor, *Neighbors in Conflict.*

6. Eisinger, "Ethnic Conflict," 17–18.

7. However, as the experience of the Irish and the Jews in American politics suggests, that early radicalism would not preclude subsequent political incorporation. See Eisinger, "Ethnic Conflict," and Ira Katznelson, *City Trenches,* 118.

8. *New York Times,* March 28, 1968, 40.

9. Amiri Baraka interview.

10. *New York Times,* March 28, 1968, 87.

11. Castells, *City and the Grassroots,* 50; Woodard, "Making of the New Ark," 128.

12. *Washington Post,* April 9, 1968, A3.

13. Matusow, *Unraveling of America,* 396.

14. *Washington Post,* April 7, 1968, 1.

15. Ibid., April 9, 1968, A3.

16. Unfortunately, Whitney Young died unexpectedly in Africa after the Atlanta summit. See Whitney Young's approach to Black Power and Pan-Africanism in Baraka, *African Congress,* 35–43.

17. Bullins, "The King Is Dead," 23–24.

18. Sellers, *River of No Return,* 67–80.

19. Wills, *Second Civil War,* 16, 18, 40. For Gelston's savage attack on Gloria Richardson, see Sellers, *River of No Return,* 70.

20. Drake, "Patterns of Interracial Conflict in 1968," 40; O'Reilly, *Racial Matters.*

21. Porambo, *No Cause for Indictment,* 194, 192. Huey Newton of the Black Panthers had similar thoughts.

22. *New York Times,* Sunday, April 14, 1968, 60.

23. Ibid., 60.

24. Stone, *Black Political Power in America,* 125.

25. Sitkoff, *Struggle for Black Equality,* 156; Brauer, *Kennedy and the Second Reconstruction,* 142, 252–59; Chafe, *Unfinished Journey,* 212.

26. Porambo, *No Cause for Indictment,* 273.

27. Ibid.

28. Ibid., 275.

29. Vailsburg looks like a finger jutting out of the city, wedged between Irvington, Maplewood, South Orange, and East Orange.

30. Porambo, *No Cause for Indictment,* 202–3.

31. Ibid., 203.

32. Ibid.

33. Ibid., 267.

34. Ibid., 269.

35. Sun Tzu, *Art of War*, 131.

36. *New York Times*, June 22, 1968, 28.

37. *Newark Evening News*, June 20, 1968, 17.

38. Subsequently, the United Brothers supported a third black candidate, Leon Ewing, for another seat on the city council.

39. *Newark Sunday News*, June 23, 1968, 20.

40. The major exception to this criticism is Manning Marable.

41. W. J. Wilson, *Power, Racism, and Privilege*, 97, 113–14. McAdam, *Political Process and the Development of Black Insurgency*, 108, follows Wilson's approach.

42. W. J. Wilson, *Declining Significance of Race*; W. J. Wilson, *Truly Disadvantaged*.

43. Draper, *Rediscovery of Black Nationalism*.

44. *Newark Sunday News*, June 23, 1968, 20.

45. Ibid.

46. The Housing and Urban Development Acts provide for a "project area committee" for each urban renewal site; one site was the Central Ward's NJR-32.

47. *Newark Sunday News*, June 23, 1968, 20.

48. Van Deburg, *New Day in Babylon*, 64–82.

49. *Newark Sunday News*, June 23, 1968, 20.

50. Ibid.

51. Ibid.

52. *Star Ledger*, June 22, 1968, 3.

53. *New York Times*, June 22, 1968. While the *New York Times* guessed the audience was 400, the *Star Ledger* (June 22, 1968, 3) estimated 600.

54. This writer's recollection of that speech.

55. *Newark Evening News*, June 24, 1968, 8.

56. Ibid.

57. Ibid.

58. Karenga was the leader of the 1968 National Black Power Conference in Philadelphia.

59. The first was in Washington, D.C., in 1966; the second in Newark, N.J., in 1967.

60. *Philadelphia Inquirer*, August 29, 1968, 44.

61. Ibid., August 30, 1968, 7.

62. Ibid., August 31, 1968, 7.

63. Ibid., September 2, 1968, 1.

64. Ibid.

65. Ibid.

66. Baraka, "Creation of the New Ark," Baraka Files, KWOF, 75.

67. Ibid.

68. Bingham interview; Karenga interview.

69. Tucker interview.

70. In some studies of Black Power, any quote, even if out of context, will do to caricature the behavior of these leaders and to make them look like fools.

71. Bingham/Mshauri interview, 1985.

72. Sun Tzu, *Art of War*, 131.

73. Allen, *Black Awakening*, 140–41.

74. Llorens, "Ameer (LeRoi Jones) Baraka," 77.

75. Ibid.

76. Baraka, *Raise*, 162.

77. Llorens, "Ameer (LeRoi Jones) Baraka," 77.

78. Van Deburg, *New Day in Babylon*, 216; Kofsky, *Black Nationalism and the Revolution in Music*, 65–66; Breitman, *By Any Means Necessary*, 63–64.

79. Graham, *Civil Rights Era*, 304.

80. Peace for their antiwar stand on Vietnam, and power for Black Power.

81. Stone, *Black Political Power in America*, 286. Meanwhile, Imperiale and Giuliano gathered 71 percent in the North Ward and 51 percent in the East Ward.

82. Stone, *Black Political Power in America*, 286.

83. Curvin, "Persistent Minority," 68–69.

84. See Przeworski and Sprague, *Paper Stones*; Winant, *Racial Formation*.

85. In Swahili, "Kawaida" means tradition or custom; Karenga defined it as tradition and reason. For a similar Pan-African approach to tradition and modernity, see the statement by South African writer Pixley ka Izaka Seme, a founder of the ANC, in Fredrickson, *Black Liberation*, 118.

CHAPTER FOUR

1. Katznelson, *City Trenches*; Castells, *City and the Grassroots*.

2. Essien-Udom and Essien-Udom, "Malcolm X: An International Man."

3. Kenneth O'Reilly's *Racial Matters* is the most comprehensive study of this.

4. Newton, *Revolutionary Suicide*, 65–66. That study group propelled its members in at least three directions: US, the Black Panthers for Self-Defense, and the Revolutionary Action Movement (RAM).

5. Newton, "Huey Newton Talks to the Movement," 50–66.

6. Hilliard, *This Side of Glory*, 163.

7. Newton, "Huey Newton Talks to the Movement," 50.

8. The Black Panthers saw the enemy as capitalism, which supported white colonialism; see P. S. Foner, *The Black Panthers Speak*.

9. Hilliard, *This Side of Glory*, 172. See also Newton, *Revolutionary Suicide*; Carmichael, *Stokely Speaks*.

10. Llorens, "Ameer (LeRoi Jones) Baraka," 77; Baraka, "Nationalism Vs PimpArt," in *Raise*, 125–32. The Yippies were the Youth International Party, a countercultural group.

11. Forman, *Making of Black Revolutionaries*, 528; for another version of those meetings, see Baraka, *Autobiography of LeRoi Jones* (1984), 279.

12. Nakawa interview.

13. O'Reilly, *Racial Matters*.

14. Baraka, *Autobiography of LeRoi Jones* (1984), 278.

15. Ibid., 278–79.

16. Amina Baraka interview.

17. This is similar to the Nation of Islam protocol toward Elijah Muhammad.

18. Baraka, "Creation of the New Ark," Baraka Files, KWOF, 80.

19. Llorens, "Ameer (LeRoi Jones) Baraka," 70–71.

20. Baraka, *Autobiography of LeRoi Jones* (1984), 277–78.

21. Akiba interview.

22. Sales, *From Civil Rights to Black Liberation*, 151.

23. Garvin interview.

24. Shakur, *Assata: An Autobiography*, 223–24; E. Brown, *Taste of Power*; see also Wallace, *Black Macho and the Myth of the Superwoman*.

25. Scheer, *Eldridge Cleaver*, 142–43.

26. Bibi Amina Baraka, "Coordinator's Statement," in Baraka, *African Congress*, 177.

27. For a review of the literature, see Walby, "Woman and Nation," 81–100; A. Davis, *Women, Race, and Class*; Jayawardena, *Feminism and Nationalism in the Third World*; Yuval-Davis and Anthias, *Woman-Nation-State*.

28. Viz., Walters, "New Black Political Culture," 8; Harding, *The Other American Revolution*, 215.

29. Transcript of Bingham/Mshauri interview, November 27, 1984, 43.

30. Ibid.

31. Transcript of Bingham/Mshauri interview, December 4, 1984, 1–2; Weiss, *Farewell to the Party of Lincoln*, 321.

32. Transcript of Bingham/Mshauri interview, November 27, 1984, 34.

33. Ibid., 8.

34. Ibid., 7.

35. Transcript of Hamm interview, 11.

36. Ibid., 12.

37. Ibid., 15. In his poetry and writing, Baraka replaced Newark with New Ark, with all its new connotations.

38. Ibid., 20.

39. P. S. Foner, *Organized Labor and the Black Worker*, 412.

40. Geschwender, *Class, Race, and Worker Insurgency*, 94–95.

41. For a history of this unique pattern of race and class, see Katznelson, *City Trenches*.

42. Transcript of Nguvu interview, 4.

43. Ibid., 1–2.

44. Ibid., 11.

45. Ibid., 25.

46. Ibid., 29.

47. Ibid.

48. Ibid., 31.

49. Ibid., 33.

50. For example, Jalia was recruited by Muminina Anasa, and Jaribu was recruited by Simba Songea.

51. Amina Baraka interview; Jalia interview.

52. Nakawa interview. This particular observation is drawn from roundtable discussions led by Tamu Bess between the women veterans of US and CFUN, 1985–86.

53. Talk by one of the original Last Poets, Abiodun Oyewole, at University of Pennsylvania, 1988.

54. Baraka, *Autobiography of LeRoi Jones* (1984), 281.

55. Ibid.

56. *New York Times*, March 11, 1970, 36.

57. Ibid., May 29, 1970, 26.

58. Curvin, "Persistent Minority," 69.

59. Ibid., 70; Baraka, *Autobiography of LeRoi Jones* (1984), 281; Bingham/Mshauri interview. Curvin, Baraka, and Bingham agree with Wheeler's assessment that Gibson had already won the convention's endorsement.

60. *Star Ledger*, November 15, 1969, 5.

61. Ibid., November 14, 1969, 5.

62. Ibid.

63. Ibid., November 15, 1969, 5.

64. Ibid., November 14, 1969, 5.

65. Ibid., November 15, 1969, 5.

66. Ibid.

67. For the distinctions between competitive and expressive politics applied to Reconstruction, see Perman, *Road to Redemption*.

68. *New York Times*, February 6, 1970, 28.

69. Ibid.

70. Unfortunately, the white vigilantes shot into the Chicago van and stopped that student exchange.

71. Baraka, "Creation of the New Ark," Baraka Files, KWOF, 105.

72. Ibid.

73. Ibid., 111.

74. *New York Times*, June 16, 1970, 1.

75. Ibid., 50.

76. Ibid.

77. Ibid.

78. *New York Times*, May 24, 1970, 1, 38.

79. Baraka, "Creation of the New Ark," Baraka Files, KWOF, 111.

80. Ibid.

81. Ibid., 112.

82. Ibid. Baraka is probably referring to the photograph that appeared on the front cover and page 23 of the July 28, 1967, issue of *Life* magazine.

83. Baraka, "Creation of the New Ark," Baraka Files, KWOF, 113.

84. Curvin, "Persistent Minority," 77.

85. Ibid., 78.

86. Ibid., 77–78; quote taken from the *New York Times*, June 14, 1970, 77.

87. Vander Zanden, *Social Psychology*, 334–37, quote on 334.

88. Ibid., 337.

89. Calvin West was on trial with Mayor Addonizio in the federal corruption case.

90. "Fifty Black Ministers Endorse Addonizio," *New York Times*, April 8, 1970, 20.

91. This is similar to the classic mistake V. I. Lenin speaks of in *"Left-Wing" Communism, An Infantile Disorder*, as he welcomes attacks on Bolshevism because the controversy made this ideology the main topic of discussion in the elections.

92. *New York Times*, June 18, 1970, 54.

93. Ibid., June 17, 1970, 34.

94. Ibid.

CHAPTER FIVE

1. PAIGC stands for the African Party for the Independence of Guinea and Cape Verde in Portuguese; PDG for the Democratic Party of Guinea in French.

2. Woodard, "Making of the New Ark," 28–40.

3. Gibson, *African Liberation Movements.*

4. Poinsett, "It's Nation Time!" 98–106.

5. Pinkney, *Red, Black and Green,* 132–33.

6. Baraka, *African Congress,* 3.

7. See Baraka, *African Congress.*

8. "Ron Karenga Convicted, Gets Ten Year Sentence," *Herald Dispatch,* June 3, 1971, 1, 1C; Baraka, *Autobiography of LeRoi Jones* (1997), 404; Nakawa interview; Scott Ngozi Brown's study of Karenga's US Organization in forthcoming Ph.D. dissertation, Cornell University.

9. Baraka, *African Congress,* 170.

10. Ibid., 168.

11. Ibid.

12. Ibid., 169.

13. A list of these organizations appears in ibid., 469–75.

14. Baraka, "Congress of African People: Political Liberation Council Organizing Manual," chart on page 11, Congress of African People Files, KWOF; Baraka, "The Pan-African Party and the Black Nation," chart on page 29. Los Angeles was not included because Karenga's US Organization was under siege.

15. For the record, the leaders Maisha Ongoza of Philadelphia and Dalila Kudura of Albany were women.

16. Baraka, *African Congress,* 170.

17. Ibid., 118–19.

18. Baraka, *Raise,* 163.

19. Baraka, *African Congress,* 117.

20. Ibid.

21. Ibid.

22. Ibid., 117–18.

23. *New York Times,* May 28, 1972, 3.

24. Revolutionary Workers League, "Draft: ALSC and the Black Liberation Movement," KWOF, 23.

25. Ibid.

26. *New York Times,* May 26, 1972, 3.

27. Drake, "Introduction," 12.

28. Ibid.

29. *Washington Post,* May 28, 1972, 4.

30. Ibid., 1. They reported another "police" estimate of 12,000 black people.

31. Ibid., 4.

32. Ibid., 1.

33. Ibid., 4.

34. Ibid.; following quotes of that day from same source.

35. Black activists unofficially renamed the Washington Monument grounds after the slain Congolese hero, Patrice Lumumba.

36. Baraka, *Autobiography of LeRoi Jones* (1997), 417. For conservative ideas, see Baraka, *African Congress*, 177–80.

37. "Black Women's United Front, Jan. 25—Detroit," *Unity and Struggle*, January 2, 1975, 1.

38. See poster illustration in *Forward: Journal of Marxism-Leninism-Mao Zedong Thought* 3 (January 1980): 113.

39. "Black Women's United Front—Forward with the Struggle!" *Unity and Struggle*, November 1, 1975, 7–8.

40. Revolutionary Communist League, "'Unity and Struggle'—History of the Revolutionary Communist League (M-L-M)," 14–15.

41. Viz., Harding, *There Is a River*, 185–86.

42. Karenga, "Joanne Little Case," 37–38.

43. Compare this with "movement center" concept in Morris, *Origins of the Civil Rights Movement*, 40.

44. Ahmed, formerly Max Stanford, founded the Revolutionary Action Movement (RAM) in the 1960s.

45. Baraka, *Strategy and Tactics*, 18–19.

46. Ibid., 2.

47. This emphasis on cadre development was influenced by Baraka's reading of the writings of Maulana Karenga, Sekou Toure, and Mao Zedong.

48. Baraka, *Strategy and Tactics*, 4.

49. Ibid., 13.

50. Ibid., 14.

51. Ibid. Note here the male rhetorical exclusion of black women, though women were pivotal to the revitalization process.

52. Walters, *Black Presidential Politics in America*, 88.

53. *New York Times*, September 4, 1971, 24.

54. Ibid.

55. Ibid.

56. Ibid.

57. Richard Hatcher's address in Baraka, *African Congress*, 64–72.

58. Marable, *Race, Reform and Rebellion*, 137.

59. Mr. Sutton was Malcolm X's attorney.

60. Baraka, "Toward the Creation of Political Institutions for All African Peoples: From Gary to Miami" (hereafter cited as "From Gary to Miami").

61. Ibid.

62. Hampton and Fayer, *Voices of Freedom*, 579–80.

63. Baraka, "From Gary to Miami," 6–7.

64. *New York Times*, June 22, 1968, 28; Woodard, "Making of the New Ark," 127.

65. Baraka, "From Gary to Miami," 8.

66. *Amsterdam News*, March 11, 1972, S2.

67. Chafe, *Civilities and Civil Rights*.

68. *New York Times*, March 6, 1972, 28.

69. See also the analysis by Castells, *City and the Grassroots*, 57.

70. In Newark, N.J., the situation was so bad that when the 1967 rebellion started the *Star Ledger* had to promote an office boy, Stanley E. Terrell, to become their first black reporter to go out and cover the story (Terrell interview).

71. Rev. Sharper had been unseated from Newark's city council by Sharpe James, the Black Convention candidate, in 1970.

72. *New York Times*, January 16, 1972, 66.

73. These black conventions and assemblies represented the crystallization of what Barrington Moore has called "the creation of an effective political presence" (Moore, *Injustice*, 81–82).

74. Hampton and Fayer, *Voices of Freedom*, 572.

75. Ibid.

76. *Washington Post*, March 11, 1972, A2.

77. *New York Times*, March 10, 1972, 20.

78. Also see Katznelson, *Black Men, White Cities*, 72–85, 112–13, 176–77.

79. *New York Times*, March 11, 1972, 12. Farrakhan, however, did not speak.

80. Walters, "New Black Political Culture," 8.

81. "Black Delegates Seek More Contacts," *New York Times*, March 19, 1972, 42.

82. Hampton and Fayer, *Voices of Freedom*, 573.

83. *New York Times*, March 19, 1972, 42.

84. Ibid.

85. Ibid.

86. Hampton and Fayer, *Voices of Freedom*, 574–75.

87. *New York Times*, March 12, section 4, page 1.

88. Ibid., March 11, 1972, 12.

89. Hampton and Fayer, *Voices of Freedom*, 574–75.

90. Franklin, *From Slavery to Freedom*, 463.

91. *Washington Post*, March 12, 1972, A2.

92. *New York Times*, March 12, 1972, 1, 38.

93. *Washington Post*, March 12, 1972, A2.

94. The stage of the Atlanta Congress was shared by Jesse Jackson, Whitney Young, Imamu Baraka, and Louis Farrakhan.

95. Poinsett, "Black Political Strategies for '72," 66.

96. Hampton and Fayer, *Voices of Freedom*, 576.

97. *New York Times*, March 12, 1972, 1, 38.

98. *Newsweek*, March 27, 1972, 30.

99. *New York Times*, March 12, 1972, 1, 38.

100. This writer's observations that night, acting as a secretary for Amiri Baraka noting each state's concerns.

101. *New York Times*, March 13, 1972, 30; the suit was named in honor of Kenneth Kaunda, president of Zambia.

102. Ibid.

103. Ibid.

104. Ibid.

105. Ibid.

106. Hampton and Fayer, *Voices of Freedom*, 580.

107. Ibid., 580–81.

108. "Model Pledge," Appendix B1, in *National Black Political Agenda*, 50.

109. *Newsweek*, March 27, 1972, 30.

110. *National Black Political Agenda*, 23.

111. Ibid., 9.

112. Ibid., 11.

113. Ibid., 17.

114. Ibid., 19.

115. Ibid., 21.

116. Ibid., 14.

117. Ibid., 7.

118. Editorial, *Amsterdam News* (New York, N.Y.), March 18, 1972.

119. Ibid.

120. Paul Delany, "Conciliator at Black Parley," *New York Times*, March 13, 1972, 30.

121. Harding, *The Other American Revolution*, 215.

122. Ibid., 216; Marable, *Race, Reform and Rebellion*, 138.

123. Cronon, *Black Moses*, 37.

CHAPTER SIX

1. According to John Hutchinson, this kind of belief is at the core of the politics of cultural nationalism. See his "Cultural Nationalism and Moral Regeneration."

2. Baraka, *Black Value System*, 7–8.

3. Ibid., 14.

4. Ronald Sullivan, "Gain in Power by LeRoi Jones Shown in Newark Poverty Vote," *New York Times*, June 19, 1971, 15. For a more detailed account of this election, see Woodard, "Making of the New Ark," 379–92.

5. "Housing Development, CAP Yajenga Nchi," 2, Newark Congress of African People File, KWOF.

6. Ibid., 1.

7. Ibid., 3–4.

8. Ibid., 2.

9. The essential document for this story is the *Kawaida Towers Inquiry*, conducted by the National Black Assembly Law and Justice Committee in April of 1973 (in Kawaida Towers Inquiry File, KWOF).

10. Ibid., 6.

11. Temple of Kawaida press release, October 8, 1972.

12. Ibid.

13. Curvin, "Persistent Minority," 208.

14. Mitchell telegraphed the committee at the last moment, saying that he was delayed by a bill on the floor of Congress; see *Kawaida Towers Inquiry*, 1.

15. "Racial Epithets Are Hurled at Negro Kawaida Workers," *Asbury Park (N.J.) Press*, January 6, 1973.

16. *Kawaida Towers Inquiry*, 26–27.

17. Ibid., 28–29.

18. WNBC-TV Editorial: Kawaida Towers, telecast, November 30, 1972 (copy in KWOF).

19. Kawaida Towers press release, March 9, 1973.

20. Kawaida Towers press release written by Imamu Amiri Baraka, November 27, 1972.

21. Joseph F. Sullivan, "Redden to Resign Jan. 1; Scores Newark Officials," *New York Times*, December 1, 1972, 1.

22. "Baraka Forces Net Police Chief in Coup," *Black News Service* (Washington, D.C.), December 4, 1972.

23. Joseph F. Sullivan, "Redden to Resign Jan. 1; Scores Newark Officials," *New York Times*, December 1, 1972, 1, 81.

24. Kawaida Towers press release, March 20, 1973.

25. Joseph F. Sullivan, "Redden to Resign Jan. 1; Scores Newark Officials," *New York Times*, December 1, 1972, 81.

26. Ibid.

27. Richard Phalon, "Sponsor Fights to Kill Tax Abatement for Kawaida," *New York Times*, December 1, 1972, 81.

28. Ibid.

29. Ibid.

30. Ibid.

31. Ibid.

32. This writer's recollection of that meeting.

33. Ibid.

34. Baraka, *Autobiography of LeRoi Jones* (1984), 304.

35. Ibid.

36. Transcript of Nguvu interview, 56.

37. One honest NJHFA civil servant informed the Kawaida Towers development team that there was no technical justification for Lucarelli's proposal to eliminate the balconies; that move actually would have lost rental income for the apartment building.

38. See "NJHFA Memorandum to Joseph Chieppa from George Feddish on the subject of Kawaida Redesign, December 30, 1975," in Project Evaluation, HFA No. 6, Kawaida Towers, KWOF.

39. Transcript of Bingham/Mshauri interview, November 27, 1984, 26–27.

40. Baraka, *Autobiography of LeRoi Jones* (1984), 302.

41. Johnston was later investigated for improprieties connected with gambling debts he owed the Mafia; finally he was forced to resign as of July 1982. See David Hardy, "Crime-Figure Loans Tied to Housing Unit," *Daily News*, n.d. 1982, 2, 24, Kawaida Files, KWOF.

42. Kawaida Towers Files, KWOF. Later, the letter was released to the press by the Temple of Kawaida.

43. Joseph F. Sullivan, "Baraka Assails Newark Council," *New York Times*, November 19, 1974, 94.

44. Ibid.

45. "City Council Led by Council Crooks Harris and Allen Blocking Housing in Central Ward!!" *Unity and Struggle*, December 1974, 3, 6, 7.

46. Ibid., 7.

47. Letter from Mayor Kenneth Gibson to City Clerk Re: Applications for Tax Abatement, Kawaida Community Development II, Inc., January 7, 1975, Kawaida Towers Files, KWOF.

48. Tex Novellino and Stanley E. Terrell, "Baraka and Six Are Arrested at Council Meeting," *Star Ledger*, February 6, 1975, 16.

49. See Baraka, *New Era in Our Politics*.

50. Joseph F. Sullivan, "Newark Officials Divide on Baraka: Gibson Backs His Housing Plan, but Council Rejects Tax-Abatement Bid," *New York Times*, February 7, 1975, 67.

51. Tex Novellino and Stanley E. Terrell, "Baraka and Six Are Arrested at Council Meeting," *Star Ledger*, February 6, 1975, 16.

52. Ibid.

53. Ibid.

54. Ibid.

55. Ibid.

56. For more details, see Woodard, "Making of the New Ark," 446–52.

57. Curvin, "Persistent Minority," 215.

58. Ibid.

59. For a similar analysis, see Allen, *Black Awakening*.

CONCLUSION

1. Bingham/Mshauri interviews explain that the slogan originated in the streets during work details.

2. Van Deburg, *New Day in Babylon*.

3. Ali A. Mazrui's lecture in *World Culture and the Black Experience* is quoted in Toll, *The Resurgence of Race*, 4.

4. Karenga, *Introduction to Black Studies*.

5. Levine, *Black Culture and Black Consciousness*, 152–53; Yinger, *Ethnicity*, 307–9; Fasold and Labov et al., "Are Black and White Vernaculars Diverging?" 3–80; Van Deburg, *New Day in Babylon*, 219–20; Massey and Denton, *American Apartheid*, 162–63.

6. A. D. Smith, *Nationalism in the Twentieth Century*, chap. 7.

7. Ibid., 166–83.

8. A. R. Hirsch, "Black Ghettos."

9. Galishoff paraphrased in Woodard, "Making of the New Ark," 77–78; quote from Galishoff, *Safeguarding the Public Health*, 3.

10. Kozol, *Savage Inequalities*; Philpott, *The Slum and the Ghetto*; Massey and Denton, *American Apartheid*.

11. Castells, *City and the Grassroots*, 54.

12. Bowles and Gintis, *Schooling in Capitalist America*.

13. MacLeod, *Ain't No Makin' It*; Bourgois, *In Search of Respect*; Willis, *Learning to Labor*; Katz, *Improving Poor People*.

14. O'Reilly, *Racial Matters*, 281–83; FBI memorandum, October 9, 1970, "From:

FBI Director to Newark SAC, re: Everett Leroy Jones," Amiri Baraka Collection, Box 9, Moorland-Spingarn Research Center, Howard University.

15. Hechter, *Internal Colonialism.*
16. Cruse, *Crisis of the Negro Intellectual,* 151.
17. P. S. Foner, *Frederick Douglass: Selections from His Writings,* 61.

Bibliography

DOCUMENTS
Atlanta, Ga.
    Dr. Martin Luther King Jr. Memorial Center
       Dr. Martin Luther King Jr. Papers (now at Stanford University)
Boston, Mass.
    Blackside, Inc.
       Civil Rights Archives, *Eyes on the Prize* section
          Gary Convention Files
Bronxville, N.Y.
    Komozi Woodard Office Files (KWOF), Sarah Lawrence College
       African Free School Files
       African Liberation Support Committee Files
       Amiri Baraka Files
          Baraka, Amiri. "The Creation of the New Ark," unpublished manuscript, ca. 1973–1974.
          ———. "Kawaida, The Doctrine of Maulana Karenga," mimeograph produced by Congress of African People, Newark, N.J., 1974.
       Central Ward Court Case Files
          Komozi, Cheo. "Federal Probe Studies Newark Housing Authority's Role in Urban Renewal Conspiracy," draft press release, ca. 1974–1975.
       CFUN Files
          Customs and Concepts of the Committee for Unified Newark, pamphlet produced by Congress of African People, Newark, 1972.
       Congress of African People Files
       Cricket Files
       "Get on Board the Freedom Train": Proceedings of the Founding Convention of the National Negro Labor Council, Cincinnati, Ohio, October 27–28, 1951 (photocopy of pamphlet).
       Harry Haywood Files
          Leaguc of Struggle for Negro Rights, *Equality, Land and Freedom: A Program for Negro Liberation*, pamphlet, n.d.
          Haywood, Harry. "Remarks on the Chicano Question," unpublished paper, May 1981.
       Jihad Files
       Karenga, Maulana. "Malcolm X: His Life and Legacy," tape of lecture delivered on May 21, 1989.
       Kasisi Nakawa File
       Katznelson, Ira. "Reinventing Liberalism: Bidding The New Deal Goodbye," April 13, 1993, unpublished manuscript.
       Kawaida Files
       Kawaida Towers Files

Letter from Mayor Kenneth Gibson to City Clerk Re: Applications for Tax Abatement, Kawaida Community Development II, Inc., January 7, 1975.

Kawaida Towers Inquiry File

Kawaida Towers Inquiry, conducted by National Black Assembly Law and Justice Committee, Monday, April 16, 1973, at the Gateway Hotel in Newark, N.J.

KT/R-32 (Kawaida Towers/Redevelopment Tract 32) File

"Memorandum of understanding between Kawaida Temple and Pilgrim Baptist Church regarding disposition of housing development in R-32 N.J.," August 7, 1972.

Kwanzaa Files

National Black Assembly Files

Elimu, Cheo. "Party Leadership: Its Role and Method of Selection," mimeograph, July 3–5, 1971.

Newark Congress of African People File

"Housing Development, CAP Yajenga Nchi [English trans.: CAP Builds the Nation]," in untitled brown binder, n.d. [ca. 1972].

NJR-32 (New Jersey Redevelopment-Tract 32) Files

Project Evaluation, HFA No. 6, Kawaida Towers, File/Binder

"New Jersey Housing Finance Agency Memorandum from George Feddish to Joseph Chieppa, Re: Kawaida Redesign, December 30, 1975."

Revolutionary Worker's League. "Draft: ALSC and the Black Liberation Movement," unpublished manuscript, n.d.

Temple of Kawaida Press Releases File

United Brothers Files

Unity and Struggle Newspaper File (1974–1978 issues)

US Publications File

WNBC-TV, "Editorial: Kawaida Towers," telecast, November 30, 1972.

Evanston, Ill.

Deering Collection, Northwestern University Library

LeRoi Jones/Amiri Baraka Files

Unity and Struggle Newspaper, 1973–1976 issues

Newark, N.J.

Main Branch, Newark Public Library

Newark Collection

New Haven, Conn.

Beinecke Library, Yale University

James Weldon Johnson Collection

Langston Hughes Papers

Correspondence: LeRoi Jones/Amiri Baraka Files

New York, N.Y.

AFRAM

Black Power Conference Resolutions

Schomburg Center for Research in Black Culture, New York Public Library

Schomburg Collection
>Larry P. Neal Papers
>Hubert H. Harrison Papers
>National Negro Congress Files
Princeton, N.J.
>Seeley G. Mudd Manuscript Library
>>Wolak, Edward J. "A Political Study of the Negro in Newark, New Jersey," Senior thesis, Princeton University, May 1948.
Washington, D.C.
>Moorland-Spingarn Research Center, Howard University
>>Amiri Baraka Collection
>>*Unity and Struggle Newspaper*
>>*CFUN Newsletter*

INTERVIEWS

Unless otherwise noted, all interviews were conducted by the author.

Akiba, Muminina. April 5, 1985, Newark, N.J.

Aljuwani, Shakoor. 1985–95, Brooklyn, N.Y.

Aljuwani, Tamu. 1985, Brooklyn, N.Y.

Anderson, Sam. May 1990, New York, N.Y.

Babu, Abdulrahman Mohammad. November 1990, New York, N.Y.

Baraka, Amina. August 19, 1986, Newark, N.J.

Baraka, Amiri. January 4, 1986, Newark, N.J. (assisted by Vanessa Whitehead)

Bess, Tamu. 1985, New York, N.Y.

Bingham, Russell (Baba Mshauri). November 27, 1984, and December 4, 1984, Newark, N.J. (assisted by Nicole Morris, Tanya Sutton, and Vanessa Whitehead)

Campbell, Eugene. May 13, 1985, Newark, N.J. (assisted by Nicole Morris and Vanessa Whitehead)

Clarke, John Henrik. August 1985, New York, N.Y. (assisted by Nicole Morris and Vanessa Whitehead)

Cruse, Harold. 1988, Philadelphia, Pa.

Dahmer, Dennis. 1991, McComb, Miss.

Dennis, David. 1991, Chicago, Ill., and McComb, Miss.

Du Uwewa, Muminina. January 11, 1986, Newark, N.J.

Garvin, Vicki. 1983, Newark, N.J.; 1992, Bronxville, N.Y.

Hamm, Larry. March 11, 1985, Newark, N.J. (assisted by Nicole Morris and Anita Rich)

Hayes, Curtis. 1991, McComb, Miss.

Haywood, Harry. 1979–84, Newark, N.J.

Holman, Wynona. December 14, 1984, Newark, N.J. (assisted by Nicole Morris, Tanya Sutton, and Vanessa Whitehead)

Imarisha, Malaika. 1988, New York, N.Y.

Jackson, Maisha. October 26, 1985, Philadelphia, Pa.

Jalia, Muminina. 1985–86, Newark, N.J.

Kamau, Ndugu. 1988, New York, N.Y.
Karenga, Maulana. December 27, 1985, Newark, N.J.
McDew, Charles. 1991, McComb, Miss.
Majadi, Jeledi. January 24, 1986, Newark, N.J.
Mfalme, Cheo. December 13, 1985, Newark, N.J.
Moses, Bob. 1991, Chicago, Ill., and McComb, Miss.
Nakawa, Kasisi. November 16, 1985, Newark, N.J.
Nash, Diane, 1991, McComb, Miss.
Nguvu, Saidi. November 15, 1985, Newark, N.J.
Oyewole, Obiodun. 1988, Philadelphia, Pa.
Reynolds, Sgt. William. 1984, Newark, N.J. (assisted by Kuza Woodard)
Sales, William. May 1990, New York, N.Y.
Salimu, Muminina. March 22, 1986, Newark, N.J.
Seale, Bobby. 1986–88, Philadelphia, Pa.
Taalamu, Cheo. May 4, 1985, Newark, N.J. (assisted by Carole Whitehead)
Thazabu, Malaika. January 25, 1986, Newark, N.J. (assisted by Nicole Morris and
    Vanessa Whitehead)
Tucker, Donald. January 31, 1986, Newark, N.J.
Ture, Kwame (Stokely Carmichael). February 1990, Philadelphia, Pa.
Turner, James. February 16, 1986, Newark, N.J.
Ward, Eulius. February 7, 1986, Newark, N.J.
Wesley, Richard. May 3, 1986, Montclair, N.J. (assisted by Vanessa Whitehead)

NEWSPAPERS, MAGAZINES, AND JOURNALS
Amsterdam News
Asbury Park (N.J.) Press
Black Newark / Unity and Struggle
Black News Service
Black Panther Newspaper
Black Scholar
Black Theater Review
Chicago Black World / Negro Digest
Chicago Tribune
The Drama Review
Ebony
Forward
Jet
Liberator
Life
Los Angeles Herald Dispatch
Muhammad Speaks
Newark Evening News
Newark Star Ledger
New Jersey Afro-American
Newsweek

New York Times
Philadelphia Inquirer
Washington Post

GOVERNMENT PUBLICATIONS

City Planning Commission. *Master Plan: 1964 City of Newark, N.J.* Newark, N.J.: Hardam Printing, 1913.

Department of Commerce. *U.S. Bureau of the Census, Negro Population, 1790–1915.* Washington, D.C., 1918.

National Advisory Commission on Civil Disorders. *Report of the National Advisory Commission on Civil Disorders.* Washington, D.C.: Government Printing Office, 1968.

U.S. Bureau of the Census. *Recent Trends in Social and Economic Conditions of Negroes in the United States.* Washington, D.C.: Government Printing Office, July 1968.

U.S. Bureau of the Census. *Urban Atlas, Tract Data for SMSA: Newark, New Jersey.* Folio G1257 N5 U5, 1975.

BOOKS, PAMPHLETS, AND PUBLISHED PROCEEDINGS

Achebe, Chinua. *A Man of the People.* London: Heinemann, 1966.

Allen, Robert L. *Black Awakening in Capitalist America.* New York: Anchor, 1970.

——. *Reluctant Reformers.* Washington, D.C.: Howard University Press, 1974.

Anderson, Benedict. *Imagined Communities.* London: Verso, 1983.

Anderson, Jervis. *This Was Harlem.* New York: Farrar, Straus, Giroux, 1982.

Anthony, Earl. *Picking Up the Gun.* New York: Dial, 1970.

——. *Spitting in the Wind.* Malibu, Calif.: Roundtable Publishing, 1990.

Aptheker, Herbert. *Afro-American History: The Modern Era.* Secaucus, N.J.: Citadel, 1971.

——, ed. *A Documentary History of the Negro People in the United States.* Vol. 1. Secaucus, N.J.: Citadel, 1951.

Baker, Houston A., Jr. "Generational Shifts and the Recent Criticism of Afro-American Literature." In *Paradigms in Black Studies: Intellectual History, Cultural Meaning and Political Ideology,* edited by Abdul Alkalimat. Chicago: Twenty-First Century Books, 1990.

Baldwin, James. *The Fire Next Time.* New York: Dell, 1962.

Banton, Michael. "1960: A Turning Point in the Study of Race Relations." *Daedalus* 103, no. 2 (1974): 31–44.

Baraka, Amiri. *The Autobiography of LeRoi Jones.* New York: Freundlich, 1984.

——. *The Autobiography of LeRoi Jones.* 2d ed., rev. and enl. Chicago: Lawrence Hill, 1997.

——. "Black and Angry." *Newsweek,* July 10, 1972, 35.

——. *A Black Value System.* Newark, N.J.: Jihad Publications, 1969.

——. *It's Nation Time.* Chicago: Third World Press, 1970.

——. *A New Era in Our Politics.* Newark, N.J.: Jihad Publications, 1974.

——. "The Pan-African Party and the Black Nation." *Black Scholar* (March 1971): 24–32.

———. *Raise*. New York: Random House, 1971.

———. *Strategy and Tactics of a Pan-African Nationalist Party*. Newark, N.J.: CFUN, 1971.

———. "Toward the Creation of Political Institutions for All African Peoples: From Gary and Miami—Before and After." *Black World* 21, no. 12 (Oct. 1972): 54–78.

———, ed. *African Congress: A Documentary of the First Modern Pan-African Congress*. New York: William Morrow, 1972.

Baraka, Amiri, and Amina Baraka. *The Music*. New York: William Morrow, 1987.

Baraka, Amiri, and Larry Neal, eds. *Black Fire*. New York: William Morrow, 1968.

Barbaro, Fred. "Political Brokers." *Society* 9 (September–October 1972): 42–54.

Barbour, Floyd B., ed. *The Black Power Revolt*. Boston: Porter Sargent, 1968.

———. *The Black Seventies*. Boston: Porter Sargent, 1970.

Barth, Frederick. *Ethnic Groups and Boundaries*. Boston: Little, Brown, 1969.

Bayor, Ronald H. *Neighbors in Conflict: The Irish, Germans, Jews, and Italians of New York City, 1929–1941*. Baltimore: Johns Hopkins University Press, 1978.

Bell, Howard H. *A Survey of the Negro Convention Movement, 1830–1861*. New York: Arno, 1969.

———, ed. *Search for a Place: Black Separatism and Africa, 1860*. Ann Arbor: University of Michigan Press, 1969.

Bennett, Lerone, Jr. *The Negro Mood*. Chicago: Johnson, 1964.

Benston, Kimberly W. *Baraka: The Renegade and the Mask*. New Haven: Yale University Press, 1976.

———, ed. *Imamu Amiri Baraka (LeRoi Jones): A Collection of Critical Essays*. Englewood Cliffs, N.J.: Prentice-Hall, 1978.

Berlin, Ira. *Slaves Without Masters*. New York: Vintage, 1974.

Blauner, Robert. *Racial Oppression in America*. New York: Harper and Row, 1972.

Bloom, Jack M. *Class, Race, and the Civil Rights Movement*. Bloomington: Indiana University Press, 1987.

Blyden, Edward W. *Christianity, Islam and the Negro Race*. Baltimore: Black Classics, 1994.

Bourgois, Philippe. *In Search of Respect*. New York: Cambridge University Press, 1995.

Bowles, Samuel, and Herbert Gintis. *Schooling in Capitalist America: Educational Reform and the Contradictions of Economic Life*. New York: Basic, 1976.

Bracey, John H., Jr., August Meier, and Elliott Rudwick, eds. *Black Nationalism in America*. Indianapolis: Bobbs-Merrill, 1970.

Brauer, Carl M. *John F. Kennedy and the Second Reconstruction*. New York: Columbia University Press, 1977.

Breitman, George, ed. *By Any Means Necessary*. New York: Pathfinder, 1970.

———. *Malcolm X Speaks: Selected Speeches and Statements*. 2d ed. New York: Pathfinder, 1989.

Brisbane, Robert. *Black Activism*. Valley Forge: Judson, 1974.

Brown, Claude. *Manchild in the Promised Land*. New York: Macmillan, 1965.

Brown, Elaine. *A Taste of Power: A Black Woman's Story*. New York: Pantheon, 1992.

Brown, Lloyd W. *Amiri Baraka*. Boston: Twayne, 1980.

Brundage, W. Fitzhugh. *Lynching in the New South.* Urbana: University of Illinois Press, 1993.

Bullins, Ed. "The King Is Dead." *Drama Review* 12, no. 4 (Summer 1968): 23–24.

Burk, Robert Fredrick. *The Eisenhower Administration and Black Civil Rights.* Knoxville: University of Tennessee Press, 1984.

Cabral, Amilcar. *Return to the Source.* New York: African Information Service, 1973.

———. *Revolution in Guinea: Selected Texts.* New York: Monthly Review Press, 1969.

Carmichael, Stokely. *Stokely Speaks.* New York: Vintage, 1971.

Carmichael, Stokely, and Charles V. Hamilton. *Black Power: The Politics of Liberation.* New York: Vintage, 1967.

Carr, E. H. *Nationalism: A Report by a Study Group of Members of the Royal Institute of International Affairs.* London: Oxford University Press, 1939.

Carson, Clayborne. "Civil Rights Reform and the Black Freedom Movement." In *The Civil Rights Movement in America*, edited by Charles W. Eagles. Jackson: University Press of Mississippi, 1986.

———. *In Struggle: SNCC and the Black Awakening of the 1960s.* Cambridge: Harvard University Press, 1981.

Carson, Clayborne, David J. Garrow, Gerald Gill, Vincent Harding, and Darlene Clark Hine, eds. *The Eyes on the Prize Civil Rights Reader.* New York: Penguin, 1991.

Castells, Manuel. *The City and the Grassroots.* Berkeley: University of California Press, 1983.

Cell, John W. *The Highest Stage of White Supremacy: The Origins of Segregation in South Africa and the American South.* Cambridge: Cambridge University Press, 1982.

Cesaire, Aimé. *Letter to Maurice Thorez.* Paris: Presence Africaine, 1957.

Chafe, William H. *Civilities and Civil Rights.* New York: Oxford University Press, 1980.

———. *The Unfinished Journey: America Since World War II.* New York: Oxford University Press, 1991.

Clark, Kenneth B. *Dark Ghetto.* New York: Harper and Row, 1965; reprint, 1967.

Clarke, John Henrik. "Journey to the Sierra Maestra." *Freedomways* (Spring 1961): 32–35.

———. "The New Afro-American Nationalism." *Freedomways* 1 (Fall 1961): 3.

———, ed. *Malcolm X: The Man and His Times.* Trenton: African World Press, 1990.

———. *Marcus Garvey and the Vision of Africa.* New York: Vintage, 1974.

Coakley, John, ed. *The Social Origins of Nationalist Movements: The Contemporary West European Experience.* London: Sage, 1992.

Committee for a Unified Newark (CFUN). *Customs and Concepts of the Committee for Unified Newark.* Newark: Congress of African People, 1972.

Connor, Walker. "The Politics of Ethnonationalism." *Journal of International Affairs* 27, no. 1 (1973): 1–21.

Coser, Lewis A. *The Functions of Social Conflict.* Glencoe, Ill.: Free Press, 1956.

Cronon, E. David. *Black Moses: The Story of Marcus Garvey and the Universal Negro Improvement Association.* Madison: University of Wisconsin Press, 1969.

———, ed. *Marcus Garvey*. Englewood-Cliffs, N.J.: Prentice-Hall, 1973.

Cruse, Harold. *The Crisis of the Negro Intellectual*. New York: William Morrow, 1967.

———. *Rebellion or Revolution?* New York: William Morrow, 1968.

Curry, Leonard P. *The Free Black in Urban America, 1800–1850: The Shadow of the Dream*. Chicago: University of Chicago Press, 1981.

Curvin, Robert. "The Persistent Minority: The Black Political Experience in Newark." Ph.D. diss., Princeton University, 1975. Ann Arbor, Mich.: UMI, 1975.

Davis, Angela. *Women, Race, and Class*. London: Women's Press, 1981.

Davis, F. James. *Who Is Black?* University Park: Pennsylvania State University Press, 1993.

Dayal, Rajeshwar. *Mission for Hammerskjöld: The Congo Crisis*. Princeton, N.J.: Princeton University Press, 1976.

Dittmer, John. *Black Georgia in the Progressive Era*. Urbana: University of Illinois Press, 1980.

———. "The Education of Henry McNeal Turner." In *Nineteenth Century Black Leaders*, edited by Leon Litwack and August Meier. Urbana: University of Illinois Press, 1988.

———. *Local People*. Urbana: University of Illinois Press, 1994.

Doob, Leonard W. *Patriotism and Nationalism: Their Psychological Foundations*. New Haven: Yale University Press, 1964.

Drake, St. Clair. "Introduction." In *Black American Radicals and the Liberation of Africa: The Council on African Affairs, 1937–1955*, edited by Hollis R. Lynch. Ithaca, N.Y.: Africana Studies and Research Center, Cornell University, 1978.

———. "The Patterns of Interracial Conflict in 1968." In *Black America, 1968: The Year of Awakening*. New York: Publishers Co., 1969.

Draper, Theodore. *The Rediscovery of Black Nationalism*. New York: Viking, 1970.

Du Bois, W. E. B. *Black Reconstruction in America, 1860–1880*. New York: Atheneum, 1935; reprint, 1970.

———. *The Philadelphia Negro*. Philadelphia: University of Pennsylvania, 1899.

———. *The Souls of Black Folk*. New York: Vintage, 1903; reprint, 1990.

———. *The World and Africa*. New York: International Publishers, 1947; reprint, 1965.

Ebony Magazine. *The Black Revolution*. Special issue reprint. Chicago: Johnson, 1970.

Eisinger, Peter. "Ethnic Conflict, Community Building, and the Emergence of Ethnic Political Traditions in the U.S." In *Urban Ethnic Conflict: A Comparative Approach*, edited by Susan E. Clarke and Jeffrey L. Obler. Chapel Hill: University of North Carolina Press and Institute for Research in Social Science, 1976.

Essien-Udom, Ruby M., and E. U. Essien-Udom. "Malcolm X: An International Man." In *Malcolm X: The Man and His Times*, edited by John Henrik Clarke. Trenton: African World Press, 1990.

Fanon, Frantz. *Toward the African Revolution*. New York: Grove, 1967.

———. *The Wretched of the Earth*. New York: Grove, 1966.

Fasold, Ralph W., and William Labov, et al. "Are Black and White Vernaculars Diverging?" *American Speech: A Quarterly of Linguistic Usage* 62 (Spring 1987): 3–80.

Feagin, Joe R., and Harland Hahn. *Ghetto Revolts*. New York: Macmillan, 1973.

Fogelson, Robert M. *Violence as Protest: A Study of Riots and Ghettos*. Westport, Conn.: Greenwood, 1980.

Foner, Eric. *Nothing But Freedom*. Baton Rouge: Louisiana State University Press, 1983.

——. *Reconstruction*. New York: Harper and Row, 1988.

Foner, Eric, and John A. Garraty, eds. *The Reader's Companion to American History*. Boston: Houghton Mifflin, 1991.

Foner, Philip S. *Organized Labor and The Black Worker, 1619–1973*. New York: International Publishers, 1974.

——, ed. *The Black Panthers Speak*. Philadelphia: J. B. Lippincott, 1970.

——. *Frederick Douglass: Selections from His Writings*. New York: International Publishers, 1945.

——. *The Life and Writing of Frederick Douglass*. Vol. 2. New York: International Publishers, 1950.

——. *Paul Robeson Speaks*. Secaucus, N.J.: Citadel, 1978.

Forman, James. *The Making of Black Revolutionaries*. Washington, D.C.: Open Hand Publishing, 1985.

Fox-Piven, Frances, and Richard Cloward. *Poor People's Movements*. New York: Vintage, 1979.

Franklin, John Hope. *From Slavery to Freedom*. New York: Knopf, 1988.

Franklin, John Hope, and August Meier, eds. *Black Leaders of the Twentieth Century*. Urbana: University of Illinois Press, 1982.

Frazier, E. Franklin. "Garvey as a Mass Leader." In *Marcus Garvey*, edited by E. David Cronon. Englewood Cliffs, N.J.: Prentice-Hall, 1973.

——. *Race and Culture Contacts in the Modern World*. New York: Knopf, 1957.

Fredrickson, George. *The Arrogance of Race*. Middletown, Conn.: Wesleyan University Press, 1988.

——. *The Black Image in the White Mind*. Middletown, Conn.: Wesleyan University Press, 1987.

——. *Black Liberation: A Comparative History of Black Ideologies in the United States and South Africa*. New York: Oxford University Press, 1995.

Freidel, Frank. *F.D.R. and the South*. Baton Rouge: Louisiana State University Press, 1965.

Galishoff, Stuart. *Safeguarding the Public Health, Newark 1895–1918*. Westport, Conn.: Greenwood, 1975.

Gann, L. H., and Peter Duignan, eds. *Colonialism in Africa, 1870–1960*. Cambridge: Cambridge University Press, 1970.

Garrow, David. *Bearing the Cross, Martin Luther King and the SCLC*. New York: William Morrow, 1987.

Gellner, Ernest. *Nations and Nationalism*. Oxford, Eng.: Blackwell, 1983.

——. *Thought and Change*. London: Weidenfeld and Nicholson, 1964.

Genovese, Eugene. *Roll, Jordan, Roll*. New York: Oxford University Press, 1974.

Geschwender, James A. *Class, Race, and Worker Insurgency: The League of Revolutionary Black Workers*. Cambridge: Cambridge University Press, 1977.

Gibson, Richard. *African Liberation Movements*. London: Oxford University Press, 1972.

Gillette, William. *Retreat from Reconstruction, 1869–1879.* Baton Rouge: Louisiana State University Press, 1979.

Goodwyn, Lawrence. *The Populist Moment.* Oxford: Oxford University Press, 1978.

Gordon, Milton M. *Assimilation in American Life: The Role of Race, Religion, and National Origins.* New York: Oxford University Press, 1964.

Graham, Hugh Davis. *The Civil Rights Era.* New York: Oxford University Press, 1990.

Grossman, James R. *Land of Hope.* Chicago: University of Chicago, 1989.

Gutman, Herbert. *The Black Family in Slavery and in Freedom, 1750–1925.* New York: Pantheon, 1976.

Halisi, Imamu. *The Kitabu.* Los Angeles: Saidi Publications/US Organization, 1971.

Hall, Raymond L. *Black Separatism in the United States.* Hanover, N.H.: University Press of New England, 1978.

Hampton, Henry, and Steve Fayer, eds. *Voices of Freedom: An Oral History of the Civil Rights Movement from the 1950s through the 1980s.* New York: Bantam, 1990.

Harding, Vincent. *The Other American Revolution.* Los Angeles: Center for Afro-American Studies, UCLA, 1980.

———. *There Is a River.* New York: Harcourt Brace Jovanovich, 1981.

Harris, William. *The Harder We Run.* New York: Oxford University Press, 1982.

Harris, William J., ed. *The LeRoi Jones/Amiri Baraka Reader.* New York: Thunder's Mouth Press, 1988.

Harrison, Hubert H. *The Negro and the Nation.* New York: Cosmo-Advocate Publishing, 1917.

———. *When Africa Awakes.* New York: Porro Press, 1920.

Harvey, David. *The Urban Experience.* Baltimore: Johns Hopkins University Press, 1989.

Hawley, Willis D. *Nonpartisan Elections and the Case for Party Politics.* New York: Wiley, 1973.

Hayden, Tom. *Rebellion in Newark: Official Violence and Ghetto Response.* New York: Vintage, 1967.

Haywood, Harry. *Black Bolshevik.* Chicago: Liberator Press, 1978.

———. *Negro Liberation.* New York: International Publishers, 1948. Reprint, Chicago: Liberator Press, 1976.

Heberle, Rudolf. *Social Movements: An Introduction to Political Sociology.* New York: Appleton-Century-Crofts, 1951.

Hechter, Michael. *Internal Colonialism.* Berkeley: University of California Press, 1975.

Henriksen, Thomas H. "African Intellectual Influences on Black Americans: The Role of Edward W. Blyden." *Phylon,* (September 1975): 279–90.

Herod, Agustina, and Charles C. Herod. *Afro-American Nationalism: An Annotated Bibliography of Militant, Separatist and Nationalist Literature.* New York: Garland, 1986.

Hertz, Frederick. *Nationality in History and Politics: A Psychology and Sociology of National Sentiment and Nationalism.* New York: Humanities Press, 1944.

Hill, Robert, comp. *The Crusader.* New York: Garland, 1987.

Hilliard, David. *This Side of Glory*. Boston: Little, Brown, 1993.

Himes, Joseph. "The Functions of Racial Conflict." *Social Forces* 45 (September 1966): 1–10.

Hirsch, Arnold R. "Black Ghettos." In *The Reader's Companion to American History*, edited by Eric Foner and John A. Garraty. Boston, 1991.

———. *Making the Second Ghetto: Race and Housing in Chicago, 1940–1960*. Cambridge: Cambridge University Press, 1983.

Hirsch, Susan E. *Roots of the American Working Class: The Industrialization of Crafts in Newark*. Philadelphia: University of Pennsylvania Press, 1978.

Hite, Gregory Nelson. "The Hottest Places in Hell: Catholic Participation in the Selma Voting Rights Campaign, 1962–1965." Master's thesis, University of Virginia, 1994.

Hobsbawm, Eric. *The Age of Extremes*. New York: Vintage, 1994; reprint, 1996.

Hoetink, Harmannus. "National Identity and Somatic Norm Image." In *Ethnicity and Nation-Building: Comparative, International, and Historical Perspectives*, edited by Wendell Bell and Walter E. Freeman. Beverly Hills, Calif.: Sage, 1974.

———. "National Identity, Culture, and Race in the Caribbean." In *Racial Tensions and National Identity*, edited by Ernest Q. Campbell. Nashville: Vanderbilt University Press, 1972.

———. *The Two Variants in Caribbean Race Relations*. London: Oxford University Press, 1967.

Holt, Thomas. *Black over White*. Urbana: University of Illinois Press, 1977.

Horton, James Oliver. *Free People of Color: Inside the African American Community*. Washington, D.C.: Smithsonian Institution Press, 1993.

Hudson, Theodore R. *From LeRoi Jones to Amiri Baraka: The Literary Works*. Durham, N.C.: Duke University Press, 1973.

Huggins, Nathan. *Harlem Renaissance*. New York: Oxford University Press, 1971.

Huggins, Nathan I., Martin Kilson, and Daniel M. Fox, eds. *Key Issues in the Afro-American Experience*. Vol. 2. New York: Harcourt, 1971.

Hutchinson, John. "Cultural Nationalism and Moral Regeneration." In *Nationalism*, edited by John Hutchinson and Anthony D. Smith. Oxford: Oxford University Press, 1994.

———. *The Dynamics of Cultural Nationalism*. London: Aleen and Urwin, 1987.

Hutchinson, John, and Anthony D. Smith, eds. *Ethnicity*. London: Oxford University Press, 1996.

———. *Nationalism*. London: Oxford University Press, 1994.

Jackson, Kenneth T. *Crabgrass Frontier*. New York: Oxford University Press, 1985.

———. *The Ku Klux Klan in the City, 1915–1930*. New York: Oxford University Press, 1967.

———. "Race, Ethnicity, and Real Estate Appraisal." In *American Vistas, 1877 to the Present*, edited by Leonard Dinnerstein and Kenneth T. Jackson. New York: Oxford University Press, 1983.

Jackson, Kenneth T., and Barbara B. Jackson. "The Black Experience in Newark, the Growth of the Ghetto, 1870–1970." In *New Jersey Since 1860: New Findings and Interpretations*, edited by William C. Wright. Trenton: New Jersey Historical Commission, 1972.

James, Winston. *Holding Aloft the Banner of Ethiopia: Caribbean Radicalism in Early Twentieth-Century America*. London: Verso, 1998.

Jayawardena, Kumari. *Feminism and Nationalism in the Third World*. London: Zed, 1986.

Johnson, Chalmers. *Peasant Nationalism and Communist Power: The Emergence of Revolutionary China, 1937–1945*. Stanford: Stanford University Press, 1962.

Jones, LeRoi. *Black Magic: Poetry, 1961–1967*. New York: Bobbs-Merrill, 1969.

——. *Black Music*. New York: William Morrow, 1968.

——. *Blues People*. New York: William Morrow, 1963.

——. *Home: Social Essays*. New York: Ecco, 1998.

Jordan, Winthrop D. "American Chiaroscuro: The Status and Definition of Mulattoes in the British Colonies." *William and Mary Quarterly* 19, no. 2 (April 1962): 185–200.

——. *White Over Black: American Attitudes Toward the Negro, 1550–1812*. Chapel Hill: University of North Carolina Press, 1968.

Kaplan, Harold. *Urban Renewal Politics: Slum Clearance in Newark*. New York: Columbia University Press, 1963.

Karenga, Maulana. "Afro-American Nationalism." Ph.D. diss., U.S. International University, San Diego, Calif., 1976. Ann Arbor: UMI, 1976.

——. *Introduction to Black Studies*. Los Angeles: University of Sankore Press, 1982.

——. "Joanne Little Case: In Defense of Sis. Joanne: For Ourselves and History." *Black Scholar* 6, no. 10 (July/August 1975): 36–42.

Katz, Michael B. *Improving Poor People*. Princeton: Princeton University Press, 1995.

——. *In the Shadow of the Poorhouse: A Social History of Welfare in America*. New York: Basic, 1986.

Katzman, David. *Before the Ghetto*. Urbana: University of Illinois Press, 1977.

Katznelson, Ira. *Black Men, White Cities*. Chicago: University of Chicago Press, 1976.

——. *City Trenches*. Chicago: University of Chicago Press, 1981.

Kilson, Martin. "The Emerging Elites of Black Africa, 1900–1960." In *Colonialism in Africa, 1870–1960*, vol. 2, edited by L. H. Gann and Peter Duignan. Cambridge: Cambridge University Press, 1970.

——. "Political Change in the Negro Ghetto, 1900–1940's." In *Key Issues in the Afro-American Experience*, vol. 2, edited by Nathan I. Huggins, Martin Kilson, and Daniel M. Fox. New York: Harcourt, 1971.

Kirby, John B. *Black Americans in the Roosevelt Era: Liberalism and Race*. Knoxville: University of Tennessee Press, 1980.

Klingman, Peter D. "The National Negro Convention Movement, 1864–1872: Black Leadership Attitudes toward the Republican Party." Master's thesis, University of Florida, 1969.

Kofsky, Frank. *Black Nationalism and the Revolution in Music*. New York: Pathfinder, 1970.

Kozol, Jonathan. *Savage Inequalities*. New York: Crown, 1991.

Kusmer, Kenneth. *A Ghetto Takes Shape*. Urbana: University of Illinois, 1978.

Lacey, Henry C. *To Raise, Destroy, and Create: The Poetry, Drama, and Fiction of Imamu Amiri Baraka (LeRoi Jones)*. Troy, N.Y.: Whitston, 1981.

Laue, James H. "A Contemporary Revitalization Movement in American Race Relations: The 'Black Muslims.'" *Social Forces* 42 (March 1964): 315–24.

Lee, Don L. *Black Pride.* Detroit: Broadsides, 1967.

———. *Think Black.* Detroit: Broadsides, 1967.

Lerner, Daniel. *The Passing of Traditional Society.* Glencoe, Ill.: Free Press, 1958.

Levine, Lawrence W. *Black Culture and Black Consciousness.* New York: Oxford University Press, 1977.

———. "Marcus Garvey and the Politics of Revitalization." In *Black Leaders of the Twentieth Century*, edited by John Hope Franklin and August Meier. Urbana: University of Illinois Press, 1982.

Lewis, David Levering. *When Harlem Was in Vogue.* New York: Oxford University Press, 1979.

Lincoln, C. Eric. *The Black Muslims in America.* Chicago: University of Chicago Press, 1961.

Litwack, Leon. *Been in the Storm So Long.* New York: Vintage, 1980.

———. *North of Slavery.* Chicago: University of Chicago Press, 1961.

Litwack, Leon, and August Meier, eds. *Nineteenth Century Black Leaders.* Urbana: University of Illinois Press, 1988.

Llorens, David. "Ameer (LeRoi Jones) Baraka." In *The Black Revolution* (*Ebony* special issue), 65–78. Chicago: Johnson, 1970.

Logan, Rayford W. *The Negro in American Life and Thought: The Nadir, 1877–1901.* London, 1954. Reprint, New York: Da Capo Press, 1997.

Lynch, Hollis R. *Black American Radicals and the Liberation of Africa: The Council on African Affairs, 1937–1955.* Ithaca: Africana Studies and Research Center, Cornell University, 1978.

———. *Edward Wilmot Blyden: Pan-Negro Patriot, 1832–1912.* London: Oxford University Press, 1967.

———. "Pan-Negro Nationalism in the New World, Before 1862." In *The Making of Black America*, vol. 1, edited by August Meier and Elliott Rudwick. New York: Atheneum, 1969.

McAdam, Doug. *Political Process and the Development of Black Insurgency, 1930–1970.* Chicago: University of Chicago Press, 1982.

McAdoo, Bill. *Pre–Civil War Black Nationalism.* Brooklyn, N.Y.: David Walker, 1985.

Mace, James E. *Communism and the Dilemmas of National Liberation.* Cambridge: Harvard University Press, 1983.

MacLeod, Jay. *Ain't No Makin' It.* Boulder, Colo.: Westview, 1995.

Malcolm X. *The Autobiography of Malcolm X.* New York: Ballantine, 1965.

Marable, Manning. *Race, Reform and Rebellion: The Second Reconstruction in Black America.* Jackson: University Press of Mississippi, 1984.

Massey, Douglas S., and Nancy Denton. *American Apartheid: Segregation and the Making of the Underclass.* Cambridge: Harvard University Press, 1993.

Matusow, Allen J. *The Unraveling of America.* New York: Harper and Row, 1984.

Meier, August. *Negro Thought in America, 1880–1915.* Ann Arbor: University of Michigan, 1966.

Mikell, Gwendolyn. "Class and Ethnic Political Relations in Newark, N.J.: Blacks and Italians." In *Cities of the U.S.*, edited by Leith Mullings. New York: Columbia University Press, 1987.

Miller, Floyd. *The Search for a Black Nationality: Black Colonization and Emigration, 1787–1863*. Urbana: University of Illinois Press, 1975.

Mollenkopf, John H. *The Contested City*. Princeton: Princeton University Press, 1983.

Moore, Barrington, Jr. *Injustice: The Social Bases of Obedience and Revolt*. White Plains, N.Y.: M. E. Sharpe, 1978.

Morris, Aldon D. *The Origins of the Civil Rights Movement: Black Communities Organizing for Change*. New York: Free Press, 1984.

Moses, Wilson J. *Alexander Crummell: A Study of Civilization and Discontent*. Amherst: University of Massachusetts Press, 1992.

——. *The Golden Age of Black Nationalism*. New York: Oxford University Press, 1988.

——, ed. *Classical Black Nationalism*. New York: New York University Press, 1996.

Mtumi, James, and Clyde Halisi, eds. *The Quotable Karenga*. Los Angeles: US Organization, 1967.

Naison, Mark. *Communists in Harlem During the Depression*. Urbana: University of Illinois, 1983.

Nash, Gary. *Forging Freedom*. Cambridge: Harvard University Press, 1988.

The National Black Political Agenda. Washington, D.C.: National Black Political Convention, Inc., 1972.

Neal, Larry. "The Black Contribution to American Letters: Part II, The Writer as Activist, 1960 and After." In *The Black American Reference Book*, edited by Mabel M. Smythe. Englewood Cliffs, N.J.: Prentice-Hall, 1976.

——. "New Space/The Growth of Black Consciousness in the Sixties." In *The Black Seventies*, edited by Floyd B. Barbour. Boston: Porter Sargent, 1970.

——. "The Social Background of the Black Arts Movement." *Black Scholar* (January/February 1987): 11–22.

Newton, Huey P. "Huey Newton Talks to the Movement about the Black Panther Party, Cultural Nationalism, SNCC, Liberals and White Revolutionaries." In *The Black Panthers Speak*, edited by Philip S. Foner. Philadelphia: J. B. Lippincott, 1970.

——. *Revolutionary Suicide*. New York: Ballantine, 1973.

Ngugi wa Thiong'o. *Writing Against Neocolonialism*. Trenton, N.J.: Red Sea, 1986.

Nyerere, Julius K. *Ujamaa – Essays on Socialism*. New York: Oxford University Press, 1968.

Omi, Michael, and Howard Winant. *Racial Formation in the United States*. London: Routledge and Kegan Paul, 1986.

O'Reilly, Kenneth. *Racial Matters: The FBI's Secret Files on Black America, 1969–1972*. New York: Free Press, 1989.

Padmore, George. *Pan-Africanism or Communism*. New York: Doubleday, 1971.

Painter, Nell Irvin. *Exodusters: Black Migrations to Kansas after Reconstruction*. New York: W. W. Norton, 1976.

——. "Martin R. Delany: Elitism and Black Nationalism." In *Nineteenth Century Black Leaders*, edited by Leon Litwack and August Meier. Urbana: University of Illinois Press, 1988.

Park, Robert, and Ernest Burgess. *The City*. Chicago: University of Chicago Press, 1925.

Patterson, Orlando. "Going Separate Ways: The History of an Old Idea," *Newsweek*, October 30, 1995, 43.

———. *Slavery and Social Death*. Cambridge: Harvard University Press, 1982.

Payne, Charles M. *I've Got the Light of Freedom: The Organizing Tradition and the Mississippi Freedom Struggle*. Berkeley: University of California Press, 1995.

Pease, Jane H., and William H. Pease. *They Who Would Be Free*. New York: Atheneum, 1974.

Perman, Michael. *The Road to Redemption: Southern Politics, 1869–1879*. Chapel Hill: University of North Carolina Press, 1984.

Perry, Jeffrey B. "Hubert Henry Harrison, 'The Father of Harlem Radicalism': The Early Years—1883 through the Founding of the Liberty League and 'The Voice' in 1917." 2 vols. Ph.D. diss., Columbia University, 1986. Ann Arbor: UMI, 1986.

Philpott, Thomas. *The Slum and the Ghetto*. Belmont, Calif.: Wadsworth, 1991.

Pierce, Paulette. "The Roots of the Rainbow Coalition." *Black Scholar* 19, no. 2 (March/April 1988): 2–16.

Pierson, George Wilson. *Tocqueville and Beaumont in America*. New York: Oxford University Press, 1938.

Pinkney, Alphonso. *Red, Black and Green: Black Nationalism in the U.S.* Cambridge: Cambridge University Press, 1976.

Poinsett, Alex. "Black Political Strategies for '72." *Ebony* 27, no. 4 (1972): 66–74.

———. "It's Nation Time! Congress of African People Proposes Models for Worldwide Black Institutions." *Ebony* 26, no. 2 (December 1970): 98–106.

Popper, Samuel H. "Newark, N.J., 1870–1910: Chapters in the Evolution of an American Metropolis." Ph.D. diss., New York University, 1951.

Porambo, Ron. *No Cause for Indictment: An Autopsy of Newark*. New York: Holt, 1971.

Price, Clement Alexander. "The Afro-American Community of Newark, 1917–1947: A Social History." Ph.D. diss., Rutgers University, 1975. Ann Arbor: UMI, 1975.

Przeworski, Adam, and John Sprague. *Paper Stones: A History of Electoral Socialism*. Chicago: University of Chicago Press, 1986.

Raines, Howell, ed. *My Soul Is Rested*. New York: Penguin, 1977.

Randall, Dudley. "A Report on the Black Arts Convention: Assembly in Detroit." *Negro Digest* (August 1966): 54.

———. "The Second Annual Black Arts Convention." *Negro Digest* (November 1967): 42–48.

Redkey, Edwin S. *Black Exodus*. New Haven: Yale University Press, 1969.

Reilly, Charlie, ed. *Conversations with Amiri Baraka*. Jackson: University Press of Mississippi, 1994.

Revolutionary Communist League. "'Unity and Struggle'—History of the Revolutionary Communist League (M-L-M)." *Forward* no. 3 (1980).

Roediger, David R. *Towards the Abolition of Whiteness*. London: Verso, 1994.

———. *The Wages of Whiteness: Race and the Making of the American Working Class*. London: Verso, 1991.

Rusinow, Dennison. *The Yugoslav Experiment, 1948–1974*. Berkeley: University of California Press, 1977.

Sales, William, Jr. *From Civil Rights to Black Liberation: Malcolm X and the Organization of Afro-American Unity*. Boston: South End Press, 1994.

Samatar, Said S. *Oral Poetry and Somali Nationalism*. Cambridge: Cambridge University Press, 1982.

Samuels, Wilfred David. "Five Afro-Caribbean Voices in American Culture, 1917–1929: Hubert H. Harrison, Wilfred A. Domingo, Richard B. Moore, Cyril V. Briggs, and Claude McKay." Ph.D. diss., University of Iowa, 1977. Ann Arbor: UMI, 1977.

Scheer, Robert, ed. *Eldridge Cleaver: Post-Prison Writings and Speeches*. New York: Ramparts and Random House, 1969.

Sears, David O., and T. M. Tomlinson. "Riot Ideology in Los Angeles: A Study of Negro Attitudes." *Social Science Quarterly* 49 (December 1968): 485–503.

Sellers, Cleveland. *The River of No Return*. New York: William Morrow, 1973.

Shakur, Assata. *Assata: An Autobiography*. Chicago: Lawrence Hill, 1987.

Sitkoff, Harvard. *A New Deal for Blacks*. New York: Oxford University Press, 1978.

———. *The Struggle for Black Equality, 1954–1980*. New York: Hill and Wang, 1981.

Smith, Anthony D. "'Ideas' and 'Structure' in the Formation of Independence Ideals." *Philosophy of the Social Sciences* 3 (1973): 19–39.

———. "Nationalism: A Trend Report and Bibliography." *Current Sociology* 21 (1973).

———. *Nationalism in the Twentieth Century*. New York: New York University Press, 1979.

———, ed. *Ethnicity and Nationalism*. Leiden, Netherlands: E. J. Brill, 1992.

———. *Nationalist Movements*. London, 1976. New York: St. Martin's, 1977.

Smith, M. G. *The Economy of Hausa Communities of Zaria*. London: Colonial Social Science Research Council, 1955.

———. *The Plural Society in the British West Indies*. Berkeley: University of California Press, 1965.

Smythe, Mabel M., ed. *The Black American Reference Book*. Englewood Cliffs, N.J.: Prentice-Hall, 1976.

Sollors, Werner. *Amiri Baraka/LeRoi Jones: The Quest for a "Populist Modernism."* New York: Columbia University Press, 1978.

Spellman, A. B. "Revolution in Sound." In *The Black Revolution* (*Ebony* special issue), 81–96. Chicago: Johnson, 1970.

Stellhorn, Paul A. "Depression and Decline: Newark, New Jersey, 1929–1941." Ph.D. diss., Rutgers University, 1975.

Stone, Chuck. *Black Political Power in America*. New York: Dell, 1970.

———. "The National Conference on Black Power." In *The Black Power Revolt*, edited by Floyd B. Barbour. Boston: Porter Sargent, 1968.

Stuckey, Sterling. *Going Through the Storm: The Influence of African American Art in History*. New York: Oxford University Press, 1994.

———. *Slave Culture: Nationalist Theory and the Foundations of Black America*. New York: Oxford University Press, 1987.

———, ed. *The Ideological Origins of Black Nationalism in America*. Boston: Beacon, 1972.

Sun Tzu. *The Art of War*. New York: Oxford University Press, 1963.

Symmons-Symnolewicz, Konstantin. *Modern Nationalism: Toward a Consensus in Theory.* New York: Polish Institute of Arts and Science in America, 1968.

———. *Nationalist Movements: A Comparative View.* Meadville, Pa.: Maplewood, 1970.

Teaford, Jon C. *The Twentieth-Century American City: Problem, Promise, and Reality.* Baltimore: Johns Hopkins University Press, 1986.

Thompson, Mindy. *The National Negro Labor Council: A History.* Occasional Paper No. 27. New York: American Institute for Marxist Studies, 1978.

Toll, William. *The Resurgence of Race.* Philadelphia: Temple University Press, 1979.

Tomlinson, T. M., and Diana L. TenHouten. "Los Angeles Riot Study Method: Negro Reaction Survey." Los Angeles: Institute of Government and Public Affairs at UCLA, 1967.

Van Deburg, William L. *New Day in Babylon: The Black Power Movement and American Culture, 1965–1975.* Chicago: University of Chicago, 1991.

———, ed. *Modern Black Nationalism: From Marcus Garvey to Louis Farrakhan.* New York University Press, 1997.

Van den Berghe, Pierre. *Race and Racism.* New York: Wiley, 1967.

Vander Zanden, James W. *Social Psychology.* New York: Random House, 1981.

Wade, Richard C. "The Negro in Cincinnati, 1800–1830." *Journal of Negro History* 39 (1954): 43–57.

Walby, Sylvia. "Woman and Nation." In *Ethnicity and Nationalism*, edited by Anthony D. Smith. Leiden, Netherlands: E. J. Brill, 1992.

Wallace, Michele. *Black Macho and the Myth of the Superwoman.* London: Verso, 1990.

Walters, Ronald W. *Black Presidential Politics in America: A Strategic Approach.* Albany: SUNY Press, 1988.

———. "The New Black Political Culture." *Black World* 21, no. 12 (Oct. 1972): 4–17.

Weaver, Robert C. "The New Deal and the Negro: A Look at the Facts." *Opportunity* 13 (July 1935).

Weisbort, Robert. *Freedom Bound.* New York: Penguin, 1990.

Weiss, Nancy J. *Farewell to the Party of Lincoln: Black Politics in the Age of FDR.* Princeton: Princeton University Press, 1983.

Wesley, Charles. "Lincoln's Plan for Colonizing the Emancipated Negro." *Journal of Negro History* 4 (January 1919): 1–21.

Williamson, Joel. *After Slavery.* New York: W. W. Norton, 1965.

———. *New People.* New York: Free Press, 1980.

Willis, Paul. *Learning to Labor.* New York: Columbia University Press, 1977.

Wills, Garry. *The Second Civil War: Arming for Armageddon.* New York: New American Library, 1968.

Wilson, David A. "Nation Building and Revolutionary War." In *Nation Building*, edited by Karl W. Deutch and William J. Foltz. New York: Atherton, 1963.

Wilson, William J. *The Declining Significance of Race.* Chicago: University of Chicago Press, 1976.

———. *Power, Racism, and Privilege.* New York: Free Press, 1973.

———. *The Truly Disadvantaged.* Chicago: University of Chicago Press, 1988.

Winant, Howard. *Racial Conditions.* Minneapolis: University of Minnesota Press, 1994.

Wirth, Louis. "Types of Nationalism." *American Journal of Sociology* 41 (July 1935–May 1936): 723–37.

Wolak, Edward J. "A Political Study of the Negro in Newark, New Jersey." Senior thesis, Princeton University, May 1948.

Wolters, Raymond. *Negroes and the Great Depression.* Westport, Conn.: Greenwood, 1970.

Wood, Peter H. *The Black Majority.* New York: W. W. Norton, 1974.

Woodard, Komozi. "The Making of the New Ark: Imamu Amiri Baraka (LeRoi Jones), the Newark Congress of African People, and the Modern Black Convention Movement. A History of the Black Revolt and the New Nationalism, 1966–1976." Ph.D. diss., University of Pennsylvania, 1991. Ann Arbor: UMI, 1991.

Woodson, Carter G. *A Century of Negro Migration.* Washington, D.C.: Associated Publishers, 1918.

———. "The Negroes in Cincinnati Prior to the Civil War." *Journal of Negro History* 1 (1916): 1–22.

Woodward, C. Vann. *The Strange Career of Jim Crow.* New York: Oxford University Press, 1966.

Wright, Nathan, Jr. *Black Power and Urban Unrest.* New York: Holt, Rinehart and Winston, 1967.

———. *Ready to Riot.* New York: Holt, Rinehart and Winston, 1967.

Wright, William C., ed. *New Jersey Since 1860: New Findings and Interpretations.* Trenton, N.J.: New Jersey Historical Commission, 1972.

Yinger, J. Milton. *Ethnicity.* Albany: SUNY Press, 1994.

Yuval-Davis, Nira, and Floya Anthias, eds. *Woman-Nation-State.* London: Macmillan, 1989.

Zunz, Olivier. *The Changing Face of Inequality.* Chicago: University of Chicago Press, 1982.

Index

132–33; on neo-African architecture, 225–29

Barrett, David. *See* Mtetezi, Kaimu

BARTS. *See* Black Arts Repertory Theater/School

BCD. *See* Black Community Defense and Development

Belafonte, Harry, 148, 194, 200

Berlin Conference (1884), 23

Bibb, Henry and Mary, 15

Bingham, Russell (Baba Mshauri), 89, 125–26, 247

Black abolitionists, 13–17

Black aesthetic, xiii, 225

Black Agenda: welfare and, xiv, 102–3, 142–43, 197, 204, 264, 266; character of, 1–3; education and, 6, 73, 77–78, 102–3, 107, 135, 143, 197, 198, 204, 213, 220, 264–66; employment and, 36, 95, 102–3, 142–43; economics and, 75, 107, 115, 142, 189, 213, 220, 224; health issues, 77, 101–3, 142–43, 198, 204, 214; drugs and, 77, 143; and fundraising, 102, 104, 109, 144–49, 200, 243–44, 246, 247; at Newark Black Political Convention, 102–4; communications as part of, 107, 134, 143, 168, 189, 198–99, 213–14, 220, 226; agenda-building process of, 142–43, 196–98; environmental issues and, 189, 213; opposition to, 201–3; at Gary, 203–16; and foreign policy, 213, 215; environmental racism and, 214; as foundation of convention movement, 256; contemporary challenges of, 265. *See also* Gary Agenda

Black and Puerto Rican Convention, 1, 2, 114, 139, 140–43, 256

Black Arts Convention, 1, 66

Black Arts Movement: as second Black Renaissance, xi–xiii; influence on Modern Black Convention Movement of, 1, 62, 144, 259–60; and color caste, 13; demise of, 43; and Detroit Black Arts Convention, 66; newspapers inspired by, 67; wall murals as

element of, 67; and Spirit House, 70, 85, 139; impact of Karenga and Baraka's meeting on, 85; and Last Poets, 139; impact of, on 1970 election campaign, 144. *See also* Black Arts Repertory Theater/School

Black Arts Repertory Theater/School (BARTS), 63–68, 225

Black Arts West, 66, 70, 133

Black Community Defense and Development (BCD), 88, 121–22, 166

Black Congress, 72, 118

Black consciousness: and Black Arts Movement, xi, 51; role of institutional racism in, xiv; impact of group conflict on, xiv, 5, 97; influence of international developments on, xv; impact of urbanization on, xv, 6; impact of migration on, xv, 6, 22, 25–26, 31–32; and political mobilization, xv, 153–54; in context of slavery, 5; and situation of racial oppression, 5; and distinct identity, 6; role of, in ghetto formation, 6, 31–33; and Booker T. Washington, 24; and soul food, 32; and music and dance, 32; and Malcolm X, 59, 60; and militancy, 70; role of urban uprisings in, 70–71; and CAP, 74, 221–22, 243; impact of community mobilization on, 92; and Martin Luther King Jr., 93–94; and self-transformation, 125–33; and youth, 128–29; and 1970 election campaign victory, 155; effect of African Liberation Day on, 176; and national scope of convention movement, 197

Black Convention Movement: classical, 9, 13–17. *See also* Modern Black Convention Movement

Black ethos, xv, 6, 32–34, 59, 139, 145

Black freedom movement: fusion with Black Nationalism of, xiii, 7; spread of, 4–5, 7; viewed as irrational and dysfunctional, 6; scholarship about, 6, 7; role of civil rights revolution in, 7; protracted nature of, 8; hetero-

geneous character of, 8; Harry
Haywood defines, 8–9; united front
quality of, 9; and phases of black
nationality formation, 10–11; and
ethnogenesis, 10–13; impact of Modern Black Convention Movement on,
92; stages of, 161; moves toward Left,
180; and sexism, 180–84; trajectory
of, 255–70
Black Liberation Center, 105
Black Muslims, 26
Black nationalism. *See* Cultural
nationalism
Black Panther Party: as component
of Black Power, xiv, 260; and rivalry,
4; roots of, 41, 43, 61–63; and grassroots political organization, 70, 73; in
Oakland, 71–74; founding of, 72; in
Harlem, 73; and Robert F. Williams,
73; debates with US Organization,
105–6, 116–19, 165; and Los Angeles
shoot-out, 119–20; and Young Lords,
139; and Imperiale and Newark
Rebellion, 153; and CAP, 169; and
involvement in African Liberation
Day, 178; at Gary, 207
Black political conventions, 37, 93,
101–7, 197–200, 256
Black political party: call for, 91–92,
106, 108, 167–68, 178; CFUN as,
113; and 1972 election campaign,
186–88; and party building, 193–94;
and Eastern Regional CAP, 189–90;
and Gary Agenda, 207–10
Black political strategy: components of,
xiv, 1; of Baraka and Martin Luther
King Jr., 94; and CAP, 162–72; at
"East" Conference, 186–88; at Northlake Summit, 191–94; at National
Conference of Black Elected Officials,
194–99
Black Power: as call for political experimentation, 41–42; and SNCC origins
of concept of, 42; and Malcolm X, 50;
and West Coast experiments, 69–74;
politics of, 74; and Newark Black

Power experiment, 92; and Martin
Luther King Jr., 93–94; divisions
within, 116–17; themes of, 128; and
1970 election campaign, 145, 153–54;
and Eastern Regional CAP, 190; disintegration of, 252–54; strategy of,
256; trajectory of, 255–70
Black Power Conferences: in Washington, 1, 85; in Newark, 43–44, 84–89;
in Philadelphia, 92, 95, 107–13; 1967
National Black Power Conference,
93; influence on youth of, 128; in
Bermuda, 162; "East" Conference,
185–86; Eastern Regional CAP, 189–
90. *See also* Black and Puerto Rican
Convention; Gary convention
Black Power Congress, international,
86
Black Power organizations, 70–77 passim; produced by fusion, xiii; aims of,
xiii; impact on community of, xiv; agitational effect of slogans of, xiv, 69,
71. *See also* Black Panther Party; Black
Power Congress, international; Committee for a Unified NewArk; Congress of African People
Black presidential strategy, 187, 190–94
Black Revolt: internationalism of, xv,
17, 29, 159–80, 215, 268, 269–70; role
in cultural nationalism, 3–4; roots of,
41–42; Baraka's introduction to, 49;
Malcolm X's role in, 60; in Newark,
74–75; effect of Martin Luther King
Jr.'s assassination upon, 94, 110; and
police intimidation in Newark, 100;
and SNCC, 105; and gun cultism,
105; and CFUN, 108–10; white political reaction to, 112; cultural revolution as a component of, 117; and
debate between US Organization and
Black Panther Party, 116–17; and
New Ark Fund, 144; and founding of
CAP, 162–63; and effect of rupture
between CFUN and US Organization, 165–67; and gender discrimination, 180, 184; as roots of Gary con-

Conference, 87; to Philadelphia Convention, 107; to Black and Puerto Rican Convention, 142; to CAP, 162; to "East" Conference, 185–86; to Eastern Regional CAP, 190; to Northlake Summit, 191–92; to Democratic National Convention, 192, 202, 207–8; women as, 197; to Gary Convention, 204–6, 209–12

Dellums, Ronald, 195, 205

Democrats, 21, 22–23, 40, 106, 112, 125–26, 185, 193–94, 205–10 passim

Detroit, Mich.: black population in, 26, 32; Detroit Black Arts Convention, 66; rebellion in, 73; following King's assassination, 96; Detroit League of Revolutionary Black Workers, 129–30; and BWUF, 181–82

Diggs, Charles, Jr., 175–78 passim, 191–96 passim, 203, 205–7, 209, 217

Discrimination, racial, 15, 27, 28, 35, 36, 58, 78, 30

Dodge Revolutionary Union Movement (DRUM), 78

Douglass, Frederick, xi, 15–16, 17, 179, 270

Draper, Theodore, 3, 102

Du Bois, W. E. B., 1, 4, 11, 12, 13, 23–25, 29, 36–38, 175, 198

"The East," 185–89

Eisenhower, Dwight D., 39, 56

Elections: of 1876, 20; of 1968, 101, 112–13; of 1970, 115, 140, 142–53; of 1972, 185–88, 191–99; of 1974, 246

Emancipation, 16

Equality, racial, 22, 27, 40, 44–45, 97, 203, 244

Essex County, N.J., 2; as site of Atlantic City and Democratic National Convention, 40; Essex County Political Convention, 197–200; and Kawaida Towers, 223; See also Newark, N.J.

Ethnogenesis, 10–13

Fanon, Frantz, 1, 43, 50, 56, 116, 255

Farmer, James, 40

Farrakhan, Louis, 3, 164, 203

Fauntroy, Walter, 176, 178, 186, 191, 199–200, 202, 203

FBI (Federal Bureau of Investigation), 116, 119, 153, 172, 240, 267

Forman, James, 105, 118

Forten, James, 14

Frazier, E. Franklin, 11

Fredrickson, George, 18–19

Free Southern Theater, 67

Furaha, Muminina, 133

Garnet, Henry Highland, 15, 16, 19

Garvey, Marcus: and UNIA, 4, 26, 260; and Garvey Movement, 11, 26, 269; and Hubert Harrison, 25; and decline of Garveyism, 28; and impact of ghetto formation, 32; influence on UN incident participants, 58; and parents of Malcolm X, 60; and Baraka's vision of CAP, 170–71

Garvin, Vicki, 36, 275 (n. 119)

Gary Agenda, 3; "East" Conference as model for, 189; National Black Political Agenda, 196–99, 212–16, 218; building process of, 196–216; opposition to, 201–3

Gary convention, 3, 42, 43–44, 184–85, 203–18; and National Black Political Assembly, 160, 168, 185–86; groundwork for, 168; and origins of CAP, 168; strategy and tactics of, 186–88; impact of Baraka's self-criticism upon, 188–89; role of Shirley Chisholm in, 192; Baraka's role in, 196, 203, 210–12, 216–18; leadership of, 196, 203–7, 210–12, 216–18; and grassroots mobilization and agenda building, 196–99, 206–7, 210–14; delegates to, 202, 204–6, 209–11; creation of national political community, 203–7; key issues of, 268–69

Genocide, 95, 110

Ghetto: and black ethos, 6, 26; and

grassroots intelligentsia, 7; second ghetto, 8, 11, 30–35, 42, 115, 236; and new ghetto leadership, 43; and internal colonialism, 44; uprisings in, 70–71, 73, 256; violence in, 80–84; and politics of Modern Black Convention Movement, 102–3; and urban crisis in Newark, 198–99; transformation of, 224–30; expanding boundaries of, 241, 244; and contemporary situation, 260; Black Power strategy surrounding, 261–62. *See also* Newark Rebellion; Urban crisis

Gibson, Mayor Kenneth: and 1970 election campaign, 44, 115, 143–44, 148–49; and United Brothers, 89; and 1970 victory, 150–53, 190; and Atlanta CAP, 164; at Black Leadership Unity Conference, 185; containment policy of, 222–23; lack of leadership of, 232, 235; critics of, 238; intervention in Kawaida crisis, 240; betrayal of CAP by, 246–48, 251–53

Gibson, Richard, 52, 54

Ginsberg, Allen, 52

Goodman, Andrew, 130

Grass roots: fusion of, xiii; momentum of, 5; and Malcolm X's message, 7; fusion with college-educated elites, 7; and bourgeois vs. cultural nationalism, 30–31; and women, 40; and Black Arts Movement, 43; and Newark, 49; and Malcolm X, 50, 62; and Black Panther Party, 70, 73; and black urban uprisings, 71; and Newark Black Political Convention, 101; and collapse of CFUN, 116; mobilization during 1970 election campaign, 144, 150; and ALSC, 175; and mobilization for Gary convention, 196–99, 206–7, 210–14; of urban masses and black nationalists, 256; facing contemporary challenges, 265

Great Migration, 11, 12–13, 22, 25–26

Greenwich Village, 42, 52

Gregory, Dick, 141, 148, 176–77

Group conflict, xiv–xv; theory of, 7–8, 92–93

Guinea, 161

Guinea-Bissau, 161–62, 171, 173, 175, 215, 269

Hamer, Fannie Lou, 20, 40

Hamm, Larry, 128

Hampton, Fred, 207

Harlem: black nationalism in, 24–25, 32, 42, 43, 58; and UN incident, 57–58; Writers Guild of, 58; and Malcolm X, 60; and BARTS, 63–68; and Last Poets, 139

Harlem Renaissance, xii, 13, 25–26, 32

Harris, Earl, 89, 143, 150–51, 246–53

Harrison, Hubert H., 4, 24–25, 27

HARYOU-ACT, 66

Hatcher, Richard: at Black and Puerto Rican Convention, 142; endorsement of, 147–48, 216–17; at Atlanta CAP, 164; at Northlake, 190–94; at Gary convention, 196, 203, 205; calls for black political party, 207–10; at National Conference of Black Elected Officials, 195

Hayden, Tom, 82–84

Hayes-Tilden Compromise of 1876 ("Gentlemen's Agreement"), 20

Haywood, Harry, xii, 8–9, 10, 26, 27, 38, 49, 69

Hekalu Mwalimu (Temple of the Teacher), 225–26

Henry, Hayward, 164, 189, 220

Hill, Jaribu, 133

Hilliard, David, 117

House Un-American Activities Committee (HUAC), 37–38

Housing for African Americans: conditions of, 34, 142–43; and Black Panther's program, 73; impact of King's assassination, 95; and Newark Black Political Convention, 102–3; and urban crisis, 197–99, 204; and urban renewal, 198; and U.S. Department of Housing and Urban Development

(HUD), 205, 230, 246, 248, 281
(n. 46); and Gary agenda, 214. *See also*
Kawaida Towers; Newark Housing
Authority; NJR-32
Howard University, 51, 52, 55, 57, 185,
189, 196
Huggins, John, 119–20
Hughes, Langston, xi, 27, 37–38
Hutchings, Phil, 77, 105–6

Imperiale, Anthony, 97–100, 110, 112,
138, 150, 153, 231–35, 236, 240, 243,
281 (n. 81)
Imperialism, 23, 27, 215
Inequities, racial, 34, 35–36
Institutional racism, xiv, 8, 30, 34–38,
44–45, 238
Intellectuals, black, 49, 50, 51, 52–54
Internal colonialism, 44; during Recon-
struction, 22; created by New Deal,
30–36; and Black Power, 71; and poli-
tics of cultural nationalism, 116–17;
in Newark, 153; and founding of
CAP, 160–61; and Black Agenda, 213;
transformation into neocolonialism,
254; and the contemporary ghetto
situation, 260, 263; in Ireland, 268;
resistance to, 270
International Ladies' Garment Workers'
Union, 27
Irish ethnicity, 7, 92–93
Irish Republican Brotherhood, 26
Islam, 23, 62. *See also* Nation of Islam
Italian Americans: and control of
Newark government, 75, 103, 152;
conflict in Newark, 97–99, 153; and
Kawaida Towers, 229–32, 240, 246;
and labor unions, 235–36

Jackson, George, 260
Jackson, Jesse: at Newark Black Power
Conference, 85; at Third National
Black Power Conference, 107; and
1970 election campaign, 147, 148–49,
153; and CAP founding, 164–65; and
National Black Political Assembly,

185; at Northlake, 190; at National
Conference of Black Elected Officials,
191, 195; at Gary, 203, 207–9
Jackson, Maynard, 191
Jackson, Samuel C., 205–6
James, Sharpe, 143, 151, 252–53, 287
(n. 71)
Johnson, James Weldon, 25
Johnson, Lyndon B., 95
Jones, Absolom, 14
Jones, Hettie Cohen, 52
Jones, LeRoi. *See* Baraka, Amiri
Jordan, Barbara, 191, 204
Jordan, Vernon, 191
Justice Department, U.S., 237, 240

Kansas Exodus, 11, 21
Karenga, Haiba, 166
Karenga, Maulana: founds US Organization, 43, 70; names Baraka, 59;
and cultural nationalism, 71–72; principles of cultural revolution of, 72,
113, 117; meets Baraka, 85; involvement in National Black Power Conferences, 85–86, 107–8, 120; leads
convention movement, 92; involvement in Newark Black Political Convention, 104–5; and United Brothers,
107–10; influences Baraka, 109–
10, 118, 120–21, 286 (n. 47); and
Kawaida, 113; breaks with CFUN,
116–22, 165–67; on US/Black Panther disputes, 116–17, 118; and Los
Angeles shoot-out, 119–20; imprison-
ment of, 120, 166; and women's political issues, 124; and Eldridge Cleaver,
124; and gender discrimination,
183–84
Kawaida: defined, 72, 113, 120–21,
282 (n. 85); and Karenga's break with
Baraka, 165. *See also* Kawaida Community Development; Temple of
Kawaida
Kawaida Community Development, 2,
5, 44, 222–54 passim
Kawaida Towers, 224–54; and Newark

Moorish Science Temple, 40, 26
Moses, Bob, 40
Mozambique, 175, 215, 269
Mshauri, Baba. *See* Bingham, Russell
Mtetezi, Kaimu, 89, 126, 223
Muhammad, Balozi Zayd, iv, v, vi, 110,
    121–22, 166, 220. *See also* Black Com-
    munity Defense and Development
Muhammad, Elijah, 26, 60, 164, 254,
    282 (n. 17)
Muhammad, Saludin, 186
Music, xi, 61, 66, 267; blues, 33; jazz,
    64–65
Muslims, 267. *See also* Nation of Islam

Name changes: post-emancipation,
    16–17; and spread of nationalism, 51,
    59, 89, 126, 151. *See also* Nationality
    formation
Nasser, Gamal Abdel, 54
National Association for the Advance-
    ment of Colored People (NAACP):
    in Harlem, 25; hegemony of, 32, 36;
    protests New Deal, 35; and civil rights
    movement, 39, 40; and first Black
    Power convention, 87; alliances of,
    111, 118; and National Black Assem-
    bly, 185; boycotts Gary convention,
    201–2, 211
National Black Assembly (NBA),
    212–19 passim, 233–45 passim, 254,
    258
National Black Political Agenda. *See*
    Gary Agenda
National Committee of Inquiry, 194
National Guard, 82, 94
Nationalism: defined, 9; heterogeneous
    nature of, 9; essential components,
    9; revolutionary nationalism, 38; of
    Patrice Lumumba and Congo Crisis,
    54–58. *See also* African liberation;
    Cultural nationalism; Nationality
    formation
Nationality formation: defined, iv,
    9–10; strategy of, xiii; role of urban
    uprisings in, xiii, 4–5, 40; and fusion

between small circles and grass roots,
    xiii, 7; impact of black conventions
    on, xiv; black institutional strategy of,
    xiv, 6; role of racial oppression in, xiv,
    6, 8; role of ghetto formation in, xiv,
    6, 23, 24–25, 26, 30, 34; role of con-
    flict with urban bureaucracies in, xiv,
    75, 115; role of collapsed government
    and business services in, xiv, 115; role
    of group conflict in, xiv–xv, 5, 7, 8, 78,
    97; impact of migration on, xv; role
    of international developments in, xv;
    influence of urban population concen-
    tration on, xv, 23, 30, 115; overview of
    specific process of, 1–3, 92–93; orga-
    nizations and institutions of, 2; funda-
    mental issues of, 3–4; urban origins
    of, 5–6; propositions about, 5–10; and
    development of national community,
    6; paradoxical role of assimilation in,
    6; role of language community in, 6;
    and rising educational levels, 6; role of
    intelligentsia in, 6–7; role of students
    in, 7; role of grass roots in, 7; acceler-
    ation of, 7, 8, 115; role of Modern
    Black Convention Movement in, 9;
    phases of, 10–42, 51; and ethnogene-
    sis, 11–13; role of class formation
    in, 12–13, 23, 24, 26, 35–38, 78; role
    of church in, 14, 23, 32; and names,
    16–17, 125–26, 265; and KKK, 21;
    and *Souls of Black Folk*, 23; and black
    folk culture, 31–34; and race records
    and blues, 33, and labor exploitation,
    35–38; and communism, 38; and vot-
    ing rights, 40; trajectory of, 43; and
    American apartheid, 44; role of auto-
    biography in, 51, 63; role of Congo`
    Crisis in, 54–58; role of Malcolm X
    in, 59–63; in Newark, 76, 93; theories
    of, 92–93, 102–3, 128, 130, 142; role
    of United Brothers in, 93; and
    CFUN, 113, 115; and cooperative
    economics, 115; and youth, 128–29;
    and hegemony of white supremacy,
    131; impact of 1970 election cam-

paign victory on, 154; national scope
of, 159–72; and anticolonialism, 173–
80; and antisexism, 180–84; and Gary
convention, 184–218; and 1972 election campaign, 185–88; romanticism
v. bureaucratic, 261. *See also* Cultural
nationalism; Cultural nationalism:
politics of
National Maritime Union, 38
National Negro Congress, 4, 29–30
National Negro Labor Council, 36–37
National Urban League, 3, 25, 69, 87,
95, 107, 164, 185, 191; local chapters,
140
National Welfare Rights Organization,
181, 191, 234
Nation of Islam, xiv, 26, 59–60, 72, 123,
132, 164, 254, 260, 282 (n. 17)
Nat Turner Park (Newark), 245–46
Neal, Larry, 51, 62–63, 65, 67, 72, 167
New Ark, 224–30
Newark, N.J.: and Newark Black Political Convention, 1; Black Power origins in, 2; black population in, 26, 32;
changing government structure of,
37; Baraka's return to, 43; 1967 uprising in, 43; and grass roots, 49, 50,
116; and Black Arts festival, 66; post-
war white flight from, 75; and Medical School Crisis, 75–77, 125; economic decay of, 76; and civil rights,
76; Italian American governance of,
76, 97–98, 103, 152; unemployment
in, 77; and Model Cities Act, 77; and
1967 National Black Power Conference, 84–90, 93; and Black Power
experiment, 92; and 1968 Black Political Convention, 93, 106–7; Martin
Luther King's visit to, 93–95; and
uprisings following King's assassination, 96; and police force, 96, 99–100;
and 1968 special election, 97; racial
confrontations in, 97, 99, 241–42;
Puerto Rican community within, 98,
99; as political arena, 99; and SNCC,
105; and founding of CFUN, 108;

impact of 1968 elections upon, 112;
and the development of expressive
politics, 114; and black/Puerto Rican
alliance, 114–15; need for black institutions in, 128; and mobilization of
youth, 126–28; and Mutual Defense
Pact, 138–40; and New Ark Fund,
144–49; and 1970 election campaign,
144–55; and CAP, 168, 219; and
school names, 198; urban crisis in,
198–99, 222–24; expanding boundaries of ghetto in, 241, 244. *See also*
Committee for Unified Newark;
Kawaida Towers; Newark Housing
Authority; Newark Rebellion
Newark City Council: 238–41 passim,
246–53, 287 (n. 71)
Newark City Hall, 75, 77, 249–53
New Ark Fund, 144
Newark Housing Authority, 75, 103,
199, 224, 228, 244, 248–49, 252
Newark Rebellion, 43, 76, 78–84, 143,
149, 153, 287 (n. 70)
NewArk Student Federation, 2, 128
New Deal, 22, 30, 31, 35–36
New Jersey Housing Finance Agency
(NJHFA), 230, 243–44, 245, 249, 250,
252, 289 (n. 37)
New Lafayette Theater, 67
Newspapers, African American: *Black
Newark*, 2, 135; *Unity and Struggle*, 2,
135, 249–50; *The Messenger*, 25; *Cru-
sader*, 25; *Village Voice*, 54; *New York
Times*, 57, 87, 97, 101, 197, 217, 238–
39, 249; *The Liberator*, 58; *Muhammad
Speaks*, 59; inspired by Black Arts
Movement, 67; *Washington Post*, 95;
Asbury Park Press, 235
Newton, Huey P., 4, 34, 43, 62, 70–73
passim, 97, 116–18, 280 (n. 21)
New York City: Patrice Lumumba's visit
to, 55; and UN incident, 57–59; and
Malcolm X's assassination, 62; and
founding of Black Panther Party, 72;
and Last Poets, 139; and CAP, 168;
and Black Political Convention at the

Karenga and Baraka in, 109; and grass roots, 109; resisting white racism, 111; and 1968 election in Newark, 112–13, 140; and collapse of CFUN, 121; revised leadership of, 124; and Earl Harris, 247; as foundation of convention movement, 256. *See also* Committee for Unified Newark

United Brothers of Mahwah, 129–30

United Community Corporation, 223, 226

United Freedom Party, 141

United Nations, 54, 56, 57–59, 73, 87

United Sisters, 88, 122

United States Department of Housing and Development. *See* HUD

Universal Negro Improvement Association (UNIA), 4, 26, 28

Urban crisis: and Black Agenda, 143, 198–99, 208, 256; in Newark, 222–24. *See also* Kawaida Towers; Newark, N.J.

Urbanization, xiii, 1, 3; as source of nationality formation, 4–6; and migrations, 6, 11, 75; and race riots, 15; and black population growth, 25–26, 168, 262. *See also* Ghetto; Migration; Nationality formation

Urban uprisings, 1, 11, 30–34, 41, 94–95. *See also* Newark Rebellion

US Organization: as component of convention movement, xiv; founding of, 71–72, 260; debates with Black Panther Party, 105–6, 116–19; and Third National Black Power Convention, 107; collapse of, 120; and political issues of women, 124; rupture with CFUN, 165–67; and gun cultism, 166; and polygamy, 180–81. *See also* Karenga, Maulana

Vallani, Ralph, 229, 230, 231

Van Deburg, William, 111

Veterans, in CFUN movement, 133

Vietnam, 38, 108, 169, 215

Violence: and antimigration legislation, 15; and Congo Crisis, 55; and UN incident, 57; following Larry Neal's murder, 67; and urban uprisings, 70–71, 78–84; following King's assassination, 94; surrounding US/Panther disputes, 105, 116, 118; surrounding collapse of CFUN triumvirate, 121; following 1970 elections, 150, 153, 284 (n. 170); surrounding rupture of CFUN and US Organization, 166; and shattered political vision, 222–24; and Kawaida Towers, 235, 237–38, 241–43. *See also* Police brutality

Vogelman, Irving, 233

Voter registration, black, 102, 104, 109, 112, 140, 168, 191

Voter turnout, black: 1968 election in Newark, 112; 1970 election in Newark, 150, 153

Voting, black: and Black Power vision, 42; and Malcolm X, 60; and SNCC, 72; and ballot-or-bullet debate, 92, 101–2; and Newark Black Political Convention, 101–2; and Kenneth Gibson campaign, 115; and Northlake Summit strategy, 191–94. *See also* Voter registration; Voter turnout

Voting Rights Act, 11, 41

Walker, David, 14

Wallace, George, 97–99

Ward, Eulius "Honey," 89, 223

Warren, Earl, 39

Washington, Booker T., 24, 60

Washington, D.C., 19, 32, 95, 176–78, 215–16

Watts, Dan, 58

Watts Rebellion, 41, 70, 71, 73, 96

West, Calvin, 152

West, Levin, 152

Westbrooks, Dennis, 151

Weusi, Jitu, 186, 220

Wheeler, Harry, 89, 101, 141, 151

White Citizens' Councils, 39

White liberals, 40, 54, 69, 95, 97, 228–30, 233, 235–36

White supremacy, 15, 22, 39. *See also* Racism

Wilcox, Preston, 234

Wiley, George, 191

Wilkins, Roy, 201

Williams, Henry Sylvester, 23

Williams, Hosea, 194

Williams, Junius, 89

Williams, Robert F., 25, 50, 52, 53, 54, 58, 73, 86

Wills, Gary, 96

Wilson, Harold (Kasisi Mhisani), 109, 132, 224–25

Women's leadership: at 1974 Afrikan Women's Conference, 18; Rosa Parks, 39–40; confronts Adlai Stevenson, 57; by Amina Baraka, 59; at National Black Power Conference, 88–89; and United Brothers, 89; and modernization of cultural nationalism, 122–24; at Soul Sessions, 132; in CFUN, 133–34, 135–37; at Black and Puerto Rican Convention, 140, 142; of BWUF, 180–84; and grass roots, 197

Women's Political Council, 39

Women's political issues: discrimination in workplace as, 27, 36; and Third National Black Power Convention, 107; within CFUN, 123; communalism as, 135, 137; and BWUF, 180–84; polygamy as one of, 180–81; increased acknowledgment of, 197, 286 (n. 47)

Wonder, Stevie, 148

Woods, Dessie X., and Cheryl S. Todd, 183

Wright, Nathan, 107

Wright, Richard, xi, xii

Young, Andrew, 191, 194

Young, Coleman, 36

Young, Whitney, Jr., 3, 95, 107–8, 162–64, 280 (n. 16)

Youth Organization of Black Unity (YOBU), 181

Zimbabwe. *See* Rhodesia